Test Bank

for

Barlow and Durand's

Abnormal Psychology
An Integrative Approach
Fourth Edition

Michael Goodstone
State University of New York, Farmingdale

Marilyn Blumenthal
State University of New York, Farmingdale

THOMSON

WADSWORTH

Australia • Canada • Mexico • Singapore • Spain • United Kingdom • United States

Printed in the United States of America
1 2 3 4 5 6 7 08 07 06 05 04

Printer: Globus Printing

0-534-63368-4

For more information about our products,
contact us at:
Thomson Learning Academic Resource Center
1-800-423-0563

For permission to use material from this text or product, submit a request online at
http://www.thomsonrights.com.
Any additional questions about permissions can be submitted by email to **thomsonrights@thomson.com.**

Thomson Wadsworth
10 Davis Drive
Belmont, CA 94002-3098
USA

Asia
Thomson Learning
5 Shenton Way #01-01
UIC Building
Singapore 068808

Australia/New Zealand
Thomson Learning
102 Dodds Street
Southbank, Victoria 3006
Australia

Canada
Nelson
1120 Birchmount Road
Toronto, Ontario M1K 5G4
Canada

Europe/Middle East/South Africa
Thomson Learning
High Holborn House
50/51 Bedford Row
London WC1R 4LR
United Kingdom

Latin America
Thomson Learning
Seneca, 53
Colonia Polanco
11560 Mexico D.F.
Mexico

Spain/Portugal
Paraninfo
Calle/Magallanes, 25
28015 Madrid, Spain

TABLE OF CONTENTS

About the Authors

Michael Goodstone, Ph.D., is a psychologist with specialization in industrial/organizational psychology and clinical psychology. As an expert on the development and validation of tests and measures, he has served as a consultant to many different types of organizations including financial services, manufacturing, power utilities, temporary services, health care and academia. Dr. Goodstone is currently an Assistant Professor of Psychology at the State University of New York at Farmingdale where he teaches Abnormal Psychology and courses related to industrial/organizational psychology.

Marilyn Blumenthal, Ph.D., is a Professor of Psychology at SUNY Farmingdale where she has taught Abnormal Psychology for more than 25 years. She is also a licensed clinical psychologist specializing in women's issues and bereavement. Dr. Blumenthal has made presentations on stress at seminars for midlife/menopausal women and has conducted workshops on coping with aging parents and with the death of parents. She has researched student self-disclosure of psychological problems in the college classroom and is currently exploring family disconnection issues.

The current test bank is an outgrowth of a workshop called "Publishers' Test Banks: Do They Pass the Test?" which Drs. Blumenthal and Goodstone presented at the annual SUNY Farmingdale Teaching of Psychology Conference in 1999. For many years, both Dr. Goodstone and Dr. Blumenthal have been concerned about the quality, reliability and validity of test banks provided to adopters of Abnormal Psychology textbooks. In response to negative student feedback, these professors systematically analyzed published questions and distractors for content, relevance, length, consistency, and syntax. Each item in the current Barlow and Durand Test Bank has been carefully constructed to meet specified criteria.

The authors wish to acknowledge the support and encouragement of their spouses, Lori and Lee, during the time consuming process of preparing the Barlow and Durand Test Bank.

EXPLANATION OF SYMBOLS

SAMPLE QUESTION:

p. 2, b, obj 1, FACT, LOW, WWW

1. According to the authors of your textbook, the definition of a psychological disorder <u>always</u> includes:

   a. stress
   b. impaired functioning in an individual
   c. culturally expected responses
   d. psychotic symptoms

p. 2 – textbook page on which related content can be found. (Questions labeled CD referrer to content found on the *Abnormal Psychology Live!* CD-ROM that accompanies the text.

b – correct answer to the question

obj 1 – the number of a specific Learning Objective in the Instructor's Manual

FACT – type of question (<u>FACT</u>UAL, <u>CO</u>NCEPTUAL or <u>APPLIED</u>)

LOW – level of difficulty (LOW, <u>MODE</u>RATE or HIGH)

WWW – indicates that the question, the correct answer and explanations of why the other choices are incorrect can be found at http://psychstudy.wadsworth.com

Note: Following each chapter are sample questions from the student Study Guide written by David A. Santogrossi, Purdue University.

MULTIPLE CHOICE

1. According to the authors of your textbook, the definition of a psychological disorder is associated with:
   a. stress
   b. impaired functioning
   c. culturally expected responses
   d. psychotic symptoms

   ANS: B   DIF: 1   REF: p. 2   OBJ: 1 TYPE: FACT/WWW

2. In regard to the criteria that define abnormality, it would be correct to state that:
   a. no one criterion has yet been developed that fully defines abnormality
   b. personal distress is the one criterion that defines abnormality
   c. the criteria differ depending on the cause of the psychological disorder
   d. the criteria differ depending on whether the individual has a psychological disorder or a psychological dysfunction

   ANS: A   DIF: 5   REF: p. 2   OBJ: 1 TYPE: CON

3. The criterion that a particular behavior be atypical or not culturally expected is insufficient to define abnormality because:
   a. behavior that occurs infrequently is considered abnormal in every culture
   b. society is less willing to tolerate eccentricity in people who are productive
   c. behaviors vary very little from one culture to another
   d. many people behave in ways that deviate from the average but this doesn't mean that they have a disorder

   ANS: D   DIF: 5   REF: p. 4   OBJ: 1 TYPE: CON

4. Which of the following degrees is earned by a psychiatrist?
   a. Ph.D.
   b. Ed.D.
   c. M.D.
   d. Psy.D.

   ANS: C   DIF: 1   REF: p. 5   OBJ: 1 TYPE: FACT/WWW

5. It is 1975 and Ivan is an idealistic young Russian student. He joins a group protesting various government policies and criticizes the leader of the Communist Party. For his dissident political views, Ivan will probably be:
   a. forced to work for the Communist Party
   b. incarcerated in a maximum security prison
   c. given psychological tests to determine if he is mentally ill
   d. committed to a mental institution

   ANS: D   DIF: 5   REF: p. 4   OBJ: 1 TYPE: APP

6. The typical profile or prototype of a disorder reflects the _____ as described in DSM-IV.
   a. theoretical perspectives on abnormality
   b. treatments for mental disorders
   c. causes of mental illness
   d. diagnostic criteria for psychological disorders

   ANS: D   DIF: 3   REF: p. 5   OBJ: 1 TYPE: CON

7. The scientific study of psychological disorders is called:
   a. psychopathology
   b. psychoanalysis
   c. pseudoscience
   d. parapsychology

   ANS: A   DIF: 1   REF: p. 5   OBJ: 1 TYPE: FACT

8. After college graduation two of your friends are interested in careers in the helping professions. Anna wants to become a psychiatrist; Carl plans on becoming a psychologist. Since you are taking a course in Abnormal Psychology, they ask you for career advice. You would tell:
   a. Anna to apply to medical school and Carl to study psychology at the graduate level
   b. Carl to apply to medical school and Anna to study psychology at the graduate level
   c. both of them to apply to medical school
   d. both of them to apply to graduate school

   ANS: A   DIF: 3   REF: p. 5   OBJ: 2 TYPE: APP

9. All of the following are ways in which mental health professionals might function as scientist-practitioners EXCEPT:
   a. analyzing their own motivations and reasons for helping people with psychological problems
   b. evaluating their own assessments and treatments for effectiveness
   c. conducting research leading to new information about mental disorders and their treatments
   d. using the most current diagnostic and treatment procedures

   ANS: A   DIF: 5   REF: p. 5   OBJ: 2 TYPE: APP

10. As used by clinical psychologists, the term "presenting problem" is used to indicate the problem that:
    a. the patient thinks is most severe
    b. has lasted the longest amount of time
    c. the therapist thinks is most severe
    d. first brought the individual to therapy

    ANS: D   DIF: 3   REF: p. 6   OBJ: 2 TYPE: CON

11. A male college student began feeling sad and lonely. Although still able to go to classes and work at his job, he finds himself feeling down much of the time and he worries about what is happening to him. Which part of the definition of abnormality applies to his situation?
    a. personal distress
    b. cultural factors
    c. impaired functioning
    d. violation of societal norms

    ANS: A   DIF: 3   REF: p. 3   OBJ: 1 TYPE: APP/CON

12. Statistical data are often relevant when discussing psychological disorders. For example, a researcher might want to know how many new cases of depression are diagnosed each year, a figure called the _____ of the disorder.
    a. prevalence
    b. incidence
    c. recurrence
    d. ratio

    ANS: B   DIF: 3   REF: p. 6   OBJ: 2 TYPE: CON

13. Psychological disorders can be described as following a typical course or individual pattern. For example, schizophrenia follows a chronic course, while mood disorders, including depression, follow a(n) _____ course.
    a. episodic
    b. time-limited
    c. guarded
    d. insidious

    ANS: A   DIF: 3   REF: p. 6   OBJ: 2 TYPE: CON

14. If a psychological disorder is said to have an acute onset, it means that the symptoms developed:
    a. suddenly
    b. atypically
    c. gradually
    d. following a previous period of recovery

    ANS: A   DIF: 3   REF: p. 6   OBJ: 2 TYPE: CON

15. When 20 year-old Larry was first diagnosed with schizophrenia, his family wanted to know if and how the disorder would progress and how it would affect him in the future. In medical terms, the family wanted to know Larry's _____.
    a. diagnosis
    b. prognosis
    c. psychosocial profile
    d. pathology

    ANS: B   DIF: 3   REF: p. 7   OBJ: 1 TYPE: APP

16. Developmental psychopathology refers to the study of changes in:
    a. abnormal behavior
    b. normal behavior
    c. children's behavior, both normal and abnormal
    d. normal adolescent behavior

    ANS: A   DIF: 1   REF: p. 7   OBJ: 1 TYPE: FACT

17. As part of the integrative multidimensional perspective of the textbook, treatments for mental disorders are described:
    a. in general terms
    b. in association with specific disorders
    c. in separate chapters that focus on different treatment approaches
    d. only for severe cases

    ANS: B   DIF: 3   REF: p. 7   OBJ: 4 TYPE: CON

18. At various times in history, in an attempt to explain problematic, irrational behavior, humans have focused on supernatural causes that include all of the following EXCEPT:
    a. magnetic fields
    b. demons and evil spirits
    c. bodily humors
    d. the moon and stars

    ANS: C   DIF: 3   REF: p. 8   OBJ: 3 TYPE: CON

19. The biological and psychological models or theories of abnormality derived originally from the ancient Greek concept in which the:
    a. mind was considered separate from the body
    b. flow of bodily fluids affected behavior and personality
    c. female reproductive organs were associated with psychopathology
    d. movement of the planets influenced human behavior

    ANS: A   DIF: 5   REF: p. 8   OBJ: 3 TYPE: CON/WWW

20. Since the time of ancient Greece, the concept of a psyche or soul was similar to that of the:
    a. brain
    b. mind
    c. body
    d. blood

    ANS: B   DIF: 1   REF: p. 8   OBJ: 3 TYPE: CON

21. Towards the end of the 14th century and continuing into the 15th century, the causes of "madness" were generally attributed to:
    a. toxins in the blood
    b. religious delusions
    c. brain disease
    d. demons and witches

    ANS: D   DIF: 3   REF: p. 8   OBJ: 3 TYPE: CON

22. In regard to the turbulent political and religious events of the 14th and 15th centuries, which of the following accurately describes the attitudes of the Catholic Church toward mentally ill people?
    a. they were considered to be suffering from religious delusions and were cared for by members of the church communities
    b. they were seen as possessed by evil spirits and blamed for all misfortunes
    c. they were regarded as basically good individuals who were not responsible for their abnormal behavior
    d. they were provided with medical treatments and sometimes hospitalized because mental illness was regarded as equivalent to physical illness

    ANS: B   DIF: 5   REF: p. 8   OBJ: 3 TYPE: APP

23. During the Middle Ages, as well as at other times, mentally ill people were sometimes forced to undergo the religious ritual called exorcism in order to:
    a. cure the mental illness by making the individual more religious
    b. build up muscle strength and make the person healthier
    c. rid the individual's body of evil spirits
    d. prove that the person was not a witch

    ANS: C   DIF: 3   REF: p. 8   OBJ: 3 TYPE: CON

24. The treatment given to the mentally ill King Charles VI of France showed that the causes of his disorder were attributed to _____ phenomena.
    a. natural
    b. supernatural
    c. both natural and supernatural
    d. neither natural nor supernatural

    ANS: C   DIF: 5   REF: p. 9   OBJ: 3 TYPE: APP

25. As noted in the textbook, the young girl in the movie, "The Exorcist," was:
    a. diagnosed with a brain tumor
    b. diagnosed with a seizure disorder
    c. forced to submit to an exorcism before receiving any medical or psychological treatments
    d. forced to submit to an exorcism after medical and psychological conditions were ruled out

    ANS: D   DIF: 5   REF: p. 9   OBJ: 3 TYPE: APP

26. The belief of homophobic people that the "sin" of homosexuality has resulted in HIV/AIDS is related to the historical concept of _____ as a cause of madness.
    a. divine punishment
    b. faith healing
    c. hysteria
    d. sorcery

    ANS: A   DIF: 5   REF: p. 10   OBJ: 3 TYPE: APP

27. The inexplicable phenomenon called mass hysteria that occurred during the Middle Ages was associated with all of the following EXCEPT:
    a. St. Vitus' Dance
    b. tarantism
    c. insect bites
    d. poisonous snakes

    ANS: D   DIF: 3   REF: p. 10   OBJ: 3 TYPE: CON

28. One hot and humid night one of your friends suggests doing some really crazy things. You look up at the sky and then say: "It must be the full moon." Your statement reflects the concept from which the word _____ is derived.
    a. lunatic
    b. idiot
    c. maniac
    d. psychopath

    ANS: A   DIF: 3   REF: p. 11   OBJ: 3 TYPE: APP

29. The historic belief that the movements and/or positions of the moon, the stars, and the planets influence human behavior is still held by followers of the pseudoscience called _____.
    a. graphology
    b. parapsychology
    c. astronomy
    d. astrology

    ANS: D   DIF: 3   REF: p. 11   OBJ: 3 TYPE: CON/WWW

30. The Greek physician Hippocrates (400 BC) suggested that psychological disorders could be negatively influenced by factors such as:
    a. family stress
    b. supernatural forces
    c. religion
    d. birth order

    ANS: A   DIF: 3   REF: p. 11   OBJ: 3 TYPE: CON

31. Which of the following is NOT one of the causes of psychopathology suggested by the Greek physician Hippocrates (400 BC)?
    a. head injury
    b. brain pathology
    c. genetics
    d. spirit possession

    ANS: D   DIF: 3   REF: p. 11   OBJ: 3 TYPE: CON

32. You are listening to old musical tunes including "My Melancholy Baby." Your friends are impressed when you tell them that "melancholic," referring to a depressive personality, derives from a Greek word meaning:
   a. blood
   b. phlegm
   c. yellow bile
   d. black bile

   ANS: D   DIF: 5   REF: p. 12   OBJ: 3 TYPE: APP

33. According to Hippocrates' humoral theory, the "choleric" personality is:
   a. hot-tempered
   b. easy going
   c. kind
   d. cheap

   ANS: A   DIF: 3   REF: p. 12   OBJ: 3 TYPE: CON

34. Based on Hippocrates' humoral theory, "sanguine" describes a person who is:
   a. pessimistic
   b. pale
   c. cheerful
   d. humorous

   ANS: C   DIF: 3   REF: p. 12   OBJ: 3 TYPE: CON

35. Bloodletting, a treatment devised centuries ago to restore the balance of humors, was accomplished with the use of:
   a. needles
   b. leeches
   c. tourniquets
   d. bacteria

   ANS: B   DIF: 3   REF: p. 12   OBJ: 3 TYPE: CON

36. In ancient Greece, a woman suffering from "hysteria" might be told that her condition could be cured by:
   a. marriage
   b. pregnancy
   c. childbirth
   d. divorce

   ANS: A   DIF: 3   REF: p. 12   OBJ: 3 TYPE: APP

37. In ancient Greece, "humoral excesses" thought to be causing psychological disorders were treated by:
   a. increasing or decreasing the person's exposure to heat, dryness, moisture or cold
   b. herbal remedies
   c. decreasing both caloric and liquid intake
   d. lowering the person's body temperature for extended periods of time

   ANS: A   DIF: 5   REF: p. 12   OBJ: 3 TYPE: APP

38. Induced vomiting was a 17th century treatment for depression. As described in "Anatomy of Melancholy," (1621) this could be accomplished by eating:
   a. raw meat
   b. ice
   c. coal
   d. tobacco

   ANS: D   DIF: 3   REF: p. 12   OBJ: 3 TYPE: CON

39. Somatoform disorders, a current DSM-IV classification that evolved from the concept of "hysteria" affect:
   a. adult males only
   b. adult females only
   c. both males and females of any age
   d. children only

   ANS: C   DIF: 3   REF: p. 12   OBJ: 3 TYPE: CON

40. In keeping with an accepted treatment for mental illness in the 14th century, a physician treating King Charles VI of France had him moved to the countryside in order to:
   a. be closer to a hospital that treated mental illness
   b. keep him away from his family
   c. restore the balance in his humors
   d. cure him of hysteria

   ANS: C   DIF: 5   REF: p. 9   OBJ: 3 TYPE: APP

41. In an attempt to rid the body of the excessive humors thought to be causing psychological disorders, physicians throughout history have used treatments such as:
   a. bloodletting
   b. induced seizures
   c. exorcism
   d. drilling through the skull

   ANS: A   DIF: 5   REF: p. 12   OBJ: 3 TYPE: APP/WWW

42. The concept of hysteria, which traditionally meant physical symptoms for which no organic pathology could be found, is now associated with which DSM-IV classification?
   a. anxiety disorders
   b. neurosis
   c. PMS
   d. somatoform disorders

   ANS: D   DIF: 5   REF: p. 12   OBJ: 3 TYPE: APP

43. The traditional tendency to stigmatize women as "hysterical" derived from Hippocrates' concept of:
   a. the "wandering uterus"
   b. an "incompetent cervix"
   c. "penis envy"
   d. "pelvic dysfunction"

   ANS: A   DIF: 5   REF: p. 12   OBJ: 3 TYPE: APP

44. Until the 1970s hysterical disorders were diagnosed only in women. In fact the term "hysteria" derives from the Greek *hysteron* which means:
   a. ovary
   b. uterus
   c. pregnancy
   d. vagina

   ANS: B   DIF: 3   REF: p. 12   OBJ: 3 TYPE: FACT

45. The first significant supporting evidence for a biological cause of a mental disorder was the 19th century discovery that the psychotic disorder called general paresis was caused by the same bacterial microorganism that causes _____ .
   a. malaria
   b. Alzheimer's disease
   c. syphilis
   d. hysteria

   ANS: C   DIF: 3   REF: p. 12   OBJ: 3 TYPE: CON

46. In the 19th century United States, John Gray, a well-known psychiatrist, believed that mental illness was due to:
   a. psychological factors
   b. physical causes
   c. social/environmental influences
   d. unknown influences

   ANS: B   DIF: 1   REF: p. 13   OBJ: 3 TYPE: FACT

47. In the 1930s when insulin shock therapy was deemed too risky as a treatment for mental disorder, _____ began to be used instead.
   a. bromides
   b. electroconvulsive therapy
   c. megavitamin therapy
   d. moral therapy

   ANS: B   DIF: 3   REF: p. 13   OBJ: 3 TYPE: APP

48. The first effective medications for severe psychotic disorders were developed in the:
   a. late 19th century
   b. early 20th century
   c. 1950s
   d. 1990s

   ANS: C   DIF: 1   REF: p. 13   OBJ: 3 TYPE: FACT

49. In the 1800s, an important research and clinical publication read by psychiatrists in the United States was titled:
   a. Case Studies in Mental Illness
   b. American Journal of Madness
   c. American Journal of Insanity
   d. Lunatics in America

   ANS: C   DIF: 5   REF: p. 13   OBJ: 3 TYPE: FACT

50. With the discovery of the major tranquilizers called _____, psychotic symptoms, including hallucinations, delusions, and aggressiveness, were able to be controlled.
   a. neuroleptics
   b. benzodiazepines
   c. bromides
   d. opiates

   ANS: A   DIF: 3   REF: p. 13   OBJ: 3 TYPE: CON

51. Benzodiazepines, or "minor" tranquilizers, such as Valium and Librium are effective in reducing the symptoms of:
   a. depression
   b. anxiety
   c. schizophrenia
   d. hysteria

   ANS: B   DIF: 3   REF: p. 13   OBJ: 3 TYPE: FACT

52. In the late 1800s the emphasis on a biological cause of mental disorder resulted ironically in reduced interest in treatments for mental patients because it was thought that:
   a. physicians should devote more time to the physically ill
   b. patients would improve more rapidly if they were not hospitalized
   c. the hospital staff was not adequately trained to administer new treatments
   d. mental illness due to brain pathology was incurable

   ANS: D   DIF: 5   REF: p. 14   OBJ: 3 TYPE: CON

53. In contrast to the asylums of the early 18th century, the psychosocial approach called moral therapy advocated all of the following EXCEPT:
   a. restraint and seclusion
   b. normal social interaction
   c. individual attention from the hospital staff
   d. lectures on interesting subjects for hospitalized patients

   ANS: A   DIF: 1   REF: p. 14   OBJ: 3 TYPE: APP

54. After Philippe Pinel systematically introduced moral therapy as a treatment in mental hospitals in France, a similar type of socially facilitative environment was first established in a US hospital by:
   a. Benjamin Rush
   b. William Tuke
   c. Joseph von Medina
   d. Manfred Sakel

   ANS: A   DIF: 3   REF: p. 15   OBJ: 3 TYPE: APP

55. After the mid 1800s, moral therapy declined as a treatment for the mentally ill because:
   a. the number of patients in mental institutions also declined
   b. immigrants caused an increase in the mental hospital population
   c. the number of people available to staff mental hospitals increased
   d. new biologically based treatments became available

   ANS: B   DIF: 5   REF: p. 15   OBJ: 3 TYPE: APP

56. You have been asked to give a report on the mental hygiene movement and its foremost crusader Dorothea Dix, who campaigned for more humane treatment of the insane. After mentioning all of her accomplishments you note the unforeseen consequence of her efforts, namely:
   a. a decrease in the number of mental patients in institutions, forcing many to close
   b. an increase in the number of mental patients resulting in insufficient staff to care for them
   c. a change from custodial care to moral therapy for institutionalized patients
   d. more patients receiving psychotherapy and less receiving medication

   ANS: B   DIF: 5   REF: p. 15   OBJ: 3 TYPE: APP/WWW

57. Anton Mesmer, an early 18th century physician, purported to be effecting cures in patients by unblocking their flow of a bodily fluid he called "animal magnetism." In fact, any effectiveness of his methods was actually due to:
   a. undetectable magnetic fields
   b. chemically induced humoral balance
   c. mental telepathy
   d. the power of suggestion

   ANS: D   DIF: 5   REF: p. 16   OBJ: 3 TYPE: APP

58. A "double blind" experiment to ascertain the effectiveness of animal magnetism therapy was conducted by:
   a. Philippe Pinel
   b. Anton Mesmer
   c. Sigmund Freud
   d. Benjamin Franklin

   ANS: D   DIF: 3   REF: p. 16   OBJ: 3 TYPE: FACT

59. Which of the following accurately describes the patients of Freud and Breur after they received hypnotherapy for their psychological disorders?
    a. feelings of relief and improvement
    b. decreased emotionality while in the hypnotic state
    c. accurate post-hypnotic recall
    d. increased understanding of the causes of their psychological disorder

    ANS: A   DIF: 3   REF: p. 17   OBJ: 3 TYPE: CON

60. Realizing that patients were often unaware of material previously recalled under hypnosis, Charcot, Breuer and Freud hypothesized the existence of _____ , a concept considered one of the most important developments in the history of psychopathology.
    a. neurosis
    b. the unconscious mind
    c. the Electra complex
    d. catharsis

    ANS: B   DIF: 5   REF: p. 17   OBJ: 3 TYPE: APP

61. In using hypnosis to treat patients with psychological disorders, Freud discovered:
    a. that it is therapeutic to recall and relive emotionally traumatic events
    b. that patients are unable to process emotionally charged information
    c. that hypnosis was less effective than mesmerism
    d. the existence of conscious memories

    ANS: A   DIF: 5   REF: p. 17   OBJ: 3 TYPE: CON

62. In the classic case of Anna O. in 1895, the neurologist Breuer treated her "hysterical" symptoms by using:
    a. hydrotherapy
    b. hypnosis
    c. faith healing
    d. the placebo effect

    ANS: B   DIF: 3   REF: p. 17   OBJ: 3 TYPE: CON

63. Which of the following is NOT included as part of Freud's structure of the mind?
    a. id
    b. psyche
    c. superego
    d. ego

    ANS: B   DIF: 1   REF: p. 18   OBJ: 3 TYPE: FACT

64. In Freudian theory "libido" and "thanatos" represent the two basic but opposing drives of:
    a. life and death
    b. sex and celibacy
    c. good and evil
    d. pleasure and pain

    ANS: A   DIF: 3   REF: p. 18   OBJ: 3 TYPE: CON

65. You have just read a newspaper article about a savage rape and murder. You wonder how someone could commit such a horrible crime. Then you recall from your study of Freudian theory that according to Freud, anyone could be a killer or rapist if _____ impulses are not well controlled.
    a. egoistic
    b. phallic
    c. id
    d. mesmeric

    ANS: C   DIF: 5   REF: p. 18   OBJ: 3 TYPE: APP

66. Although Freud conceptualized the libido as the life energy within the id, many people think of it as the:
    a. death instinct
    b. sex drive
    c. conscience
    d. Oedipal conflict

    ANS: B   DIF: 1   REF: p. 18   OBJ: 3 TYPE: CON

67. According to psychoanalytic theory, the _____ develops early in life to insure that we can adapt to the demands of the real world while still finding ways to meet our basic needs.
    a. ego
    b. superego
    c. libido
    d. ideal self

    ANS: A   DIF: 5   REF: p. 18   OBJ: 3 TYPE: CON/WWW

68. According to psychoanalytic theory, the id operates on the "pleasure principle," which means that it:
    a. adheres to social rules and regulations
    b. thinks in an unemotional, logical and rational manner
    c. is sexual, aggressive, selfish, and envious
    d. utilizes secondary process thinking

    ANS: C   DIF: 5   REF: p. 18   OBJ: 3 TYPE: CON

69. A classmate in your psychology course is worried about the selfish and sometimes dangerous drives of the id. You respond by saying that:
    a. each of us develops an ego to help us behave more realistically
    b. id fantasies never become reality
    c. psychologists disproved Freud's theories a long time ago
    d. since id impulses are usually part of consciousness awareness, we can learn to control them

    ANS: A   DIF: 5   REF: p. 18   OBJ: 3 TYPE: APP

70. According to psychoanalytic theory, the role of the ego involves:
    a. counteracting the aggressive and sexual drives of the id
    b. maximizing pleasure and reduce tension
    c. mediating conflict between the id and the superego
    d. utilizing fantasy and primary process thinking

    ANS: C   DIF: 5   REF: p. 18   OBJ: 3 TYPE: CON

71. If you were asked to explain Freud's structure of the mind to a friend who was unfamiliar with psychology, you might use an organizational analogy in which the id would be the employee who comes to work late and takes very long lunch hours, the superego would be the building security guard, and the ego would be:
    a. a newly hired employee
    b. a recently fired employee
    c. a manager
    d. a salesperson

    ANS: C   DIF: 5   REF: p. 18   OBJ: 3 TYPE: APP

72. According to psychoanalytic theory, the conflicts between the id and the superego often lead to feelings of:
    a. anxiety
    b. desire
    c. depression
    d. anger

    ANS: A   DIF: 3   REF: p. 18   OBJ: 3 TYPE: CON

73. According to Freudian theory, anxiety is a signal for the ego to marshal its mechanisms of defense, which function as:
    a. reality-based actions
    b. unconscious protective processes
    c. conscious efforts to maintain control
    d. primitive emotional responses

    ANS: B   DIF: 1   REF: p. 18   OBJ: 3 TYPE: FACT

74. As used in modern terminology to reflect coping styles, defense mechanisms:
    a. can be either adaptive or maladaptive
    b. are always maladaptive
    c. are never adaptive
    d. are always self-defeating

    ANS: A   DIF: 3   REF: p. 19   OBJ: 3 TYPE: CON

75. Which of the following is an example of the maladaptive, self-defeating type of defensive mechanism?
    a. a phobia
    b. sublimation
    c. a hallucinatory experience
    d. amnesia

    ANS: A   DIF: 3   REF: p. 19   OBJ: 3 TYPE: CON

76. In which of the following defense mechanisms does an individual unconsciously block disturbing wishes, thoughts or experiences from awareness?
    a. rationalization
    b. reaction formation
    c. repression
    d. displacement

    ANS: C   DIF: 1   REF: p. 19   OBJ: 3 TYPE: FACT

77. In which of the following defense mechanisms does an individual falsely attribute his or her own unacceptable feelings, impulses, or thoughts to another person?
    a. denial
    b. projection
    c. displacement
    d. sublimation

    ANS: B   DIF: 3   REF: p. 19   OBJ: 3 TYPE: CON

78. Mrs. B. received a very poor rating by her supervisor who had been constantly criticizing her in front of her coworkers. When she got home, her kids ran up to greet her all talking at once. She responded by yelling: "Leave me alone! Can't you see I'm tired?" According to psychoanalytic theory, this is an example of the defense mechanism known as:
    a. displacement
    b. projection
    c. repression
    d. rationalization

    ANS: A   DIF: 3   REF: p. 19   OBJ: 3 TYPE: APP/WWW

79. A 4-year-old girl sucks her thumb, a teenager binges on food, and an adult woman bites her fingernails. According to the Freudian theory of psychosexual development, all three are fixated at the _____ stage.
    a. oral
    b. anal
    c. phallic
    d. genital

    ANS: A   DIF: 1   REF: p. 19   OBJ: 3 TYPE: APP

80. The Oedipus complex, the psychosexual conflict that occurs at the phallic stage of development, is characterized by a three- to five-year-old boy who:
    a. represses his need for genital self-stimulation
    b. loves his mother but has feelings of anger and envy toward his father
    c. loves his father but has feelings of anger and envy toward his mother
    d. fantasizes about tragic Greek heroes

    ANS: B   DIF: 3   REF: p. 19   OBJ: 3 TYPE: CON

81. The Electra complex, the psychosexual conflict that occurs at the phallic stage of development in girls, is characterized by:
    a. castration anxiety
    b. Oedipal conflicts
    c. penis envy
    d. latency lust

    ANS: C   DIF: 3   REF: p. 19   OBJ: 3 TYPE: CON

82. Which of the following is NOT related to the "collective unconscious" in Carl Jung's psychoanalytic theory?
    a. accumulated wisdom of society
    b. genetic inheritance of personality traits
    c. individual storage of cultural memories
    d. passing of memories from one generation to another

    ANS: B   DIF: 3   REF: p. 20   OBJ: 3 TYPE: CON

83. Borderline Personality Disorder, in which some behavior "borders" on being out of touch with reality, was first associated with the ideas of:
    a. Otto Kernberg
    b. Sigmund Freud
    c. Alfred Adler
    d. Carl Jung

    ANS: A   DIF: 5   REF: p. 20   OBJ: 3 TYPE: CON

84. In their theories about human nature, psychoanalysts Carl Jung and Alfred Adler both:
    a. regarded human nature as possessing many negative qualities
    b. completely accepted Freud's ideas
    c. believed that there were no barriers to the internal and external growth of the individual
    d. emphasized a strong drive toward individual self-actualization

    ANS: D   DIF: 5   REF: p. 20   OBJ: 3 TYPE: CON

85. Anna Freud (1895-1982), a well-known psychoanalyst who developed the concept of "ego psychology," was Sigmund Freud's:
    a. wife
    b. sister
    c. cousin
    d. daughter

    ANS: D   DIF: 1   REF: p. 20   OBJ: 3 TYPE: FACT

86. All of the following are included in the psychoanalytic theories of Carl Jung EXCEPT:
    a. collective unconscious
    b. sexual drives
    c. spiritual and religious drives
    d. introversion/extroversion

    ANS: B   DIF: 1   REF: p. 20   OBJ: 3 TYPE: FACT

87. Which of the following is an accurate statement about "stage" theories of development?
    a. In Freudian theory, sexual arousal and interest occur during the latency stage.
    b. In Erikson's theory, development occurs across the life span.
    c. In Freudian theory, intrapsychic conflicts are resolved in early childhood.
    d. In Erikson's theory, the final stage of development begins at about age 50.

    ANS: B   DIF: 3   REF: p. 20   OBJ: 3 TYPE: CON

88. In psychoanalytic psychotherapy it is important for patients to:
    a. keep their thoughts and feelings to themselves
    b. make eye contact with the psychoanalyst
    c. describe the content of their dreams to the analyst
    d. remain emotionally detached from the analyst

    ANS: C   DIF: 5   REF: p. 20   OBJ: 3 TYPE: CON

89. Psychodynamic psychotherapy differs from classical (Freudian) psychoanalysis in that it:
    a. emphasizes the goal of personality reconstruction
    b. requires a long term commitment on the part of the person being analyzed
    c. focuses on social and interpersonal issues
    d. considers past experiences important

    ANS: C   DIF: 5   REF: p. 21   OBJ: 3 TYPE: CON

90. Most mental health professionals are aware that psychoanalysis as a treatment technique:
    a. is basically unscientific
    b. has been proven effective
    c. has been subject to careful measurement criteria
    d. is noted for consistency in analytic interpretation

    ANS: A   DIF: 5   REF: p. 21   OBJ: 3 TYPE: CON/WWW

91. The concepts of "self-actualizing" and "hierarchy of needs" are most closely associated with the theories of:
    a. Abraham Maslow
    b. Carl Rogers
    c. Carl Jung
    d. Melanie Klein

    ANS: A   DIF: 1   REF: p. 21, 22   OBJ: 3 TYPE: FACT

92. Which of the following is NOT associated with the humanistic theories of Carl Rogers?
    a. unconditional positive regard
    b. hierarchy of needs
    c. empathy
    d. person-centered therapy

    ANS: B   DIF: 1   REF: p. 22   OBJ: 3 TYPE: FACT

17

93. Humanistic therapists regard _____ as the single most positive influence in facilitating human growth.
    a. therapist interpretation of the patient's verbalizations
    b. relationships (including the therapeutic relationship)
    c. self-esteem
    d. intellectual and moral development

    ANS: B   DIF: 3   REF: p. 22   OBJ: 3 TYPE: CON

94. The systematic development of a scientific approach to psychopathology is represented by:
    a. humanistic psychology
    b. psychoanalysis
    c. Jungian psychology
    d. the behavioral model

    ANS: D   DIF: 3   REF: p. 22   OBJ: 3 TYPE: CON

95. Which method reflects the first general application of the behavioral method to psychopathology?
    a. introspection (Titchener)
    b. dream analysis (Freud)
    c. systematic desensitization (Wolpe)
    d. conditioning of a fear response (Pavlov)

    ANS: C   DIF: 5   REF: p. 24   OBJ: 3 TYPE: APP

96. Someone you know has been having a lot of difficulty because of irrational fears. Knowing that you are studying abnormal psychology, this person asks if you know of an effective and well-established treatment. You advise her that _____, based on the mid 20th century work of Joseph Wolpe, is a successful anxiety reduction procedure.
    a. systematic desensitization
    b. person centered therapy
    c. exorcism
    d. aversive conditioning

    ANS: A   DIF: 5   REF: p. 24   OBJ: 3 TYPE: APP/WWW

97. Which well known behavioral scientist is the author of The Behavior of Organisms (1938), Walden Two (1948), and Beyond Freedom and Dignity (1971)?
    a. John Watson
    b. Ivan Pavlov
    c. B.F. Skinner
    d. Edward L. Thorndike

    ANS: C   DIF: 1   REF: p. 24   OBJ: 3 TYPE: FACT

98. When scientific principles of psychology are applied to clinical problems or psychopathology the procedures implemented are called:
    a. clinical psychology
    b. behavior therapy
    c. scientific psychology
    d. the law of effect

    ANS: B   DIF: 5   REF: p. 24   OBJ: 3 TYPE: APP

99. The continual interaction of biological, psychological and social influences and their effect on behavior is called the _____ approach.
   a. sociocultural
   b. psychobiological/biopsychological
   c. systematic
   d. multidimensional integrative

   ANS: D   DIF: 3   REF: p. 26   OBJ: 4 TYPE: CON

100. As described on the "Abnormal Psychology Live" CD, Ivan Pavlov's ideas were brought to the United States in the early 20th century by:
   a. John B. Watson   c. B.F. Skinner
   b. Carl Jung   d. Mary Cover Jones

   ANS: A   DIF: 2   REF: CD

101. Behaviorists John Watson and B.F. Skinner believed that both animal and human behavior are the result of:
   a. conditioning   c. unconscious motivation
   b. sorcery   d. self-actualization

   ANS: A   DIF: 2   REF: CD

102. DSM-IV-TR, an updated version of the Diagnostic and Statistical Manual of Mental Disorders, was published in:
   a. 1996   c. 2000
   b. 1999   d. 2002

   ANS: C   DIF: 1   REF: p. 29   OBJ: 1 TYPE:FACT

103. Ivan Pavlov, a Russian physiologist, based his theories of conditioning on the results of experiments he conducted on:
   a. humans   c. rats
   b. pigeons   d. dogs

   ANS: D   DIF: 2   REF: CD

ESSAY

1. Discuss the criteria for abnormality and the meanings of psychological disorder, psychological dysfunction and "culturally expected" behavior.

2. Using examples from the case histories in Chapter 1, discuss whether psychological disorders are qualitatively different from normal behavior or just extreme expressions of normal behavior.

3. Describe the process of becoming a mental health professional. Discuss the differences among the following: psychiatrist, psychologist, psychiatric social worker, nurse practitioner. For each profession list the credentials, the educational background, and the professional responsibilities of scientist-practitioners. **WWW**

4. Compare and contrast the three traditional models of abnormal behavior: supernatural, psychological, and biological. Mention significant events and persons in the historical development of each model.

5. Describe the phenomenon of mass hysteria. Give historical and modern examples. Compare ideas regarding the etiology of this type of behavior.

6. Describe the work of the reformers Dorothea Dix and Philippe Pinel. Discuss whether their efforts were effective in improving conditions of the mentally ill.

7. Explain psychoanalytic theory. Refer to concepts such as anxiety, defense mechanisms and psychosexual development. Use examples to illustrate these concepts.

8. Compare and contrast classical psychoanalysis and psychodynamic psychotherapy. Note the criticisms of classical psychoanalysis and explain why it is more of historical than of current interest.

9. Explain how humanistic psychology and the behavioral model developed. Compare behavior therapy and humanistic therapy, noting significant contributors to each.

10. Explain the concept of a multidimensional integrative approach to psychopathology. Compare the ancient Greek view of the separation of mind and body with the current emphasis on biological etiology and brain-behavior interaction.

11. Using the information on the "Abnormal Psychology Live" CD, describe the historical events that culminated in the development of behaviorism in the United States. In your answer, make specific reference to the contributions of Pavlov, Watson, and Skinner.

REF: CD

MULTIPLE CHOICE

1. Which of the following is not an aspect of the definition of psychological disorders?
   a. the atypical response element, which states that a deviation from normal behavior is evidence of a psychological disorder
   b. the psychodynamic element, which suggests that abnormal behavior is the result of poor ego defense mechanisms
   c. the distress element, in which personal discomfort signals the presence of a psychological disorder
   d. the impairment in functioning element, which defines a psychological disorder based on a disruption in ability to carry out normal tasks

   ANS: B

2. The scientist-practitioner model of psychology focuses on
   a. the psychologist's use of scientific principles to study which treatments are most effective and to decide which treatment to use.
   b. the psychologist's use of statistics, such as prevalence and incidence, to diagnose clients.
   c. the exchange of information between scientists.
   d. the use of drugs in clinical practice.

   ANS: A

3. Louie was barking like a dog and walking on his hands and knees. A professional thought the cause of Louie's problem was that he had an excess of a particular neurotransmitter, and prescribed a drug for him. The professional is most likely a _____, operating under the _____ model of abnormal behavior.
   a. clinical psychologist, psychological
   b. psychiatric nurse, supernatural
   c. psychiatric social worker, behavioral
   d. psychiatrist, biological

   ANS: D

4. The phenomenon in which entire groups of people simultaneously begin to behave abnormally is known as
   a. mass hysteria.
   b. exorcism.
   c. lunacy.
   d. melancholy.

   ANS: A

5. The elements of person-centered therapy include
   a. hypnosis and catharsis.
   b. reinforcement and shaping.
   c. rest and relaxation.
   d. unconditional positive regard and empathy.

   ANS: D

6. Your best friend tells you she has just gotten a job in a Veteran's Administration hospital where she will administer and interpret tests, diagnose and treat mental disorders, and continue her research on chronic disorders. All of her training in _____ has paid off.
   a. nursing.
   b. psychiatry.
   c. social work.
   d. clinical psychology.
   e. counseling.

   ANS: D

7. Alarmingly, in some areas where the rate of new cases of AIDS had been declining, it has begun increasing again. The statistic that tells us this information is
   a. incidence.
   b. correlation.
   c. deviation.
   d. prevalence.

   ANS: A

8. Therapist Dr. X (not her real name) is working with a client who is heavily involved with body-piercing. The client enjoys it but Dr. X thinks the amount is so excessive she considers it abnormal behavior. She is employing which definition of abnormality?
   a. dysfunction
   b. culturally inappropriate or unexpected
   c. impairment
   d. distress

   ANS: B

9. Tim owns a cat who licks her chops when she hears cellophane catfood packets being opened. This is not a skill she or her wild ancestors learned in the jungle. According to a classical conditioning account, the cellophane sound is
   a. a conditioned stimulus.
   b. an unconditioned stimulus.
   c. a conditioned response.
   d. an unconditioned response.
   e. an instrumental operant

   ANS: A

10. Human behavior, both normal and abnormal, is the result of biological, psychological, and social factors _____.
   a. competing
   b. operating independently
   c. interacting
   d. conflicting

   ANS: C

MULTIPLE CHOICE

1. The best description of the multidimensional integrative approach to understanding psychopathology is that it is based on:
    a. biological and psychological causes
    b. biological causes only
    c. learned helplessness and social learning theory
    d. the physical structure and chemical processes of the brain

    ANS: A   DIF: 3   REF: p. 31   OBJ: 1 TYPE: CON

2. Within the multidimensional integrative approach to understanding psychopathology, learned helplessness is considered a _____ dimension.
    a. biological   c. emotional
    b. psychological   d. psychological

    ANS: C   DIF: 3   REF: p. 31   OBJ: 1 TYPE: CON

3. The basis of the multidimensional integrative approach to understanding psychopathology is that each dimension (psychological, biolgical, emotional, etc.):
    a. operates independently   c. builds on the dimension that preceeds it
    b. is sufficient to cause pathology   d. is influenced by the other dimensions

    ANS: D   DIF: 1   REF: p. 31   OBJ: 1 TYPE: CON

4. Your uncle spent most of his teen years in a hospital undergoing treatment for a severe physical illness. As an adult, he is rather shy and withdrawn, particularly around women. He has been diagnosed with social phobia and you believe that it is entirely due to lack of socialization during his teen years. Your theory or model of what caused his phobia is:
    a. multidimensional
    b. integrative
    c. one-dimensional
    d. biological

    ANS: C   DIF: 1   REF: p. 31   OBJ: 1 TYPE: APP

5. According to the multidimensional integrative approach to psychopathology, the following statement is true for most psychological disorders:
    a. if one monozygotic twin has a particular disorder, the other twin will definitely have the disorder as well
    b. monozygotic twins are no more likely to share psychological disorders than any other siblings
    c. monozygotic twins are no more likely to share disorders than any other two people selected at random from the population
    d. if one monozygotic twin has a particular psychological disorder, the other twin is more likely to have the disorder than the rest of the population

    ANS: D   DIF: 5   REF: p. 34   OBJ: 2 TYPE: APP

6. The most accurate way to think of genes is that they:
   a. set boundaries for our development
   b. determine both our physical and psychological characteristics
   c. determine physical but not psychological characteristics
   d. actually have very little to do with any of the characteristics that we display

   ANS: A   DIF: 3   REF: p. 34   OBJ: 2 TYPE: FACT/WWW

7. Referring to behavior and personality as polygenic means that both are:
   a. influenced by only a few genes, but each has a large effect
   b. influenced by many genes, with each individual gene contributing a relatively small effect
   c. influenced by individual genes only rarely
   d. a result of our genetic structure only

   ANS: B   DIF: 3   REF: p. 35   OBJ: 2 TYPE: FACT

8. The procedures referred to as quantitative genetics are used to:
   a. determine the effects of multiple genes   c. correct genetic abnormalities
   b. provide genetic counseling   d. test the multidimensional integrative
                                                       model

   ANS: A   DIF: 3   REF: p. 35   OBJ: 2 TYPE: FACT

9. Most psychological disorders appear to be influenced by many individual genes rather than caused by one single gene, a process referred to as:
   a. multigenic
   b. polygenic
   c. unigenic
   d. morphogenic

   ANS: B   DIF: 3   REF: p. 35   OBJ: 2 TYPE: FACT

10. The most recent estimate of the contribution of genetics to the development of general cognitive ability (IQ) is approximately:
    a. 20%
    b. 60%
    c. 80%
    d. zero

    ANS: B   DIF: 1   REF: p. 35   OBJ: 2 TYPE: FACT

11. The most recent estimates of the contribution of genetics to the development of personality characteristics such as shyness or activity level are approximately:
    a. 10 - 20%
    b. 30 - 50%
    c. 75 - 85%
    d. zero

    ANS: B   DIF: 1   REF: p. 35   OBJ: 2 TYPE: FACT

12. According to recent estimates, genetic contributions to the development of most psychological disorders are:
    a. below 50%
    b. above 50%
    c. different for each disorder (estimates range from 0 to 100%)
    d. nonexistent

    ANS: A   DIF: 1   REF: p. 35   OBJ: 2 TYPE: FACT

13. Recent evidence regarding the genetic influence on most psychological disorders has shown that:
    a. single genes are usually responsible for psychological disorders
    b. genes that influence psychopathology are usually recessive
    c. there is no evidence that genes influence psychopathology
    d. multiple genes interact, with each gene contributing a small effect

    ANS: D   DIF: 1   REF: p. 35   OBJ: 2 TYPE: FACT

14. In the diathesis-stress model, "diathesis" refers to:
    a. an inherited disorder
    b. conditions in the environment that can trigger a disorder depending upon how severe the stressors are
    c. an inherited tendency or condition that makes a person susceptible to developing a disorder
    d. the inheritance of multiple disorders

    ANS: C   DIF: 1   REF: p. 36   OBJ: 2 TYPE: FACT/WWW

15. In the diathesis-stress model, "stress" refers to:
    a. life events, in combination with an inherited tendency, that trigger a disorder
    b. inherited tendencies, in combination with life events, that trigger a disorder
    c. defective genes
    d. exposure to very unusual and extreme environmental conditions

    ANS: A   DIF: 1   REF: p. 36   OBJ: 2 TYPE: FACT

16. According to the diathesis-stress model, psychopathology is the result of the:
    a. interaction between normal and defective or damaged genes
    b. stress level of an individual and how stress is managed in a person's life
    c. family history of an individual
    d. interaction of an inherited tendency and events in the person's life

    ANS: D   DIF: 3   REF: p. 36   OBJ: 2 TYPE: FACT

17. According to the diathesis-stress model, monozygotic twins raised in the same household will:
    a. not necessarily have the same disorders because of potential differences in their diathesis
    b. have the same disorders because their diathesis and stress are exactly the same
    c. not necessarily have the same disorders because of potential differences in their stress
    d. have no more likelihood of sharing a disorder than any other two randomly selected individuals from the population

    ANS: C   DIF: 3   REF: p. 37   OBJ: 2 TYPE: APP

18. According to the diathesis-stress model, which statement is true?
    a. given a certain level of stress, a disorder will develop
    b. once a diathesis for a particular disorder is inherited, the disorder will eventually develop
    c. an individual's inherited tendencies will influence the stressful life events the person encounters
    d. it is possible to inherit a diathesis and never develop a disorder

    ANS: D   DIF: 3   REF: p. 37   OBJ: 2 TYPE: APP

19. The model that describes the development of psychopathology as a combination of an inherited predisposition and the events that have occurred in the individual's life is called:
    a. diathesis-stress
    b. genetic
    c. bio-behavioral
    d. psychoanalytic

    ANS: A   DIF: 3   REF: p. 37   OBJ: 2 TYPE: FACT

20. The idea that our inherited tendencies influence the probability that we will encounter stressful life events is a characteristic of the:
    a. diathesis-stress model
    b. reciprocal gene-environment model
    c. genetic model
    d. psycho-social model

    ANS: B   DIF: 3   REF: p. 38   OBJ: 2 TYPE: FACT

21. In the landmark study by Caspi et. al. (2003), the researchers studied stressful life events and genetics of 847 individuals. For individuals who had at least four stressful life events, the risk of major depression:
    a. remained unchanged regardless of genetic   c. halved if they possessed two short alleles
       make up   of the gene being studied
    b. doubled if they possessed two short alleles d. was entirely related to the genetic make-
       of the gene being studied   up and not the number of life stressors

    ANS: B   DIF: 3   REF: p. 37   OBJ: 2 TYPE: FACT

22. Recent studies such as Caspi (2003) and Hariri (2002) demonstrate that psychopathology and behavior in general are the result of:
    a. interactions between our genetics and   c. genetics more than environmental
       environment   influences
    b. environmental influences more than   d. neurotransmitters
       genetics

    ANS: A   DIF: 3   REF: p. 37   OBJ: 2 TYPE: FACT

23. John has inherited a personality trait that makes him more likely to keep to himself than to socialize. As a result he does not have many friends and spends a lot of time alone. If John were to develop depression, the model that would probably best explain this situation and the cause of his depression is:
a. diathesis-stress
b. biological
c. reciprocal gene-environment
d. interpersonal

ANS: C   DIF: 5   REF: p. 38   OBJ: 2 TYPE: APP/WWW

24. Some people may be genetically predisposed to seek out difficult relationships. These difficult relationships may contribute to their experience of depression. This is an example of the:
a. diathesis-stress model
b. reciprocal gene-environment model
c. genetic model
d. quantitative genetics

ANS: B   DIF: 3   REF: p. 38   OBJ: 2 TYPE: CON

25. Research studies using the procedure called "cross fostering" have shown that genetically emotional and reactive young animals raised by calm mothers tended to be:
a. calm
b. emotional and reactive
c. calm but emotional and reactive when raising their own young
d. emotional and reactive but calm when raising their own young

ANS: A   DIF: 3   REF: p. 39   OBJ: 2 TYPE: FACT

26. Looking at the findings of many cross fostering studies (Francis et al., 1999, Suomi, 1999, Tienari, et al., 1994) it appears that positive interventions such as good parenting in early life may:
a. have little effect in terms of preventing psychopathology in those geentically predisposed to such conditions
b. dramatically change the genetics of individuals genetically predisposed to psychopathology
c. have a greater effect on future generations than on the individual exposed to the "good parenting"
d. override the genetically influenced tendency to develop psychopathology in later life

ANS: D   DIF: 5   REF: p. 39   OBJ: 2 TYPE: CON

27. Some of the most recent research studies regarding genetic vs. environmental causes of disorders in animals and humans have suggested:
a. genetic influences are greater than originally observed because positive environmental conditions do not prevent disorders
b. genetics and the environment share equal roles in the development of all psychological disorders
c. the relative contributions of genetics and the environment in the development of psychological disorders are different for lower animals than for humans
d. genetic influences may have been overstated by previous studies, i.e., without sufficient environmental stress, the genetic predisposition may never be activated

ANS: D   DIF: 5   REF: p. 38   OBJ: 2 TYPE: FACT

28. The central nervous system is made up of the:
    a. brain and spinal cord
    b. brain only
    c. spinal cord only
    d. nerves leading to and from the brain

    ANS: A   DIF: 1   REF: p. 41   OBJ: 3 TYPE: FACT

29. The brain and the spinal cord comprise the:
    a. peripheral nervous system
    b. somatic nervous system
    c. parasympathetic nervous system
    d. central nervous system

    ANS: D   DIF: 1   REF: p. 41   OBJ: 3 TYPE: FACT

30. The area between the axon of one neuron and the dendrite of another neuron is the:
    a. axon terminal
    b. soma
    c. synaptic cleft
    d. transmission cleft

    ANS: C   DIF: 1   REF: p. 42   OBJ: 3 TYPE: FACT

31. The synaptic cleft is the area between the:
    a. soma of one neuron and the dendrite of another neuron
    b. axon of one neuron and the dendrite of another neuron
    c. axon of one neuron and the soma of another neuron
    d. somas of two neurons

    ANS: B   DIF: 1   REF: p. 42   OBJ: 3 TYPE: FACT

32. Neurotransmitters are important because they:
    a. allow neurons to send signals to other neurons
    b. maintain the oxygenation of the brain
    c. prevent the development of psychopathology
    d. allow the brain to maintain its structural integrity

    ANS: A   DIF: 1   REF: p. 42   OBJ: 3 TYPE: FACT

33. The chemicals that allow transmission of signals between neurons are called:
    a. re-uptake inhibitors
    b. hormones
    c. neurotransmitters
    d. genes

    ANS: C   DIF: 1   REF: p. 42   OBJ: 3 TYPE: FACT

34. GABA, dopamine and norepinephrine are all examples of:
   a. electrical brain waves
   b. neurons
   c. neurotransmitters
   d. areas of the brain

   ANS: C   DIF: 1   REF: p. 42   OBJ: 3 TYPE: FACT

35. Most automatic functions, e.g., breathing, sleeping and motor coordination, are controlled by the part of the brain called the:
   a. brain stem
   b. forebrain
   c. cortex
   d. frontal lobes

   ANS: A   DIF: 3   REF: p. 44   OBJ: 3 TYPE: FACT

36. Recent research has associated the _____ with autism. This is also the part of the brain that controls motor coordination.
   a. reticular activating system (RAS)
   b. medulla
   c. pons
   d. cerebellum

   ANS: D   DIF: 3   REF: p. 44   OBJ: 3 TYPE: FACT

37. The part of the brain stem that regulates vital activities such as heartbeat, breathing and digestion is the:
   a. cerebellum
   b. reticular activating system (RAS)
   c. hindbrain
   d. thalamus

   ANS: C   DIF: 1   REF: p. 44   OBJ: 3 TYPE: FACT

38. Functions of the limbic system include control or regulation of:
   a. basic body functions such as breathing
   b. sleep cycles
   c. emotional experiences, expressions, impulse control and basic drives such as aggression, sex, hunger and thirst
   d. body posture, coordinated movement and involuntary responses such as reflexes and other automatic processes

   ANS: C   DIF: 3   REF: p. 44   OBJ: 3 TYPE: FACT

39. About 80% of the neurons contained in the brain are located in the:
   a. cerebral cortex
   b. brain stem
   c. midbrain
   d. basal ganglia

   ANS: A   DIF: 1   REF: p. 44   OBJ: 3 TYPE: FACT

40. The ability to plan, think, reason and create is located in the part of the brain called the:
    a. thalamus
    b. midbrain
    c. cerebral cortex
    d. brain stem

    ANS: C   DIF: 1   REF: p. 44   OBJ: 3 TYPE: FACT

41. The part of the brain that makes humans most distinct from other animals is the:
    a. thalamus
    b. midbrain
    c. brain stem
    d. cerebral cortex

    ANS: D   DIF: 3   REF: p. 44   OBJ: 3 TYPE: FACT

42. The significance of the human cerebral cortex is that, in comparison to the brains of animals, it makes our _____.
    a. instincts stronger
    b. thoughts distinct
    c. motor responses faster
    d. immune functioning superior

    ANS: B   DIF: 3   REF: p. 44   OBJ: 3 TYPE: FACT/WWW

43. For most people, verbal and cognitive processes are usually controlled by the:
    a. left hemisphere of the cortex
    b. right hemisphere of the cortex
    c. entire cortex
    d. midbrain

    ANS. A   DIF: 3   REF: p. 44   OBJ: 3 TYPE: FACT

44. For most people, perception and the creation of images are usually handled by the:
    a. left hemisphere of the cortex
    b. entire cortex
    c. midbrain
    d. right hemisphere of the cortex

    ANS: D   DIF: 3   REF: p. 44   OBJ: 3 TYPE: FACT

45. The part(s) of the brain most associated with memory, thought and reasoning is(are) the:
    a. occipital lobes
    b. brain stem
    c. left parietal lobe
    d. frontal lobes

    ANS: D   DIF: 3   REF: p. 44   OBJ: 3 TYPE: FACT

46. The peripheral nervous system is made up of the:
   a. endocrine system
   b. brain stem and cortex
   c. somatic and autonomic nervous system
   d. brain and spinal cord

   ANS: C   DIF: 1   REF: p. 44   OBJ: 3 TYPE: FACT

47. The major function of the peripheral nervous system is to:
   a. carry messages to and from the central nervous system
   b. process information received from the central nervous system
   c. regulate arousal
   d. control hormonal activity

   ANS: A   DIF: 1   REF: p. 44   OBJ: 3 TYPE: FACT

48. The part of the autonomic nervous system primarily responsible for our "fight or flight" response to stress is the:
   a. parasympathetic nervous system
   b. sympathetic nervous system
   c. endocrine system
   d. cortex

   ANS: B   DIF: 1   REF: p. 45   OBJ: 3 TYPE: FACT

49. Balancing the "fight or flight" response to stress and returning the body to a state of "normal arousal" is a function of the:
   a. sympathetic nervous system
   b. parasympathetic nervous system
   c. endocrine system
   d. cortex

   ANS: B   DIF: 1   REF: p. 46   OBJ: 3 TYPE: FACT

50. When those studying the brain speak of brain circuits, they are referring to:
   a. electrical pathways in the brain   c. neurotransmitter pathways
   b. physical brain structures   d. brain stem activity

   ANS: A   DIF: 3   REF: p. 46   OBJ: 3 TYPE: FACT

51. Virtually all drugs that are used to treat psychopathology work by influencing:
   a. neurotransmitters
   b. electrical conductivity of neurons
   c. brain structure
   d. neuronal structure

   ANS: A   DIF: 1   REF: p. 46   OBJ: 4 TYPE: FACT

52. According to your text's discussion of how neurotransmitters such as serotonin work, the term "biochemical imbalance" for the cause of disorders such as depression is probably:
    a. an oversimplification
    b. about accurate
    c. completely incorrect
    d. a perfect description

    ANS: A   DIF: 3   REF: p. 47   OBJ: 4 TYPE: CON

53. Drugs that increase the activity of a neurotransmitter are called:
    a. agonists
    b. antagonists
    c. enhancers
    d. psychotropics

    ANS: A   DIF: 3   REF: p. 47   OBJ: 4 TYPE: FACT

54. Drugs that decrease the activity of a neurotransmitter are called:
    a. agonists
    b. blockers
    c. re-uptake inhibitors
    d. antagonists

    ANS: D   DIF: 3   REF: p. 47   OBJ: 4 TYPE: FACT

55. Drugs that interfere with the re-uptake of a neurotransmitter are called:
    a. agonists
    b. antagonists
    c. blockers
    d. enhancers

    ANS: A   DIF: 3   REF: p. 47   OBJ: 4 TYPE: FACT

56. The neurotransmitter associated with regulation of mood, behavior and thought processes is:
    a. GABA
    b. norepinephrine
    c. serotonin
    d. dopamine

    ANS: C   DIF: 3   REF: p. 47   OBJ: 4 TYPE: FACT

57. The neurotransmitter associated with inhibition of anxiety is:
    a. norepinephrine
    b. dopamine
    c. serotonin
    d. GABA

    ANS: D   DIF: 3   REF: p. 48   OBJ: 4 TYPE: FACT

58. The neurotransmitter thought to regulate or moderate certain behavioral tendencies rather than directly influencing specific patterns of behavior or psychological disorders is:
    a. norepinephrine
    b. GABA
    c. dopamine
    d. serotonin

    ANS: A   DIF: 3   REF: p. 48   OBJ: 4 TYPE: FACT

59. The neurotransmitter associated with both schizophrenia and Parkinson's disease is:
    a. GABA
    b. norepinephrine
    c. dopamine
    d. serotonin

    ANS: C   DIF: 1   REF: p. 49   OBJ: 4 TYPE: FACT

60. Extremely low activity levels of serotonin are associated with:
    a. aggression, suicide and impulsive behavior
    b. schizophrenia
    c. anxiety disorders and general feelings of nervousness
    d. mania

    ANS: A   DIF: 3   REF: p. 47   OBJ: 4 TYPE: FACT

61. Extremely low levels of GABA are associated with:
    a. decreased anxiety
    b. increased depression
    c. increased anxiety
    d. decreased depression

    ANS: C   DIF: 3   REF: p. 48   OBJ: 4 TYPE: FACT

62. Extremely low levels of dopamine activity are associated with:
    a. muscle rigidity, tremors and impaired judgement
    b. schizophrenia
    c. pleasure seeking
    d. exploratory behaviors

    ANS: A   DIF: 3   REF: p. 49   OBJ: 4 TYPE: FACT

63. Recent research and increased understanding about the role of neurotransmitters in psychopathology point out that:
    a. each psychological disorder is caused by a deficit in a specific neurotransmitter
    b. chemical imbalances of the brain are the cause of psychopathology
    c. simple cause/effect conclusions stating that an individual neurotransmitter abnormality causes a disorder are incomplete
    d. neurotransmitters have very little to do with psychopathology for most individuals but may be the single cause of disorders for others

    ANS: C   DIF: 3   REF: p. 50   OBJ: 4 TYPE: CON/WWW

64. In the 1992 studies conducted by Baxter et al., OCD patients were provided with cognitive-behavioral therapy (exposure and response prevention) but no drugs. This study is important because brain imaging showed that:
    a. the neurotransmitter circuits of the brain had been normalized
    b. the patients' OCD symptoms improved without changes in neurotransmitter function
    c. neither OCD symptoms nor neurotransmitter function had improved
    d. neurotransmitter circuits are the direct and only cause of OCD

    ANS: A   DIF: 3   REF: p. 51   OBJ: 4 TYPE: FACT

65. What is one of the conclusions generally drawn from the 1990s studies of OCD, brain imaging and cognitive-behavioral therapy by Baxter et al., and the follow up studies by Schwartz, et al.?
    a. neurotransmitters affect how people feel and act
    b. drugs are the only way to impact faulty neurotransmitter circuits
    c. neurotransmitters are a result of how people feel and act, not a cause
    d. psychosocial factors such as therapy affect neurotransmitters

    ANS: D   DIF: 3   REF: p. 51   OBJ: 4 TYPE: FACT

66. In a recent study (Petrovic, Kalso, Peterson & Ingvar, 2002), subjects were exposed to a painful stimulus (heat to the hand) under three conditions: 1. opiate medication, 2. placebo (sugar pill) medication, and 3. no medication. Brain scans indicated that a subject's experience of reduced pain with the placebo is due to:
    a. activation of brain regions identical to those activated by opiate medication
    b. activation of brain regions that are overlapping, but not identical, to those activated by opiate medication
    c. psychological expectation since a placebo does not activate brain regions associated with pain control
    d. similarities in activated brain regions during the "no medication" condition

    ANS: B   DIF: 3   REF: p. 51   OBJ: 4 TYPE: FACT

67. Insel, Champoux, Scanlan and Scoumi (1986) raised one group of rhesus monkeys with the ability to control things in their environment and another group of monkeys who had no control of their environment (e.g., when they would receive treats and toys). When injected with a drug that produces a feeling of severe anxiety, the monkeys:
    a. raised with a sense of control appeared angry and aggressive while the monkeys raised without a sense of control appeared very anxious
    b. raised with a sense of control appeared anxious while the monkeys raised without a sense of control appeared angry and aggressive
    c. in both groups appeared anxious
    d. in both groups appeared angry and aggressive

    ANS: A   DIF: 5   REF: p. 52   OBJ: 4 TYPE: FACT

68. The significance of the study conducted by Insel, Champoux, Scanlan and Scoumi (1986), in which rhesus monkeys were raised either with a sense of control or without a sense of control and later exposed to an anxiety-inducing drug is that chemicals such as neurotransmitters:
    a. have very direct effects on behavior
    b. influence behavior in different ways depending upon the psychological history of the individual
    c. influence individuals in fairly direct and consistent ways regardless of the psychological history of the individual
    d. have few reliable and consistent effects on observed behavior

    ANS: B   DIF: 5   REF: p. 52   OBJ: 4 TYPE: CON/WWW

69. The most recent research evidence suggests that the relationship between the brain (structure, function, neurotransmitters) and psychosocial factors (socialization, rearing, life events) is best described as:
    a. a system where our brains directly influence our behavior and psychosocial factors but not the other way around
    b. an interaction where the brain affects our psychosocial factors and psychosocial factors impact our brain
    c. a system where our behavior and psychosocial factors impact our brain but not the other way around
    d. far too complex to ever understand whether one system influences the other

    ANS: B   DIF: 5   REF: p. 53   OBJ: 4 TYPE: CON

70. When comparing the brains of rats raised in a rich environment requiring lots of learning and motor behavior with the brains of rats raised as "couch potatoes" (Greenough, 1990), the cerebellums of the more active rats:
    a. contained more neuronal connections and dendrites
    b. contained fewer neuronal connections but more axons and dendrites
    c. were less likely to possess pathological neurotransmitter circuits
    d. were exactly the same as the inactive rats

    ANS: A   DIF: 5   REF: p. 52   OBJ: 4 TYPE: FACT

71. Studies regarding rat learning and brain structure by Greenough, (1990) and Wallace, et al. (1992), suggest that:
    a. early experiences such as learning cause physical changes in the brain
    b. psychopathology is the result of early learning experiences
    c. while psychopathology is often a result of early life experiences, it is generally due to the physical changes in the brain that such experiences cause
    d. genetically caused brain structure problems can be corrected by positive life experiences

    ANS: A   DIF: 3   REF: p. 53   OBJ: 4 TYPE: CON

72. One conclusion that can be drawn from the studies regarding rat learning and brain structure (Greenough, 1990; Wallace, et al, 1992) is that:
    a. early psychological experience affects the development of the nervous system and will absolutely determine whether or not the individual will develop a psychological disorder later in life
    b. early psychological experience does not result in physical changes to the nervous system but can still influence whether or not one develops a psychological disorder
    c. early psychological experience affects the development of the nervous system and influences vulnerability to psychological disorders later in life
    d. early psychological experience has little to do with brain structure or later development of psychopathology

    ANS: C   DIF: 5   REF: p. 53   OBJ: 4 TYPE: CON

73. Regarding biological influences on the development of psychopathology, the most accurate statement is:
    a. both genetics and life events play a part in the development of brain structure and function that can affect vulnerability to psychopathology
    b. life events can only cause changes in brain structure or function for those with genetic defects
    c. early life events play a much greater role in the development of brain structure or function than genetics
    d. vulnerability to psychopathology has little to do with the brain changes associated with genetics or early life events

    ANS: A   DIF: 3   REF: p. 53   OBJ: 4 TYPE: CON

74. When one examines the current state of knowledge regarding genetics and life experience effects on brain structure and function, the best overall conclusion is that most psychological disorders are:
    a. the result of a complex interaction of genetics and faulty neurotransmitter circuits
    b. the result of stressful early life experiences and the negative effects such experiences have on brain structure or function
    c. the result of both biological and psychosocial factors
    d. beyond our current ability to understand in any meaningful way

    ANS: C   DIF: 3   REF: p. 53   OBJ: 4 TYPE: CON

75. Learned helplessness is demonstrated in laboratory animals by:
    a. creating aversive stimuli (such as electrical shocks to the foot) that the animal can control
    b. creating aversive stimuli (such as electrical shocks to the foot) that the animal cannot control
    c. creating pleasant stimuli (such as a food pellet) that the animal cannot control
    d. creating pleasant stimuli (such as a food pellet) that the animal can control

    ANS: B   DIF: 3   REF: p. 55   OBJ: 5 TYPE: FACT

76. Placing a rat in a cage where electrical shocks, over which the rat has no control, are occasionally administered through the floor is a way to create:
    a. social learning
    b. learned helplessness
    c. unconscious learning
    d. negative neurotransmitter pathways
    e. one angry rat

    ANS: B   DIF: 3   REF: p. 55   OBJ: 5 TYPE: FACT

77. It is important to understand the process of how learned helplessness is created in laboratory animals because learned helplessness in animals resembles the human disorder of:
    a. panic disorder
    b. depression
    c. mania
    d. schizophrenia

    ANS: B   DIF: 3   REF: p. 55   OBJ: 5 TYPE: FACT

78. The behavior of an individual who believes that no matter how hard she studies, she will never succeed in college can best be explained by:
    a. personality disorder
    b. faulty neurotransmitter circuits
    c. learned helplessness
    d. internal conflicts

    ANS: C   DIF: 1   REF: p. 55   OBJ: 5 TYPE: CON

79. In a study by Levy, Slade, Kunkel, & Kasl (2002) individuals between the ages of 50 and 94 who had positive views about themselves as well as positive attitudes towards aging:
    a. lived four years longer than those without   c. were found to be less likely to have heart
       such positive attitudes.   disease.
    b. lived seven and a half years longer than   d. were found to be more likely to be
       those without such positive attitudes.   involved with positive community
                                                          activities.

    ANS: B   DIF: 3   REF: p. 55   OBJ: 5 TYPE: FACT

80. The work of Albert Bandura regarding modeling helps us to understand the development of psychopathology because it demonstrates that animals:
    a. can learn patterns of behavior by observing others
    b. must learn through direct experience such as classical or operant conditioning
    c. will only learn behavior patterns if they are reinforced by a model
    d. acquire all of their behavior patterns by imitating the actions of others

    ANS: A   DIF: 3   REF: p. 55   OBJ: 5 TYPE: CON/WWW

81. One important contribution of the work of Albert Bandura regarding modeling or observational learning is that:
    a. much of our learned behavior depends upon our interactions with those around us
    b. our learned behavior has much more to do with the types of consequences (reinforcements and punishments) of our actions than our interactions with those around us
    c. it is impossible to learn behavioral patterns without observing those around us
    d. learning acquired through observation is much more resistant to extinction than behavior acquired through classical or operant conditioning

    ANS: A   DIF: 5   REF: p. 55   OBJ: 5 TYPE: CON

82. The major difference between the modern cognitive science idea of the unconscious and Freud's view of the unconscious is that Freud saw the unconscious as _____ where modern cognitive science views the unconscious as _____.
    a. the function of the id; the result of multiple neuronal pathways interacting with the stimuli presented to the individual
    b. a seething caldron of emotional conflicts; neuronal pathways interacting with the stimuli presented to the individual
    c. the function of the superego; ability to process, store and act upon information without awareness
    d. a seething caldron of emotional conflicts; ability to process, store and act upon information without awareness

    ANS: D   DIF: 3   REF: p. 56   OBJ: 5 TYPE: CON

83. According to modern cognitive science, the unconscious:
    a. clearly exists in much the same way that Freud imagined
    b. may or may not exist as it is impossible to study material that we are not aware of
    c. clearly does not exist
    d. clearly exists but in a very different way than Freud imagined

    ANS: D   DIF: 3   REF: p. 56   OBJ: 5 TYPE: CON/WWW

84. In the Stroop color naming paradigm, a patient with a blood phobia would be expected to name the color of the printed word "wound":
    a. more quickly than a neutral word
    b. in about the same time it takes to name the color of a neutral word
    c. more slowly than a neutral word
    d. with a great deal of difficulty or not at all

    ANS: C   DIF: 5   REF: p. 56   OBJ: 5 TYPE: APP

85. Strong emotional reactions such as extreme fear are generally experienced as unpleasant to the individual. In panic disorder, for example, patients may experience these sensations quite frequently. The primary function of human capability for such strong emotion appears to be:
    a. survival
    b. recreation
    c. empathy
    d. creativity

    ANS: A   DIF: 3   REF: p. 57   OBJ: 5 TYPE: APP

86. Emotion is generally thought to be comprised of :
    a. behavior, physiology, and cognition
    b. mood and affect
    c. cognition, behavior and affect
    d. behavior physiology and mood

    ANS: A   DIF: 3   REF: p. 57   OBJ: 5 TYPE: FACT

87. You and a friend are lost while walking on a street in a foreign city. A stranger approaches and you are concerned that the stranger may try to mug you. Your friend assumes that the stranger is approaching to give you directions. As the stranger approaches, you experience fear but your friend experiences relief. Your different emotional reactions can be explained by the _____ theory of emotion.
    a. physiological
    b. neurological
    c. affective
    d. cognitive

    ANS: D   DIF: 3   REF: p. 58   OBJ: 5 TYPE: APP

88. The relationship between emotion and health is demonstrated by the fact that:
    a. panic is related to poor concentration
    b. people with chronic diseases are often angry about their care
    c. those in poor physical health almost always develop psychological disorders
    d. anger increases risk of heart disease

    ANS: D   DIF: 3   REF: p. 59   OBJ: 5 TYPE: FACT

89. Studies examining the effects of anger and hostility on the cardiovascular system have demonstrated that anger results in:
    a. decreased pumping efficiency of the heart
    b. increased pumping efficiency of the heart
    c. heart changes similar to those found when exercising
    d. few if any measurable changes in the heart

    ANS: A   DIF: 1   REF: p. 59   OBJ: 5 TYPE: FACT

90. The "evil eye," Latin American *susto*, and the Haitian phenomenon of voodoo death are currently viewed as examples of the:
    a. unsubstantiated myths that people can become ill without physical cause
    b. power of the social environment on our physical and psychological health
    c. power of the supernatural model of psychopathology
    d. isolated cultural phenomena with little practical significance

    ANS: B   DIF: 3   REF: p. 60   OBJ: 6 TYPE: CON/WWW

91. The fact that women are more likely to suffer from insect phobias than men is most likely due to:
    a. biological differences
    b. differences in neurochemical pathways
    c. cultural expectations
    d. genetic influences

    ANS: C   DIF: 1   REF: p. 61   OBJ: 6 TYPE: CON

92. Anxious males tend to have a higher rate of alcoholism than females. One likely explanation for this difference is that men are:
    a. more likely to use alcohol to deal with anxiety rather than admit they are afraid
    b. less likely to be fearful of becoming alcoholic
    c. exposed to alcohol more often than women are
    d. more likely to see alcohol as a good long term solution to problems such as anxiety

    ANS: A   DIF: 1   REF: p. 61   OBJ: 6 TYPE: CON

93. The influences of culture and gender on psychopathology are most clearly evident in the disorder of:
    a. anorexia
    b. panic disorder
    c. bipolar disorder
    d. depression

    ANS: A   DIF: 1   REF: p. 61   OBJ: 6 TYPE: CON

94. People who have many social contacts and live their lives continually interacting with others:
    a. develop more infections and have poorer overall health
    b. have not been found to differ on any health outcome
    c. often suffer from psychological disorders such as dependency
    d. live longer and healthier lives

    ANS: D   DIF: 1   REF: p. 61   OBJ: 6 TYPE: FACT/WWW

95. Research exposing subjects to the virus that causes the common cold (Cohen, Doyle, Skoner, Rabin, and Gwaltney (1997), demonstrated that:
    a. the lower the individual's socialization, the lower the chances of contracting a cold
    b. the greater the individual's socialization, the lower the chances of contracting a cold
    c. extent of socialization and chances of contracting a cold were unrelated
    d. the quality of social contact predicted whether the individual would contract a cold, but the frequency of social contact did not

    ANS: B   DIF: 3   REF: p. 62   OBJ: 6 TYPE: FACT

96. Regarding the research on socialization and health, the safest conclusion is that:
    a. social support is important but mostly for those individuals who are at high risk for various physical or psychological disorders
    b. having a supportive group of people around us is important to our physical health but not our psychological well being
    c. having a supportive group of people around us is important to our psychological well being but not our physical health
    d. having a supportive group of people around us is one of the most important parts of maintaining our physical and mental health

    ANS: D   DIF: 5   REF: p. 62   OBJ: 6 TYPE: CON

97. In a study conducted by Haber and Barchas (1983), monkeys were injected with amphetamine, a central nervous system stimulant. Comparison of the drug's effects on the dominant versus submissive monkeys demonstrated that the effects of brain chemicals such as drugs are:
    a. different for individual animals depending upon their place in the social hierarchy
    b. the same for all animals regardless of their place in the social hierarchy
    c. the same for all animals except for those with a biological predisposition for aggression
    d. different for individual animals but the differences appear to be random

    ANS: A   DIF: 5   REF: p. 63   OBJ: 6 TYPE: CON

98. Depression and schizophrenia seem to appear in all cultures but tend to be characterized by different symptoms within individual cultures. For example, depression in western culture is generally characterized by feelings of guilt and inadequacy where in developing countries it is characterized by physical distress such as fatigue or illness. This is most likely due to:
    a. genetic differences between individuals living in different cultures
    b. differences in treatment provided in different cultures
    c. reasons that our current methods of study are incapable of understanding
    d. the fact that social and cultural factors influence psychopathology

    ANS: D   DIF: 5   REF: p. 62   OBJ: 6 TYPE: CON

99. Research with the elderly has found that depression is more likely in those individuals who:
    a. have frequent social contacts
    b. live in group settings
    c. have fewer social contacts
    d. receive increased attention from their families when they are sick

    ANS: C   DIF: 1   REF: p. 62   OBJ: 6 TYPE: FACT

100. Given the role of social factors in psychological disorders and the fact that psychological disorders are still associated with social stigma (people tend to think that the disorder is something to be ashamed of), there is a much greater chance that people with psychological disorders will:
    a. be far more easily treated than those with physical disorders
    b. seek help for their disorders but be more likely to receive insufficient treatment than those with physical illness
    c. be ignored by mental health professionals when they seek help
    d. not seek and receive the treatment and support of others that are most needed for recovery

    ANS: D   DIF: 1   REF: p. 63   OBJ: 6 TYPE: CON

101. When we compare the incidence of psychological disorders across countries and cultures, we find that:
    a. there is remarkable similarity in the rates of various disorders in different countries and cultures
    b. all western countries have a similar rate of common disorders but this is not true for developing countries
    c. developing countries have a much higher rate of psychological disorder than western countries
    d. there are enormous differences in the rates of various disorders in different countries and cultures

    ANS: D   DIF: 3   REF: p. 63   OBJ: 6 TYPE: FACT

102. Political strife, war and suffering in a country tend to _____ the rate of psychological disorders in the country.
    a. decrease
    b. have little effect on
    c. have unpredictable effects on
    d. increase

    ANS: D   DIF: 1   REF: p. 63   OBJ: 6 TYPE: FACT

103. A lifespan psychologist would point out that the only way to understand a patient's disorder is to understand how the individual:
    a. developed from a childhood to adulthood
    b. developed during the psychosexual stages
    c. resolved conflicts in early life
    d. sees himself/herself as part of a family, a community and a culture

    ANS: A   DIF: 1   REF: p. 64   OBJ: 6 TYPE: FACT

104. When therapists ask patients how they are feeling and how they are experiencing their disorder today, it is essentially taking "snap-shots" of their lives at the moment. This approach to understanding psychopathology is criticized as incomplete by:
    a. lifespan psychologists
    b. cognitive-behaviorists
    c. humanists
    d. all mental health workers

    ANS: A   DIF: 1   REF: p. 64   OBJ: 7 TYPE: CON

105. In an experiment by Kolb, Gibb, and Gorny (2003), animals of varying ages were placed in complex environments. Their findings suggest that:
    a. the impact of the environment on the brain is different at varying stages of life
    c. environments that are beneficial to the aged may be harmful to the young
    b. the impact of the environment on the brain is significant but uniform throughout the life span
    d. the environment has little effect on the brain throughout the lifespan

    ANS: A   DIF: 3   REF: p. 64   OBJ: 7 TYPE: CON

106. The fact that some behaviors can be symptoms of many different disorders (e.g., delusions can be a result of amphetamine abuse or of schizophrenia) is an example of:
    a. equifinality
    b. psychopathology
    c. pathogenesis
    d. orthogonal causation

    ANS: A   DIF: 5   REF: p. 64   OBJ: 7 TYPE: FACT

107. The term equifinality refers to the fact that:
    a. once a process has begun, it will always lead to a final outcome
    b. many causes of psychopathology are equal in influence
    c. a number of paths can lead to the same outcome
    d. all forms of psychopathology have similar causes

    ANS: C   DIF: 5   REF: p. 64   OBJ: 7 TYPE: FACT

108. During Dr. Barlow's "Abnormal Psychology Live" presentation, he explains that the study of the causes of psychopathology is very complex because:
    a. our research methods are very limited
    b. the science of psychology is only a little over 100 years old
    c. every patient is an individual and pathology may be caused by unique factors in each patient
    d. psychological and biological influences interact so we can't understand them in isolation

    ANS: D   DIF: 2   REF: CD

109. In the "Abnormal Psychology Live" presentation, Dr. Barlow expalins that while brain chemicals and drugs impact behavior, it is also true that psychological intervention:
    a. impacts brain function and structure
    b. is a powerful tool to change behavior
    c. is a more limited but safer way to change behavior
    d. may one day be found to influence brain function and structure too

    ANS: A   DIF: 2   REF: CD

ESSAY

1. Describe the diathesis-stress model. Use the model to explain how one monozygotic twin suffers from clinical depression while the other does not.

2. Explain the difference between the modern cognitive science view of the unconscious and the Freudian idea of the unconscious.   **WWW**

3. Explain why is it considered too simplistic to say that disorders like depression are caused by too little serotonin or that schizophrenia is caused by too much dopamine.

4. Psychoactive medications (drugs that impact our thoughts, emotions and behavior) usually work as either agonists or antagonists for various neurotransmitters. Explain how both an agonist and an antagonist operate on a neurotransmitter. Explain the process of re-uptake inhibition and the effect it has on a neurotransmitter.

5. Describe the basic components of the multidimensional integrative model. What are the dimensions and what does the term integrative mean in this model?

6. Name three important neurotransmitters and describe what impact each one is thought to have on human experience.

7. Describe learned helplessness. How is it developed in laboratory animals and how does it help us to understand human depression?

8. Several studies (Baxter et al., 1992, Brody, et al, 2001, Leuchter et al., 2002, Petrovic et al., 2002) have demonstrated the ability of psychological/environmental factors to influence brain function. Discuss the methods used in one or more of these studies and explain the resulting implications of this type of research for understanding the causes of psychopathology in humans.

9. Socialization is considered one of the most important parts of human experience. Describe some of the research findings that demonstrate the importance of relationships to our psychological well being.

10. Describe the concept of equifinality. What does this concept say regarding the causes of psychopathology?

11. In Dr. Barlow's "Abnormal Psychology Live" presentation, he appears very optimistic about our ability to make progress in our current and future understanding of the causes of psychopathology. At the same time he indicates that such understanding will not come from simple, one dimensional models. Based on Dr. Barlow's presentation, explain what you think the future will bring regarding our understanding for the causes of psychopathology.

REF: CD

Study Guide

MULTIPLE CHOICE

1. The part of the nervous system that is activated in times of stress is the _____ nervous system.
   a. parasympathetic
   b. somatic
   c. sympathetic
   d. central

   ANS: C

2. Obsessive-compulsive disorder appears to be linked to the area of the brain called the _____. The implications of this finding are that _____.
   a. orbital frontal cortex; although the disorder is related to a particular brain circuit, the causes of the disorder are not necessarily completely biological.
   b. orbital frontal cortex; the disorder is probably due only to brain damage in this area.
   c. occipital lobe; although the disorder is related to a particular brain circuit, the disorder causes the abnormalities in the brain.
   d. occipital lobe; the disorder is most likely due to purely psychological causes.

   ANS: A

3. Research indicates that the relationship between psychological treatment and brain circuits is such that
   a. psychological treatment works regardless of the brain circuit activity.
   b. psychological treatment can alter brain circuits.
   c. brain circuit activity alone determines the response to psychological treatment.
   d. psychological treatment is not effective due to the changes in the brain caused by mental disorders.

   ANS: B

4. According to the principle of prepared learning, humans
   a. are genetically predisposed to know certain things.
   b. inherit a capacity to learn certain things that are beneficial to the survival of the species.
   c. ready to learn to read by the age of six.
   d. are unable to learn the same things that rats learn.

   ANS: B

5. Beck's cognitive-behavioral therapy focuses on
   a. free association.
   b. internal conflicts.
   c. modifying beliefs and attitudes.
   d. self-actualization.

   ANS: C

6. The endocrine system is important because it
    a. produces the neurotransmitters that determine bodily growth.
    b. produces hormones that are implicated in some psychological problems.
    c. produces the hormones that directly cause some psychological disorders.
    d. is the main controller of the entire nervous system.

    ANS: B

7. Judy's blood-injury-injection phobia described in the text was likely caused by
    a. a biological predisposition
    b. behavioral influences
    c. social influences
    d. all of the above

    ANS: B

8. Which part of the brain gives humans the capacity to think, plan, and reason?
    a. cerebellum
    b. thalamus
    c. limbic system
    d. cerebral cortex

    ANS: D

9. Which of the following could result in learned helplessness?
    a. being in a stressful situation one cannot control
    b. being in a stressful situation and refusing to control it
    c. being in control and then encountering stressors
    d. perceiving control when none is present

    ANS: A

10. Equifinality refers to the idea that
    a. different paths may lead to the same outcome.
    b. a psychological disorder is caused by more than one factor.
    c. a disorder will have a different prognosis, depending on the individual.
    d. the same disorder can have multiple symptoms.

    ANS: A

MULTIPLE CHOICE

1. The systematic evaluation of psychological, biological and social factors in a person with a possible mental disorder is known as clinical _____.
   a. assessment
   b. interpretation
   c. validation
   d. standardization

   ANS: A   DIF: 1   REF: p. 69   OBJ: 1 TYPE: CON

2. The process of determining whether an individual's symptoms meet the criteria for a specific psychological disorder is called:
   a. prognosis
   b. diagnosis
   c. classification
   d. analysis

   ANS: B   DIF: 3   REF: p. 69   OBJ: 1 TYPE: CON

3. The text revision of the *Diagnostic and Statistical Manual of Mental Disorders* (DSM-IV-TR) was published in:
   a. 1985
   b. 1990
   c. 1994
   d. 2000

   ANS: D   DIF: 1   REF: p. 69   OBJ: 5 TYPE: FACT

4. The *Diagnostic and Statistical Manual of Mental Disorders* is a publication of the:
   a. American Psychological Association
   b. International Association of Psychologists
   c. American Psychiatric Association
   d. National Institutes of Mental Health

   ANS: C   DIF: 1   REF: p. 69   OBJ: 5 TYPE: FACT

5. Which of the following factors is typically NOT part of a clinical assessment?
   a. psychological
   b. social
   c. biological
   d. astrological

   ANS: D   DIF: 3   REF: p. 69   OBJ: 2 TYPE: CON

6. In the first interview with Frank, a patient described in the textbook, he stated that he had been having intrusive thoughts that he tried to prevent by performing certain movements. Based on this information, you might predict that Frank would be diagnosed with:
   a. major depressive disorder
   b. obsessive-compulsive disorder
   c. a personality disorder
   d. schizophrenia

   ANS: B   DIF: 5   REF: p. 70, 91   OBJ: 2 TYPE: APP

7. According to Brian, the discharged Army veteran described in your textbook, he identified himself as homosexual because:
   a. gay men approached him frequently
   b. his homosexual experiences were very satisfying
   c. he believed others thought he was "queer"
   d. women rejected him

   ANS: C   DIF: 5   REF: p. 70   OBJ: 2 TYPE: APP

8. In the textbook case study, Brian, the 20 year-old who identified himself as a homosexual, was referred for a psychological evaluation because of:
   a. anxiety symptoms
   b. sexual problems
   c. depressive episodes
   d. aggressive behavior

   ANS: B   DIF: 3   REF: p. 70   OBJ: 2 TYPE: APP

9. During the interview with the Army veteran named Brian (described in your textbook), he stated that he was homosexual and also said that:
   a. others thought he was straight
   b. he had homosexual friends
   c. he wanted to be straight
   d. there was one particular man that he was attracted to

   ANS: C   DIF: 3   REF: p. 70   OBJ: 2 TYPE: APP

10. The process of clinical assessment results in narrowing the focus to:
    a. concentrate on problem areas that seem most relevant
    b. consider a broad range of problems
    c. cover all possible problems
    d. concentrate on all problem areas equally

    ANS: A   DIF: 5   REF: p. 70   OBJ: 1 TYPE: CON

11. If you had been the therapist conducting a diagnostic interview with Frank, the patient described in the textbook that was having intrusive thoughts, you would have observed that he:
    a. looked attentively at the therapist
    b. suffered from a seizure disorder
    c. frequently closed his eyes
    d. spoke in a loud, threatening manner

    ANS: C   DIF: 3   REF: p. 70   OBJ: 2 TYPE: APP

12. Which of the following is **NOT** one of the three basic concepts that help determine the value of a psychological assessment procedure?
    a. reliability
    b. classification
    c. validity
    d. standardization

    ANS: B   DIF: 1   REF: p. 71   OBJ: 1 TYPE: CON

13. A patient who had recurrent headaches, fatigue, and loss of appetite received different diagnoses about this condition from several psychologists. In terms of assessment, this indicates a problem with _____.
    a. reliability
    b. classification
    c. validity
    d. standardization

    ANS: A   DIF: 5   REF: p. 71   OBJ: 1 TYPE: APP

14. In terms of psychological assessment, which of the following describes the concept of validity?
    a. two or more "raters" get the same answers
    b. an assessment technique is consistent across different measures
    c. scores are used as a norm for comparison purposes
    d. an assessment technique measures what it is designed to measure

    ANS: D   DIF: 3   REF: p. 71   OBJ: 1 TYPE: CON/WWW

15. Mr. J., a 40 year-old recent immigrant to the United States comes from a working-class background and is just learning to speak English. He applies for a job and is given a test. His score is compared to others who have taken the test, mostly young college graduates whose native language is English. Mr. J. thinks this is unfair. In fact, this is an issue of _____.
    a. reliability
    b. classification
    c. validity
    d. standardization

    ANS: D   DIF: 5   REF: p. 71   OBJ: 1 TYPE: APP

16. In trying to understand and help an individual with a psychological problem, the psychologist will obtain detailed information about the person's life as part of a:
    a. physical exam
    b. clinical interview
    c. mental status exam
    d. brain scan

    ANS: B   DIF: 3   REF: p. 71   OBJ: 2 TYPE: CON/WWW

17. As part of a psychological assessment, a *mental status exam* is used to find out how a person thinks, feels and behaves; its primary purpose, however, is to determine:
    a. if a psychological disorder might be present
    b. what type of treatment should be used
    c. which medication would be most effective
    d. whether the individual also has a medical condition

    ANS: A   DIF: 3   REF: p. 72   OBJ: 2 TYPE: CON

18. In a *mental status exam* a psychologist evaluates an individual's thought processes by:
    a. asking the person to read aloud
    b. listening to what the person says
    c. reading what the person has written
    d. evaluating the person's dreams

    ANS: B   DIF: 3   REF: p. 72   OBJ: 2 TYPE: CON

19. In a *mental status exam*, the term "sensorium" indicates a person's:
    a. general awareness of his or her surroundings
    b. level of emotional sensitivity
    c. ability to make reasonable judgments
    d. impairment in visual or auditory functioning

    ANS: A   DIF: 3   REF: p. 72   OBJ: 2 TYPE: CON

20. Determining mood and affect is an important part of the *mental status exam*. Although both of these terms refer to feeling states of the individual, it would be correct to say that mood is more _____ than affect.
    a. pervasive
    b. severe
    c. changeable
    d. frequent

    ANS: A   DIF: 5   REF: p. 72   OBJ: 2 TYPE: CON

21. If an individual were observed to be laughing during a funeral service, it could be said that his or her affect was _____.
    a. blunted
    b. inappropriate
    c. flat
    d. pervasive

    ANS: B   DIF: 1   REF: p. 72   OBJ: 2 TYPE: APP

22. A *mental status exam* covers all of the following categories EXCEPT:
    a. intellectual functioning
    b. appearance
    c. behavior
    d. physical symptoms

    ANS: D   DIF: 1   REF: p. 72   OBJ: 2 TYPE: CON

23. In regard to a *mental status exam*, which of the following questions is NOT related to the concept of sensorium?
    a. What is today's date?
    b. Where are you?
    c. Who are you?
    d. How old are you?

ANS: D   DIF: 1   REF: p. 72   OBJ: 2 TYPE: CON

24. In a *mental status exam*, it is important to determine if the individual's sensorium is clear and if he or she is "oriented times three." This refers to:
    a. person, place and time
    b. day, month and year of birth
    c. ability to follow directions
    d. spatial orientation

ANS: A   DIF: 5   REF: p. 72   OBJ: 2 TYPE: CON

25. The initial assessment of the patient in your textbook named Frank, who was anxious about his job and his marriage, revealed that he:
    a. had intrusive thoughts
    b. was disoriented
    c. showed inappropriate affect
    d. had a low intelligence level

ANS: A   DIF: 5   REF: p. 73   OBJ: 2 TYPE: APP

26. All of the following apply to a clinical interview conducted by a psychologist EXCEPT:
    a. attempts to facilitate communication
    b. uses nonthreatening ways of seeking information
    c. keeps patient information confidential in all circumstances
    d. applies appropriate listening skills

ANS: C   DIF: 5   REF: p. 73   OBJ: 2 TYPE: CON

27. In a clinical interview, the law regarding "privileged communication" does NOT apply if the patient:
    a. threatens self-harm or harm to another person
    b. relates a history of sexual abuse
    c. has been mentally ill for more than five years
    d. is hospitalized in a psychiatric facility

ANS: A   DIF: 3   REF: p. 73   OBJ: 2 TYPE: CON

28. The Anxiety Disorders Interview Schedule for DSM-IV is an example of a:
    a. personality inventory
    b. semistructured clinical interview
    c. projective test
    d. behavioral intervention

ANS: B   DIF: 3   REF: p. 74   OBJ: 2 TYPE: CON

29. Which of the following medical conditions might also produce symptoms of behavioral disorders or symptoms that mimic psychological disorders?
    a. hyperthyroidism
    b. cocaine withdrawal
    c. both of these
    d. neither of these

    ANS: C   DIF: 5   REF: p. 74   OBJ: 2 TYPE: APP

30. As part of a behavioral assessment, psychologists sometimes use _____ settings when it is not possible to do direct observation in a naturalistic setting.
    a. imagel
    b. empirical
    c. analog
    d. virtual

    ANS: C   DIF: 3   REF: p. 76   OBJ: 2 TYPE: FACT

31. The reactivity phenomenon of self-monitoring procedures has been shown to:
    a. increase desired behaviors
    b. decrease undesired behaviors
    c. both increase desired behaviors and decrease undesired behaviors
    d. neither increase desired behaviors nor decrease undesired behaviors

    ANS: C   DIF: 5   REF: p. 77   OBJ: 2 TYPE: CON

32. When observational data are being collected, the observer's presence may cause a person to behave differently, a phenomenon known as:
    a. reactivity
    b. structuring
    c. recording
    d. monitoring

    ANS: A   DIF: 5   REF: p. 77   OBJ: 2 TYPE: CON

33. In discussing monitoring procedures, which of the following is an example of the reactivity phenomenon?
    a. A man begins to eat less after joining a clinic weight loss program in which each participant's weight is recorded weekly by a staff member.
    b. After joining a fitness club, a woman stops exercising in her home and instead walks 2 miles a day by herself.
    c. A man changes his brand of cigarettes after his father dies of lung cancer.
    d. On parents' visiting day in a classroom, the previously well-behaved children continue to show good behavior.

    ANS: A   DIF: 5   REF: p. 77   OBJ: 2 TYPE: APP

34. Many popular magazines include "psychological" or "personality" tests to help readers better understand themselves or others. According to the textbook, most of these tests are:
    a. reliable
    b. valid
    c. for entertainment only
    d. informative and educational

    ANS: C   DIF: 3   REF: p. 77   OBJ: 3 TYPE: APP/WWW

35. Which of the following describes a personality inventory?
    a. determines the possible contribution of brain damage to the person's condition
    b. uses imaging to assess brain structure and/or function
    c. assesses long-standing patterns of behavior
    d. ascertains the structure and patterns of cognition

    ANS: C   DIF: 2   REF: p. 79   OBJ: 3 TYPE: CON

36. Which of the following describes an intelligence test?
    a. determines the possible contribution of brain damage to the person's condition
    b. uses imaging to assess brain structure and/or function
    c. assesses long-standing patterns of behavior
    d. ascertains the structure and patterns of cognition

    ANS: D   DIF: 2   REF: p. 81   OBJ: 3 TYPE:CON

37. Which of the following describes a neuropsychological test?
    a. determines the possible contribution of brain damage to the person's condition
    b. uses imaging to assess brain structure and/or function
    c. assesses long-standing patterns of behavior
    d. ascertains the structure and patterns of cognition

    ANS: A   DIF: 2   REF: p. 82   OBJ: 3 TYPE:CON

38. Which of the following describes a neurobiological test?
    a. determines the possible contribution of brain damage to the person's condition
    b. uses imaging to assess brain structure and/or function
    c. assesses long-standing patterns of behavior
    d. ascertains the structure and patterns of cognition

    ANS: B   DIF: 3   REF: p. 83-84   OBJ: 3 TYPE:CON

39. The projective type of psychological tests is based on _____ theory.
    a. behavioral
    b. cognitive
    c. humanistic
    d. psychoanalytic

    ANS: D   DIF: 3   REF: p. 78   OBJ: 3 TYPE: FACT/WWW

40. When an individual describes what he or she sees in the ambiguous stimuli of the Rorschach test, it is assumed that the person's _____ thoughts are revealed.
    a. unconscious
    b. conscious
    c. preconscious
    d. postconscious

    ANS: A   DIF: 5   REF: p. 78   OBJ: 3 TYPE: APP

41. A psychoanalytic therapist who wants to assess the unconscious thoughts and feelings of a patient would be most likely to use the _____ test.
    a. MMPI
    b. Bender Visual-Motor Gestalt Test
    c. Rorschach inkblot test
    d. Halstead-Reitan Neuropsychological Battery

    ANS: C   DIF: 5   REF: p. 78   OBJ: 3 TYPE: CON/WWW

42. Use of the Rorschach test has long been considered controversial because of all of the following concerns EXCEPT:
    a. the test is based on psychoanalytic theory
    b. there is little or no data regarding its reliability or validity
    c. the inkblots have been changed many times since the test was developed
    d. until recently there were no standardized procedures for administering the test

    ANS: C   DIF: 5   REF: p. 78   OBJ: 3 TYPE: CON

43. The Comprehensive System, a more standardized version of the Rorschach inkblot test, was developed in the 1970s by:
    a. Paul Meehl
    b. Herman Rorschach
    c. John Exner
    d. Alfred Binet

    ANS: C   DIF: 1   REF: p. 78   OBJ: 3 TYPE: FACT

44. The Comprehensive System of administering and scoring the Rorschach inkblot test specifies all of the following EXCEPT:
    a. how the cards with the inkblots should be presented
    b. exactly what the psychologist administering the test should say
    c. the way in which the test taker's responses should be recorded
    d. the amount of time allowed for each inkblot card to be presented

    ANS: D   DIF: 5   REF: p. 78   OBJ: 3 TYPE: APP

45. The Comprehensive System for administering and scoring the Rorschach inkblot test was developed because:
    a. a lack of standardized procedures affects the way the test taker responds to the questions
    b. it was discovered that inter-rater reliability had increased significantly
    c. Hermann Rorschach was dissatisfied with the way his test was being given
    d. the previous scoring system was found to be difficult and time consuming

    ANS: A   DIF: 5   REF: p. 78   OBJ: 3 TYPE: CON

46. The Thematic Apperception Test differs from the Rorschach inkblot test in that the person taking the TAT is asked to use his or her imagination to:
    a. tell a complete story about a picture
    b. draw a picture based on a story that is read aloud by the examiner
    c. write down responses after reading a short story
    d. tell a story and draw a picture about it

    ANS: A   DIF: 3   REF: p. 78   OBJ: 3 TYPE: CON

47. Which of the following is an accurate statement about the Thematic Apperception Test?
    a. most psychologists interpret responses to the TAT cards in the same way
    b. high inter-rater reliability exists among those administering the test
    c. the TAT is used as a diagnostic test because validity is high
    d. many clinicians use the TAT to encourage people to talk more openly about their lives

    ANS: D   DIF: 3   REF: p. 79   OBJ: 3 TYPE: CON/WWW

48. In regard to projective tests, research has found that most clinicians:
    a. do not use projective tests
    b. have their own ways of administering and scoring the tests
    c. use standardized procedures when administering and scoring the tests
    d. rely on these tests to diagnose psychopathology

    ANS: B   DIF: 3   REF: p. 79   OBJ: 3 TYPE: APP

49. "The questions make sense to the person reading them and the wording of the questions seems to fit the type of information desired." In regard to personality inventories, which type of validity is defined by the preceding statement?
    a. predictive
    b. face
    c. construct
    d. analytic

    ANS: B   DIF: 3   REF: p. 79   OBJ: 3 TYPE: CON

50. In regard to the questions used on personality inventories, which of the following reflects the position of psychologist Paul Meehl?
    a. the meaning of the questions should be apparent to the reader
    b. the questions should have surface validity
    c. the wording and content of the questions is most relevant
    d. the answers to the questions and what they predict is most important

    ANS: D   DIF: 5   REF: p. 79   OBJ: 3 TYPE: APP

51. As an assessment measure, the MMPI is considered unique because it is:
    a. data based
    b. theory based
    c. based on the biological model
    d. based on the humanistic approach

    ANS: A   DIF: 3   REF: p. 79   OBJ: 3 TYPE: CON

52. If you were asked to compare and contrast the MMPI and the Rorschach inkblot test, you could say correctly that:
    a. responses are interpreted individually in the MMPI
    b. the pattern of responses is evaluated in the MMPI
    c. the Rorschach test is more tedious and time consuming for the patient to complete
    d. the Rorschach test more accurately predicts psychopathology

    ANS: B   DIF: 5   REF: p. 79   OBJ: 3 TYPE: APP

53. Since the MMPI is _____ the assessment concept known as reliability is increased.
    a. often interpreted by computer
    b. made up of many scales
    c. non-sexist
    d. well-researched

    ANS: A   DIF: 3   REF: p. 79   OBJ: 3 TYPE: CON

54. All of the following refer to MMPI-2 scales EXCEPT:
    a. BIZ (bizarre mentation)
    b. CYN (cynicism)
    c. PSA (psychamuria)
    d. WRK (work interference)

    ANS: C   DIF: 1   REF: p. 80   OBJ: 3 TYPE: FACT

55. An individual taking the MMPI who falsifies answers in order to look good will probably have a high score on the _____ scale.
    a. Cannot-Say (?)
    b. Lie (L)
    c. Infrequency (F)
    d. Defensiveness (K)

    ANS: B   DIF: 3   REF: p. 79   OBJ: 3 TYPE: APP

56. On the original version of the MMPI, a pattern of responses indicating that a person is aggressive, unreliable, and irresponsible would result in a high score on the _____ scale.
    a. Psychopathic deviation (Pd)
    b. Paranoia (Pa)
    c. Hysteria (Hy)
    d. Social Introversion (Si)

    ANS: A   DIF: 3   REF: p. 80-81   OBJ: 3 TYPE: CON

57. The MMPI-A, a new version of the Minnesota Multiphasic Personality Inventory, has been developed specifically for testing:
    a. children with ADHD
    b. children with autism
    c. adults
    d. adolescents

    ANS: D   DIF: 1   REF: p. 80   OBJ: 3 TYPE: FACT

58. While taking the MMPI, James S. made an attempt to give himself an unrealistic positive image by falsifying answers and trying to appear as though he had no psychological problems. On the four MMPI scales that determine the validity of each test administration, you could accurately state that James S. probably had high scores on the:
    a. L and F scales only
    b. F scale only
    c. L and K scales only
    d. Cannot Say scale only

    ANS: C   DIF: 5   REF: p. 80   OBJ: 3 TYPE: APP

59. The MMPI-2, a more recent version of the personality inventory, has been updated to reflect all of the following EXCEPT:
    a. cultural diversity
    b. gender equality
    c. contemporary issues
    d. sexual values

    ANS: D   DIF: 3   REF: p. 80   OBJ: 3 TYPE: CON

60. The calculation of an IQ, previously done by using a child's mental age, is now done by using a deviation IQ. This means that the child's score is compared to the scores of others:
    a. of the same age
    b. in the same grade
    c. who took the test at the same time
    d. with the same level of intelligence

    ANS: A   DIF: 5   REF: p. 81   OBJ: 3 TYPE: CON

61. In regard to IQ tests, which of the following statements is NOT true?
    a. IQ and intelligence are the same thing.
    b. An IQ test has predictive validity with respect to academic success.
    c. IQ tests measure abilities such as attention, memory, reasoning and perception.
    d. Psychologists have different theories about which skills and abilities constitute intelligence.

    ANS: A   DIF: 5   REF: p. 81-82   OBJ: 3 TYPE: CON

62. The performance scales on the WISC-III (Weschler Intelligence Scale for Children) measure all of the following EXCEPT:
    a. vocabulary and knowledge of facts
    b. psychomotor abilities
    c. ability to learn new relationships
    d. non-verbal reasoning

    ANS: A   DIF: 3   REF: p. 82   OBJ: 3 TYPE: FACT

63. Neuropsychological tests are used to assess whether or not an individual might:
    a. be mentally retarded
    b. have a brain dysfunction
    c. have had a psychotic episode
    d. be in a depressed state

    ANS: B   DIF: 3   REF: p. 82   OBJ: 3 TYPE: APP/WWW

64. If it were important to determine the exact location of brain impairment, which of the following tests would most likely be used?
    a. Bender Visual-Motor Gestalt Test
    b. Halstead-Reitan Neuropsychological Battery
    c. Gall Phrenological Brain Scan
    d. Stanford-Binet Intelligence Scale

    ANS: B   DIF: 5   REF: p. 82   OBJ: 3 TYPE: APP

65. Although abnormalities in the structure and functioning of the brain can be detected by neuroimaging techniques, current research is also looking at:
    a. a possible association of these abnormalities with psychological disorders
    b. using brain imaging techniques as a treatment for psychological disorders
    c. preventing psychological disorders with neuroimaging techniques
    d. changing brain functioning from abnormal to normal

    ANS: A   DIF: 5   REF: p. 83   OBJ: 4 TYPE: APP

66. Recent research involving PET scans has shown that patients with Alzheimer's disease have:
    a. increased dopamine reuptake in the occipital lobes
    b. increased serotonin levels in the temporal lobes
    c. reduced glucose metabolism in the parietal lobes
    d. reduced amino acid production in the frontal lobes

    ANS: C   DIF: 5   REF: p. 84   OBJ: 4 TYPE: APP

67. In addition to MRI, PET, and CT, there are other brain imaging techniques currently in use or now being developed. Which of the following is NOT one of these newer neuroimaging techniques?
    a. fMRI
    b. MEG
    c. SPECT
    d. EEG

    ANS: D   DIF: 1   REF: p. 84   OBJ: 4 TYPE: FACT

68. A primary diagnostic technique for identifying seizure disorders is the:
    a. EEG
    b. DOT
    c. GSR
    d. ERP

    ANS: A   DIF: 3   REF: p. 84   OBJ: 4 TYPE: FACT

69. According to the textbook, assessment of psychophysiological response to emotional stimuli is important in treating all of the following EXCEPT:
   a. sexual dysfunctions
   b. posttraumatic stress disorder
   c. hypertension
   d. cancer

   ANS: D   DIF: 5   REF: p. 85   OBJ: 4 TYPE: CON

70. One important advantage of using a classification and diagnostic system like DSM-IV is that knowing a patient's diagnosis:
   a. helps the therapist to develop a treatment plan and prognosis
   b. allows patients to fully participate in their own treatment
   c. permits the insurance company to have access to patients' records
   d. allows the therapist to see the patient as an individual

   ANS: A   DIF: 3   REF: p. 86   OBJ: 5 TYPE: CON

71. Believing that it would not helpful, a therapist refuses to use the DSM-IV nor any other diagnostic system. One problem that we may expect for this therapist is that it may be hard to:
   a. apply what has been learned from treating other patients with similar problems
   b. think of patients as individuals
   c. monitor the progress of patients in therapy
   d. convince patients that mental disorders do not define an individual's personality

   ANS: A   DIF: 5   REF: p. 86   OBJ: 5 TYPE: APP

72. The dimensional approach to classification of mental disorders differs from the categorical approach because the dimensional system provides:
   a. lists of symptoms that are associated with all of the forms of psychopathology that are currently believed to exist
   b. diagnostic labels based on the presence of specific symptoms
   c. information that is used to determine the cause and treatment of the disorder
   d. scales that indicate the degree to which patients are experiencing various cognitions, moods and behaviors

   ANS: D   DIF: 3   REF: p. 87   OBJ: 5 TYPE: CON

73. Most people who are correctly diagnosed with a DSM-IV disorder like Major Depressive Episode will:
   a. usually have at least some of the same symptoms as others with the disorder
   b. always have at least five of the same symptoms as others with the disorder
   c. typically have very few of the same symptoms as others with the disorder
   d. usually experience all of the same symptoms as others with the disorder

   ANS: A   DIF: 3   REF: p. 88   OBJ: 5 TYPE: CON

74. Several clinicians interview a patient and use a new diagnostic system to independently provide the same diagnosis. We can say that it appears the new diagnostic system is:
    a. reliable
    b. valid
    c. both reliable and valid
    d. neither reliable nor valid

    ANS: A   DIF: 5   REF: p. 88   OBJ: 5 TYPE: APP

75. The crucial test as to whether a diagnostic system has a high degree of validity is that it should result in:
    a. an effective treatment plan
    b. all clinicians reaching the same diagnosis for the patient
    c. the accurate diagnostic label for the patient
    d. the same diagnostic label regardless of when the patient is evaluated

    ANS: C   DIF: 5   REF: p. 88   OBJ: 5 TYPE: APP/WWW

76. In 1980, the first widely accepted nosology of mental disorders relying on precise descriptions of disorders was introduced as:
    a. DSM-II
    b. DSM-III
    c. DSM-III-R
    d. DSM-IV

    ANS: B   DIF: 1   REF: p. 89   OBJ: 5 TYPE: FACT

77. An important change in the DSM versions that followed DSM-III was:
    a. the lack of a presumed theoretical cause for each disorder
    b. a change from a dimensional to a categorical system
    c. greater emphasis on validity and less concern for reliability
    d. the inclusion of the humanistic view of pathology

    ANS: A   DIF: 3   REF: p. 89   OBJ: 5 TYPE: CON

78. One of the important changes from DSM-III-R to DSM-IV reflects our greater understanding of the multiple causes and influences on various mental states and disorders. This change is:
    a. less distinction between organically (physically) caused and psychologically based disorders in DSM-IV
    b. more distinction between organically (physically) caused and psychologically based disorders in DSM-IV
    c. more distinction between neurosis and psychosis in DSM-IV
    d. less emphasis on the types of treatment that might be appropriate for each disorder in DSM-IV

    ANS: A   DIF: 5   REF: p. 90   OBJ: 5 TYPE: CON

79. The best way to have a general idea about a patient's overall level of functioning is to look at DSM-IV Axis:
    a. I
    b. II
    c. III
    d. V

    ANS: D   DIF: 1   REF: p. 90   OBJ: 5 TYPE: FACT

80. Using the multiaxial system of DSM-IV, disorders such as Major Depressive Episode, anxiety disorders and learning disorders are coded on:
    a. Axis I
    b. Axis II
    c. Axis III
    d. Axis IV

    ANS: A   DIF: 3   REF: p. 90   OBJ: 5 TYPE: CON

81. In the DSM-IV, medical conditions are coded on _____.
    a. Axis I
    b. Axis II
    c. Axis III
    d. Axis V

    ANS: C   DIF: 1   REF: p. 90   OBJ: 5 TYPE: FACT

82. A patient's depression began following a recent divorce and subsequent homelessness. The events of divorce and homelessness are coded on _____ in DSM-IV.
    a. Axis II
    b. Axis III
    c. Axis IV
    d. Axis V

    ANS: C   DIF: 3   REF: p. 90   OBJ: 5 TYPE: APP

83. The best way to have a general idea of a patient's overall level of functioning in life is to look at DSM-IV Axis _____.
    a. I
    b. II
    c. III
    d. V

    ANS: D   DIF: 3   REF: p. 91   OBJ: 5 TYPE: FACT/WWW

84. One of the problems with a diagnostic and classification system like the DSM-IV is that:
    a. individuals are often assigned more than one psychological disorder at one time
    b. diagnosis is difficult because it is hard to tell how much discomfort a particular symptom is causing the patient
    c. the criteria for many mental disorders are almost identical to each other
    d. it attempts to maximize validity at the cost of reliability

    ANS: A   DIF: 3   REF: p. 91   OBJ: 5 TYPE: CON

85. In classifying mental disorders, we no longer use labels such as moron, imbecile or idiot because:
    a. labels can take on a negative meaning
    b. people will refuse treatment for mental disorders that have a negative connotation
    c. mental health professionals are reluctant to assign a diagnosis that upsets people
    d. disorders can change more frequently than changes in classification systems

    ANS: A   DIF: 3   REF: p. 92-93   OBJ: 5 TYPE: APP

86. All of the following are potential dangers of assigning a diagnostic label EXCEPT:
    a. the patient may lose self-esteem
    b. the patient's prognosis (future course of the disorder) becomes difficult to predict
    c. family and friends may see the patient as the disorder rather than an individual
    d. health care workers may see the patient as the disorder rather than an individual

    ANS: B   DIF: 3   REF: p. 93   OBJ: 5 TYPE: APP/WWW

87. Before establishing a new DSM diagnostic category, e.g., mixed anxiety-depression, all of the following would be considered EXCEPT:
    a. whether an appropriate form of therapy currently exists for the condition
    b. the possibility that the symptoms are better accounted for by existing disorders
    c. the degree of suffering and impairment that the symptoms cause
    d. whether there are significant numbers of people who experience the symptoms

    ANS: A   DIF: 3   REF: p. 93-94   OBJ: 5 TYPE: CON

88. According to the authors of your textbook (Barlow and Durand), the future of DSM classification is most likely to include a greater emphasis on:
    a. the dimensional approach
    b. the categorical approach
    c. a theoretical approach, e.g., psychoanalytic, humanistic or behavioral
    d. economic considerations of diagnosis

    ANS: A   DIF: 3   REF: p. 89   OBJ: 5 TYPE: CON

89. The terms taxonomy and nosology refer to:
    a. scientific classification
    b. the accuracy of a diagnostic system
    c. the reliability of a grouping of clinical symptoms
    d. theoretical ideas that cannot be tested objectively

    ANS: A   DIF: 1   REF: p. 86   OBJ: 5 TYPE: FACT

90. DSM-IV-TR is based on a _____ classification system.
    a. dimensional
    b. categorical
    c. prototypical
    d. psychoanalytic

    ANS: C   DIF: 1   REF: p. 88   OBJ: 5 TYPE: FACT

91. A classical categorical approach to diagnosis is:
    a. more useful in psychology than in medicine
    b. more useful in medicine than in psychology
    c. not appropriate in either medicine or psychology
    d. equally useful in medicine and psychology

    ANS: B   DIF: 3   REF: p. 87   OBJ: 5 TYPE: CON

92. The classical categorical approach to diagnosis assumes that each person with a particular disorder will:
    a. be helped by recognizing the cause of the disorder
    b. experience very few of the same symptoms
    c. respond to the same treatments equally
    d. experience the same symptoms with little or no variation

    ANS: D   DIF: 5   REF: p. 88   OBJ: 5 TYPE: CON

93. The dimensional approach to diagnosis is characterized by:
    a. quantification of patients' experiences using scales measuring several areas such as anxiety or depression
    b. lists of symptoms that patients must experience for the diagnosis to be assigned
    c. essential elements that all patients must report for the diagnosis to be assigned but allowance for specific nonessential variations as well
    d. a theoretical explanation for the underlying cause of the disorder that is assumed to be shared by all patients experiencing similar symptoms

    ANS: A   DIF: 3   REF: p. 87   OBJ: 5 TYPE: CON

94. In contrast to previous editions of DSM, the fourth edition integrates possible social and cultural influences on diagnosis. All of the following questions relate to these influences EXCEPT:
    a. Does the clinician understand the cultural significance of the patient's disorder?
    b. Does the patient accept Western models of disease or disorder?
    c. Is it acceptable in the patient's culture to be physically ill but not mentally ill?
    d. Do the symptoms of the patient's disorder meet the criteria for a DSM-IV diagnosis?

    ANS: D   DIF: 5   REF: p. 91   OBJ: 5 TYPE: APP

95. In the Hispanic subculture, *ataques de nervios* is a type of _____ disorder.
    a. depressive
    b. psychotic
    c. anxiety
    d. manic

    ANS: C   DIF: 3   REF: p. 91   OBJ: 5 TYPE: FACT

96. Controversy continues concerning inclusion of "premenstrual dysphoric disorder" in future editions of DSM because of issues related to:
    a. religion
    b. racism
    c. stigmatization
    d. pregnancy and birth

    ANS: C   DIF: 3   REF: p. 94   OBJ: 5 TYPE: CON

97. Assume that it is not the 21st century but rather the 1st century and you are a female who has been having some vague pains in various parts of your body. In fact, sometimes you can hardly move due to the pain. Most likely a knowledgeable medical practitioner, e.g., Hippocrates, would diagnose you with a condition called:
   a. neurasthenia
   b. ataque de nervios
   c. hysteria
   d. psychogenic pain disorder

   ANS: C   DIF: 3   REF: p. 94   OBJ: 5 TYPE: APP

98. If you were asked to support the inclusion of "Premenstrual Dysphoric Disorder" (previously called LLPDD) as a DSM diagnostic category, which of the following statements would you NOT include?
   a. About 5% of women with Premenstrual Syndrome (PMS), a similar but less severe disorder, suffer from incapacitating symptoms.
   b. There are several treatments for the biological abnormalities associated with PMDD.
   c. Many women with no other psychological disorders meet the criteria for PMDD.
   d. PMDD is primarily either a gynecological or an endocrinological disorder.

   ANS: D   DIF: 5   REF: p. 94-95   OBJ: 5 TYPE: APP

99. Hysteria, a "female" condition characterized by physical complaints without medical basis, was thought to result from a(n):
   a. displaced ovary
   b. wandering uterus
   c. enlarged womb
   d. missing cervix

   ANS: B   DIF: 1   REF: p. 94   OBJ: 5 TYPE: CON

100. Assume that it is the year 2010 and that "premenstrual dysphoric disorder" has been included in "DSM-V." A young woman named Debra has been having severe mood swings and other problems just prior to the beginning of her menstrual period. However she is reluctant to go to a clinician because she is concerned that she might be diagnosed as having a(an) _____ problem.
   a. gynecological
   b. psychiatric
   c. endocrine
   d. hormonal

   ANS: B   DIF: 3   REF: p. 95   OBJ: 5 TYPE: APP

ESSAY

1. Describe the major objectives and procedures of clinical assessment. Be sure to include the typical activities of the assessor and the intended outcomes of the process.

2. Describe the concepts of reliability and validity. Why are the reliability and the validity of an assessment procedure important?

3. Describe the major objectives and typical procedures of the mental status exam. Be sure to include the typical activities of the examiner and the intended outcomes of the process.

4. Discuss the concept of confidentiality and the limits of confidentiality with regard to clinical assessment. Be sure to include the situations that would cause a clinician to break confidentiality.

5. Projective tests such as the Thematic Apperception Test and the original Rorschach inkblot test are often criticized with regard to their reliability. Explain why the reliability of these tests may not be as good as a personality measure such as the MMPI.

6. A psychiatrist orders a series of tests including an IQ test, personality inventory (MMPI), neuropsychological test (Halstead-Reitan) and a brain scan (CT scan) for a 10-year-old boy who has recently been acting aggressively. Explain what each test measures and how the psychiatrist would use the results of each test to help diagnose or rule out potential causes of the boy's behavior.

7. Describe the influence of culture on the experience of psychopathology. Why is it important for the clinician to acknowledge and appreciate the patient's culture before determining a diagnosis? **WWW**

8. The DSM-IV is based on a multiaxial system. Explain the content of each axis and its contribution to understanding the patient.

9. Labeling a patient with a diagnosis is often referred to as a "double-edged sword" as the diagnostic label can both help and hurt the patient. Explain the advantages and disadvantages (to the patient) of a diagnostic label.

10. Describe the controversy surrounding "premenstrual dysphoric disorder" and its possible inclusion in a future DSM edition. Discuss both the benefits and the disadvantages to women of legitimizing PMDD as a mental disorder.

11. Describe how the different mental health professionals arrived at a diagnosis of panic disorder in the case described on the "Abnormal Psychology Live" CD. Include a brief discussion of the symptoms that were mentioned, the treatments that were discussed and the expected prognosis.

    REF: CD

MULTIPLE CHOICE

1. One advantage of a formal observation, as compared to an informal observation, is that
   a. formal observations are easier to make.
   b. formal observations rarely require the use of naturalistic settings.
   c. formal observations are more reliable, due to the focus on behaviors that are both observable and measurable.
   d. formal observations give more information about an individual.

   ANS: C

2. On the MMPI, results are assessed according to
   a. how the pattern of answers corresponds to that of people diagnosed with a specific disorder.
   b. how often the individual refers to specific ideas, such as aggression or sexuality.
   c. the degree of emotionality associated with results.
   d. how often an individual responds to questions that reflect aggression or some other concept.
   e. the responder's personality and appearance

   ANS: A

3. The CAT scan neuroimaging technique
   a. uses X-rays to portray brain structures
   b. uses magnetic fields to portray brain structures
   c. follows tracer elements in the nervous system
   d. uses magnetic fields to portray brain functions
   e. studies brains of domestic felines

   ANS: A

4. This instrument measures brain wave activity, by recording the electrical activity of the brain.
   a. CAT scan
   b. MRI
   c. EEG
   d. SPECT

   ANS: C

5. The classical and dimensional approaches to nosology differ in that
   a. the classical approach uses categories and the dimensional approach uses prototypes.
   b. the classical approach uses prototypes and the dimensional approach uses profiles.
   c. the classical approach diagnoses based on the presence of symptoms and the dimensional approach notes the degree of severity of symptoms.
   d. the classical approach places individuals in categories; the dimensional approach places symptoms in categories.

   ANS: C

6. According to the textbook, DSM-IV is based on the
   a. classical system of nosology.
   b. dimensional system of nosology.
   c. categorical system of nosology.
   d. prototypical system of nosology.

   ANS: A

7. The purpose of standardization is
   a. to make a diagnosis predictive.
   b. to increase the scores on a test.
   c. to determine whether a technique is appropriate.
   d. to make techniques consistent and comparable.
   e. to increase measurement subjectivity.

   ANS: D

8. Comorbidity refers to
   a. a disorder that manifests itself in several ways.
   b. the same disorder being diagnosed for two members of a family.
   c. more than one disorder diagnosed for the same individual.
   d. the severity of a particular disorder.
   e. disorders that can cause death.

   ANS: C

9. Emily has been evaluated by three different professionals, each of whom offers a different diagnosis. She wonders whether the field has any standards because their judgments obviously lack
   a. statistical significance.
   b. clinical utility.
   c. reliability.
   d. clinical significance.
   e. statistical utility.

   ANS: C

10. We can use a computer to score polygraph tracings to eliminate human judgment and error and, thus, increase _____. To call this system a "lie detector" is a question of _____.
    a. validity; ethics
    b. validity; standardization
    c. sensitivity; reliability
    d. reliability; validity

    ANS: D

MULTIPLE CHOICE

1. Your friend has trouble making commitments in relationships and you believe that this is because her parents had a bitter divorce when she was young. Your belief that a child who lives through a bitter parental divorce will have trouble making commitments in relationships as an adult would be considered a(n):
   a. hypothesis
   b. independent variable
   c. empirical conclusion
   d. applied theory

   ANS: A   DIF: 1   REF: p. 101   OBJ: 1 TYPE: APP

2. Of the following, the hypothesis that would not be appropriate given the concept of testability is:
   a. behavior is influenced by the rewards that follow the behavior
   b. children who view aggression are more likely to act in an aggressive manner
   c. invisible forces influence our behavior every day
   d. personality traits can be influenced by genetics

   ANS: C   DIF: 3   REF: p. 101   OBJ: 1 TYPE: APP

3. A hypothesis is defined as a(n):
   a. theory
   b. empirical conclusion
   c. research study
   d. educated guess

   ANS: D   DIF: 1   REF: p. 101   OBJ: 1 TYPE: FACT

4. The dependent variable in a research study is the variable that:
   a. is expected to influence or change the variable being studied
   b. empirical result of the study
   c. is expected to be changed or influenced in the study
   d. forms the most important component of the hypothesis

   ANS: C   DIF: 1   REF: p. 100   OBJ: 1 TYPE: FACT

5. The independent variable in a research study is the variable that:
   a. is expected to be changed or influenced in the study
   b. is expected to influence or change the dependent variable
   c. empirical result of the study
   d. forms the most important component of the hypothesis

   ANS: B   DIF: 1   REF: p. 100   OBJ: 1 TYPE: FACT

6. A researcher is testing the effects of sunlight on depression. The independent variable is:
   a. sunlight
   b. depression
   c. the assumption that light affects mood
   d. the research design

   ANS: A   DIF: 1   REF: p. 100   OBJ: 1 TYPE: APP

7. A researcher is testing the effects of sunlight on depression. The dependent variable is:
   a. sunlight
   b. the assumption that light affects mood
   c. the research design
   d. depression

   ANS: D   DIF: 1   REF: p. 100   OBJ: 1 TYPE: APP

8. In regard to research design, all of the following statements are true EXCEPT:
   a. independent variables are hypothesized to have an impact on dependent variables
   b. independent variables are generally manipulated by the researcher
   c. dependent variables are hypothesized to have an impact on independent variables
   d. dependent variables are generally measured by the researcher

   ANS: C   DIF: 3   REF: p. 100   OBJ: 1 TYPE: FACT/WWW

9. Any factor in a research study that makes the results uninterpretable is called a(n):
   a. independent variable
   b. confound
   c. dependent variable
   d. confluence

   ANS: B   DIF: 1   REF: p. 101   OBJ: 1 TYPE: FACT

10. While studying the impact of nutrition on intelligence, a researcher has one group of rats on a vitamin rich diet while the other rat group eats Big Macs. While observing the rats run a complicated maze, the researcher notes that the vitamin enhanced rats' maze is more brightly lit than the Big Mac rats' maze. The difference in lighting in this study is a(n):
    a. confound
    b. independent variable
    c. dependent variable
    d. hypothesis

    ANS: A   DIF: 5   REF: p. 101   OBJ: 1 TYPE: APP

11. Studies that have significant confounds are said to be low in:
    a. external validity
    b. internal validity
    c. fidelity
    d. empirical validity

    ANS: B   DIF: 3   REF: p. 101   OBJ: 1 TYPE: FACT/WWW

12. Internal validity is defined as:
    a. the extent to which the results of a study can be explained by the dependent variable
    b. the degree to which the hypothesis is supported by the study
    c. the overall quality of the research
    d. the extent to which the results in a study can be explained by the independent variable

    ANS: D   DIF: 3   REF: p. 101   OBJ: 1 TYPE: FACT

13. A researcher separates the participants into two groups. Group A receives an active medication and Group B receives an empty capsule that looks and feels like the real medication. Group B is the:
    a. treatment group
    b. analog group
    c. control group
    d. experimental group

    ANS: C   DIF: 1   REF: p. 101   OBJ: 1 TYPE: APP

14. Researchers use control groups to:
    a. make comparisons to the treatment group
    b. give all research participants an equal chance to participate in the study
    c. control the hypothesis
    d. randomize the experiment

    ANS: A   DIF: 1   REF: p. 101   OBJ: 1 TYPE: FACT

15. The purpose of random assignment is to make sure that:
    a. each research participant spends an equal amount of time in the treatment and control groups
    b. each research participant has an equal chance of being in the treatment or control group
    c. everyone in each group is exactly the same on the independent variable
    d. everyone in each group is exactly the same on the dependent variable

    ANS: B   DIF: 1   REF: p. 102   OBJ: 1 TYPE: FACT

16. The reason that researchers cannot allow participants to decide whether to be in the control or treatment group is that this procedure may result in differences between the treatment and control group participants that:
    a. have nothing to do with the independent variable
    b. are a direct result of the independent variable
    c. have nothing to do with the dependent variable
    d. are a direct result of the dependent variable

    ANS: A   DIF: 5   REF: p. 102   OBJ: 1 TYPE: CON

17. Randomization is used to assign research participants to groups in order to:
    a. prevent assembling groups that differ in a way that may influence the research outcome
    b. make sure that all participants in the study are the same on the dependent variable when the study is concluded
    c. make sure that all participants are the same on the independent variable before the study begins
    d. prevent any differences in the way the independent variable is manipulated for all research subjects

    ANS: A   DIF: 2   REF: p. 102   OBJ: 1 TYPE: FACT

18. External validity refers to the:
    a. degree that the dependent variable was changed in the study
    b. power of the independent variable to cause a change in the dependent variable
    c. extent to which findings apply to individuals or situations other than those studied
    d. overall quality of the study

    ANS: C   DIF: 1   REF: p. 101   OBJ: 1 TYPE: FACT

19. A researcher studies the impact of stress on college students' exam scores. Whether the results of this study help us to understand the relationship between job performance and stress level of real-life organizational workers is a question of:
    a. internal validity
    b. study confounds
    c. external validity
    d. the original research hypothesis

    ANS: C   DIF: 3   REF: p. 101   OBJ: 1 TYPE: APP

20. The more a researcher controls _____ validity by restricting the study to participants who are similar to one another, the less _____ validity the study will generally have.
    a. internal; external
    b. external; internal
    c. internal; clinical
    d. external; clinical

    ANS: A   DIF: 5   REF: p. 101   OBJ: 1 TYPE: CON

21. Analog research models:
    a. are conducted outside of the laboratory   c. are correlational
    b. generally utilize case studies to maximize   d. create laboratory conditions that are
       similarity to the phenomenon under study   comparable to the phenomenon under
                                                             study

    ANS: D   DIF: 1   REF: p. 102   OBJ: 1 TYPE: FACT

22. Statistical significance determines whether an observed difference between a treatment and control group is likely due to:
    a. random assignment
    b. external validity
    c. chance
    d. confounds

    ANS: C   DIF: 3   REF: p. 102   OBJ: 1 TYPE: FACT

23. In research, the term clinical significance refers to:
    a. whether the effects observed in the study are due to chance
    b. the external validity of the study
    c. how large the effect of the treatment is
    d. randomization of the sampling procedure

    ANS: C   DIF: 1   REF: p. 102   OBJ: 1 TYPE: FACT/WWW

24. A researcher studying the effect of a dietary supplement on sleep finds that research participants who take the supplement sleep an average of 7 hours and 25 minutes per night while participants who were given a placebo pill with no active ingredients in it sleep for an average of 7 hours and 20 minutes. These findings are clearly:
    a. statistically significant
    b. not clinically significant
    c. not valid
    d. clinically significant

    ANS: B   DIF: 3   REF: p. 102   OBJ: 1 TYPE: APP

25. In research studies, the term "effect size" refers to:
    a. how much each treated and untreated person in the study changes
    b. the power of the statistical tests that are used to detect the impact of the independent variable
    c. how many subjects are included in a particular study
    d. the degree of external validity that the study has

    ANS: A   DIF: 2   REF: p. 102   OBJ: 1 TYPE: FACT

26. In well-designed research studies, medications that enhance serotonin functioning have been found to help patients recover from episodes of depression. Given the realities of the patient uniformity myth, it would be a mistake to conclude that:
    a. most depressed patients will be helped substantially by these medications
    b. all depressed patients will be helped by these medications
    c. research can help us determine which treatments should be used for specific disorders
    d. medication can be an appropriate treatment for a psychological disorder

    ANS: B   DIF: 3   REF: p. 103   OBJ: 1 TYPE: APP

27. Joe is suffering from a severe an anxiety disorder. His psychiatrist prescribes a medication that has been found in many research studies to help reduce anxiety. Joe takes the medication but his anxiety level does not improve at all. Since the anxiety medication did not work, Joe concludes that his psychiatrist must be wrong and he must be suffering from some other disorder. The problem with Joe's conclusion is that he is failing to consider the:
    a. patient uniformity myth
    b. internal validity of the research studies
    c. lack of clinical significance of many research findings
    d. external validity of the prior research

    ANS: A   DIF: 5   REF: p. 103   OBJ: 1 TYPE: APP

28. The type of study that generally does not follow the scientific method and typically contains many confounds is the:
    a. case study
    b. correlation model
    c. true experiment
    d. longitudinal study

    ANS: A   DIF: 1   REF: p. 103   OBJ: 2 TYPE: FACT

29. One of the major problems with the case study method is that it is too easy to make false conclusions based on:
    a. statistical significance
    b. unreliable measures
    c. poorly defined dependent variables
    d. coincidence

    ANS: D   DIF: 1   REF: p. 104   OBJ: 2 TYPE: FACT

30. The most accurate description of the correlational model is:
    a. manipulation of an independent variable to measure the effects on a dependent variable
    b. in-depth examination of many variables associated with a small number of individuals
    c. statistical examination of the relationships between variables
    d. statistical examination of the cause of changes in a dependent variable

    ANS: C   DIF: 1   REF: p. 104   OBJ: 2 TYPE: FACT

31. When studying family functioning, it has been observed that marital discord often increases as child behavior problems increase in the family. Using the correlational model:
    a. it is possible to determine that marital problems generally cause child behavior problems
    b. it is not possible to determine whether marital discord causes child behavior problems, whether child behavior problems cause marital discord, or whether both may be true
    c. it is possible to determine whether marital problems cause child behavior problems or whether child behavior problems cause marital problems, but it is not possible to determine whether both may be true
    d. it is possible to determine whether any or all observed effects may be causing changes on any of the variables being studied

    ANS: B   DIF: 3   REF: p. 104   OBJ: 2 TYPE: APP

32. As a child's age increases, so does her height. This is an example of a(n):
    a. negative correlation
    b. zero correlation
    c. causal correlation
    d. positive correlation

    ANS: D   DIF: 1   REF: p. 104   OBJ: 2 TYPE: APP/WWW

33. The more time one spends exercising, the less one generally weighs. The correlation between time on a treadmill each month and overall body weight would represent a(n):
    a. positive correlation
    b. zero correlation
    c. negative correlation
    d. causal correlation

    ANS: C   DIF: 1   REF: p. 104   OBJ: 2 TYPE: APP

34. The correlation between the amount of time a college student studies and the student's height in inches is:
    a. positive
    b. negative
    c. zero
    d. causal

    ANS: C   DIF: 1   REF: p. 104   OBJ: 2 TYPE: APP

35. Every incremental increase in variable A is associated with an exactly equal sized increase in variable B. The correlation between these two variables is:
    a. +1.00
    b. -1.00
    c. 0
    d. causal

    ANS: A   DIF: 1   REF: p. 104   OBJ: 2 TYPE: FACT

36. Every incremental increase in variable A is associated with an exactly equal sized <u>decrease</u> in variable B. The correlation between these two variables is:
    a. + 1.00
    b. - 1.00
    c. 0
    d. causal

    ANS: B   DIF: 1   REF: p. 104   OBJ: 2 TYPE: FACT

37. We would generally expect that the correlation between the number of hours that a student studies for her tests and her exam grades would have a correlation of approximately:
    a. - .50
    b. 1.00
    c. .50
    d. 0

    ANS: C   DIF: 1   REF: p. 104   OBJ: 2 TYPE: APP

38. Epidemiology is the study of:
    a. the effectiveness of the correlational model in determining cause
    b. research methods
    c. various forms of therapy
    d. incidence, distribution and consequences of a problem in a population

    ANS: D   DIF: 1   REF: p. 105   OBJ: 2 TYPE: FACT

39. Epidemological researchers such as Delisi, Maurizio, Yost, et al., 2003, who assessed men and women in Manhattan following the terrorist attacks of September 11, 2001, generally used the research method called the:
    a. correlational model
    b. case study
    c. experiment
    d. longitudinal study

    ANS: A   DIF: 3   REF: p. 106   OBJ: 2 TYPE: FACT

40. The basis of an experiment is:
    a. manipulation of a dependent variable
    b. examining the relationship between an independent and a dependent variable
    c. manipulation of an independent variable
    d. in depth fact gathering regarding many variables

    ANS: C   DIF: 1   REF: p. 106   OBJ: 2 TYPE: FACT

41. A researcher manipulates an independent variable and observes the effects on a dependent variable in a(n):
    a. correlational study
    b. case study
    c. experiment
    d. epidemiological study

    ANS: C   DIF: 1   REF: p. 106   OBJ: 2 TYPE: FACT

42. While trying to discover the nature of the relationship between stress and blood pressure, a researcher asks participants to complete a difficult task. The researcher monitors the participants' blood pressure while some are exposed to noisy distractions and others stay in a quiet environment. This type of research study is a(n):
    a. correlational study
    b. experiment
    c. case study
    d. placebo control study

    ANS: B   DIF: 3   REF: p. 106   OBJ: 2 TYPE: APP

43. One of the hallmarks of the experimental method that makes it different from a correlational study is that in an experiment:
a. we observe what happens in the natural world
b. the researcher is unaware of the independent variable
c. a variable is manipulated in a way that would not have occured naturally
d. there are multiple control groups

ANS: C   DIF: 3   REF: p. 106   OBJ: 2 TYPE: FACT

44. When a control group is used in experimental research, the members of the control group will be treated exactly the same as the:
a. treatment group except that they will be exposed to the independent variable
b. treatment group in every way
c. control group in any other psychology study
d. treatment group except that they will not be exposed to the independent variable

ANS: D   DIF: 3   REF: p. 106   OBJ: 2 TYPE: FACT

45. The purpose of a control group in experimental research is to:
a. control for the expectation of some research subjects that they will improve just because they are in a research study
b. determine whether a treatment or independent variable actually influenced change in the independent variable
c. determine statistical significance
d. control the dependent variable

ANS: B   DIF: 1   REF: p. 106   OBJ: 2 TYPE: FACT

46. Placebos are used in experiments to:
a. control for the variability of individuals who tend to volunteer for research studies
b. control for the expectations of some research participants that they will improve just because they are in a research study
c. help determine whether an independent variable actually causes a statistically significant change in a dependent variable
d. make certain that the treatment and control group are randomly selected

ANS: B   DIF: 1   REF: p. 107   OBJ: 2 TYPE: FACT

47. In a typical drug study, some research participants are given an active medication and others are given a sugar pill. The subjects given the sugar pill are in the:
a. placebo control group
b. treatment group
c. independent variable group
d. dependent variable group

ANS: A   DIF: 1   REF: p. 107   OBJ: 2 TYPE: APP

48. In a double-blind study:
   a. the participants are not aware of who is in the treatment and control groups but the researcher providing the treatment does know
   b. neither the researcher providing the treatment nor the participants are aware of who is in the treatment and who is in the control group
   c. neither the researcher providing the treatment nor the research participants can ever be made aware of the research findings
   d. the research participants are not aware that they are participating in a research study

   ANS: B   DIF: 1   REF: p. 107   OBJ: 2 TYPE: FACT

49. It can be important to use a double blind procedure in a research study to prevent the:
   a. independent variable from influencing the dependent variable
   b. confusion of correlation with causation
   c. participants' expectations from biasing the expectations of the researcher
   d. researcher's expectations from biasing the outcome

   ANS: D   DIF: 3   REF: p. 107   OBJ: 2 TYPE: FACT/WWW

50. Of the following, researchers use _____ to attempt to control for the phenomenon called the "allegiance effect" which occurs when experimenter bias influences research outcomes.
   a. correlation studies   c. epidemiological studies
   b. double-blind control   d. placebo pills

   ANS: A   DIF: 3   REF: p. 107   OBJ: 2 TYPE: FACT

51. The following is an example of treatment outcome research:
   a. examining the changes in serotonin levels from taking Prozac
   b. determining whether the active ingredients in a medication actually have any impact on the function of the brain
   c. exploring the parts of cognitive-behavioral therapy homework that are most difficult for patients to perform
   d. examining the impact of Prozac on depression

   ANS: D   DIF: 5   REF: p. 108   OBJ: 2 TYPE: APP

52. The following is an example of treatment process research:
   a. examining the impact of Prozac on depression
   b. determining how many therapy sessions it takes for most anxiety patients to feel better
   c. examining the impact of Prozac on serotonin levels
   d. determining which treatment reduces patients' anxiety in the fewest number of sessions

   ANS: C   DIF: 5   REF: p. 108   OBJ: 2 TYPE: APP

53. Single-case experimental designs utilize several strategies such as _____ to improve their internal validity.
   a. repeated measures
   b. process measures
   c. random assignment
   d. placebo controls

   ANS: A   DIF: 3   REF: p. 108   OBJ: 2 TYPE: FACT

54. One important difference between a typical case study and the single-case experiment is that during the single-case experiment, behavior is generally:
    a. manipulated
    b. controlled by the experimenter
    c. measured more than once
    d. observed in the natural environment

    ANS: C   DIF: 3   REF: p. 108   OBJ: 2 TYPE: FACT

55. The advantage of using a withdrawal design as part of a single-case experiment is that the researcher can:
    a. counterbalance the research design with additional measures to improve internal and external validity
    b. control for the placebo effect
    c. conduct a true double blind experiment
    d. determine whether improvements gained with treatment are lost when the treatment is withheld

    ANS: D   DIF: 1   REF: p. 109   OBJ: 2 TYPE: CON

56. One of the problems of using a withdrawal design as part of a single-case experiment is the:
    a. difficulty of measuring changes that are associated with removal of a treatment
    b. confounding factor of the placebo effect when the treatment is removed
    c. ethical issue of removing treatment that appears to be helping the patient
    d. impossibility of removing the treatment equally for the treatment and control subjects

    ANS: C   DIF: 1   REF: p. 109   OBJ: 2 TYPE: FACT

57. A child is having temper tantrums at home, at school and at his grandparents' house. After working with the parents for a while, the therapist believes that the child is being rewarded for his tantrums in each setting because his teacher, parents and grandparents generally give him what he wants just to make him stop yelling. The therapist devises a plan to stop his tantrums but first implements the plan at home, then the following week at school, and finally at the grandparents' home several weeks later. From a research perspective, this is an example of:
    a. withdrawal method
    b. multiple baseline
    c. placebo control
    d. external validity

    ANS: B   DIF: 5   REF: p. 109   OBJ: 2 TYPE: APP

58. The single-case experimental design is primarily criticized as having limited:
    a. reliability
    b. external validity
    c. usefulness
    d. measures

    ANS: B   DIF: 3   REF: p. 110   OBJ: 2 TYPE: FACT

59. An important advantage of the multiple baseline design over the withdrawal design for evaluating treatments is that multiple baseline:
   a. has greater internal validity
   c. does not require the removal of a potentially helpful treatment
   b. has greater external validity
   d. does not require the artificial intervention of the researcher

   ANS: C   DIF: 3   REF: p. 111   OBJ: 3 TYPE: FACT

60. A phenotype is defined as an individual's:
   a. hidden characteristics
   b. observable characteristics
   c. genetic influences
   d. unique genetic make-up

   ANS: B   DIF: 1   REF: p. 111   OBJ: 3 TYPE: FACT

61. A genotype is defined as an individual's:
   a. unique genetic make-up
   b. recessive genes
   c. hidden characteristics
   d. observable features and behavior

   ANS: A   DIF: 1   REF: p. 111   OBJ: 3 TYPE: FACT

62. Mary looks nothing like her mother, but Mary's daughter grows up to look exactly like Mary's mother. In other words, grandmother and granddaughter look alike. The fact that Mary's daughter looks like her (Mary's) mother but she herself doesn't is a good example of the:
   a. difference between genotype and phenotype
   b. influence of environment on genes
   c. fact that we really have no idea of how genes work
   d. diathesis-stress model

   ANS: A   DIF: 3   REF: p. 111   OBJ: 3 TYPE: CON

63. At this point, we know much more about the _____ of psychological disorders than the _____ of psychological disorders.
   a. genotype; phenotype
   b. phenotype; genotype
   c. behavioral causes; social influences
   d. social influences; behavioral causes

   ANS: B   DIF: 1   REF: p. 111   OBJ: 3 TYPE: FACT

64. One reason that we can expect rapid increases in our understanding of the genetic influences of psychopathology over the next several years is the:
   a. success of the human genome project
   b. development of powerful new statistical techniques
   c. recent availability of fast, new generation computers
   d. new brain scanning technology

   ANS: A   DIF: 1   REF: p. 111   OBJ: 3 TYPE: FACT

65. At this point, the human genome project has been successful in producing:
    a. a complete listing of each human gene and its function
    b. little if any success in mapping the structure and location of human genes
    c. a rough draft of the mapping of all human genes
    d. some success in mapping the structure of human genes, but little success in mapping gene locations
    e. nice blue denim pants

    ANS: C   DIF: 3   REF: p. 111   OBJ: 3 TYPE: FACT

66. Family studies are often used to help determine whether a psychological disorder has a genetic component. Which of the following patterns is typical for a disorder that is influenced by genetics?
    a. siblings of the person with the disorder are more likely to have the disorder than cousins, and cousins are just as likely to have the disorder as the general public
    b. siblings of the person with the disorder will almost always have the same or similar disorders and cousins are more likely than the general public to have disorders
    c. siblings of the person with the disorder are more likely than cousins to have the disorder and cousins are more likely to have the disorder than the general public
    d. siblings will almost always have the same or similar disorders, though cousins may have a similar rate of the disorder as the general public

    ANS· C   DIF: 1   REF: p. 111   OBJ: 3 TYPE: CON

67. While conducting a family study, a researcher determines that the siblings and parents of the person with a disorder are much more likely than the general public to have the disorder although cousins, uncles and grandparents are only moderately more likely to have the disorder than the general public. This is an example of a disorder with:
    a. no genetic component
    b. a single gene influence
    c. a genetic component
    d. strong environmental and very weak genetic components

    ANS: C   DIF: 3   REF: p. 111   OBJ: 3 TYPE: APP/WWW

68. One of the major problems of using family studies to determine the genetic components of psychological disorders is that family members may have similar disorders due to:
    a. shared genes
    b. common diet factors
    c. physical similarities
    d. the fact that they live together

    ANS: D   DIF: 1   REF: p. 112   OBJ: 3 TYPE: FACT

69. Adoption studies are often used when attempting to study the influence of genetic factors on psychological disorders because these studies allow examination of genetic influences of psychopathology:
    a. without the typical confound of common biological parents
    b. using more sophisticated statistical techniques
    c. through direct examination of genetic causes
    d. without the typical confound of siblings raised in the same environment

    ANS: D   DIF: 3   REF: p. 112   OBJ: 3 TYPE: CON

70. Monozygotic twins allow for unique genetic studies because they:
    a. have identical genes
    b. always share the same environment
    c. share approximately 50% of the same genes
    d. are usually raised in similar ways

    ANS: A   DIF: 1   REF: p. 112   OBJ: 3 TYPE: FACT

71. Combining the monozygotic and adoption studies, researchers often study monozygotic twins raised in different families. Using this method, similarities in behaviors, traits and psychological disorders between monozygotic twins raised apart helps researchers determine:
    a. the effects of adoption on a child's psychological functioning
    b. whether it is detrimental to separate twins at birth
    c. whether genes or adoption impact psychopathology
    d. the effects of genes

    ANS: D   DIF: 3   REF: p. 112   OBJ: 3 TYPE: CON

72. Given what we know about the effects of genes and the environment, which of the following pairs of children would be expected to be most similar in terms of overall personality, psychological disorders and intelligence?
    a. monozygotic twins, one raised in a wealthy family living in a modern city and the other raised in poverty in a developing nation
    b. adopted children from different biological families raised in the same home
    c. biological siblings raised in the same house
    d. biological siblings, each adopted immediately after birth, one raised in Chicago and the other raised in New York City

    ANS: C   DIF: 5   REF: p. 112   OBJ: 3 TYPE: APP

73. Family, twin and adoption studies can identify all of the following EXCEPT:
    a. whether a particular form of psychopathology is influenced by genes
    b. whether a particular form of psychopathology is influenced by the environment
    c. identification and location of a gene associated with psychopathology
    d. approximate degree of influence of genetics for a specific psychological disorder

    ANS: C   DIF: 1   REF: p. 112   OBJ: 3 TYPE: FACT/WWW

74. Which type of study must be conducted to identify the location of specific genes associated with psychopathology?
    a. association
    b. family
    c. twin
    d. adoption

    ANS: A   DIF: 1   REF: p. 112   OBJ: 3 TYPE: FACT

75. Which type of study must be conducted to identify the location of specific genes associated with psychopathology?
    a. family study
    b. twin analysis
    c. adoption study
    d. genetic linkage analysis

    ANS: D   DIF: 1   REF: p. 112   OBJ: 3 TYPE: FACT

76. The implication of the fact that genetic linkage studies frequently fail to replicate when subsequent researchers repeat the study in different families is that:
    a. the human genome is not well mapped
    b. researchers need to be more careful with their methods
    c. the environment is a more powerful influence on most forms of complex psychopathology than genetics
    d. it is doubtful that there are single gene causes for complex disorders

    ANS: D   DIF: 5   REF: p. 113   OBJ: 3 TYPE: CON

77. A researcher studying a family with a history of obsessive compulsive disorder (OCD) records data for each person in the family with OCD and for those who have been diagnosed with OCD in the past. The researcher is particularly interested in determining if family members who now have OCD or who were previously diagnosed with OCD share any other inherited characteristics. The researcher is conducting a(n):
    a. association study
    b. chromosome analysis
    c. genetic linkage analysis
    d. family DNA analysis

    ANS: C   DIF: 5   REF: p. 113   OBJ: 3 TYPE: APP

78. Genetic linkage analysis has not yet provided the types of answers scientists hope for in terms of understanding the specific genetic causes of psychopathology. The most likely reason that this type of analysis has not been as promising as hoped is that the genetic influences of psychopathology are:
    a. impossible to understand until the entire human genome is sequenced
    b. difficult to understand with the limited statistical models available
    c. based on more than single gene defects
    d. insignificant in comparison to the power of the environment

    ANS: C   DIF: 5   REF: p. 113   OBJ: 3 TYPE: CON

79. An association study of the genetic influences of psychopathology compares people with and without a specific disorder in terms of:
    a. shared environments
    b. inherited characteristics other than the disorder
    c. family history
    d. inherited tendencies to behave in a specific manner

    ANS: B   DIF: 5   REF: p. 113   OBJ: 3 TYPE: FACT

80. A researcher collects data comparing people <u>with and without</u> a particular disorder. The researcher is particularly interested in inherited tendencies that are not part of the disorder but that occur with much greater frequency in the people afflicted with the disorder. The researcher is conducting a(n):
    a.   genetic linkage analysis
    b.   association study
    c.   family study
    d.   DNA analysis

    ANS: B   DIF: 3   REF: p. 113   OBJ: 3 TYPE: FACT

81. One of the research methods used to help determine the typical course and progression of a disorder like schizophrenia is a _____ study.
    a.   family
    b.   group
    c.   randomized control group
    d.   longitudinal

    ANS: D   DIF: 1   REF: p. 114   OBJ: 4 TYPE: APP

82. Longitudinal and/or cross-sectional research is often necessary to determine:
    a.   how disorders change and progress over a typical patient's lifetime
    b.   the genetic causes of a particular disorder
    c.   the environmental causes of a particular disorder
    d.   if a particular treatment is appropriate for patients suffering from a specific disorder

    ANS: A   DIF: 1   REF: p. 114   OBJ: 4 TYPE: FACT/WWW

83. The two most frequently used methods in prevention research for examining psychopathology across time are:
    a.   longitudinal and case study
    b.   case study and experimental
    c.   longitudinal and cross-sectional
    d.   experimental and cross-sectional

    ANS: C   DIF: 3   REF: p. 114   OBJ: 4 TYPE: FACT

84. As described in your text, Brown and Finn (1982) found that attitudes regarding alcohol were somewhat different for 12-year-olds, 15-year-olds, and 17-year-olds. All measures were taken during the same year from children of different ages. This type of research is an example of the research method called:
    a.   longitudinal
    b.   cross-sectional
    c.   experimental
    d.   case-study

    ANS: B   DIF: 1   REF: p. 113   OBJ: 4 TYPE: APP

85. A researcher is studying how depression tends to be experienced by people of different ages. The researcher interviews depressed adolescents, young adults, individuals in their 30s and 50s and those over 70 years old. The research design being used is called:
   a. cross-sectional
   b. longitudinal
   c. experimental
   d. case-study

   ANS: A   DIF: 1   REF: p. 113   OBJ: 4 TYPE: APP

86. A researcher is studying how anxiety tends to be experienced by people of different ages. The researcher interviews depressed adolescents, young adults, individuals in their 30s and 50s and those over 70. The individuals in each age group represent a:
   a. treatment group
   b. control group
   c. longitudinal group
   d. cohort

   ANS: D   DIF: 1   REF: p. 113   OBJ: 4 TYPE: FACT

87. One significant limitation of the cross-sectional design is called the "cohort effect." This relates to the fact that:
   a. experience is confounded with participation the study
   b. age is confounded with experience
   c. genetics and experience are confounded
   d. reliable statistics cannot be computed for cohort groups

   ANS: B   DIF: 1   REF: p. 113   OBJ: 4 TYPE: FACT

88. Age and experience are confounded while using the cross-sectional design. This means that it cannot be determined if:
   a. findings for cohort groups are due to their similar experiences or similar age
   b. findings are due to the fact that age and life experience tend to be correlated
   c. differences across groups are due to differences in assignment to the treatment conditions
   d. differences across groups are due to age, experience, or the experimental manipulation

   ANS: A   DIF: 3   REF: p. 113   OBJ: 4 TYPE: CON

89. Use of a cross-sectional design would be appropriate in trying to find an answer to all of the following questions EXCEPT:
   a. How does panic disorder differ in children and adults?
   b. Are the cognitive triggers for panic disorder different in children and adults?
   c. What early behaviors did adult panic disorder patients tend to display when they were young?
   d. Does exposure therapy tend to be more or less effective when it is used in the treatment of children versus adults?

   ANS: C   DIF: 5   REF: p. 113   OBJ: 4 TYPE: APP/WWW

90. The research design most helpful in determining how individuals with particular disorders change over time is the:
    a. longitudinal method
    b. cross-sectional design
    c. family study
    d. association study

    ANS: A   DIF: 1   REF: p. 114   OBJ: 4 TYPE: FACT

91. One reason that cross-sectional studies are more common than longitudinal studies is the fact that:
    a. cross-sectional studies involve large numbers of subjects
    b. longitudinal studies involve very sophisticated statistical procedures
    c. cross-sectional studies take many years to complete
    d. longitudinal studies take many years to complete

    ANS: D   DIF: 1   REF: p. 114   OBJ: 4 TYPE: CON

92. Which research method often suffers from losing research participants due to high drop out rates or even death?
    a. cross-sectional study
    b. longitudinal study
    c. family study
    d. twin study

    ANS: B   DIF: 1   REF: p. 114   OBJ: 4 TYPE: FACT

93. In cross-cultural research, the independent or treatment variable is generally the:
    a. culture
    b. disorder
    c. method used to treat the disorder
    d. success of the treatment

    ANS: A   DIF: 3   REF: p. 115   OBJ: 5 TYPE: FACT

94. One of the most important reasons to conduct cross-cultural research in psychopathology is that:
    a. we can gain a better appreciation for the virtues of various cultures by examining how psychopathology is viewed by different cultures
    b. the stigma of psychopathology can be removed by understanding that psychopathology exists in all cultures
    c. genetic influences of disorders can be best determined through careful comparison of the different environmental stressors found in various cultures
    d. we can understand more about psychopathology by understanding how culture impacts the experience of various disorders

    ANS: D   DIF: 3   REF: p. 115   OBJ: 5 TYPE: CON

95. One of the problems in trying to understand how psychopathology may be "caused" by cultural influences is that similarities in the way individuals of a culture experience psychopathology:
    a. are confounded by the cross-cultural methods used to study psychopathology
    b. may be due to the culture or to common genetic factors
    c. cannot be understood by those outside of the culture
    d. generally do not exist

    ANS: B   DIF: 3   REF: p. 115   OBJ: 5 TYPE: CON

96. Which of the following are potential problems when conducting cross-cultural research in the area of psychopathology?
    a. different cultures may describe or experience similar psychological sensations in very different ways
    b. the level of "abnormality" that is considered acceptable may differ greatly across cultures
    c. treatment models developed in one culture may be unacceptable according to another culture's customs and values
    d. all of these

    ANS: D   DIF: 1   REF: p. 115   OBJ: 5 TYPE: CON

97. The most influential and successful research generally utilizes:
    a. multiple well controlled, double-blind experiments
    b. a combination of well controlled correlational studies and cross-sectional research
    c. a program of multiple research designs over a period of time
    d. multiple cross-sectional and longitudinal designs over a period of time

    ANS: C   DIF: 1   REF: p. 116   OBJ: 6 TYPE: CON

98. A new research study is published and becomes the "hot story" in the news today. This story concerns you because the researchers report that they are the first scientists to find a higher incidence of depression in individuals who are taking a particular vitamin--the same vitamin that your physician has had you taking for years. While this may be cause for you to investigate further, you probably shouldn't panic because:
    a. your physician will call you if there is anything to worry about
    b. research like this is rarely accurate
    c. without replication, the finding could just be due to coincidence
    d. unless it was a double-blind experiment, the results are probably in error

    ANS: C   DIF: 3   REF: p. 116   OBJ: 6 TYPE: APP

99. The function of replication in research is to:
    a. better define independent and dependent variables
    b. improve the research design
    c. rule out coincidence
    d. enhance the external validity of the study

    ANS: C   DIF: 1   REF: p. 117   OBJ: 6 TYPE: FACT/WWW

100. Which type of problem is shared by the placebo control method and the withdrawal design method?
    a. lack of control of the independent variable
    b. ethical concern of withholding treatment from those who need it
    c. ethical issue of tricking people into thinking that they will get better
    d. the fact that the individual will likely respond to the unique circumstances of the research setting

    ANS: B   DIF: 1   REF: p. 117   OBJ: 6 TYPE: FACT

101. According to the requirements of "informed consent," research participants in a blind, placebo controlled study will be told:
    a. that they may or may not receive an active treatment
    b. that they will not receive active treatment until the research study is over
    c. if they are in the placebo group or the treatment group
    d. only that they are participants in a research study and that they can quit at any time

    ANS: A   DIF: 3   REF: p. 117   OBJ: 6 TYPE: FACT

102. The basic components of informed consent are:
    a. competence, volunteerism, full information and comprehension
    b. volunteerism and comprehension
    c. competence, volunteerism, comprehension and knowledge of results
    d. anonymity, volunteerism, full information and comprehension

    ANS: A   DIF: 3   REF: p. 117   OBJ: 6 TYPE: FACT

103. Your psychology professor is conducting research and desperately needs more research participants because the existing subjects keep running from the building screaming! She tells the class that everyone must be a subject to get a grade in the class and that there are no exceptions. In terms of ethical treatment of research subjects, her policy would:
    a. violate the informed consent concept of competence
    b. be acceptable as long as her procedures were presented to the institutional review board
    c. be acceptable if she carefully explained the experiment to each participant and did allow participants to quit if they were uncomfortable during the procedure
    d. violate the informed consent concept of volunteerism

    ANS: D   DIF: 1   REF: p. 117   OBJ: 6 TYPE: APP

104. When conducting research with schizophrenic adults:
    a. informed consent is not necessary
    b. informed consent must be given by a mentally competent family member or guardian
    c. it is difficult to meet the requirements of informed consent
    d. it is necessary to have the research procedures approved by the American Psychological Association

    ANS: C   DIF: 3   REF: p. 117   OBJ: 6 TYPE: APP

105. With regard to deception of research participants:
    a. it is not allowed under any circumstances
    b. the researcher must tell the participants about the deception after the study
    c. the researcher must obtain approval of the procedure from a special national review board
    d. the researcher need only tell the participants about the deception if not telling them would place the participants in any harm

ANS: B   DIF: 3   REF: p. 117   OBJ: 6 TYPE: FACT

106. In Dr. Barlow's "Abnormal Psychology Live" presentation for Chapter 4-Research Methods, he discusses the importance of using independent evaluators when assessing participants involved with psychopathology research studies. The reason that the researchers or therapists involved with the study do not perform the evaluations themselves is that:
    a. it would violate the participant's confidentiality
    b. those involved with the research might be biased
    c. it would violate ethical standards for researchers
    d. those involved with the research could not meet the requirements for informed consent

ANS: B   DIF: 2   REF: CD

ESSAY

1. Define the term hypothesis and write two different testable hypotheses regarding possible causes of depression.

2. Describe the case study as a research method. Explain several advantages and disadvantages of the case study as a research method.

3. Describe correlational research. Explain the statistic used to represent the relationship between variables and the advantages and limitations of the correlational method. **WWW**

4. Describe the experiment as it is used in group research. Explain the procedures, advantages and disadvantages of the experiment as a research method.

5. Discuss how typical research findings demonstrating the effect of an independent variable (such as a medication) on an average amount of improvement experienced by the group studied (such as overall reduced feelings of depression) might contribute to the patient uniformity myth. What potential problems may exist for individuals treated by health care providers acting on the research finding that "the average improvement for group treated with the medication was 50% better than the improvement noted for the control group"?

6. Describe the difference between the statistical and clinical significance of research findings. Explain why it is important to make a distinction between statistical and clinical significance when interpreting research findings.

7. Explain how family studies are used to help determine the role of genetic factors in psychopathology. Describe the limitations of family studies in determining the genetic factors influencing psychopathology.

8. Explain the unique ways that monozygotic twins raised in separate environments help us to understand the genetic influences of psychopathology.

9. Describe how either genetic linkage studies or association studies are conducted and how these studies may help identify the specific locations of genes influencing a particular form of psychopathology.

10. Describe the procedures of the cross-sectional and longitudinal research methods. What are the uses and limitations of each of these methods?

11. Describe each of the four components of informed consent for research participants. Explain why it may be difficult to satisfy informed consent when the research participants are mentally retarded adults.

12. Explain the importance of studying cross-cultural psychopathology. Describe at least two significant obstacles to studying a disorder across different cultures.

Study Guide

MULTIPLE CHOICE

1. When developing an hypothesis, one important consideration is
   a. whether or not it is correct.
   b. testability.
   c. internal validity.
   d. external validity.

   ANS: B

2. Confounds, or factors that make it difficult to interpret accurately the results of a study, directly affect
   a. reliability.
   b. external validity.
   c. internal validity.
   d. whether the results are published.

   ANS: C

3. Which of the following demonstrates the placebo effect?
   a. Wanda is getting a drug to control her anxiety; therefore, her younger brother wants to get a drug.
   b. Eugene's therapist gave him an inactive medication, which she claimed would cure his insomnia. Eugene sleeps better when he takes this pill.
   c. Harvey is suffering from depression, but treatment is not available. Eventually, his depression dissipates.
   d. Hillary's therapist doesn't know how to cure her schizophrenia, but tries a variety of techniques, none of which works.

   ANS: B

4. All of these are strategies used in single-case study designs to improve internal validity EXCEPT
   a. repeated measurement.
   b. withdrawal.
   c. control groups.
   d. multiple baselines

   ANS: C

5. Dagwood discovered that the more intelligent a person is, the more books that person has at home. From this, Dagwood inferred that books make one more intelligent, so he rushed to the bookstore and spent hundreds of dollars on books for his home library in hopes of increasing his intelligence. Dagwood could have saved his money, because
   a. intelligence comes first, not the books.
   b. it would have been cheaper just to buy books at garage sales.
   c. based simply on a correlation between books and intelligence, it is impossible to determine directionality of causation.
   d. none of the above; excuse me while I run to the bookstore.

   ANS: C

6. Epidemiological research is useful because it
   a. directly identifies the causes of disorders.
   b. tells researchers the relationship between two variables.
   c. provides examples of cases when treatment was effective.
   d. tells the extent of a disorder in the population.

   ANS: A

7. Your research finds a correlation between schizophrenia and income level in the population, with more people in poverty displaying the disorder. Which of the following represents the third variable issue?
   a. schizophrenic individuals may be less able to report their incomes accurately
   b. both schizophrenia and low income may be caused by the same gene
   c. schizophrenia may cause poverty, or poverty may cause schizophrenia
   d. the correlation may not be a direct one
   e. schizophrenia is only one of three causes

   ANS: A

8. In an experiment with depressed patients, doctors gave some participants antidepressant pills while others received an identical pill with no active ingredients. Neither doctors nor patients knew who got what. If both groups improved substantially but equally, this is strong evidence
   a. the "active ingredient" has no effect.
   b. any effect of the antidepressant pill is due to patients' expectations.
   c. of the need for placebo controls in drug research.
   d. the placebo effect can be significant.
   e. all of the above

   ANS: E

9. "My parents used to beat me all the time and I turned out OK." What is wrong with this "evidence" favoring harsh physical discipline?
   a. The case study results may not be generalizable to other people.
   b. The dependent variable, or outcome measure, is poorly defined.
   c. A judge may not be objective and reliable.
   d. all of the above

   ANS: D

10. A newspaper article reports research showing that people who are single or divorced are more likely to suffer from chronic disease and to die earlier than married people. From this research we can correctly conclude
   a. unmarried people are unhappy and suffer more stress than people with partners, and these factors lead to more physical disability.
   b. if you wish to live longer, you should get married.
   c. people who suffer from chronic disease and die early are less likely to find a marriage partner.
   d. singles bars are full of deadly germs.
   e. none of the above

   ANS: E

MULTIPLE CHOICE

1. Which of the following characterizes the mood-state known as anxiety?
    a. positive mood state
    b. reduced heart rate
    c. apprehension about the future
    d. muscle relaxation

    ANS: C   DIF: 1   REF: p. 121   OBJ: 1 TYPE: FACT

2. Anxiety is closely related to which of the following psychological disorders?
    a. schizophrenia
    b. depression
    c. dementia
    d. psychosis

    ANS: B   DIF: 1   REF: p. 121   OBJ: 1 TYPE: CON

3. The "flight or fight" response that is triggered by anxiety primarily involves the _____ nervous system.
    a. autonomic
    b. parasympathetic
    c. peripheral
    d. somatic

    ANS: A   DIF: 1   REF: p. 122   OBJ: 1 TYPE: CON

4. "I've got to get out of here right now, or I may not make it!" This statement is most likely to be said by someone experiencing a(n):
    a. episode of depression
    b. future oriented mood state
    c. fear reaction
    d. parasympathetic "surge"

    ANS: C   DIF: 5   REF: p. 122   OBJ: 1 TYPE: APP

5. According to the textbook, the experience of fear can be described as a(n):
    a. immediate emotional reaction to danger
    b. type of claustrophobia
    c. neurotic response
    d. culturally specific phenomenon

    ANS: A   DIF: 3   REF: p. 122   OBJ: 1 TYPE: CON

6. Mrs. Pan has an anxiety disorder in which she has occasional panic attacks when shopping at the mall. This type of panic attack is referred to as:
   a. uncued
   b. situationally predisposed
   c. cued
   d. situationally bound

   ANS: B   DIF: 3   REF: p. 122   OBJ: 2 TYPE: CON

7. Which type of panic attack is most closely related to phobias?
   a. situationally predisposed
   b. situationally bound
   c. unexpected
   d. uncued

   ANS: B   DIF: 3   REF: p. 122   OBJ: 2 TYPE: FACT/WWW

8. According to the DSM-IV-TR criteria, the symptoms of a panic attack develop abruptly and reach a peak within _____ minute(s).
   a. 1
   b. 10
   c. 30
   d. 60
   e. none of the above

   ANS: B   DIF: 1   REF: p. 123   OBJ: 2 TYPE: FACT

9. Physiological assessments of panic attacks recorded in the laboratory indicate an increase in all of the following EXCEPT:
   a. heartbeat
   b. finger temperature
   c. muscle tension
   d. stomach contractions

   ANS: D   DIF: 1   REF: p. 123   OBJ: 2 TYPE: FACT

10. Which of the following is an accurate statement about anxiety?
    a. An inherited tendency can make us tense or uptight.
    b. A single gene makes us vulnerable to anxiety.
    c. Panic disorder does not "run in families."
    d. Stress is a direct cause of panic disorder.

    ANS: A   DIF: 3   REF: p. 123   OBJ: 1 TYPE: CON/WWW

11. Which of the following neurotransmitter systems is associated not only with anxiety, but also with depression?
    a. GABA-benzodiazepine
    b. noradrenergic
    c. serotonergic
    d. corticotropin releasing factor (CRF) system

    ANS: D   DIF: 5   REF: p. 124   OBJ: 1 TYPE: CON

12. The area of the brain most often associated with anxiety is the:
    a. limbic system
    b. reticular activating system
    c. occipital lobe
    d. corpus callosum

    ANS: A   DIF: 1   REF: p. 124   OBJ: 1 TYPE: FACT/WWW

13. According to Jeffrey Gray, a British neuropsychologist, the behavioral inhibition system (BIS) is
    activated by danger signals _____, resulting in the experience of anxiety.
    a. ascending from the brain stem
    b. descending from the cortex
    c. arising from both the brain stem and the cortex
    d. within the amygdala only

    ANS: C   DIF: 3   REF: p. 124   OBJ: 1 TYPE: CON

14. According to recent research (Johnson et al., 2000), an increased risk of developing anxiety
    disorders was found among teenagers who:
    a. smoked pot more than once per week
    b. smoked 20 or more cigarettes daily
    c. drank alcohol every day
    d. used anabolic steroids for 6 months or more

    ANS: B   DIF: 5   REF: p. 125   OBJ: 2 TYPE: APP

15. The recent research by Johnson et al., (2000), on cigarette smoking by teenagers indicates the
    possibility that:
    a. brain circuits are permanently "wired"
    b. neurotransmitter systems operate independently of non-biological influences
    c. sensitivity of brain circuits can be affected by environmental factors
    d. respiratory disorders cause changes in neurotransmitter systems

    ANS: C   DIF: 5   REF: p. 125   OBJ: 1 TYPE: APP

16. Recent research by Barlow (2002) and others indicates that vulnerability to anxiety disorders is
    related to:
    a. one's sense of control over environmental events
    b. the number of unexpected occurrences in one's life
    c. the number of siblings in one's family
    d. genetic or biological factors only

    ANS: A   DIF: 3   REF: p. 125   OBJ: 1 TYPE: APP

17. According to recent research on comorbidity by Brown and Barlow (2002) and others, at the time
    of assessment of an anxiety disorder, _____ of patients also had at least one other anxiety or
    depressive disorder.
    a. 15%
    b. 25%
    c. 55%
    d. 75%

    ANS: C   DIF: 1   REF: p. 126   OBJ: 3 TYPE: FACT

18. Which of the following terms is most associated with generalized anxiety disorder (GAD)?
    a. fear
    b. panic
    c. worry
    d. emotion

    ANS: C   DIF: 1   REF: p. 127   OBJ: 3 TYPE: FACT

19. All of the following are symptoms of generalized anxiety disorder (GAD) EXCEPT:
    a. muscle tension
    b. mental agitation
    c. worrying about minor daily events
    d. hypersomnia

    ANS: D   DIF: 3   REF: p. 128   OBJ: 3 TYPE: CON

20. Research studies have found that generalized anxiety disorder (GAD) is particularly prevalent among:
    a. young adult males
    b. teenage girls
    c. the elderly
    d. mid-life males

    ANS: C   DIF: 1   REF: p. 129   OBJ: 3 TYPE: FACT

21. Which physiological measure consistently distinguishes individuals with generalized anxiety disorder (GAD) from nonanxious normal subjects?
    a. increased muscle tension
    b. increased heart rate
    c. decreased EEG beta activity
    d. heightened autonomic arousal

    ANS: A   DIF: 5   REF: p. 129   OBJ: 5 TYPE: FACT

22. Findings from cognitive science combined with biological data indicate that the developmental model for generalized anxiety disorder includes all of the following EXCEPT:
    a. inherited tendency to be tense
    b. sense of control over life events
    c. stress leading to apprehension and vigilance
    d. autonomic restriction

    ANS: B   DIF: 3   REF: p. 130   OBJ: 5 TYPE: CON

23. For generalized anxiety disorder (GAD) the typical pharmacological treatment of choice has been the category of drugs known as:
    a. benzodiazepines
    b. SSRIs
    c. tricyclics
    d. MAO inhibitors

    ANS: A   DIF: 1   REF: p. 130   OBJ: 6 TYPE: FACT

24. Barlow and others (1992) have developed a cognitive-behavioral treatment for generalized anxiety disorder (GAD) that helps the patient:
    a. avoid feelings of anxiety as well as the negative images associated with those feelings
    b. confront anxiety-provoking thoughts and images
    c. adjust medication levels as needed to cope with the anxiety
    d. analyze the unconscious sources of the anxiety

    ANS: B   DIF: 3   REF: p. 131   OBJ: 6 TYPE: APP

25. Agoraphobic avoidance behavior appears to be determined by:
    a. how recently the last panic attack occurred
    b. the extent to which the person expects another panic attack to occur
    c. the number of panic attacks the person has had in the past
    d. how severe the panic attacks have been

    ANS: B   DIF: 5   REF: p. 132   OBJ: 3 TYPE: CON/WWW

26. Which of the following is an accurate statement about panic disorder with or without agoraphobia?
    a. An individual who suffers through an agoraphobic situation rather than avoiding it entirely is not considered agoraphobic.
    b. Most individuals with panic disorder will also avoid internal sensations that produce physiological arousal.
    c. Approximately 75% of those with agoraphobia are male.
    d. Women are more likely than men to cope with panic disorder by drinking alcohol.

    ANS: B   DIF: 5   REF: p. 134   OBJ: 3 TYPE: CON

27. Nocturnal panic attacks generally occur when an individual is:
    a. in REM sleep
    b. having a nightmare
    c. deeply asleep
    d. dreaming

    ANS: C   DIF: 1   REF: p. 135   OBJ: 3 TYPE: FACT

28. The phenomenon known as "isolated sleep paralysis" is most likely to occur in _____ who suffer from panic disorder.
    a. Caucasians
    b. African-Americans
    c. Latinos
    d. Asians

    ANS: B   DIF: 1   REF: p. 136   OBJ: 3 TYPE: FACT

29. Agoraphobia, which has come to mean "fear of going out," derives from the Greek word *agora,* meaning:
    a. marketplace
    b. home
    c. travel
    d. safe

    ANS: A   DIF: 1   REF: p. 123   OBJ: 3 TYPE: FACT

30. A teenage girl had recently been having panic attacks while shopping at the mall. She was sitting in her room feeling very depressed. To cheer her up, a friend suggested that they both go to an exercise class. Shortly after the warm-up started, however, she had another panic attack. What is the best explanation for this occurrence?
    a. She was angry with the friend for insisting that she go out.
    b. The medication that had been prescribed for her was only treating the depression, not the anxiety.
    c. The physical sensations experienced during exercise had become an internal cue for panic to occur.
    d. The exercise class was an unconditioned stimulus that resulted in a panic attack.

ANS: C   DIF: 5   REF: p. 137   OBJ: 3 TYPE: APP/WWW

31. An individual who suffers from panic disorder might become anxious about climbing stairs, exercising or being in hot rooms because these activities produce sensations similar to those accompanying a panic attack. In psychological terms, the exercise and hot rooms have become:
    a. conditioned stimuli
    b. unconditioned stimuli
    c. conditioned responses
    d. unconditioned responses

ANS: A   DIF: 5   REF: p. 137   OBJ: 3 TYPE: APP

32. In a study on anxiety by Ehlers and Breuer (1992), patients with panic disorder and others in a control group were asked to estimate how fast their hearts were beating. Since individuals with panic disorder pay close attention to their internal somatic sensations, you would correctly predict that they were _____ than the control group in estimating heart rate.
    a. more accurate
    b. less accurate
    c. faster
    d. slower

ANS: A   DIF: 3   REF: p. 138   OBJ: 3 TYPE: APP

33. In treating panic disorder, all of the following types of medications are used EXCEPT:
    a. tricyclic antidepressants
    b. SSRIs
    c. opiates
    d. benzodiazepines

ANS: C   DIF: 1   REF: p. 138   OBJ: 6 TYPE: FACT

34. What is one factor that distinguishes between traditional exposure-based treatments for panic disorder and the more recent panic control treatment (PCT) developed at one of Barlow's clinics?
    a. exposure to the interoceptive sensations associated with panic attacks
    b. referral to a psychiatrist for medication monitoring
    c. traditional exposure-based treatments result in a higher rate of cures
    d. as part of PCT, the therapist accompanies the patient on "reality testing" activities

ANS: A   DIF: 3   REF: p. 139   OBJ: 6 TYPE: CON

35. Which of the following procedures is NOT part of Barlow's panic control treatment (PCT)?
    a. cognitive therapy to modify conscious or unconscious perceptions about the "dangerousness" of feared situations
    b. creation of mini panic attacks in the therapist's office
    c. exercises to elevate the heart rate or spinning to make the patient dizzy
    d. reducing agoraphobic avoidance by exposure to feared situations

    ANS: D   DIF: 3   REF: p. 139   OBJ: 6 TYPE: CON

36. In a major double-blind NIMH research study looking at the separate and combined effects of both psychological and drug treatments (Barlow et al., 2000), patients were randomized into five different treatment conditions including:
    a. psychological treatment alone (PCT)
    b. combined drug and psychological treatment
    c. placebo alone
    d. all of these

    ANS: D   DIF: 5   REF: p. 140   OBJ: 6 TYPE: APP

37. A relative of yours who suffers from panic disorder asks you what treatment would have the most long-lasting benefits. Since you have just read about the double-blind NIMH research study evaluating psychological treatments with and without medication, you tell your relative to first try:
    a. the drug imipramine
    b. psychological treatment along with medication
    c. panic control treatment that includes cognitive behavioral therapy (CBT)
    d. any available treatment since patients in all treatment conditions achieved the same long-lasting gains

    ANS: C   DIF: 5   REF: p. 140   OBJ: 6 TYPE: APP

38. All of the following are characteristics common to specific phobias EXCEPT:
    a. strong and persistent anxiety related to a specific object or situation
    b. significant attempts by the anxious individual to avoid the phobic situation
    c. recognition by the person with the phobia that the anxiety is excessive or unreasonable
    d. decreased arousal of the autonomic nervous system

    ANS: D   DIF: 3   REF: p. 141   OBJ: 3 TYPE: CON

39. Phobic reactions to all of the following are included in the natural environment subtype of specific phobias with the exception of:
    a. heights
    b. storms (including thunder and lightning)
    c. deep water
    d. animals

    ANS: D   DIF: 1   REF: p. 143   OBJ: 3 TYPE: FACT

40. Although blood-injury-injection phobia is one of the specific phobias, it differs in regard to:
    a. blood pressure and heart rate
    b. level of anxiety
    c. age and gender
    d. the sleep/wake cycle

    ANS: A   DIF: 1   REF: p. 142   OBJ: 3 TYPE: FACT

41. In the type of specific phobia called "blood-injury-injection," there is an inherited vasovagal response and a tendency to faint due to:
    a. an increase in blood pressure
    b. a decrease in blood pressure
    c. an increase in body temperature
    d. a decrease in body temperature

    ANS: B   DIF: 1   REF: p. 142   OBJ: 5 TYPE: FACT

42. Which of the following is NOT an example of a situational phobia?
    a. claustrophobia
    b. fear of flying
    c. fear of public buses
    d. animal phobia

    ANS: D   DIF: 1   REF: p. 142   OBJ: 3 TYPE: FACT

43. The main difference between situational phobia and panic disorder with agoraphobia (PDA) is:
    a. people with situational phobia never experience panic attacks outside the context of the phobic situation
    b. people with situational phobia experience panic attacks when confronted with the phobic situation as well as at other times
    c. people with PDA experience panic attacks only in specific situations
    d. people with PDA experience panic attacks only at specific times

    ANS: A   DIF: 5   REF: p. 143   OBJ: 3 TYPE: CON

44. According to your textbook, there are at least three ways of developing a phobia. Which is NOT one of these ways?
    a. experiencing a panic attack in a specific situation
    b. having a nightmare about a feared situation
    c. observing someone else experience severe fear
    d. in certain conditions, being told about danger

    ANS: B   DIF: 3   REF: p. 146   OBJ: 5 TYPE: CON

45. You are told about a child who has shown behavior consistent with "separation anxiety." In order to determine if the child actually has a disorder or whether the behavior is normal, you would first need to know:
    a. the child's age
    b. whether the child is a boy or a girl
    c. if other family members have anxiety disorders
    d. how long the child has shown this behavior

    ANS: A   DIF: 3   REF: p. 145   OBJ: 3 TYPE: CON

46. Although illness phobia resembles hypochondria, it differs in that persons with illness phobias:
    a. are fearful of acquiring a disease
    b. are fearful that they have contracted a disease
    c. are worried that they had the disease and weren't aware of it
    d. actually have the disease

    ANS: A   DIF: 3   REF: p. 143   OBJ: 3 TYPE: CON

47. During the 1990s illness phobia has become more prevalent due the increasing numbers of people who had:
    a. herpes
    b. Alzheimer's
    c. HIV/AIDS
    d. hepatitis

    ANS: C   DIF: 1   REF: p. 143   OBJ: 3 TYPE: FACT

48. The Latin term *globus hystericus* is another name for:
    a. hysteria
    b. fear of traveling
    c. choking phobia
    d. blood-injury-injection phobia

    ANS: C   DIF: 1   REF: p. 143   OBJ: 3 TYPE: FACT

49. A psychological disorder in children characterized by unrealistic and persistent worry that something will happen to the parents and that may result in refusal to leave home is called:
    a. globus hystericus
    b. school phobia
    c. situational phobia
    d. separation anxiety

    ANS: D   DIF: 3   REF: p. 144   OBJ: 3 TYPE: CON

50. In the general population approximately _____ of people have specific fears severe enough to be diagnosed as phobias.
    a. 1%
    b. 11%
    c. 31%
    d. 51%

    ANS: B   DIF: 1   REF: p. 144   OBJ: 3 TYPE: FACT

51. Which of the following is a correct match between "normal" childhood fears and the approximate age of onset?
    a. age 10: evaluation by others, anxiety over physical appearance
    b. infancy: monsters and other imaginary creatures
    c. ages 1-2: loud noises and strangers
    d. age 3: separation from parents, fears of animals and the dark

    ANS: A   DIF: 1   REF: p. 145   OBJ: 3 TYPE: FACT

52. A culture bound syndrome in Chinese cultures called *Pa-leng* (or sometimes "frigo phobia") often results in the sufferer:
    a. appearing naked in public
    b. wearing layers of clothing
    c. exercising compulsively
    d. hoarding food

    ANS: B   DIF: 3   REF: p. 145   OBJ: 3 TYPE: APP

53. According to your textbook, new techniques have made it possible to treat some phobias effectively in one:
    a. day
    b. week
    c. month
    d. year

    ANS: D   DIF: 1   REF: p. 148   OBJ: 3 TYPE: FACT

54. In regard to treatment of specific phobias, which of the following statements is correct?
    a. Structured exposure-based exercises are no longer considered necessary.
    b. Individuals with "blood" phobias must learn to relax their muscles to keep their blood pressure high enough to prevent fainting.
    c. Exposure-based exercises actually change brain functioning.
    d. Avoiding a phobic situation weakens the phobic response.

    ANS: C   DIF: 3   REF: p. 148   OBJ: 6 TYPE: CON/WWW

55. Which of the following would NOT be considered an example of social phobia?
    a. A student who is reluctant to speak up in a classroom due to fear of embarrassing herself.
    b. A male who has difficulty urinating in a public restroom when others are present.
    c. A person who can only eat comfortably when he is alone.
    d. An individual who cannot travel on public transportation without a family member present.

    ANS: D   DIF: 3   REF: p. 149   OBJ: 3 TYPE: CON

56. According to research by Kessler et al., (1994), as many as _____ of the general population suffer from social phobia at some point in their lives.
    a. 3%
    b. 13%
    c. 23%
    d. 33%

    ANS: B   DIF: 1   REF: p. 149   OBJ: 3 TYPE: FACT

57. The most prevalent psychological disorder in the general population is:
    a. social phobia
    b. agoraphobia
    c. school phobia
    d. panic disorder

    ANS: A   DIF: 1   REF: p. 149   OBJ: 3 TYPE: FACT

58. Unlike most of the anxiety disorders in which female sufferers predominate, the sex ratio is almost equal in:
    a. agoraphobia
    b. specific phobias
    c. social phobia
    d. panic disorder

    ANS: C   DIF: 1   REF: p. 149   OBJ: 3 TYPE: CON

59. The anxiety disorder called social phobia, involving anxiety about being evaluated or criticized, usually begins during:
    a. childhood
    b. adolescence
    c. young adulthood
    d. middle age

    ANS: B   DIF: 1   REF: p. 149   OBJ: 3 TYPE: FACT

60. In Japan, the anxiety syndrome termed *taijin kyo fusho* involves a fear of:
    a. performing onstage
    b. personally offending others
    c. embarrassing oneself
    d. speaking to females

    ANS: B   DIF: 3   REF: p. 150   OBJ: 3 TYPE: CON

61. Research by Lundh (1996) demonstrated that social phobics presented with pictures of faces were more likely to remember _____ expressions.
    a. smiling and pleasant
    b. critical and angry
    c. sad and tearful
    d. blank, meaningless

    ANS: B   DIF: 1   REF: p. 150   OBJ: 3 TYPE: APP

62. Which of the following drugs received FDA approval in 1999 as a treatment for social phobia?
    a. Zoloft
    b. Paxil
    c. Prozac
    d. Phenelzine

    ANS: B   DIF: 1   REF: p. 151   OBJ: 6 TYPE: FACT

63. A friend stated that when she went to a clinic, she had to spend 30 to 60 second sessions shaking her head from side to side, spinning in a chair, tensing all her muscles, hyperventilating, or breathing through a narrow straw. She is surprised that you correctly guessed that she is receiving treatment for:
    a. specific phobia
    b. social phobia
    c. panic disorder
    d. posttraumatic stress disorder

    ANS: C   DIF: 3   REF: p. 140   OBJ: 6 TYPE: APP

64. The setting for posttraumatic stress disorder to occur follows an experience accompanied by a triad of feelings, including all of the following EXCEPT:
   a. horror
   b. paranoia
   c. helplessness
   d. fear

   ANS: B   DIF: 3   REF: p. 152   OBJ: 4 TYPE: CON

65. Individuals suffering from posttraumatic stress disorder (PTSD) display a characteristic set of symptoms including all of the following EXCEPT:
   a. numbing of emotional responsiveness
   b. sudden "flashbacks" in which the traumatic event is relived
   c. decreased startle response and chronic underarousal
   d. memories and nightmares of the event

   ANS: C   DIF: 1   REF: p. 152   OBJ: 4 TYPE: FACT

66. Following the tragedy at the World Trade Center in New York City on 9/11/01, more than 100 children who lived near the scene later developed:
   a. claustrophobia
   b. agoraphobia
   c. social phobia
   d. blood-injection-injury phobia

   ANS: B   DIF: 1   REF: p. 155   OBJ: 4 TYPE: FACT

67. Which of the following is an accurate statement about posttraumatic stress disorder (PTSD)?
   a. Acute stress disorder is diagnosed instead of PTSD if a person's symptoms begin 6 months or more after the traumatic event.
   b. PTSD occurs in all individuals who experience a traumatic event.
   c. Most persons diagnosed with acute stress disorder do not eventually develop PTSD.
   d. Acute stress disorder was included as a DSM-IV diagnosis so early severe reactions to trauma could receive health insurance coverage for immediate treatment.

   ANS: D   DIF: 3   REF: p. 153   OBJ: 4 TYPE: FACT/WWW

68. In a study by Kilpatrick et al. (1985) concerning women who had experienced traumatic events, the most profound emotional impact, including suicidal ideation or attempts, occurred following:
   a. robbery
   b. rape
   c. aggravated assault
   d. auto accidents that included fatalities

   ANS: B   DIF: 1   REF: p. 154   OBJ: 4 TYPE: FACT

69. Veterans returning home to the United States after the end of the war in Vietnam experienced a high rate of posttraumatic stress disorder due in part to:
    a. high rates of drug addiction
    b. youth and inexperience
    c. absence of social support
    d. separation from family

    ANS: C   DIF: 1   REF: p. 157   OBJ: 4 TYPE: FACT

70. Although the "alarm reactions" experienced in both PTSD and panic disorder are very similar and result in conditioned responses, in panic disorder the alarm is:
    a. false
    b. real
    c. stronger
    d. weaker

    ANS: A   DIF: 1   REF: p. 157   OBJ: 4 TYPE: FACT

71. Which of the following is an accurate statement about factors affecting treatment for PTSD?
    a. psychoanalytic therapists help patients to relive emotional trauma through a process called free association
    b. victims of PTSD often repress memories of the traumatic event
    c. re-exposure to the trauma should be accomplished quickly to assure the best therapeutic response
    d. medications effective for other anxiety disorders are ineffective with PTSD

    ANS: B   DIF: 3   REF: p. 158   OBJ: 6 TYPE: APP/WWW

72. Obsessive-Compulsive Disorder is often accompanied by all of the following EXCEPT:
    a. severe generalized anxiety
    b. major depression
    c. visual hallucinations
    d. panic attacks

    ANS: C   DIF: 3   REF: p. 159   OBJ: 4 TYPE: CON

73. Actions, or sometimes thoughts, that an individual with OCD uses to reduce anxiety are called:
    a. operants
    b. fixations
    c. habits
    d. rituals

    ANS: D   DIF: 1   REF: p. 159   OBJ: 4 TYPE: FACT

74. The compulsions that an individual with OCD uses to suppress disastrous consequences or ward off intrusive thoughts can be either:
    a. behavioral or mental
    b. positive or negative
    c. biological or psychological
    d. autonomic or somatic

    ANS: A   DIF: 1   REF: p. 159   OBJ: 4 TYPE: CON

75. In regard to the anxiety disorder known as OCD, which of the following would NOT be an example of a **behavioral** compulsion?
    a. checking
    b. counting
    c. handwashing
    d. ordering

    ANS: B   DIF: 3   REF: p. 160   OBJ: 4 TYPE: FACT

76. In regard to OCD, when the term "magical" is used to refer to compulsive acts, it means:
    a. the person with OCD believes he/she is possessed
    b. compulsive behaviors are similar to superstitions
    c. the compulsions have no logical relation to the obsessions
    d. many magicians have been diagnosed with OCD

    ANS: C   DIF: 5   REF: p. 159   OBJ: 4 TYPE: FACT

77. In a 1986 study by Jenike et al., it was found that the most common obsessions in a group of 100 patients were related to:
    a. aggression
    b. sex
    c. contamination
    d. symmetry

    ANS: C   DIF: 3   REF: p. 159   OBJ: 4 TYPE: FACT

78. In regard to the obsessions seen in patients with OCD, the term "need for symmetry" refers to:
    a. doing something a number of different ways
    b. keeping things in perfect order
    c. putting everything on one's right and nothing on the left
    d. accumulation of possessions

    ANS: B   DIF: 1   REF: p. 159   OBJ: 4 TYPE: CON

79. In OCD, certain types of obsessions lead to certain types of compulsions. From the following choose the one that is a correct match between an obsession and its consequent rituals.
    a. aggression obsessions: cleaning
    b. contamination: ordering
    c. sexual obsessions: checking
    d. symmetry: hoarding

    ANS: C   DIF: 3   REF: p. 160   OBJ: 4 TYPE: FACT

80. In the case of Richard (described in the textbook), he was obsessed with the idea that if he did not eat in a certain ritualistic way, he would become possessed, an aspect of OCD that is termed:
    a. symmetrical
    b. magical
    c. logical
    d. demonic

    ANS: B   DIF: 3   REF: p. 159   OBJ: 4 TYPE: APP

81. In the case of Richard, the patient with OCD described in the textbook, he was compelled to take very small steps as he walked and to look back repeatedly. As with other types of checking compulsions, Richard was trying to:
    a. restore a sense of safety and control
    b. reduce the possibility of contamination
    c. ward off an imagined disaster
    d. make sure he didn't make a mistake

    ANS: C   DIF: 5   REF: p. 160   OBJ: 4 TYPE: APP

82. Normal, ordinary people who have occasional intrusive thoughts with bizarre, sexual or aggressive content, would not be considered to have OCD unless they find the thoughts unacceptable or even dangerous and also:
    a. use alcohol or other drugs to reduce anxiety
    b. develop insomnia and nightmares
    c. become anxious about having additional intrusive thoughts
    d. suffer from either posttraumatic stress disorder or social phobia

    ANS: C   DIF: 5   REF: p. 161   OBJ: 4 TYPE: APP

83. In regard to a type of thinking pattern found in some patients with OCD, which of the following would be an example of *thought-action fusion*?
    a. washing one's hands repeatedly to ward off germs
    b. taking only very small steps while walking to prevent others from being in danger
    c. believing that thinking about an abortion is the moral equivalent of having an abortion
    d. saving stacks of old newspapers or magazines because they might be needed some day

    ANS: C   DIF: 5   REF: p. 161   OBJ: 4 TYPE: CON

84. A young child has thoughts about hating her younger brother and wishing he would die. She becomes very anxious about these thoughts because she has developed the idea that if anything really happened to him, it would be her fault. This pattern of thinking is called:
    a. neutralizing
    b. thought-action fusion
    c. thought suppression
    d. fundamental responsibility

    ANS: B   DIF: 1   REF: p. 161   OBJ: 4 TYPE: APP

85. Tony has thoughts about hating his younger brother and wishing he would die. He becomes very anxious about these thoughts because he has developed the idea that if anything really happened to his brother, it would be his fault. For no explainable reason, Tony starts mentally counting by odd numbers each time he walks past his brother's room and discovers that this activity makes him less anxious. Tony's behavior can be described as:
    a. a phobia of going into his brother's room because he is afraid his hatred will actually hurt him
    b. a mental compulsion developed to neutralize his bad thoughts
    c. an attempt to be better in math than his brother to gain parental acceptance
    d. a compulsive ritual designed to make him like his brother more

    ANS: B   DIF: 5   REF: p. 162   OBJ: 4 TYPE: APP

86. What happens when persons with OCD attempt to neutralize or suppress disturbing, intrusive thoughts?
   a. the obsessive thoughts disappear
   b. the frequency of the obsessive thoughts increases
   c. other kinds of obsessive thinking starts to occur
   d. this strategy has no effect on the obsessive thoughts

   ANS: B   DIF: 5   REF: p. 162   OBJ: 4 TYPE: CON

87. According to several cross-cultural research studies reported in the textbook, the prevalence of OCD is:
   a. very similar across cultures
   b. lower in European countries
   c. higher in Africa nations
   d. virtually non-existent in some cultures

   ANS: A   DIF: 3   REF: p. 161   OBJ: 4 TYPE: APP

88. According to research studies reported in the textbook, persons with OCD who hold fundamentalist religious beliefs often present with:
   a. both checking and hoarding rituals
   b. a reduced sense of responsibility for their actions
   c. attitudes of inflated responsibility
   d. non-equivalence of obsessive thoughts and compulsive actions

   ANS: C   DIF: 5   REF: p. 162   OBJ: 4 TYPE: APP

89. The model of the etiology of obsessive-compulsive disorder suggests that in order for an individual to develop OCD, _____ must be present.
   a. biological vulnerability
   b. psychological vulnerability
   c. both biological and psychological vulnerabilities
   d. neither biological nor psychological vulnerabilities

   ANS: C   DIF: 3   REF: p. 162   OBJ: 5 TYPE: CON

90. In regard to pharmacological treatments for obsessive-compulsive disorder, the most effective drugs are those that inhibit the reuptake of the neurotransmitter called:
   a. serotonin
   b. dopamine
   c. noradrenaline
   d. epinephrine

   ANS: A   DIF: 3   REF: p. 162   OBJ: 5 TYPE: CON

91. In regard to treatment of obsessive-compulsive disorders, drugs that inhibit the reuptake of serotonin (SSRIs) have been found to be effective in approximately _____ of patients.
   a. 10%
   b. 30%
   c. 60%
   d. 80%

   ANS: C   DIF: 1   REF: p. 162   OBJ: 6 TYPE: FACT

92. The behavioral process in which OCD patients are not permitted to carry out their compulsions while in the presence of the anxiety producing stimulus or situation is called:
   a. exposure and ritual prevention
   b. thought stopping technique
   c. anxiety reduction therapy
   d. behavioral inhibition conditioning

ANS: A   DIF: 1   REF: p. 162   OBJ: 6 TYPE: CON

93. Which of the following is an example of the treatment technique for OCD called exposure and ritual prevention (ERP)?
   a. Carrie has an obsessive fear of contamination which has led to compulsive handwashing rituals. Her therapist is treating her by making her touch dirty laundry but not allowing her to wash for increasingly longer periods of time afterwards.
   b. Kerry has an obsessive fear of contamination which has led to compulsive handwashing rituals. Her therapist is treating her by forcing her to wash her hands repeatedly, even when she doesn't feel anxious.
   c. Kelly has religious obsessions. She feels that if she doesn't read biblical passages every hour of the day, she will do something evil. Her therapist is treating her by having her attend religious services more frequently so that good thoughts will replace the bad ones.
   d. Callie has a hoarding compulsion. She becomes anxious whenever she has to throw something away; she even keeps stuff that she doesn't need and will never use. Her therapist has arranged for all Callie's junk to be dumped when she is away from home.

ANS: A   DIF: 5   REF: p. 162   OBJ: 6 TYPE: APP/WWW

94. Research studies have shown that the therapeutic benefits of medication for OCD:
   a. are permanent
   b. are reduced when the medication is discontinued
   c. continue even when the drug is discontinued
   d. are no more effective than a placebo

ANS: B   DIF: 3   REF: p. 162   OBJ: 6 TYPE: APP

95. Research studies have shown that combining exposure and ritual prevention (ERP) with medication when treating patients with OCD:
   a. is better than drug treatment alone
   b. is better than ERP alone
   c. causes patients to discontinue treatment
   d. does not produce any additional therapeutic advantage

ANS: D   DIF: 5   REF: p. 162   OBJ: 6 TYPE: APP

96. According the textbook, treatments for obsessive-compulsive disorder have included all of the following EXCEPT:
   a. medication
   b. exposure and ritual prevention (ERP)
   c. psychosurgery
   d. shock therapy (ECT)

ANS: D   DIF: 3   REF: p. 162   OBJ: 6 TYPE: FACT/
WWW

97. Mr. J. suffers from a severe case of obsessive-compulsive disorder. His symptoms have not responded to either medication or psychological therapies. As a last resort, his therapist suggests the possibility of a psychosurgical procedure, specifically an operation called:
   a. lobotomy
   b. lobectomy
   c. cingulotomy
   d. cingulectomy

   ANS: C   DIF: 1   REF: p. 162   OBJ: 6 TYPE: FACT

98. As a last resort, both a psychiatrist and a neurosurgeon have suggested to Ms Z. that a psychosurgical procedure called a cingulotomy might relieve her severe OCD symptoms. Ms Z. asks what the success rate has been for this operation. She is told that approximately _____ of patients benefited substantially.
   a. 3%
   b. 13%
   c. 30%
   d. 53%

   ANS: C   DIF: 3   REF: p. 162   OBJ: 6 TYPE: FACT

99. In a study reported by Barlow (2001), non-clinical subjects reported all of the following obsessional and intrusive thoughts EXCEPT:
   a. "While holding a baby, having a sudden urge to kick it."
   b. "Impulse to push someone in front of a train."
   c. "Having unnatural sexual acts."
   d. "Professors who teach Abnormal Psychology must all be abnormal."

   ANS: D   DIF: 1   REF: p. 161   OBJ: 4 TYPE: FACT

100. In the integrative model of the causes of obsessive-compulsive disorder (displayed as a diagram in the textbook), anxious apprehension:
   a. is focused on recurring thoughts
   b. becomes associated with unacceptable thoughts
   c. leads to learned alarms
   d. results from biological vulnerability only

   ANS: A   DIF: 3   REF: p. 162   OBJ: 4 TYPE: CON/WWW

101. As described on the "Abnormal Psychology Live" CD, Steve's symptoms caused him to think he was having a:
   a. seizure   c. heart attack
   b. panic attack   d. stroke

   ANS: C   DIF: 1   REF: CD

102. As described on the "Abnormal Psychology Live" CD, Steve was diagnosed with:
   a. generalized anxiety disorder   c. panic disorder
   b. agoraphobia   d. social phobia

   ANS: C   DIF: 2   REF: CD

103. During a panic attack, Steve ("Abnormal Psychology Live" CD), said he felt all of the following EXCEPT:
   a. "as though I had a knot in my chest"
   b. "like I had swallowed something"
   c. "lightheaded and flushed"
   d. "sick to my stomach"

   ANS: D   DIF: 2   REF: CD

104. During the interview with Chuck ("Abnormal Psychology Live" CD), he stated that he was obsessed with having to check the stove to see if he had left it on. Chuck found his own behavior absurd because he:
   a. did not own a stove
   b. never cooked
   c. did not know how to turn it on
   d. knew he always turned it off

   ANS: B   DIF: 2   REF: CD

105. During the interview with Chuck ("Abnormal Psychology Live" CD), when asked how often he experienced obsessive thoughts, he replied:
   a. "only when I feel stressed"
   b. "all the time"
   c. "hardly ever"
   d. "several times a day"

   ANS: B   DIF: 2   REF: CD

ESSAY

1. Why is anxiety termed "a future-oriented mood-state" and fear an "alarm reaction to actual present danger"? Discuss biological and psychological similarities and differences between these emotional events. Explore the idea that fear is panic that occurs in an inappropriate setting.

2. Discuss panic disorder including symptoms, causes, and treatment. Use the etiologic integrative model in your discussion. What is a panic attack? Explain the differences between the three types of panic attacks.

3. Discuss the genetic, psychological and socio-cultural factors involved in anxiety disorders. Cite current research into the neurobiology of anxiety and panic and the role of the CRF system and other brain circuits.

4. Define generalized anxiety disorder. Compare and contrast GAD with phobic disorders, noting how avoidance behavior is manifested differently in each.

5. Define agoraphobia and discuss the concept of "safety" for a person with this condition. Note gender differences in the development of this disorder. Explain what is meant by interoceptive avoidance.

6. Describe how the five subtypes of specific phobia differ from each other. Discuss the differences between separation anxiety and school phobia. What are the specific factors involved in the development of a phobia?

7. Define social phobia, noting the typical life stage of onset, and explain how it differs from "normal" shyness. Using examples describe how social anxiety impairs functioning. What types of treatments are effective for social phobia?

8. Use the concepts of biological vulnerability and psychological vulnerability to discuss the etiologic integrative models of anxiety disorders. Choose one of the models to further illustrate the development of a particular anxiety disorder (e.g., social phobia).   **WWW**

9. Discuss the criteria for a diagnosis of posttraumatic stress disorder. What is the significance of biological vulnerability in the development of PTSD? Using the textbook case involving several family members with PTSD, discuss the differences in their symptoms and how they were treated.

10. Compare and contrast obsessive-compulsive disorder with the other anxiety disorders. Define obsession and compulsion and give examples. Explain "exposure and ritual prevention" as a treatment for OCD.

MULTIPLE CHOICE

1. Anxiety is
    a. an immediate alarm reaction to stressful situations.
    b. usually a sign of an underdeveloped ego.
    c. potentially helpful in planning for the future.
    d. always a hindrance to adaptive functioning.

    ANS: C

2. Paula has frequent panic attacks, but only when she views the national news on television. However, she does not experience a panic attack every time she sees the national news. Paula's panic attacks would be classified as
    a. unexpected
    b. situationally bound
    c. situationally predisposed
    d. justified

    ANS: C

3. Which of the following is the area of the brain most often associated with anxiety?
    a. occipital lobe
    b. orbital frontal lobe
    c. medulla
    d. limbic system

    ANS: D

4. All but which of the following may be related to nocturnal panic?
    a. nightmares
    b. slow wave sleep
    c. sleep apnea
    d. the phenomenon described as "the witch is riding you"

    ANS: A

5. The main element in psychological treatment of panic disorders is
    a. benzodiazepines
    b. hypnosis
    c. exposure to the feared symptoms
    d. teaching avoidance techniques

    ANS: C

6. A specific phobia involving motorcycles can develop as a result of a predisposition to develop fear combined with
   a. watching another person experience a motorcycle accident
   b. hearing your mother repeatedly warn you about the doom associated with motorcycles
   c. experiencing a traumatic event yourself, such as a motorcycle skid
   d. all of the above

   ANS: D

7. The most common phobia, the fear of public speaking, is an example of
   a. specific phobia.
   b. agoraphobia.
   c. social phobia.
   d. specific, situational phobia
   e. none of the above.

   ANS: C

8. Valerie tells you that she has been receiving cognitive behavioral treatment for her generalized anxiety disorder. This treatment most likely involves
   a. Bringing on the worry process during therapy sessions and confronting the anxiety-provoking images and worrisome thoughts head-on.
   b. Discussing the earliest memories of anxiety-provoking events and finding meaning in these fears.
   c. Snapping a rubber band on her wrist when she is anxious.
   d. the prescription of serotonin reuptake inhibitor medication.
   e. none of the above

   ANS: A

9. Rob presented at the clinic with complaints that he is terrified to go anywhere that does not have a bathroom for fear that he will begin vomiting and not be able to stop. He has had one panic attack and reported that a week after that attack he felt no residual effects from the attack. Rob would most likely receive a DSM-IV diagnosis of
   a. panic disorder with agoraphobia.
   b. panic disorder without agoraphobia.
   c. interoceptive agoraphobia.
   d. agoraphobia without history of panic disorder.

   ANS: B

10. What is the most prevalent psychological disorder?
    a. major depression
    b. posttraumatic stress disorder
    c. schizophrenia
    d. social phobia

    ANS: D

MULTIPLE CHOICE

1. All of the following are classified as somatoform disorders EXCEPT:
    a. dissociative identity disorder
    b. hypochondriasis
    c. conversion disorder
    d. body dysmorphic disorder

    ANS: A   DIF: 1   REF: p. 169   OBJ: 1 TYPE: FACT

2. The common aspect of all somatoform disorders is a pathological:
    a. belief that a serious medical condition will cause death
    b. belief that one's appearance is ugly
    c. concern with appearance or functioning of the body
    d. concern with the meaning of a physical pain

    ANS: C   DIF: 3   REF: p. 169   OBJ: 1 TYPE: FACT

3. Hypochondriasis exists when:
    a. normal bodily sensations are interpreted by the patient as a sign of a serious illness
    b. real physical illness is exaggerated to the point where the patient can only focus on the pain
    c. the patient has an unrealistic fear of contacting germs
    d. the patient is truly ill but does not trust the medical establishment enough to seek treatment

    ANS: A   DIF: 1   REF: p. 169   OBJ: 1 TYPE: FACT

4. An essential element of hypochondriasis is:
    a. psychosis
    b. anxiety
    c. depression
    d. dissociation

    ANS: B   DIF: 1   REF: p. 169   OBJ: 1 TYPE: FACT/WWW

5. Joe just ate six chilidogs and drank a liter of soda. If Joe is a hypochondriac, he would probably interpret any resulting stomach discomfort as:
    a. his own fault for eating so much
    b. the result of poor quality food
    c. gas pains from overeating
    d. a sign that something is seriously wrong with his stomach

    ANS: D   DIF: 1   REF: p. 170   OBJ: 1 TYPE: APP

6. The core feature of hypochondriasis is:
   a. disease conviction
   b. fear of contamination
   c. preoccupation with an imagined body defect
   d. compulsive behavior such as hand washing

   ANS: A   DIF: 1   REF: p. 170   OBJ: 1 TYPE: FACT

7. Since Jane is a hypochondriac, we can expect her to see her physician:
   a. often and feel completely reassured that there is nothing wrong with her health
   b. rarely but continue to believe that she is quite ill
   c. almost never because she does not trust physicians
   d. often but continue to be anxious about her health anyway

   ANS: D   DIF: 3   REF: p. 170   OBJ: 1 TYPE: APP

8. Jill is constantly worried that she will get sick. Although she feels fine now and believes that she is healthy, she still worries endlessly about developing a serious illness. Most likely Jill would be diagnosed with:
   a. illness phobia
   b. hypochondriasis
   c. somatization disorder
   d. body dysmorphic disorder

   ANS: A   DIF: 3   REF: p. 170   OBJ: 1 TYPE: APP

9. Although both panic disorder patients and hypochondriacs tend to misinterpret bodily sensations, patients with panic disorder:
   a. are having real physical sensations while hypochondriacs' sensations are "all in their heads"
   b. tend to fear immediate catastrophe while hypochondriacs tend to fear long-term illness
   c. are having imagined physical sensations while hypochondriacs are experiencing real physical sensations
   d. tend to ignore the symptoms of their first attacks while hypochondriacs tend to seek immediate medical treatment following the first indication of pain

   ANS: B   DIF: 5   REF: p. 170   OBJ: 1 TYPE: CON

10. With regard to a diagnosis of hypochondriasis, women are:
    a. as equally likely as men to be diagnosed
    b. less likely than men to be diagnosed
    c. more likely than men to be diagnosed
    d. more likely than men to be diagnosed during middle to late adulthood but no more likely than men to be diagnosed during teen years and early adulthood

    ANS: A   DIF: 1   REF: p. 171   OBJ: 1 TYPE: FACT

11. Disorders such as *koro* and *dhat,* that are similar to hypochondriasis, demonstrate the:
    a. influence of culture on psychopathology
    b. physical basis of many hypochondriacs' complaints
    c. difficulty of accurately diagnosing hypochondriasis
    d. influence of genetics on psychopathology

    ANS: A   DIF: 3   REF: p. 171   OBJ: 1 TYPE: CON

12. Hypochondriasis is essentially an emotional disturbance triggered by:
    a. physical pathology
    b. misinterpretation of normal physical sensations
    c. social concerns
    d. severe or unusual physical sensations

    ANS: B   DIF: 3   REF: p. 172   OBJ: 1 TYPE: CON

13. All of the following have been implicated in the development and maintenance of hypochondriasis EXCEPT:
    a. the additional attention one receives when sick
    b. a specific hypochondriac gene
    c. the high incidence of disease in the family during the hypochondriac's childhood
    d. learning to worry from family members overly concerned with health

    ANS: B   DIF: 1   REF: p. 172   OBJ: 1 TYPE: FACT

14. With regard to the treatment of hypochondriasis, some research supports the use of:
    a. classical conditioning and operant conditioning
    b. psychoanalysis
    c. cognitive-behavioral treatment and stress management
    d. humanistic therapy

    ANS: C   DIF: 1   REF: p. 173   OBJ: 1 TYPE: FACT

15. With regard to the treatment of hypochondriasis, research exploring the use of reassurance in a process called "explanatory therapy" showed that:
    a. some significant gains were achieved
    b. reassurance did not work for hypochondriacs
    c. reassurance showed some gains but they lasted less than several days
    d. the gains were so significant that participants were essentially "cured"

    ANS: A   DIF: 5   REF: p. 173   OBJ: 1 TYPE: FACT

16. In terms of anti-depressant medication treatments for hypochondriasis, the most accurate statement based on the research so far is:
    a. anti-depressants are effective
    b. anti-depressants are not effective
    c. some reports suggest that anti-depressants may be effective but placebo controlled studies have not been performed
    d. placebo controlled studies have been performed and the results suggest that anti-depressants work for some hypochondriacs but not for most

    ANS: C   DIF: 3   REF: P. 173   OBJ: 1 TYPE: FACT

17. When no physical cause can be found for pain or other symptoms, the diagnosis is usually:
    a. hypochondriasis
    b. pain disorder
    c. body dysmorphic disorder
    d. somatization disorder

    ANS: D   DIF: 3   REF: p. 173   OBJ: 1 TYPE: FACT/WWW

18. Joan and Fred both experience physical symptoms of pain and discomfort. Both have been examined by physicians and declared healthy. Joan is concerned that her pain is a sign of a serious illness while Fred is not worried that he is sick. Fred is so focused on his pain that he finds it hard to participate in normal life activities. The following statement is true:
    a. Joan has hypochondriasis; Fred has somatization disorder.
    b. Joan has somatization disorder; Fred has hypochondriasis.
    c. Both Fred and Joan have somatization disorder.
    d. Both Fred and Joan are hypochondriacs.

    ANS: A   DIF: 3   REF: p. 174   OBJ: 1 TYPE: APP

19. The percentage of the population diagnosed with somatization disorder is:
    a. very small
    b. about the same percentage as for hypochondriasis
    c. greater than the percentage for hypochondriasis
    d. completely unknown

    ANS: A   DIF: 1   REF: p. 174   OBJ: 1 TYPE: FACT

20. There appears to be a common genetic component involved in somatization disorder and:
    a. hypochondriasis
    b. antisocial personality disorder
    c. body dysmorphic disorder
    d. panic disorder

    ANS: B   DIF: 1   REF: p. 176   OBJ: 1 TYPE: FACT

21. The hypothesized connections between somatization disorder and antisocial personality disorder are:
    a. poor modeling by parents and other authority figures
    b. sibling rivalry and attention deficits
    c. pleasure seeking and impulsivity
    d. genetic defects and poor nutrition

    ANS: C   DIF: 3   REF: p. 176   OBJ: 1 TYPE: FACT

22. Which of the following are typical characteristics of patients with somatization disorder?
    a. female and impulsive
    b. female and sexually conservative
    c. male and impulsive
    d. male and aggressive

    ANS: A   DIF: 1   REF: p. 174   OBJ: 1 TYPE: FACT

23. Which of the following statements is true with regard to the treatment of somatization disorder?
    a. cognitive-behavioral treatment has been demonstrated in several studies to be the best available treatment
    b. it is relatively easy to treat as long as the patient is willing to participate in therapy
    c. assignment of a "gatekeeper" physician has been found to cure most patients
    d. it is difficult to treat and there are no treatments with proven effectiveness

    ANS: D   DIF: 3   REF: p. 177   OBJ: 1 TYPE: FACT

24. One method that is used to reduce the financial burden associated with somatization disorder is:
    a. psychoanalysis   c. exposure therapy
    b. encouraging patients to speak to family   d. assignment of a gatekeeper physician
       and friends about their symptoms

    ANS: D   DIF: 3   REF: P. 177   OBJ: 1 TYPE: FACT

25. The disorder that involves physical malfunctioning without any physical cause is called:
    a. conversion disorder
    b. hypochondriasis
    c. somatization disorder
    d. body dysmorphic disorder

    ANS: A   DIF: 1   REF: p. 177   OBJ: 2 TYPE: FACT

26. George has completely lost his sight during the past year but medical experts can find no physical reason for his blindness. This could be an example of:
    a. somatization disorder
    b. hypochondriasis
    c. conversion disorder
    d. dissociative disorder

    ANS: C   DIF: 1   REF: p. 177   OBJ: 2 TYPE: APP

27. Conversion disorder patients were conceptualized by Freud as:
    a. converting unconscious conflicts into physical symptoms
    b. converting unconscious conflicts into defense mechanisms
    c. experiencing physical symptoms as a result of the superego
    d. experiencing internal conflicts as a result of physical illness

    ANS: A   DIF: 1   REF: p. 177   OBJ: 2 TYPE: CON

28. Conversion disorder symptoms generally appear:
    a. randomly
    b. following a physical injury to the affected area
    c. shortly after a stressful event
    d. in children

    ANS: C   DIF: 3   REF: p. 178   OBJ: 2 TYPE: FACT

29. Which of the following would be typical for a patient suffering from a conversion disorder?
    a. ability to avoid walking into things even though he reports being unable to see anything
    b. ability to see some bright objects when calm, but suffering complete loss of sight during a stressful period or emergency
    c. great concern with the loss of function and belief that it is a symptom of a potentially fatal disease
    d. ability to identify everything in the visual field even though the patient reports that she is blind

    ANS: A   DIF: 3   REF: p. 178   OBJ: 2 TYPE: APP/WWW

30. In regard to diagnosing a patient's symptoms as a conversion disorder, it is:
    a. quite apparent when a patient is malingering (faking) but it is difficult to determine whether symptoms are due to real physical disorders or a conversion disorder
    b. quite apparent when a symptom is due to a real physical disorder, but it is impossible to determine the difference between a conversion disorder and patient malingering (faking)
    c. rather easy to determine the difference between symptoms that the patient fakes, those caused by real physical disorder, and symptoms caused by conversion disorder
    d. very difficult to determine whether the symptoms are due to malingering (faking), real physical disorders, or conversion disorder

    ANS: D   DIF: 3   REF: p. 178   OBJ: 2 TYPE: CON

31. The disorder called "Munchausen Syndrome by proxy" (or factitious disorder by proxy) is characterized by:
    a. deliberate actions directed toward making a child sick
    b. a parent lying to a doctor, e.g., saying that the child has had symptoms that never really existed
    c. a parent developing the same symptoms that the child has
    d. convincing a child to lie to a doctor about factitious symptoms

    ANS: A   DIF: 3   REF: p. 178   OBJ: 2 TYPE: FACT

32. Parents suspected of "Munchausen Syndrome by proxy" show all of the following typical behaviors EXCEPT:
    a. helping medical staff to discover the true nature of the child's illness
    b. developing a positive relationship with medical staff
    c. appearing extremely concerned and caring toward the child
    d. purposefully making the child sick

    ANS: A   DIF: 3   REF: p. 178   OBJ: 2 TYPE: FACT

33. In factitious disorders, the patient:
    a. voluntarily makes up symptoms with no apparent motivation
    b. is unaware that he/she is making up symptoms
    c. truly experiences symptoms with no apparent physical cause
    d. makes up symptoms in an effort to avoid work or to receive some other benefit

    ANS: A   DIF: 5   REF: p. 178   OBJ: 2 TYPE: FACT

34. The modern view of the causes of conversion disorder is:
    a. completely different from Freud's ideas of the etiology of this disorder
    b. somewhat similar to the causes that Freud described for this disorder
    c. a combination of genetic predisposition and neurobiological deficits
    d. based on social learning theory

    ANS: B   DIF: 3   REF: p. 179   OBJ: 2 TYPE: FACT

35. The causes of conversion disorder described in your textbook include all of the following processes EXCEPT:
    a. social modeling
    b. unconscious motivation
    c. stressful life events
    d. escape behavior

    ANS: A   DIF: 5   REF: p. 179   OBJ: 2 TYPE: CON

36. With regard to Freud's explanation of "la belle indifference" (the observation that conversion disorder patients are not concerned about their symptoms), research conducted by Lader and Sartorius (1968) suggests that:
    a. conversion disorder patients do display "la belle indifference" but Freud's explanation of primary gain is not supported
    b. Freud's explanation is essentially correct since there is great variability in the amount of concern that conversion disorder patients display regarding their symptoms
    c. conversion disorder patients actually are quite concerned with their symptoms so Freud's explanation of primary gain is not supported
    d. "la belle indifference" is a myth, thus validating Freud's explanation of primary gain

    ANS: C   DIF: 5   REF: p. 181   OBJ: 2 TYPE: FACT

37. Evidence for the influence of social and cultural factors in conversion disorder includes the fact that conversion disorder:
   a. is almost exclusively experienced by women
   b. is being diagnosed more frequently in our society
   c. tends to occur in lower socioeconomic groups where there is less medical knowledge
   d. tends to occur in wealthy areas where there is easy access to sophisticated medical tests

   ANS: C   DIF: 3   REF: p. 181   OBJ: 2 TYPE: FACT

38. According to your textbook, the following statement is true about research regarding the treatment of conversion disorder:
   a. there are very few systematic, controlled studies
   b. the use of medication is generally supported
   c. social support has proven to be the most important aspect of treatment
   d. Freudian methods to access the unconscious are most effective

   ANS: A   DIF: 1   REF: p. 181   OBJ: 2 TYPE: FACT

39. Your textbook authors describe a treatment plan for conversion disorder involving:
   a. in-depth exploration of psychological conflicts
   b. regression to the early psychosexual stages of development
   c. application of a strict behavioral program that includes reinforcement for each display of progress and punishment when necessary
   d. removal of any benefits that patients receive for limitations imposed by the disorder

   ANS: D   DIF: 3   REF: p. 182   OBJ: 2 TYPE: CON/WWW

40. Psychological pain disorder is diagnosed when a patient:
   a. has physical reasons for pain but psychological factors play a major role as well
   b. has significant pain with no apparent physical cause
   c. has physical reasons for pain, but knowingly exaggerates the pain to gain sympathy, attention, or some other benefit
   d. is malingering (faking) the experience of significant pain

   ANS: A   DIF: 1   REF: p. 182   OBJ: 3 TYPE: FACT

41. One important feature of pain disorder is that the pain is:
   a. real and it hurts
   b. entirely imagined
   c. entirely faked
   d. partly real and partly faked

   ANS: A   DIF: 1   REF: p. 182   OBJ: 3 TYPE: FACT

42. Joe injured his back at work several years ago. Although he was treated and considered healed by his physicians, he still complains of severe and debilitating back pain. Other than some minor scar tissue, his doctors can't find anything that could be causing more than some minor stiffness. It asppears that Joe might be diagnosed with:
    a. conversion disorder
    b. somatization disorder
    c. pain disorder
    d. hypochondriasis

    ANS: C   DIF: 3   REF: p. 182   OBJ: 3 TYPE: APP

43. One reason that it is difficult to diagnose pain disorder is that:
    a. the experience of pain usually involves some level of both physical and psychological factors
    b. pain disorder is almost the same as conversion disorder
    c. most patients lie about the degree of pain that is experienced
    d. pain is often accompanied by secondary gains such as attention or disability payments from an employer

    ANS: A   DIF: 3   REF: p. 182   OBJ: 3 TYPE: CON

44. Individuals who see themselves as having some defect in appearance even though no such defect is present are diagnosed with:
    a. conversion disorder
    b. somatoform disorder
    c. hypochondriasis
    d. body dysmorphic disorder

    ANS: D   DIF: 1   REF: p. 183   OBJ: 3 TYPE: FACT

45. During therapy for social phobia, Lisa turns to her therapist and says: "Are you kidding? I'll never be comfortable in public as long as I have this huge, crooked nose!" The therapist is shocked because Lisa actually has a completely normal looking nose. Lisa appears to have:
    a. body dysmorphic disorder
    b. conversion disorder
    c. somatoform disorder
    d. hypochondriasis

    ANS: A   DIF: 1   REF: p. 183   OBJ: 3 TYPE: APP/WWW

46. With regard to body image, people with body dysmorphic disorder:
    a. always recognize that their beliefs are irrational
    b. sometimes do not recognize that their beliefs are irrational
    c. never recognize that their beliefs are irrational
    d. only realize that their beliefs are irrational if told by a professional

    ANS: B   DIF: 3   REF: p. 183   OBJ: 3 TYPE: FACT

47. One of the problems with trying to determine the prevalence of body dysmorphic disorder (BDD) is that:
    a. patients with this disorder generally do not seek psychotherapy
    b. it is almost impossible to differentiate from conversion disorder
    c. therapists are reluctant to report statistics for this disorder
    d. many BDD patients are misdiagnosed with an anxiety disorder

    ANS: A   DIF: 3   REF: p. 184   OBJ: 3 TYPE: CON

48. In terms of seriousness, body dysmorphic disorder is:
    a. very serious with a significant suicide rate
    b. very serious because it generally leads to bipolar disorder
    c. very serious because patients usually become schizophrenic
    d. not very serious because it only involves patient perceptions

    ANS: A   DIF: 3   REF: p. 183   OBJ: 3 TYPE: FACT

49. The seemingly odd motivations of body dysmorphic disorder may be more easily understood by:
    a. examining the great lengths people go to in various cultures to alter their bodies in a manner consistent with the cultural ideals
    b. using hypnosis to explore the patient's unconscious desires to be attractive
    c. exploring the neurobiological differences between patients diagnosed with body dysmorphic disorder and those without the diagnosis
    d. examining the family histories of patients diagnosed with body dysmorphic disorder

    ANS: A   DIF: 5   REF: p. 185   OBJ: 3 TYPE: CON

50. Patients with body dysmorphic disorder are often diagnosed with another psychological disorder called:
    a. panic disorder
    b. somatization disorder
    c. conversion disorder
    d. obsessive compulsive disorder

    ANS: D   DIF: 3   REF: p. 186   OBJ: 3 TYPE: FACT

51. Looking at the treatments that have been found to be effective for body dysmorphic disorder suggests that BDD may be:
    a. a variation of conversion disorder
    b. a variation of obsessive compulsive disorder
    c. a unique form of dissociative disorder
    d. purely biological in cause

    ANS: B   DIF: 3   REF: p. 186   OBJ: 3 TYPE: FACT

52. Patients with body dysmorphic disorder often try to find relief by:
    a. undergoing plastic surgery
    b. using drugs and alcohol
    c. constantly seeking reassurance from mental health professionals
    d. trying to distract themselves from their negative thoughts

    ANS: A   DIF: 1   REF: p. 186   OBJ: 3 TYPE: FACT

53. Plastic surgery for body dysmorphic patients generally results in:
    a. little, if any, patient satisfaction
    b. an improved self-image
    c. substantial relief from the current concern, but with new concerns arising over time
    d. somatization or conversion reactions

ANS: A   DIF: 3   REF: p. 186   OBJ: 3 TYPE: FACT

54. The experience of dissociation occurs in:
    a. psychotic disorders only
    b. individuals with dissociative disorders only
    c. only in those individuals who have experienced great personal trauma
    d. certain psychological disorders as well as in non-disordered people at times

ANS: D   DIF: 1   REF: p. 187   OBJ: 4 TYPE: FACT

55. In healthy, well-adjusted individuals, dissociation typically occurs following:
    a. calm, reflective periods
    b. participation in a group activity
    c. reading or any activity that requires great concentration
    d. stress or exhaustion

ANS: D   DIF: 1   REF: p. 187   OBJ: 4 TYPE: FACT

56. Depersonalization is defined as:
    a. altered perception including loss of the sense of one's own reality
    b. altered perception involving loss of the sense of reality of the external world
    c. vivid hallucinations
    d. the feeling that one is no longer a person

ANS: A   DIF: 1   REF: p. 188   OBJ: 4 TYPE: FACT

57. Derealization is defined as:
    a. vivid hallucinations
    b. altered perception involving loss of the sense of one's own reality
    c. altered perception involving loss of the sense of reality of the external world
    d. the feeling that one is no longer a person

ANS: C   DIF: 1   REF: p. 187   OBJ: 4 TYPE: FACT

58. Jason suddenly notices that the world looks weird to him. Some objects look bigger than normal and others look smaller. Cars passing by seem oddly shaped and people appear dead or mechanical. Joe is experiencing:
    a. derealization
    b. depersonalization
    c. classic early psychosis symptoms
    d. mania

ANS: A   DIF: 1   REF: p. 187   OBJ: 4 TYPE: APP

59. While driving alone in her car, Sarah suddenly looks around and, for a moment, she can't remember where she is, how she arrived at this point on the road or even why she is driving her car. Sarah is experiencing:
    a. derealization
    b. depersonalization
    c. the early stages of what will eventually become a severe psychotic disorder
    d. symptoms of a mood disorder

    ANS: B   DIF: 1   REF: p. 187   OBJ: 4 TYPE: APP

60. The diagnosis of depersonalization disorder is:
    a. quite rare and only applied when the experience of depersonalization interferes with normal functioning
    b. quite rare but applied to anyone who experiences depersonalization
    c. fairly common since many people experience depersonalization
    d. fairly common and applied to anyone who is frightened by an experience of depersonalization

    ANS: A   DIF: 1   REF: p. 188   OBJ: 4 TYPE: FACT/WWW

61. In dissociative amnesia, the individual typically has no memory of:
    a. any events
    b. events prior to a trauma
    c. selective events, particularly those involving trauma
    d. events following a trauma, particularly those involving interpersonal issues

    ANS: C   DIF: 1   REF: p. 188   OBJ: 4 TYPE: FACT

62. In dissociative amnesia, memory loss is:
    a. always partial
    b. always complete
    c. either partial or complete
    d. associated with traumatic events only

    ANS: C   DIF: 3   REF: p. 189   OBJ: 4 TYPE: FACT

63. In dissociative fugue, the term fugue relates to:
    a. confusion
    b. flight or travel
    c. loss of consciousness
    d. hallucination

    ANS: B   DIF: 1   REF: p. 189   OBJ: 4 TYPE: FACT

64. During a fugue state, patients diagnosed with dissociative fugue:
    a. travel and typically experience memory loss during their trip
    b. travel but do not experience memory loss
    c. experience memory loss but do not travel
    d. seldom recover any sense of their own identity

    ANS: A   DIF: 3   REF: p. 189   OBJ: 4 TYPE: FACT

65. During a dissociative fugue state, it is not uncommon for individuals to:
   a. commit suicide
   b. see the world as a strange and foreign place
   c. take on a new identity
   d. contact friends and family

   ANS: C   DIF: 3   REF: p. 189   OBJ: 4 TYPE: FACT

66. A dissociative disorder that is not found in Western cultures and appears to have some similarities to dissociative fugue is:
   a. amok
   b. exorcism
   c. trance
   d. voodoo

   ANS: A   DIF: 1   REF: p. 190   OBJ: 4 TYPE: FACT

67. Dissociative trance disorder is diagnosed:
   a. only when the trance is unpredictable in terms of when it appears (i.e., individual goes into a trance without prior religious ritual)
   b. only when the trance is undesirable and considered pathological in the individual's culture
   c. only when the trance causes harm to the individual or others
   d. whenever an individual repeatedly enters a trance state

   ANS: B   DIF: 3   REF: p. 190   OBJ: 4 TYPE: FACT

68. In non-western cultures, trance and possession are:
   a. extremely rare
   b. never considered a disorder
   c. the most common forms of dissociative disorders
   d. the rarest forms of dissociative disorders

   ANS: C   DIF: 1   REF: p. 190   OBJ: 4 TYPE: FACT

69. The disorder in which more than one distinct personality exists within one individual is now called _____ in the DSM-IV.
   a. dissociative identity disorder
   b. dissociative trance disorder
   c. schizophrenia
   d. multiple personality disorder

   ANS: A   DIF: 1   REF: p. 191   OBJ: 4 TYPE: FACT/WWW

70. Individuals with dissociative identity disorder generally:
   a. have only one other distinct personality
   b. suffer a loss of their own identity that lasts several years
   c. maintain complete awareness of all of their personalities
   d. have several distinct personalities

   ANS: D   DIF: 1   REF: p. 191   OBJ: 4 TYPE: FACT

71. The defining feature of multiple personality disorder, as it was called prior to DSM-IV, is that aspects of the individual's personality are:
    a. fixated
    b. completely supressed
    c. dissociated
    d. characterized by fugue states

    ANS: C   DIF: 1   REF: P. 191   OBJ: 4 TYPE: FACT

72. With regard to dissociative identity disorder, the term "alter" refers to _____ within the individual.
    a. the "host" personality
    b. a dangerous personality
    c. the most recent personality to emerge
    d. a different personality

    ANS: D   DIF: 1   REF: p. 191   OBJ: 4 TYPE: FACT

73. In dissociative identity disorder, the "host" personality is usually the one that:
    a. is the most aggressive of the personalities
    b. asks for treatment and becomes the patient
    c. earns income for the individual
    d. is sexually provocative

    ANS: B   DIF: 1   REF: p. 191   OBJ: 4 TYPE: FACT

74. In dissociative identity disorder, the "host" personality usually:
    a. is of a gender opposite to that of the individual
    b. becomes overwhelmed trying to hold all of the personality fragments together
    c. is male
    d. is well aware of each personality and everything that happens while each personality is active

    ANS: B   DIF: 3   REF: p. 191   OBJ: 4 TYPE: FACT

75. The existence of a crossgendered alter in dissociative identity disorder is:
    a. common
    b. rare
    c. present in every patient
    d. almost never seen in this disorder

    ANS: A   DIF: 3   REF: p. 192   OBJ: 4 TYPE: FACT

76. One aspect of the DSM-IV criteria for diagnosis of dissociative identity disorder is:
    a. patient awareness of the distinct personalities
    b. existence of three or more personality fragments
    c. amnesia
    d. history of abuse

    ANS: C   DIF: 5   REF: p. 191   OBJ: 4 TYPE: FACT

77. Vanna, who is 40, apparently believes that she is a 20-year-old woman. Suddenly, however, she starts to speak and behave very differently, and says she no longer thinks of herself as "Vanna." Instead she claims to be Elise, a 10 year-old child. It is likely that Vanna has just experienced a:
    a. switch
    b. dissociative trance disorder
    c. conversion reaction
    d. schizophrenic moment

    ANS: A   DIF: 3   REF: p. 192   OBJ: 4 TYPE: APP

78. In dissociative identity disorder, the transition from one personality to another is called a:
    a. transform
    b. substitution
    c. switch
    d. alteration

    ANS: C   DIF: 1   REF: p. 192   OBJ: 4 TYPE: FACT

79. In one study, (Putnam, Guroff, Silberman, Barban, & Post, 1986) changes in physical handedness (right-handed versus left-handed) occured in _____ of dissociative identity disorder cases.
    a. 0%
    b. 75%
    c. 37%
    d. 100%

    ANS: C   DIF: 3   REF: p. 192   OBJ: 4 TYPE: FACT

80. The process of changing from one personality to another generally occurs _____ in most patients with dissociative identity disorder.
    a. slowly
    b. quickly
    c. rarely
    d. only after many warning signs that a change is about to occur

    ANS: B   DIF: 5   REF: p. 192   OBJ: 4 TYPE: FACT

81. With regard to evidence for the scientific validity of dissociative identity disorder (DID), the most accurate statement is:
    a. most DID patients are faking
    b. research suggests that faking dissociative experiences is possible
    c. it is virtually impossible to fake the types of changes that occur in dissociative identity disorder
    d. objective tests can always determine which patients are faking dissociative identity disorder

    ANS: B   DIF: 3   REF: p. 192   OBJ: 4 TYPE: FACT/WWW

82. Studies of faking, amnesia and hypnosis such as those conducted by Spanos (1996) and Spanos, James, and de Groot (1990), suggest that symptoms of dissociative identity disorder:
   a. cannot be developed through therapist suggestion and reinforcement
   b. are almost always the result of hypnotically inserted (false) memories
   c. can be developed through therapist suggestion and reinforcement
   d. are almost never the result of therapist intervention

   ANS: C   DIF: 3   REF: p. 193   OBJ: 4 TYPE: CON

83. Comparisons of optical functioning in the various personalities of dissociative identity disorder patients show changes that would be:
   a. easy to fake
   b. absolutely impossible to fake
   c. consistent with an individual who was trying to fake
   d. difficult to fake

   ANS: D   DIF: 1   REF: p. 193   OBJ: 4 TYPE: FACT

84. With regard to the studies of dissociative identity disorder (DID) described in your text regarding faking, amnesia and hypnosis, (Spanos, 1994, Spanos, James, and de Groot, 1990), as well as the studies regarding the physiological changes that occur in the different personalities (Miller, 1989, Ludwig et al., 1972, Tsai, Condie, Wu, Chang, 1999, Cardena & Gleaves, 2003), the most accurate statement is:
   a. while DID symptoms can be faked or developed through suggestion, many physiological changes observed in DID patients would be very difficult to fake
   b. DID symptoms and the many physiological changes observed in DID patients can be developed through suggestion and are easily faked
   c. while physiological changes associated with DID are relatively easy to fake, the symptoms of DID are very difficult to fake or to develop through suggestion
   d. almost all cases of DID are probably faked or developed through therapist suggestion

   ANS: A   DIF. 5   REF: p. 193   OBJ: 4 TYPE: CON

85. One distinction that may help determine those with dissociative identity disorder from individuals who are malingering (faking their symptoms) is that malingerers are:
   a. usually eager to demonstrate their   c. more likely to have many alters
      symptoms
   b. usually hiding the existance of a major life d. less likely to seek treatment
      crisis

   ANS: A   DIF: 3   REF: P. 193   OBJ: 4 TYPE: FACT

86. The average number of alter personalities observed in individuals with dissociative identity disorder is:
   a. one
   b. two
   c. fifteen
   d. one hundred

   ANS: C   DIF: 3   REF: p. 194   OBJ: 4 TYPE: FACT

87. Dissociative identity disorder is most commonly found in:
    a. females
    b. males
    c. children
    d. elderly

    ANS: A   DIF: 1   REF: p. 194   OBJ: 4 TYPE: FACT

88. The average length of time between an individual's first symptoms of dissociative identity ddisorder and the identification and diagnosis of the disorder by a professional is:
    a. one year
    b. twenty years
    c. less than a month
    d. seven years

    ANS: D   DIF: 3   REF: p. 194   OBJ: 4 TYPE: FACT

89. Without treatment, it is expected that dissociative identity disorder will last:
    a. ten years
    b. a lifetime
    c. several months
    d. twenty years

    ANS: B   DIF: 5   REF: p. 194   OBJ: 4 TYPE: APP

90. Studies examining the incidence of dissociative identity disorder in non-clinical populations (the population at large or a university population) suggest that approximately _____ percent of the general population suffer from dissociative identity disorder.
    a. .001
    b. .01 to .05
    c. .5 to 1
    d. 5

    ANS: C   DIF: 3   REF: p. 194   OBJ: 4 TYPE: FACT

91. Sue has dissociative identity disorder. It is extremely likely that she also has:
    a. at least one other psychological disorder
    b. a problem with her weight
    c. a history of problems with the law
    d. no desire to get better

    ANS: A   DIF: 3   REF: p. 194   OBJ: 4 TYPE: CON

92. Studies of comorbidity (Ellason and Ross, 1997) suggest that the average number of additional psychological disorders that individuals with dissociative identity disorder tend to have is:
    a. one
    b. two
    c. four
    d. seven or more

    ANS: D   DIF: 1   REF: p. 194   OBJ: 4 TYPE: FACT

93. The main reason why dissociative identity disorder patients tend to have many additional psychological disorders is that:
    a. the number of personalities increases the number of disorders
    b. the severe trauma of childhood leads to many problems in later life
    c. they seek attention
    d. they are substance abusers

    ANS: B   DIF: 3   REF: p. 194   OBJ: 4 TYPE: CON/WWW

94. One reason that dissociative identity disorder can be misdiagnosed as psychosis is that:
    a. auditory hallucinations are common in both disorders
    b. both disorders are in the same DSM-IV category
    c. mental health professionals generally do not believe that dissociation is possible
    d. substance abuse makes it difficult to differentiate these disorders

    ANS: A   DIF: 3   REF: p. 194   OBJ: 4 TYPE: CON

95. The common feature in almost every case of dissociative identity disorder is:
    a. hallucinations and delusions
    b. unrelenting substance abuse
    c. a history of body dysmorphic disorder
    d. a history of severe child abuse

    ANS: D   DIF: 1   REF: p. 194   OBJ: 4 TYPE: FACT

96. In some ways dissociative identity disorder can be seen as developing from an adaptive response because:
    a. the patient receives a great deal of attention
    b. family problems are identified
    c. psychologically, at least, the child can escape an intolerable situation
    d. overall physical health is improved

    ANS: C   DIF: 3   REF: p. 195   OBJ: 4 TYPE: CON

97. Of the following, which abused child would be most likely to develop dissociative identity disorder later in life?
    a. Mary - has a few good friends
    b. Susan - lives in a chaotic, non-supportive family
    c. Cindy - has a learning disability
    d. Jody - has attention deficit hyperactivity disorder

    ANS: B   DIF: 3   REF: p. 195   OBJ: 4 TYPE: APP

98. The experience of dissociation (feelings of unreality, blunting of emotional experience and physical pain) during or immediately following a life-threatening situation is:
    a. a sign of psychopathology
    b. extremely rare in non-disordered individuals
    c. not well documented
    d. a normal reaction

    ANS: D   DIF: 3   REF: p. 195   OBJ: 4 TYPE: FACT

99. A comparison of dissociative reactions in "normals" and in dissociative identity disorder patients indicates that the experience of dissociation is _____ in normal versus DID patients.
   a. very different
   b. very similar
   c. identical
   d. so different as to have no similarities at all

   ANS: A   DIF: 5   REF: p. 195   OBJ: 4 TYPE: FACT

100. One of the individual differences that appears to help explain who is likely to develop dissociative identity disorder following childhood trauma is:
   a. physical health
   b. suggestibility
   c. number of siblings
   d. number of abusers

   ANS: B   DIF: 1   REF: p. 196   OBJ: 4 TYPE: FACT

101. There is now incontrovertible evidence (Ceci, 2003; Loftus, 2003; Lilienfield et al., 1999; McNally, 2001; Schacter, 1995, Gleaves, 1996; Kluft, 1999; Spiegel, 1995) that the following statement is true with respect to the accuracy of recovered memories.
   a. False memories can be created and selective dissociative amnesia can occur for early traumatic experiences.
   b. False memories can be created but there is no evidence of selective dissociative amnesia for early traumatic experiences.
   c. False memories cannot be created and individuals do not develop selective dissociative amnesia for early trauma.
   d. False memories cannot be created but there is evidence that individuals do develop selective dissociative amnesia for early trauma

   ANS: A   DIF: 1   REF: p. 196   OBJ: 4 TYPE: CON

102. In studies conducted by Elizabeth Loftus and her colleagues (Loftus, 2003; Loftus, Coan and Pickrell, 1996), individuals were told about false events that had supposedly occurred when they were children. The results of this study indicated that:
   a. people cannot be convinced of events that did not happen
   b. people can become quite convinced of events that never happened
   c. only individuals with diagnosable disorders can be convinced of events that never happened
   d. people can become convinced of events that did not happen only during hypnosis or other dissociative states

   ANS: B   DIF: 3   REF: p. 196   OBJ: 4 TYPE: CON/WWW

103. While interviewing 129 women with documented histories of childhood sexual abuse, Willams (1994) found with extensive questioning that:
   a. every woman remembered minute details of the abuse
   b. almost none of the women recalled the abuse
   c. 38% of the women did not recall the abuse
   d. 75% of the women did not recall the abuse

   ANS: C   DIF: 5   REF: p. 197   OBJ: 4 TYPE: FACT

104. Goodman et al., (2003) interviewed 175 individuals with documented child abuse histories and found that ___ percent of the subjects remembered and reported the abuse.
a. 25
b. 53
c. 81
d. 100

ANS: C   DIF: 3   REF: P. 197   OBJ: 4 TYPE: FACT

105. The victims who are most likely to have amnesia for trauma are those who:
a. suffered infrequent and relatively minor abuse
b. suffered frequent and relatively minor abuse
c. were victims of severe abuse and trauma
d. were victims of natural disasters

ANS: C   DIF: 3   REF: p. 197   OBJ: 4 TYPE: FACT

106. The general treatment plan for dissociative identity disorder patients usually centers around:
a. integration of the personality fragments
b. hypnotic regression of the host and each alter
c. confrontation of the abuser
d. the typical substance abuse treatment model

ANS: A   DIF: 1   REF: p. 198   OBJ: 4 TYPE: FACT

107. The part of the treatment plan for dissociative identity disorder that is similar to the treatment plan for Posttraumatic Stress Disorder is:
a. integration of personality fragments
b. use of anti-psychotic medications
c. reliving and reprocessing the trauma
d. hypnotic regression to early life experiences

ANS: C   DIF: 3   REF: p. 198   OBJ: 4 TYPE: CON

108. In the "Abnormal Psychology Live" interview with Rachel, she claims that nobody (meaning none of her alters) wants responsibility for her body because:
a. none of the alters are sufficiently mature
b. there is too much desire for self destruction
c. of reasons that she can not understand
d. there is too much devastation behind it

ANS: D   DIF: 2   REF: CD

109. In the "Abnormal Psychology Live" presentation, Rachel describes how her eyes always see the world through "a fog." She attributes this to having spent "years in the darkness" and:
a. other people looking through the same eyes
b. her history of substance abuse
c. not wanting to see the world as it really is
d. the trauma of constantly switching personalities

ANS: A   DIF: 2   REF: CD

110. In the "Abnormal Psychology Live" presentation of Doug who has suffered with body dysmorphic disorder, he describes having thought about his perceived physical flaws:
    a. three to four times a day
    b. three or four hours a day
    c. about six hours a day
    d. virtually all day long

    ANS: D   DIF: 2   REF: CD

111. In the "Abnormal Psychology Live" presentation of Doug who suffered with body dysmorphic disorder, he attributes all of the following to his disorder EXCEPT:
    a. the failure of his marriage
    b. his obsessions
    c. his low self esteem
    d. his failure to seek advancement at work

    ANS: C   DIF: 2   REF: CD

ESSAY

1. Describe the similarities and differences between hypochondriasis and somatization disorders.

2. Both psychological and physical processes are involved in the perception of pain. Explain how this makes the DSM-IV diagnosis of pain disorder particularly difficult and partially subjective.

3. Explain the relationship between somatoform disorders and anxiety.

4. Joe, a hypochondriac, comes from a very concerned and loving family that takes his physical complaints quite seriously. Describe at least three recommendations that would help Joe get better. Include a rationale for each recommendation.

5. Describe some ways that a person with a conversion disorder might differ from an individual with a biologically caused physical malfunction.

6. Describe the differences and similarities between depersonalization and derealization.

7. Explain the current thinking regarding the environmental and psychological mechanisms in the development of dissociative identity disorder.

8. Describe the relationship between posttraumatic stress disorder and dissociative identity disorder. How are the two disorders similar? How are they different?

9. A 30-year-old woman "recovers" memories of childhood sexual abuse, the existence of which she was seemingly and previously unaware. Explain what is currently known about the accuracy of recovered memories. Can we determine whether these memories are accurate?   **WWW**

10. Describe the treatment that is generally used to treat patients with dissociative identity disorder. What is the rationale for each part of the treatment?

11. In the "Abnormal Psychology Live" presentation of Rachel, she questions the term mentally ill and asks whether "a way of survival is mentally ill." Describe what you think Rachel means when she questions whether "a way of survival is mentally ill". What does she mean by "a way of survival" and why would that cause her to question whether we should consider dissociative identity disorder a mental illness?

REF: CD

MULTIPLE CHOICE

1. The following symptoms are all necessary for a DSM-IV diagnosis of hypochondriasis, except
   a. significant distress in everyday functioning.
   b. misinterpretation of bodily symptoms.
   c. preoccupation with fear of acquiring a serious disease.
   d. preoccupation with fears of having a serious disease.

   ANS: C

2. Malingering differs from factitious disorder in that
   a. in malingering, symptoms are intentionally feigned and in factitious disorder they are not.
   b. family-oriented psychotherapy is a more effective treatment for factitious disorder than for malingering.
   c. malingering may include extending the symptoms to family members by proxy.
   d. in malingering, there is an identifiable external gain.

   ANS: D

3. Juanita, a therapist, believes that her feet are too big for her body and often complains that she will never have a normal social life because of her disability. She has begun to be absent from work, instead choosing to spend exorbitant amounts of time and money shopping for "foot-binding shoes." Her symptoms suggest
   a. body dysmorphic disorder.
   b. acute stress disorder.
   c. hypochondriasis.
   d. obsessive-compulsive disorder.

   ANS: A

4. A blind person is referred to a clinician by an optometrist, who can find no physical evidence for the blindness. The clinician asks the patient to perform a series of visual tasks. Following the assessment, the clinician concludes that her patient is suffering from a conversion disorder. What observation would lead to this conclusion?
   a. the patient performed at a chance level on the task.
   b. the patient demonstrated high anxiety during the visual task and performed at the level that chance would predict.
   c. the patient performed worse than chance on the visual task until given motivation to perform correctly, at which time he performed better than chance would predict.
   d. the patient performed better than chance on the visual task until given motivation to perform correctly, at which time he performed worse than chance would predict.

   ANS: C

5. Somatization disorder and antisocial personality disorder are often associated with gender and may be explained by similar underlying neurological mechanisms. Which of the following statements best describes this relationship?
   a. Behavioral inhibition and activation systems (fight/flight systems) are characterized by differing behavioral outcomes in males and females due to cultural norms.
   b. Males and females both have inhibition and activation systems, but males have better developed activation systems and females have better developed inhibition systems.
   c. Women with antisocial personality disorder may have an underlying deficit in the behavioral activation system and men with somatization disorder may have an underlying deficit in the behavioral inhibition system.
   d. None of the above.

   ANS: A

6. Somatization disorder is very difficult to treat. Which of the following is not a typical treatment approach for the disorder?
   a. reduction of help-seeking behavior.
   b. reduction of stress.
   c. traditional psychotherapy.
   d. reassurance.

   ANS: C

7. A central feature of hypochondriasis is
   a. interpretation of harmful stimuli as nonthreatening.
   b. interpretation of almost any physical sensation or symptom as threatening.
   c. a distrust of medical personnel.
   d. more acute physical sensations than someone without hypochondriasis

   ANS: B

8. A major distinction between hypochondriasis and somatization disorder is
   a. in somatization disorder the person is concerned with the symptoms themselves, whereas in hypochondriasis the person is concerned with the meaning of the symptoms.
   b. in hypochondriasis the person is concerned with the symptoms themselves, whereas in somatization disorder the person is concerned with the meaning of the symptoms.
   c. Hypochondriasis tends to run in families, whereas somatization disorder does not.
   d. There is genetic evidence for somatization disorder, whereas for hypochondriasis there is not.

   ANS: A

9. Jenna, a recently married young woman, described episodes of, "spacing out." During these episodes, she feels as if she is observing herself from outside of her body. Her experiences seem "dream-like," and she reports feeling completely separated from what is going on around her. It is likely that Jenna is experiencing _____.
   a. stress associated with being newly married
   b. post-traumatic episodes
   c. detachment disorder
   d. depersonalization disorder

   ANS: D

10. In a study of false memory, researchers asked 3-year-old girls who visited a physician's office whether they were touched in their genital area. The results of this study
    a. suggest that 60% of the children who were examined genitally, inaccurately reported that they were not examined.
    b. suggest that 60% of the children who were not examined genitally, inaccurately reported that they were.
    c. suggest that young children are not very accurate in reporting what happened to them.
    d. all of the above

    ANS: D

MULTIPLE CHOICE

1. Prior to the edition of DSM-IIIR, conditions that are currently characterized as mood disorders were referred to by several different names including all of the following EXCEPT:
   a. depressive disorders
   b. affective disorders
   c. psychotic episodes
   d. depressive neuroses

   ANS: C   DIF: 1   REF: p. 206   OBJ: 1 TYPE: FACT

2. One of the symptoms of a mood disorder is called anhedonia, which means:
   a. a feeling of worthlessness
   b. an altered pattern of sleep
   c. indecisiveness
   d. an inability to experience pleasure

   ANS: D   DIF: 1   REF: p. 206   OBJ: 1 TYPE: CON

3. Mood disorders can range from mild to severe; the most severe type of depression is called:
   a. major depressive disorder
   b. dysthymia
   c. cyclothymia
   d. profound depression

   ANS: A   DIF: 1   REF: p. 206   OBJ: 1 TYPE: CON/WWW

4. Most episodes of major depression are time-limited, i.e., lasting up to _____, although about 10% last as long as two years.
   a. 3 months
   b. 6 months
   c. 9 months
   d. 1 year

   ANS: C   DIF: 3   REF: p. 206   OBJ: 1 TYPE: FACT

5. Which of the following is a symptom of the mood disorder known as mania?
   a. clear, coherent speech
   b. hypoactive behavior
   c. fatigue
   d. grandiosity

   ANS: D   DIF: 1   REF: p. 206   OBJ: 1 TYPE: FACT

6. When used in connection with mood disorders, "flight of ideas" means:
   a. anxiety about airplane travel
   b. rapid speech expressing many exciting ideas at once
   c. limited imagination reflected in a slow way of speaking
   d. repression of all creative ideas

   ANS: B   DIF: 3   REF: p. 206   OBJ: 2 TYPE: CON

7. In comparing the length of untreated depressive episodes and untreated manic episodes, which of the following is an accurate statement?
   a. Depressive episodes generally last longer.
   b. Manic episodes generally last longer.
   c. Both types of episodes typically last about the same amount of time.
   d. This comparison cannot be made because depressive episodes are always treated.

   ANS: A   DIF: 3   REF: p. 206   OBJ: 2 TYPE: CON

8. The physical or somatic symptoms of a major depressive disorder include:
   a. changes in appetite or weight
   b. decreased ability to concentrate
   c. increased energy
   d. orgasmic feelings

   ANS: A   DIF: 1   REF: p. 206   OBJ: 1 TYPE: CON

9. Which of the following symptoms characterize a manic episode?
   a. feelings of guilt
   b. irritability
   c. anhedonia
   d. loss of energy

   ANS: B   DIF: 1   REF: p. 206   OBJ: 2 TYPE: CON

10. A 35-year-old individual named Manny has recently formulated an elaborate plan to cure AIDS with vitamin therapy. To provide funding for this cause he has withdrawn all the money from his bank account and purchased thousands of jars of vitamins and small boxes in which to put them. When he appeared at a hospital emergency room loudly demanding names of patients with AIDS, he himself was hospitalized for psychiatric observation. What is your diagnosis of Manny?
    a. major depressive episode
    b. hypomanic episode
    c. manic episode
    d. postpartum psychosis

    ANS: C   DIF: 3   REF: p. 206   OBJ: 2 TYPE: APP/WWW

11. In regard to mood disorders, which of the following is an accurate statement?
    a. An individual experiencing manic symptoms can also be depressed or anxious.
    b. Unipolar mania is more common than unipolar depression.
    c. An individual who has experienced only manic episodes in the past is unlikely to ever become depressed.
    d. Neither manic nor depressive symptoms remit on their own without treatment.

    ANS: A   DIF: 5   REF: p. 207   OBJ: 2 TYPE: CON

12. Dysphoric mania refers to a type of mood disorder in which manic episodes are:
    a. extremely severe
    b. very mild
    c. accompanied by depression or anxiety
    d. related to a medical condition

    ANS: C   DIF: 3   REF: p. 207   OBJ: 2 TYPE: CON

13. What significant finding is usually noted when comparing major depressive disorder/recurrent and major depressive disorder/single episode?
    a. family history of depression
    b. severity of symptoms
    c. more females have the single episode type
    d. more males have the recurrent episode type

    ANS: A   DIF: 3   REF: p. 208   OBJ: 5 TYPE: CON

14. An important difference between "major depressive disorder, recurrent" and "major depressive disorder, single episode" is:
    a. the single episode type is more common   c. single episode symptoms are more severe
    b. the recurrrent type is more common   d. recurrent symptoms are more severe

    ANS: B   DIF: 2   REF: p. 208   OBJ: 5 TYPE: FACT

15. Most individuals who experience a single episode of major depressive disorder will:
    a. never have another episode
    b. most likely have just one more episode
    c. probably have several episodes throughout their lives
    d. later have a manic episode

    ANS: C   DIF: 3   REF: p. 208   OBJ: 5 TYPE: CON

16. Debbie has been diagnosed with major depressive disorder, recurrent. She wants to know what to expect in the future regarding her condition. You tell her that according to recent research (Angst 1998, Angst and Preizig, 1996), the median lifetime number of major depressive episodes is:
    a. four
    b. eight
    c. twelve
    d. sixteen

    ANS: A   DIF: 1   REF: p. 208   OBJ: 5 TYPE: APP

17. According to recent research (Kessler et al., 2003; Soloman et al., 1997), the median duration of recurrent (subsequent to the first episode) major depressive episodes is:
    a. 2 months   c. 7 to 9 months
    b. 4 to 5 months   d. 11 to 12 months

    ANS: B   DIF: 5   REF: p. 208   OBJ: 5 TYPE: FACT

18. Dysthymic disorder differs from major depressive disorder because persons diagnosed with dysthymia have symptoms of depression that are:
    a. more severe
    b. longer-lasting
    c. episodic
    d. temporary

ANS: B   DIF: 3   REF: p. 208   OBJ: 3 TYPE: CON/WWW

19. Jack has experienced recurrent episodes of major depressive episodes. In the intervals between the episodes, he does not seem to return to "normal." In fact, during those periods, he has been diagnosed as dysthymic. Jack's conditions is referred to as:
    a. double depression
    b. bipolar disorder
    c. atypical depression
    d. dysfunctional dysthymia

ANS: A   DIF: 3   REF: p. 208   OBJ: 3 TYPE: APP

20. Research studies reported in your textbook indicate that during the 20th century, the age of onset for depression:
    a. increased
    b. decreased
    c. stayed about the same
    d. increased for males, decreased for females

ANS: B   DIF: 1   REF: p. 210   OBJ: 1 TYPE: CON

21. According to recent research (Kessler et al., 2003), the percentage of people age 18 to 29 that have already experienced major depression is:
    a. 10%   c. 25%
    b. 18%   d. 40%

ANS: C   DIF: 3   REF: p. 210   OBJ: 5 TYPE: FACT

22. The probability that a person will recover from a major depressive episode within 5 years approaches 90% in:
    a. all cases
    b. mild cases only
    c. severe cases only
    d. double depression only

ANS: A   DIF: 3   REF: p. 210   OBJ: 1 TYPE: FACT

23. In severe cases of depression where the episode lasts 5 years or longer, how many of these patients can be expected to recover?
    a. none
    b. about half
    c. approximately one-third
    d. all

ANS: C   DIF: 3   REF: p. 210   OBJ: 5 TYPE: CON

24. In regard to severe cases of major depressive disorder, i.e., those in which the depressive episode has lasted 5 years or more, all of the following statements are accurate EXCEPT:
    a. The episode may not entirely clear up, leaving some residual symptoms.
    b. The likelihood of a subsequent episode is high.
    c. The next episode is likely to be manic, rather than depressive.
    d. Subsequent episodes may be associated with incomplete inter-episode recovery.

    ANS: C   DIF: 5   REF: p. 210   OBJ: 1 TYPE: APP

25. In comparison to later age of onset, early onset of dysthymia (before age 21) is associated with all of the following characteristics EXCEPT:
    a. greater chronicity
    b. poorer response to treatment
    c. genetic influence
    d. better prognosis

    ANS: D   DIF: 3   REF: p. 210   OBJ: 3 TYPE: CON

26. Not only is there a high prevalence of dysthymic disorder in children but it has also been found (Kovacs et al., 1994) that three-fourths of these children will eventually be diagnosed with:
    a. bipolar disorder
    b. mania
    c. major depressive disorder
    d. cyclothymia

    ANS: C   DIF: 3   REF: p. 210   OBJ: 3 TYPE: FACT

27. Symptoms of severe depression are generally NOT considered a psychological disorder when they are associated with:
    a. a grief reaction
    b. a manic episode
    c. anxiety
    d. thoughts of suicide

    ANS: A   DIF: 3   REF: p. 211   OBJ: 3 TYPE: CON

28. Although grieving is considered a normal process it does sometimes become a psychological disorder. Which of the following cases would NOT be diagnosed as a pathological grief reaction?
    a. Mr. A experienced a death in his family. In addition to symptoms of depression, he has been having auditory hallucinations in which he hears other deceased people talking to him.
    b. Miss B. has experienced the death of a close friend. She is so depressed that she has no appetite, no energy and is suicidal.
    c. Mrs. C's dog recently died. Three weeks later her friends suggest that she get another dog "to help her get over the loss." Mrs. C. refuses and says she just isn't ready to get another dog and besides, it would be impossible to replace her beloved "Toto."
    d. Dr. D's wife died a few months ago. Recently, in addition to his depressive symptoms, he has been having paranoid delusions in which he believes that certain unnamed individuals are planning to remove his wife's body from the grave.

    ANS: C   DIF: 3   REF: p. 211   OBJ: 5 TYPE: APP

29. According to the textbook, therapeutic approaches towards helping the bereaved would involve all of the following EXCEPT:
    a. talking about the deceased loved one
    b. re-experiencing the emotions associated with the death
    c. finding meaning in the loss
    d. realizing that one cannot cope with the emotional pain

    ANS: D   DIF: 1   REF: p. 212   OBJ: 5 TYPE: CON

30. In regard to the terms used to differentiated mood disorders, cyclothymic is to dysthymic as:
    a. bipolar is to major depressive
    b. manic is to hypomanic
    c. major depressive is to bipolar
    d. Bipolar I is to Bipolar II

    ANS: A   DIF: 5   REF: p. 214   OBJ: 4 TYPE: APP

31. Jane is diagnosed with Bipolar II disorder. You can expect that she will experience:
    a. full manic episodes
    b. hypomanic episodes
    c. both manic and hypomanic episodes
    d. neither manic nor hypomanic episodes

    ANS: B   DIF: 1   REF: p. 213   OBJ: 4 TYPE: FACT

32. Manic episodes alternate with depressive episodes in the disorder called:
    a. bipolar disorder
    b. major depressive disorder
    c. pathological grief reaction
    d. postpartum psychosis

    ANS: A   DIF: 1   REF: p. 212   OBJ: 4 TYPE: FACT/WWW

33. When referring to the mood disorders called cyclothymia and dysthymia, it would be accurate to say that an individual with cyclothymia probably:
    a. would be considered "moody"
    b. cannot function normally at all
    c. has more depressive episodes
    d. has full manic episodes

    ANS: A   DIF: 3   REF: p. 214   OBJ: 4 TYPE: CON

34. One of the problems encountered by psychiatrists who prescribe medication for patients with bipolar disorder is that patients often:
    a. stop taking the medication in order to bring on a depressive state
    b. stop taking the medication in order to bring on a manic state
    c. overdose on the medication during a severe manic state
    d. become addicted to the medications during a severe manic state

    ANS: B   DIF: 3   REF: p. 214   OBJ: 4 TYPE: APP

35. All of the following words are used to describe the manic mood state EXCEPT:
    a. elated
    b. expansive
    c. energetic
    d. exhausted

ANS: D   DIF: 1   REF: p. 213   OBJ: 2 TYPE: CON

36. At various times, Cynthia, a 20 year-old college student, has been considered by her family and/or friends to be moody, high-strung, explosive, or hyperactive. Knowing the criteria for mood disorders you would diagnose Cynthia with:
    a. major depressive disorder
    b. panic disorder
    c. dysthymia
    d. cyclothymia

ANS: D   DIF: 5   REF: p. 214   OBJ: 4 TYPE: APP

37. The melancholic specifiers for depressive disorders include all of the following EXCEPT:
    a. weight loss
    b. loss of libido (sex drive)
    c. sleeping late and hypersomnia
    d. anhedonia

ANS: C   DIF: 3   REF: p. 216   OBJ: 5 TYPE: CON

38. Katie has been diagnosed with major depressive disorder. Most recently she has been lying immobile for long periods. If someone moves one of her arms to a different position, it just stays there. Katie has stopped speaking and does not appear to hear what is being said to her. What specifier would you apply to her diagnosis of major depressive disorder?
    a. chronic
    b. catatonic
    c. atypical
    d. melancholic

ANS: B   DIF: 1   REF: p. 216   OBJ: 5 TYPE: APP

39. Although catatonic symptoms occur in major depressive disorders, they are more frequently associated with:
    a. phobias
    b. somatoform disorders
    c. dissociative identity disorder
    d. schizophrenia

ANS: D   DIF: 1   REF: p. 216   OBJ: 5 TYPE: FACT

40. Individuals whose bipolar diagnosis includes a psychotic features specifier have hallucinations and/or delusions:
    a. only in the manic state
    b. only in the depressed state
    c. when they are either manic or depressed
    d. during inter-episode intervals only

    ANS: C   DIF: 1   REF: p. 216   OBJ: 5 TYPE: FACT

41. The postpartum onset specifier is used to characterize a severe manic or depressive episode with psychotic features that occurs in a woman following:
    a. childbirth
    b. a hysterectomy
    c. rape
    d. menopause

    ANS: A   DIF: 1   REF: p. 216   OBJ: 5 TYPE: CON

42. In rare tragic cases a mother suffering from postpartum depression sometimes:
    a. kills her child
    b. commits suicide
    c. murders other people's children
    d. injures the child's father

    ANS: A   DIF: 1   REF: p. 216   OBJ: 5 TYPE: FACT

43. In regard to mood disorders there are additional criteria called specifiers that are used to determine length of treatment and prognosis. Which of the following is a longitudinal course specifier?
    a. anhedonia
    b. catelepsy
    c. postpartum onset
    d. interepisode recovery

    ANS: D   DIF: 5   REF: p. 217   OBJ: 5 TYPE: CON

44. All of the following are longitudinal course specifiers for recurrent mania or depression EXCEPT:
    a. previous history of dysthymia
    b. presence of psychotic features
    c. previous history of cyclothymia
    d. full recovery between manic and depressive episodes

    ANS: B   DIF: 5   REF: p. 217   OBJ: 5 TYPE: CON

45. The "rapid cycling" specifier is added to the diagnosis of bipolar disorder when a patient has had at least _____ manic or depressive episodes within a year.
    a. 2
    b. 4
    c. 6
    d. 8

    ANS: B   DIF: 1   REF: p. 217   OBJ: 5 TYPE: CON

46. Since traditional antidepressant medication such as tricyclics may actually provoke rapid cycling in bipolar patients, mood stabilizers and _____ are often prescribed instead.
    a. antipsychotics
    b. tranquilizers
    c. anticonvulsants
    d. opiates

    ANS: C   DIF: 5   REF: p. 217   OBJ: 7 TYPE: APP/WWW

47. In studies of bipolar patients who experience rapid cycling, it has been found that as many as 90% are:
    a. female
    b. male
    c. elderly
    d. adolescents

    ANS: A   DIF: 3   REF: p. 217   OBJ: 5 TYPE: FACT

48. Which of the following statements applies to the condition known as seasonal affective disorder (SAD)?
    a. Individuals may become depressed during the winter and manic during the summer.
    b. Persons with SAD have symptoms of decreased sleep and decreased appetite.
    c. Depression in vulnerable people might be triggered by decreased production of the hormone called melatonin.
    d. SAD can be treated with phototherapy, i.e., 2 hours of exposure to bright light just before going to sleep.

    ANS: A   DIF: 5   REF: p. 217   OBJ: 5 TYPE: CON/WWW

49. In regard to the prevalence of mood disorders, it has been found consistently that:
    a. Females experience major depressive disorders less frequently than males.
    b. Men have twice as many mood disorders as women.
    c. Bipolar disorders occur equally across gender.
    d. Dysthymia occurs equally across gender.

    ANS: C   DIF: 1   REF: p. 219   OBJ: 6 TYPE: CON

50. Recent evidence (Coryell et al., 2003) indicates a higher level of _____ in bipolar patients with a rapid cycling pattern compared to those with a non-rapid cycling pattern.
    a. treatment response   c. medication side effects
    b. resistance to treatment   d. suicide

    ANS: D   DIF: 3   REF: p. 217   OBJ: 8 TYPE: FACT

51. All of the following are accurate statements about the prevalence of mood disorders in children and adolescents EXCEPT:
    a. Bipolar disorder in children is often misdiagnosed as attention deficit hyperactivity disorder (ADHD).
    b. Major depressive disorder in adolescents is primarily a female disorder.
    c. Rates of attempted suicide decrease during adolescence.
    d. Adolescents with bipolar disorder may become aggressive, impulsive, sexually provocative and accident-prone.

    ANS: C   DIF: 3   REF: p. 221   OBJ: 4 TYPE: CON

52. Being depressed _____ the risk of death in elderly patients who have had a stroke or heart attack.
    a. has no effect   c. triples
    b. doubles   d. reduces

    ANS: B   DIF: 3   REF: p. 222   OBJ: 4 TYPE: FACT

53. The presence of medical illnesses or symptoms of dementia can make the diagnosis of depression difficult in:
    a. middle aged men
    b. menopausal women
    c. highly creative individuals
    d. the elderly

    ANS: D   DIF: 1   REF: p. 221   OBJ: 5 TYPE: CON

54. Cross-cultural research indicates that due at least in part to appalling social and economic conditions, the prevalence of major depression is extremely high among:
    a. African-Americans
    b. Hispanic-Americans
    c. Asian-Americans
    d. Native Americans

    ANS: D   DIF: 3   REF: p. 222   OBJ: 6 TYPE: FACT

55. According to your textbook, researchers have been studying the life histories of American poets to determine if there is a relationship between creativity and _____.
    a. anxiety
    b. manic-depressive disorder
    c. dissociation
    d. schizophrenia

    ANS: B   DIF: 1   REF: p. 222   OBJ: 6 TYPE: APP

56. Which of the following presidents of the United States was known to have suffered from depression?
    a. George Washington
    b. Abraham Lincoln
    c. Franklin D. Roosevelt
    d. John F. Kennedy

    ANS: B   DIF: 1   REF: p. 209   OBJ: 1 TYPE: FACT

57. Many famous women in history have suffered from depression including:
    a. Queen Victoria of England
    b. Joan of Arc
    c. Eleanor Roosevelt
    d. Anna Freud

    ANS: A   DIF: 1   REF: p. 212   OBJ: 6 TYPE: FACT

58. Which of the following statements is accurate regarding the relationship between anxiety and depression?
    a. Almost all depressed patients are anxious, but not every anxious patient is depressed.
    b. Cognitive content (thinking) is more negative in anxious patients than in those with depression.
    c. A core symptom of anxiety is the inability to experience pleasure.
    d. Anxiety is often preceded by an episode of major depression.

    ANS: A   DIF: 5   REF: p. 223   OBJ: 6 TYPE: CON

59. In research looking at the biological causes of mood disorders, studies have shown that if one of a set of twins has bipolar disorder, the probability that the other twin will have a mood disorder is:
    a. 20%
    b. 40%
    c. 60%
    d. 80%

    ANS: D   DIF: 1   REF: p. 225   OBJ: 6 TYPE: FACT

60. In terms of the etiology of mood disorders, research has shown that:
    a. environmental stress plays a larger role in causing depression in men than in women
    b. genetic factors are more important in the development of depression in men in comparison to the development of depression in women
    c. genetic and environmental factors are equally contributory to mood disorders
    d. there are no sex differences in vulnerability to depression

    ANS: A   DIF: 5   REF: p. 226   OBJ: 6 TYPE: APP

61. Current research into neurotransmitter systems has produced the "permissive" hypothesis which means that:
    a. low levels of serotonin are sufficient to explain the etiology of mood disorders
    b. the norepinephrine system regulates serotonin levels; if norepinephrine is low, depression will occur
    c. when serotonin levels are low, other neurotransmitter systems become dysregulated and contribute to mood irregularities
    d. the absolute levels of neurotransmitters are more significant in mood regulation than the overall balance of the various neurotransmitters

    ANS: C   DIF: 5   REF: p. 226   OBJ: 6 TYPE: CON

62. A friend of yours tells you that he thinks he is mildly depressed but he's not sure. Knowing that you are studying abnormal psychology, he asks if there is any kind of laboratory test that could determine whether or not someone is depressed. You respond correctly with one of the following statements.
    a.   Currently there is no way of diagnosing depression with a laboratory test.
    b.   The dexamethasone suppression test is a biological test for depression.
    c.   The DST can only be used to diagnose severe cases of depression.
    d.   Cortisol levels are decreased in depression; he could have his cortisol levels checked by a blood test.

    ANS: A   DIF: 5   REF: p. 227   OBJ: 6 TYPE: APP

63. The best conclusion about the dexamethasone suppression test (DST) for the diagnosis of depression is that:
    a.   it is accurate   c.   it promises to be an effective diagnostic tool in the future
    b.   it is effective but cannot differentiate bipolar disorder from major depression   d.   it is not useful as a diagnostic tool

    ANS: D   DIF: 5   REF: p. 227   OBJ: 6 TYPE: FACT

64. One symptom of depression is an increase in sleeping. What other symptoms related to sleep occur in depression?
    a.   decreased delta (slow wave) sleep, the deepest stage of sleep
    b.   less intense REM activity
    c.   stages of deepest sleep occurring earlier in the sleep cycle
    d.   slower onset of REM sleep

    ANS: A   DIF: 5   REF: p. 227   OBJ: 6 TYPE: FACT/WWW

65. In regard to the relationship between stress and depression, all of the following statements are true EXCEPT:
    a.   The context of the life event, as well as its meaning to the individual, is more important than the nature of the event itself.
    b.   An individual's current mood state might distort earlier memories of stressful life events that precipitated the depression.
    c.   Stressful life events are strongly related to the onset of mood disorders.
    d.   Recurrent episodes of depression, but not initial episodes, are strongly predicted by major life stress.

    ANS: D   DIF: 5   REF: p. 228   OBJ: 6 TYPE: CON

66. When individuals who are biologically vulnerable to depression place themselves in high risk stressful environments, it is called:
    a.   humoral theory
    b.   the cognitive-behavioral model
    c.   the reciprocal gene-environment model
    d.   a stress-depression linkage effect

    ANS: C   DIF: 3   REF: p. 229   OBJ: 6 TYPE: CON

67. An individual who usually says, "It's all my fault," when anything goes wrong is reflecting the _____ characteristic of the depressive attributional style.
    a. global
    b. stable
    c. internal
    d. external

    ANS: C   DIF: 1   REF: p. 230   OBJ: 6 TYPE: APP/WWW

68. Martin Seligman's theory that people become anxious and depressed because they believe that they have no control over the stress in their lives, is called:
    a. the learned helplessness model
    b. cognitive-behavioral theory
    c. humanistic/existential theory
    d. the control theory of depression

    ANS: A   DIF: 3   REF: p. 230   OBJ: 6 TYPE: CON

69. In 1989, Abramson and his colleagues revised Seligman's theory of learned helplessness, changing the focus from specific attributions to _____ as the crucial factor in depression.
    a. lack of control
    b. a sense of hopelessness
    c. repressed anger
    d. a feeling of failure

    ANS: B   DIF: 3   REF: p. 230   OBJ: 6 TYPE: CON

70. A student who has been doing very well in her psychology class receives a minor critical comment on an essay that she wrote as part of an exam. The student thinks, "This is terrible. I'm probably going to fail the course." This type of cognitive error in thinking is called:
    a. arbitrary inference
    b. overgeneralization
    c. splitting
    d. dissociating

    ANS: B   DIF: 3   REF: p. 230   OBJ: 6 TYPE: APP

71. In Aaron Beck's depressive cognitive triad individuals think negatively about all of the following EXCEPT:
    a. themselves
    b. their immediate world
    c. their past
    d. their future

    ANS: C   DIF: 1   REF: p. 231   OBJ: 6 TYPE: CON

72. Regarding Beck's views on depression, which of the following definitions of cognitive errors and negative schema is NOT correct?
    a. In a self-blame schema, depressed individuals feel personally responsible for every bad thing that happens.
    b. Arbitrary inference means that a depressed individual emphasizes the positive rather than the negative aspects of a situation.
    c. In a negative self-evaluation schema, depressed individuals believe that they can never do anything correctly.
    d. Overgeneralization occurs when a small error is magnified to mean something much more significant.

    ANS: B   DIF: 5   REF: p. 231   OBJ: 6 TYPE: CON

73. According to recent research on the development of depression, dysfunctional attitudes (a negative outlook) and hopelessness attributes (explaining things negatively) constitute a _____ vulnerability to depression.
    a. biological
    b. cognitive
    c. behavioral
    d. sociological

    ANS: B   DIF: 3   REF: p. 232   OBJ: 6 TYPE: CON

74. Preliminary results of a study of cognitive vulnerability to depression (Alloy et al., 2000) found that ____ percent of the students with thought patterns classified as "high risk" for depression subsequently suffered a major depressive episode where only ____ percent of the "low risk" students subsequently experienced a major depressive episode.
    a. 17; 1   c. 40; 5
    b. 25; 15   d. 85; 10

    ANS: A   DIF: 5   REF: p. 232   OBJ: 8 TYPE: FACT

75. For individuals who had not been previously depressed, research studies indicate that a marital separation or divorce resulted in _____ .
    a. a higher rate of depression in men
    b. a higher rate of depression in women
    c. approximately equal rates of depression for males and females
    d. no symptoms of depression in either males or females

    ANS: A   DIF: 3   REF: p. 232   OBJ: 6 TYPE: FACT

76. Possible reasons for the higher rates of depression found in women include all of the following EXCEPT:
    a. culturally induced dependence and passivity
    b. sense of uncontrollability and helplessness
    c. low value placed on intimate relationships
    d. self-blame for being depressed

    ANS: C   DIF: 3   REF: p. 233   OBJ: 6 TYPE: APP

77. Possible reasons for the higher rates of depression found in women relate to the disadvantages experienced by women in the United States such as:
   a. discrimination and poverty
   b. abuse and sexual harassment
   c. both of these
   d. none of these

   ANS: C   DIF: 1   REF: p. 233   OBJ: 6 TYPE: FACT

78. Which of the following factors contribute to the integrative theory of depression?
   a. stressful life events
   b. stress hormones
   c. neurotransmitters
   d. all of these

   ANS: D   DIF: 1   REF: p. 234   OBJ: 6 TYPE: CON

79. The antidepressant medications known as imipramine (Tofranil) and amitriptyline (Elavil) are included in the class of drugs called:
   a. SSRIs
   b. tricyclics
   c. MAO inhibitors
   d. tranquilizers

   ANS: B   DIF: 1   REF: p. 236   OBJ: 7 TYPE: FACT/WWW

80. The therapeutic effects of the tricyclic antidepressants begin:
   a. immediately
   b. within 24 hours
   c. 2 to 8 weeks after starting the medication
   d. 3 months after starting the medication

   ANS: C   DIF: 1   REF: p. 236   OBJ: 7 TYPE: FACT

81. Side effects of the tricyclic antidepressants include:
   a. weight loss
   b. excessive urination
   c. sexual dysfunction
   d. insomnia

   ANS: C   DIF: 3   REF: p. 236   OBJ: 7 TYPE: FACT

82. Which of the following is a well-known and widely used selective serotonergic reuptake inhibitor (SSRI)?
   a. Prozac
   b. Valium
   c. Hypericum
   d. Thorazine

   ANS: A   DIF: 1   REF: p. 237   OBJ: 7 TYPE: FACT

83. Clinical studies have shown that 50 to 75 percent of patients taking Prozac will experience:
    a. manic episodes
    b. suicidal tendencies
    c. sexual dysfunction
    d. cardiac irregularities

    ANS: C   DIF: 1   REF: p. 237   OBJ: 7 TYPE: FACT

84. In regard to treatment of mood disorders, which of the following statements is accurate?
    a. Patients do not recover from episodes of major depression without treatment.
    b. Delaying or preventing future episodes of major depression is an important treatment goal.
    c. After a patient has experienced a major depressive episode and recovered, treatment can be discontinued.
    d. Close to 100% of patients with major depressive disorder respond to drug treatment.

    ANS: B   DIF: 3   REF: p. 238   OBJ: 7 TYPE: APP

85. Clinical studies have shown that the favorable response rate for patients taking antidepressant medications is:
    a. 25%
    b. 50%
    c. 75%
    d. 100%

    ANS: B   DIF: 1   REF: p. 238   OBJ: 7 TYPE: FACT

86. A goal of treatment for patients who have experienced major depressive disorders is delaying or preventing the next episode. In which of the following situations would this goal be least important?
    a. patients who have recovered from a major depressive episode but still have some residual symptoms
    b. patients with a past history of chronic depression (dysthymia)
    c. patients with a past history of multiple episodes of major depressive disorder
    d. patients who have had a single, brief episode of major depressive disorder and recovered without treatment

    ANS: D   DIF: 5   REF: p. 238   OBJ: 7 TYPE: APP

87. The newest drugs being developed for the treatment of depression focus on down-regulating HPA axis activity by blocking the production of cortisol or blocking a neuropeptide called Substance P. This is consistent with the _____ of the origin of depression (Nemeroff, 2002, Ranga & Krishan, 2002).
    a. cognitive hypothesis   c. stress hypothesis
    b. dopamine hypothesis   d. serotonin

    ANS: C   DIF: 5   REF: p. 238   OBJ: 7 TYPE: FACT

88. The antidepressant medication lithium is also referred to as a mood stabilizer because it:
    a. increases the availability of both dopamine and norepinephrine in the brain
    b. is less toxic than the SSRI medications
    c. helps to prevent manic episodes
    d. increases thyroid functioning, which results in improved mood stabilization

    ANS: C   DIF: 3   REF: p. 238   OBJ: 7 TYPE: APP

89. A relative of yours has been diagnosed with bipolar (manic-depressive) disorder. Your family is impressed when you mention that the preferred drug for this condition is:
    a. Prozac
    b. St. John's Wort
    c. an anticonvulsant
    d. lithium

    ANS: D   DIF: 3   REF: p. 238   OBJ: 7 TYPE: APP/WWW

90. Although the mood stabilizing drug lithium is the preferred treatment for bipolar disorder, patient compliance has been a problem. Patients often stop taking their lithium, even though it is effective in stabilizing their moods, because they:
    a. become anxious that the drug is too toxic
    b. miss the euphoric feelings that mania produces
    c. start to have panic attacks
    d. cannot afford the high cost of the medication

    ANS: B   DIF: 3   REF: p. 239   OBJ: 7 TYPE: APP

91. Although ECT (electroconvulsive therapy) has been a controversial issue for decades, it is an effective treatment for depression especially when:
    a. patients cannot afford antidepressant medication
    b. patient response to antidepressant medication is poor
    c. symptoms of depression are mild
    d. a manic-depressive patient is currently experiencing a manic episode

    ANS: B   DIF: 3   REF: p. 239   OBJ: 7 TYPE: APP

92. In comparing ECT (electroconvulsive therapy) to antidepressant medication, all of the following statements are accurate EXCEPT:
    a. Relief of symptoms occurs more rapidly with ECT
    b. Relief of symptoms occurs more rapidly with medication
    c. Short-term memory loss is a side effect of treatment with medication
    d. Psychotically depressed patients should be treated with medication, not ECT

    ANS: A   DIF: 3   REF: p. 239   OBJ: 7 TYPE: CON

93. Recent research (Grunhaus, Schreiber, Dolberg, Polak, & Dannon, 2003; Janicak et al., 2002) suggests that an equally effective alternative to electroconvulsive therapy that requires no anesthesia and appears to alter electrical activity in the brain may be:
    a. transcranial magnetic stimulation (TMS)   c. magnetic resonance stimulation (MRS)
    b. electrocranial stimulation (ECS)   d. positron cranial stimulation (PCS)

    ANS: A   DIF: 5   REF: p. 239   OBJ: 7 TYPE: FACT

94. A depressed young woman enters a psychologist's office for her first appointment. The therapist tells her that they will work together to recognize and correct her "negative thinking errors." The type of therapy that will be used here is called:
   a. Interpersonal Psychotherapy (IPT)
   b. conditional therapy
   c. cognitive therapy
   d. antidepressive therapy

   ANS: C   DIF: 1   REF: p. 239   OBJ: 7 TYPE: APP

95. Interpersonal Psychotherapy (IPT) helps depressed patients resolve relationship problems. All of the following issues are a possible focus of Interpersonal Psychotherapy EXCEPT:
   a. marital conflict
   b. death of a loved one
   c. deficits in social skills
   d. negative thinking

   ANS: D   DIF: 3   REF: p. 241   OBJ: 7 TYPE: CON

96. Recent research suggesting that it might be possible to "psychologically immunize" children against depression is based on studies in which at-risk children:
   a. who scored in the "depressed" range on psychological tests were treated with psychoanalytic therapy
   b. received the same medication as that given to a depressed family member
   c. were taught cognitive and social problem-solving skills
   d. were given sham ECT treatments

   ANS: C   DIF: 3   REF: p. 242   OBJ: 7 TYPE: APP

97. Seligman and his colleagues conducted a course in which university students at risk for depression were taught cognitive and social problem-solving skills. Students in the study were determined to be at risk for depression based on a:
   a. low score on a test of learned helplessness
   b. pessimistic cognitive style
   c. family history of depression
   d. poor response to antidepressant medication

   ANS: B   DIF: 3   REF: p. 242   OBJ: 7 TYPE: CON

98. Combining medication and psychosocial treatments for patients with depression has the following advantages:
   a. the therapeutic effects of medication are gradual, allowing the patient to learn coping skills while the drugs begin working
   b. depressed patients can usually stop taking their antidepressant medication after several sessions of psychosocial treatment
   c. the same psychologist can provide the psychosocial therapy and prescribe the necessary medication
   d. patients benefit from both rapid drug action and the psychosocial protection against recurrence or relapse

   ANS: D   DIF: 5   REF: p. 242   OBJ: 7 TYPE: APP

99. Which of the following statements about suicide is correct?
   a. The suicide rate is high among African-Americans but low among Native Americans.
   b. The suicide rate among adolescents in the U.S. is decreasing.
   c. For teenagers, suicide is the third leading cause of death after auto accidents and homicide.
   d. Females are more likely than males to die from suicide.

   ANS: C   DIF: 1   REF: p. 246   OBJ: 8 TYPE: FACT

100. Research has found that low serotonin levels may be implicated in suicidal behavior because they affect all of the following EXCEPT:
   a. impulsivity
   b. instability
   c. inertia
   d. overreactivity

   ANS: C   DIF: 3   REF: p. 248   OBJ: 8 TYPE: CON

101. Evidence for an inherited tendency towards suicidal behavior comes from research involving:
   a. the human genome project
   b. callers to suicide hotlines
   c. adoption and twin studies
   d. "psychological autopsies"

   ANS: C   DIF: 5   REF: p. 248   OBJ: 8 TYPE: CON

102. In regard to the relationship between mood disorders and suicide, which of the following statements reflects the current thinking on this issue?
   a. Suicide is often associated with psychological disorders, especially depression.
   b. All persons who attempt suicide have mood disorders.
   c. A small percentage of adolescent suicides are an expression of severe depression.
   d. Suicide is generally a response to some disappointment in people who are otherwise psychologically healthy.

   ANS: A   DIF: 5   REF: p. 248   OBJ: 8 TYPE: CON

103. Statistics on suicide indicate that approximately one-quarter to one-half of all suicides are associated with:
   a. alcohol use
   b. guns
   c. aggression
   d. work stress

   ANS: A   DIF: 1   REF: p. 248   OBJ: 8 TYPE: FACT

104. All of the following are risk factors for suicide EXCEPT:
   a. sense of hopelessness
   b. a shameful or humiliating experience
   c. previous suicide attempt(s)
   d. a vague suicidal fantasy without detailed plans

   ANS: D   DIF: 1   REF: p. 248   OBJ: 8 TYPE: CON

105. Although glorifying and romanticizing suicide in the media contributes to copycat suicides, it is more likely that the person copying the suicide is:
    a. just doing it for attention
    b. vulnerable due to an existing psychological disorder
    c. not really serious about the suicide attempt
    d. trying to impress others

    ANS: B   DIF: 3   REF: p. 249   OBJ: 8 TYPE: CON

106. Impulsive suicidal behavior is often a symptom of _____ personality disorder.
    a. schizoid
    b. borderline
    c. obsessive-compulsive
    d. paranoid

    ANS: B   DIF: 3   REF: p. 249   OBJ: 8 TYPE: FACT

107. In a randomly assigned, controlled study conducted by David Rudd and his colleagues, previously suicidal, hospitalized young adults were helped to develop social competence and more adaptive coping skills, and to recognize the emotional triggers that precipitate suicide attempts. A two-year follow up indicated continued reductions in suicidal ideation and behavior. What is the significance of this study?
    a. None of the patients in the study committed suicide.
    b. None of the patients committed suicide after the study was completed.
    c. It has been expanded into the first empirically supported psychological treatment for suicidal behavior.
    d. It is the first psychological treatment for suicidal behavior in which medication was not used.

    ANS: D   DIF: 5   REF: p. 250   OBJ: 8 TYPE: APP

108. On the "Abnormal Psychology Live" CD for Chapter 7, Barbara says that her primary depressive symptom was:
    a. agitation   c. mania
    b. suicidal thoughts   d. physically lethargy

    ANS: D   DIF: 2   REF: CD

109. Barbara, one of the patients suffering from a major depressive episode on the "Abnormal Psychology Live" CD for Chapter 7, told how she avoided relationships because she was:
    a. ashamed of how depressed she had   c. angry with her friends and family
       become
    b. afraid people would ask her to participate   d. confused as to why anyone would want to
       in activities   spend time with her

    ANS: B   DIF: 3   REF: CD

110. On the "Abnormal Psychology Live" CD for Chapter 7 Barbara described thoughts of suicide that involved:
    a. taking pills   c. driving
    b. a gun   d. tremendous anxiety

    ANS: C   DIF: 2   REF: CD

111. During Evelyn's final interview on the "Abnormal Psychology Live" CD for Chapter 7, she describes the experience of starting to feel better as:
    a. beginning to see some light
    b. being lifted above the depths of despair
    c. having fewer suicidal thoughts
    d. wanting to go home

    ANS: A   DIF: 2   REF: CD

112. During the final interview with Mary on the "Abnormal Psychology Live" CD for Chapter 7, she is clearly in a manic state with an affect that can be considered inappropriate due to her:
    a. wildly excited tone of voice
    b. lack of eye contact
    c. constant crying
    d. laughing

    ANS: D   DIF: 3   REF: CD

ESSAY

1. Compare and contrast the clinical symptoms of major depression and mania. Explain what is meant by dysphoric (or mixed) mania. **WWW**

2. Compare the two types of course modifiers for depression and how they apply to either recent or recurrent episodes. Define the psychotic, catatonic, rapid cycling and seasonal specifiers. How do these additional criteria help in determining prognosis and treatment?

3. Compare and contrast dysthymia and cyclothymia and how each differs from either major depression or bipolar disorder. Explain what is meant by double depression.

4. Explain how a grief reaction can become a pathological disorder. Is it possible to predict who will develop a pathological grief reaction?

5. Discuss what is meant by a description of someone as "moody." Explain the differences between mania and hypomania in terms of symptoms and severity.

6. Discuss the onset, symptoms, diagnosis, and treatment of postpartum depression.

7. Explain the neurobiological basis of depression. Describe the role of specific neurotransmitters implicated in mood disorders.

8. Describe several of the medical and psychological treatments for depression. Compare the treatments in terms of effectiveness.

9. Explain Aaron Beck's cognitive theory of depression. What is the cognitive triad? Give examples of the different types of cognitive errors.

10. Discuss the relationship between suicide and psychological disorders such as depression, substance abuse and personality disorders. Describe the significance of stressful life events in suicidal behavior.

MULTIPLE CHOICE

1. Which of the following would not be present during a major depressive episode?
    a. changes in appetite and sleeping habits.
    b. anxiety.
    c. anhedonia.
    d. grandiosity.

    ANS: D

2. Jenny has experienced long-standing feelings of depression that have never interfered with her productivity or functioning until now. During the past 10 days, she has experienced a depressed mood, feelings of emptiness, and a significant weight loss. Jenny confided in a neighbor that she is considering suicide. It is likely that Jenny is suffering from
    a. major depressive disorder, single episode.
    b. major depressive disorder, recurrent.
    c. double depression.
    d. dysthymia with depressive episode.

    ANS: C

3. Richard, who has not responded well to medication, experiences six or more manic and depressive cycles in a year. Diagnosed with bipolar disorder, Richard is displaying
    a. bipolar II disorder.
    b. rapid cycling pattern.
    c. seasonal patterning.
    d. inexplicable treatment response.

    ANS: B

4. Cross-cultural studies indicate that
    a. the term "depression" is universal, but symptoms of it vary across cultures.
    b. the symptoms of depression are universal, but the term "depression" varies across cultures.
    c. the symptoms and terminology of depression vary across cultures, but all cultures claim some form of the disorder.
    d. depression is most common in Western society.

    ANS: C

5. The statement that *best* describes the role of serotonin in the etiology of depression is that
    a. low levels of serotonin are solely responsible.
    b. low serotonin levels appear to have an impact, but only in relation to other neurotransmitters.
    c. elevated serotonin levels are solely responsible.
    d. fluctuating levels of serotonin are the underlying basis for depression.

    ANS: B

6. Feelings of depression
   a. are very rare and only occur in people with a genetic predisposition.
   b. only occur when triggered by a severely negative event.
   c. only occur in people between the ages of 25 and 40.
   d. are universal and experienced by everyone occasionally.

   ANS: D

7. The average duration of an untreated depressive episode is
   a. 2 years.
   b. 1 year.
   c. 6 months.
   d. 9 months.

   ANS: D

8. Which of the following people are experiencing symptoms of a manic episode?
   a. Lorraine has inflated self-esteem and grandiosity.
   b. Tevon is irritable and is experiencing flight of ideas.
   c. Valerie suddenly goes on an excessive spending spree that she clearly cannot afford.
   d. all of the above

   ANS: D

9. Dysthymic disorder is to major depressive episode as cyclothymic disorder is to
   a. major depressive episode.
   b. dysthymic disorder.
   c. bipolar disorder.
   d. none of the above

   ANS: C

10. Lyle is 23 years old. His mother dies two weeks ago and since then he has been so upset he has been unable to eat or sleep. He has been crying a great deal. The death was completely unexpected and Lyle has been alternating between feeling sad, feeling very anxious, and wanting to deny that his mother is dead. Lyle appears to be experiencing
    a. rapid cycling bipolar disorder.
    b. a major depressive episode.
    c. double depression.
    d. grief.

    ANS: D

MULTIPLE CHOICE

1. The chief motivating factor in both anorexia and bulimia is:
   a. a desire to purge
   b. an overwhelming drive to eat
   c. an overwhelming urge to be thin
   d. a desire to starve oneself

   ANS: C   DIF: 1   REF: p. 257   OBJ: 1 TYPE: FACT/WWW

2. When individuals with anorexia are evaluated over long periods of time, it has been found that the percentage of individuals who die as a result of their disorder is:
   a. 20%
   b. 5%
   c. 2%
   d. 40%

   ANS: A   DIF: 3   REF: p. 257   OBJ: 1 TYPE: FACT

3. Approximately ___ percent of anorexia deaths are due to suicide.
   a. 5
   b. 10
   c. 25
   d. 50

   ANS: D   DIF: 1   REF: p. 257   OBJ: 1 TYPE: FACT

4. The death rate (including suicide) due to eating disorders is:
   a. higher than for any other psychological disorder except depression
   b. lower than that of most psychological disorders
   c. higher than that of most psychological disorders
   d. the highest of all of the psychological disorders

   ANS: C   DIF: 3   REF: p. 257   OBJ: 1 TYPE: FACT

5. Eating disorders are most prevalent in:
   a. Western cultures where food is scarce
   b. Western cultures where food is plentiful
   c. Non-Western cultures where food is scarce
   d. Non-Western cultures where food is plentiful

   ANS: B   DIF: 1   REF: p. 257   OBJ: 1 TYPE: FACT

6. Over the past thirty years, most Western countries have experienced a dramatic:
   a. decrease in the incidence of anorexia and bulimia
   b. increase in the incidence of anorexia and bulimia
   c. increase in the incidence of anorexia but a decrease in the incidence of bulimia
   d. increase in the incidence of bulimia and no change in the rate of anorexia

   ANS: B   DIF: 1   REF: p. 257   OBJ: 1 TYPE: FACT

7. The typical profile of a patient with either anorexia or bulimia is:
   a. young, white, female, upper socioeconomic status, socially competitive environment
   b. young, white, female, any socioeconomic status, history of depression
   c. young, female, any race, any socioeconomic status, highly competitive
   d. any age, female, white, upper socioeconomic status, few friends

   ANS: A   DIF: 1   REF: p. 257   OBJ: 1 TYPE: FACT

8. Jody sometimes eats more than just about any other girl that you know. You wonder if her eating sometimes could be considered bingeing. In order to determine this, you would have to know:
   a. the caloric intake of the foods
   b. whether she is eating junk foods
   c. whether eating gets to be out of her control
   d. the situations under which she eats a great deal

   ANS: C   DIF: 3   REF: p. 260   OBJ: 1 TYPE: APP

9. The most significant feature of bulimia is:
   a. purging
   b. overeating
   c. overeating followed by an urge to vomit
   d. binge eating followed by compensatory behavior

   ANS: D   DIF: 3   REF: p. 260   OBJ: 1 TYPE: FACT

10. Susan, a woman of relatively normal weight, sometimes eats huge quantities of junk food with no ability to stop herself. She follows this with long periods of complete fasting. Based on this information, Susan would:
    a. be diagnosed with bulimia
    b. be diagnosed with anorexia
    c. not be diagnosed with any disorder because she is of normal weight
    d. not be diagnosed with bulimia because she is not purging

    ANS: A   DIF: 3   REF: p. 260   OBJ: 1 TYPE: APP

11. The approximate percentage of bulimia patients who do not purge is:
    a. 0
    b. 30%
    c. 45%
    d. 75%

    ANS: B   DIF: 5   REF: p. 260   OBJ: 1 TYPE: FACT

12. Amy is a young woman who is very competitive and comes from a high achieving, wealthy family. She is very social and likes the fact that she is quite popular. She believes that her popularity is dependent on the weight and shape of her body. Amy has a boyfriend but worries that she may care more about their relationship than he does. The feature that puts Amy most at risk for an eating disorder such as bulimia is her:
    a. belief that her weight and body shape influence her popularity
    b. belief that her boyfriend cares less about the relationship than she does
    c. successful family
    d. competitive nature

    ANS: A   DIF: 3   REF: p. 260   OBJ: 1 TYPE: CON/WWW

13. The most serious medical consequence of bulimia is potential:
    a. electrolyte imbalance
    b. salivary gland damage
    c. starvation
    d. tooth erosion

    ANS: A   DIF: 3   REF: p. 261   OBJ: 2 TYPE: FACT

14. Most individuals with bulimia are:
    a. of fairly normal body weight
    b. significantly over weight
    c. significantly under weight
    d. overweight during the development of the disorder but become underweight as the disorder progresses

    ANS: A   DIF: 1   REF: p. 261   OBJ: 1 TYPE: FACT

15. Bulimic patients often present with additional psychological disorders, particularly _____ and _____.
    a. body dysmorphic disorder; substance disorders
    b. mood disorders; sexual disorders
    c. anxiety disorders; mood disorders
    d. obsessive compulsive disorder; sexual disorders

    ANS: C   DIF: 3   REF: p. 261   OBJ: 1 TYPE: FACT

16. The core diagnostic factor in anorexia is:
    a. food refusal
    b. a binge-purge cycle
    c. intentional weight loss reaching 15% or less of expected body weight
    d. rapid, intentional weight loss and the belief that more weight needs to be lost

    ANS: C   DIF: 3   REF: p. 262   OBJ: 1 TYPE: FACT

17. The most common reason that anorexics generally do not seek treatment on their own is that they:
    a. are ashamed of their disorder
    b. fear that they will be hospitalized
    c. do not see themselves as too thin
    d. have little desire for food

    ANS: C   DIF: 3   REF: p. 262   OBJ: 1 TYPE: CON

18. The most common medical complication of anorexia is:
    a. brittle hair
    b. downy hair on limbs
    c. electrolyte imbalance
    d. cessation of menstrual cycle

ANS: D   DIF: 1   REF: p. 262   OBJ: 2 TYPE: FACT

19. Recent research (Eddy et al., 2002) suggests that the restricting and binging/purging subtypes of anorexia
    a. are really different disorders
    b. have completely different causes
    c. show few differences in severity of symptoms
    d. are useless distinctions of the same disorder

ANS: C   DIF: 5   REF: p. 262   OBJ: 1 TYPE: FACT

20. The approximate percentage of eating disorder patients who will experience depression at some point in their lives is approximately:
    a. 15%.
    b. 35%
    c. 60%
    d. 85%

ANS: C   DIF: 3   REF: p. 264   OBJ: 1 TYPE: FACT

21. Individuals who experience loss of control of their eating and consume great quantities of food but do not engage in any attempts to compensate for their binge would be diagnosed with:
    a. bulimia, non-purging type
    b. binge eating disorder
    c. obsessive-compulsive disorder
    d. buffet disorder

ANS: B   DIF: 1   REF: p. 264   OBJ: 3 TYPE: FACT

22. The best evidence that binge eating disorder (BED) may not just be a special case of bulimia is that:
    a. more males than females suffer from binge eating disorder
    b. no genetic component has been identified for binge eating disorder
    c. bulimic women outnumber bulimic men by 9:1, but this ratio is about 3:1 for BED
    d. the average age of onset is much younger for BED than it is for bulimia or anorexia

ANS: C   DIF: 3   REF: p. 264   OBJ: 3 TYPE: CON

23. The males most likely to develop an eating disorder such as bulimia are those who are:
    a. overweight
    b. depressed
    c. homosexual
    d. only children

ANS: C   DIF: 3   REF: p. 264   OBJ: 4 TYPE: FACT

24. The age range for the onset for bulimia and anorexia is typically:
    a. 13 to 19
    b. 8 to 12
    c. 20 to 26
    d. early childhood

    ANS: A   DIF: 1   REF: p. 264   OBJ: 1 TYPE: FACT

25. Studies of foreign-born students who are attending Western universities show that:
    a. anorexia and bulimia do not occur in students who were raised in countries where these disorders do not exist
    b. anorexia and bulimia are observed in some students who were raised in countries where these disorders do not exist
    c. anorexia, but not bulimia, has been observed in some students who were raised in countries where these disorders do not exist
    d. bulimia, but not anorexia, has been observed in some students who were raised in countries where these disorders do not exist

    ANS: B   DIF: 1   REF: p. 265   OBJ: 4 TYPE: FACT

26. Which of the following might help to explain the vast differences in the incidence of eating disorders among men and women?
    a. the influence of behavioral genetics
    b. the fact that boys are encouraged to play sports and girls to be active in social functions
    c. the fact that puberty brings boys' bodies closer to the societal ideal and girls' bodies further from the societal ideal
    d. the differences in the way boys and girls tend to gain weight from overeating

    ANS: C   DIF: 3   REF: p. 267   OBJ: 4 TYPE: CON

27. With regard to the risk of developing anorexia or bulimia, it is true that African American women are at:
    a. much lower risk than white women   c. the same risk as white women
    b. much higher risk than white women   d. slightly lower risk than white women

    ANS: A   DIF: 1   REF: p. 266   OBJ: 4 TYPE: FACT

28. When considering all the factors that influence the development of eating disorders, e.g., anorexia and bulimia, it is apparent that the _____ is unique when compared to factors that affect the development of other psychological disorders.
    a. strong influence of genetics
    b. role that family instability plays
    c. power of neurobiological influences
    d. influence of society and culture

    ANS: D   DIF: 1   REF: p. 267   OBJ: 4 TYPE: CON

29. Some of the most convincing evidence that helps to explain the observed increase in the incidence of anorexia and bulimia over the past thirty years is:
    a. improved diagnostic and reporting practices
    b. concurrent increases in the rate of depression
    c. the generally improved health of the society and an increased emphasis on diet and exercise
    d. the decrease in the weight of both Miss America contestants and Playboy centerfold models

    ANS: D   DIF: 3   REF: p. 268   OBJ: 4 TYPE: FACT/WWW

30. Examination of past and cross-cultural weight ideals (as demonstrated by old paintings and other art forms, for example) indicates that the weight considered ideal by society:
    a. fluctuates over time
    b. is usually unattainable for the average person
    c. is consistent with a thinner appearance
    d. is always unhealthy

    ANS: A   DIF: 3   REF: p. 269   OBJ: 4 TYPE: CON

31. The increase in the incidence of eating disorders such as anorexia and bulimia has been referred to as a "collision between our culture and our physiology." The most accurate interpretation of this statement is that:
    a. people have become too dependent on media determinations of beauty
    b. media standards of beauty are increasingly unattainable for the average woman
    c. dieting has become a fad that has been taken to an extreme
    d. society has no business telling us how to define beauty

    ANS: B   DIF: 5   REF: p. 271   OBJ: 4 TYPE: CON

32. When women are asked to identify the most attractive female body weight, they typically identify a weight that is:
    a. lower than the weight identified by men
    b. the same as the weight identified by men
    c. higher than the weight identified by men
    d. 20% lower than their own body weight

    ANS: A   DIF: 1   REF: p. 269   OBJ: 4 TYPE: FACT

33. When men are asked to identify the ideal male body, they typically select a body weight that is about:
    a. equal to their own
    b. 28 pounds more muscular than their own
    c. equal to the average male of their age
    d. 15 pounds lighter than their own

    ANS: B   DIF: 1   REF: p. 269   OBJ: 4 TYPE: FACT

34. Which of the teenage girls described below is at greatest risk for developing an eating disorder?
   a. Alice is currently on a diet; her friends also diet aggressively.
   b. Sue is of average to slightly above average weight but wants to lose a few pounds.
   c. Megan's friends are concerned about the weight she has lost since she began working out with the swim team.
   d. Jean has always been fairly thin despite the fact that she eats quite normally.

   ANS: A   DIF: 3   REF: p. 270   OBJ: 4 TYPE: APP

35. Of the following, the group in which we would expect to see the highest incidence of anorexia is:
   a. male homosexuals
   b. female body builders
   c. ballet dancers
   d. female track stars

   ANS: C   DIF: 1   REF: p. 271   OBJ: 4 TYPE: FACT

36. The families of anorexia patients are typically characterized as:
   a. dysfunctional and disorganized
   b. successful and perfectionistic
   c. reserved and quiet
   d. no different than the average family

   ANS: B   DIF: 1   REF: p. 272   OBJ: 4 TYPE: FACT

37. The families of anorexia patients are typically characterized by all of the following EXCEPT:
   a. open communication
   b. high achievement
   c. perfectionism
   d. concern with external appearances

   ANS: A   DIF: 1   REF: p. 272   OBJ: 4 TYPE: FACT/WWW

38. Which of the following young women appears to be at the highest risk for developing an eating disorder?
   a. Linda, whose mom and dad recently divorced
   b. Carla, whose family members always seem to be fighting with each other
   c. Sandy, whose family emphasizes achievement, support, and communication
   d. Bonnie, whose family is perfectionistic, successful and eager to maintain harmony

   ANS: D   DIF: 5   REF: p. 272   OBJ: 4 TYPE: APP

39. With regard to the biological influences of anorexia and bulimia, the most accurate statement is:
   a. anorexia and bulimia are culturally determined and not biologically influenced
   b. the biological influences of anorexia and bulimia have not been studied
   c. although the studies are still limited, there appears to be some biological influence in the development of anorexia and bulimia
   d. although the studies are limited, there does appear to be a large biological influence for anorexia and a very small biological influence for bulimia

   ANS: C   DIF: 3   REF: p. 272   OBJ: 4 TYPE: FACT

40. Genetic influences on eating disorders most likely involve:
    a. a specific gene for each actual eating disorder
    b. an inherited personality tendency that may make development of an eating disorder more likely
    c. multiple genes interacting in ways not yet determined that directly produce eating disordered behavior
    d. recessive genes

    ANS: B   DIF: 3   REF: p. 272   OBJ: 4 TYPE: CON

41. Which of the following statements is true with regard to drug treatments for patients with anorexia?
    a. medications have not generally been found to be effective for the treatment of anorexia
    b. antidepressants have some effectiveness in the treatment of anorexia
    c. anti-anxiety medications have some effectiveness in the treatment of anorexia
    d. anti-psychotic mediations have been found to be effective for the treatment of anorexia

    ANS: A   DIF: 1   REF: p. 273   OBJ: 5 TYPE: FACT

42. With regard to drug treatments for bulimia patients, which of the following statements is true?
    a. medications have not been found to be effective for the treatment of bulimia
    b. antidepressants have some effectiveness in the treatment of bulimia
    c. benzodiazipine medications have some effectiveness in the treatment of bulimia
    d. anti-psychotic medications have been found to be effective for the treatment of bulimia

    ANS: B   DIF: 1   REF: p. 274   OBJ: 5 TYPE: FACT

43. One major problem with the use of medication in the treatment of bulimia is that:
    a. well controlled studies have not found medication more effective than a placebo
    b. the beneficial effects of the medication may be short-term
    c. side effects make most patients discontinue the medication
    d. patients refuse to take their medication

    ANS: B   DIF: 1   REF: p. 274   OBJ: 5 TYPE: FACT

44. An early stage of Mary's cognitive-behavioral treatment for bulimia will likely involve:
    a. antidepressant medication
    b. family therapy
    c. small, frequent meals
    d. in-patient treatment

    ANS: C   DIF: 3   REF: p. 275   OBJ: 5 TYPE: APP

45. An important aspect of the cognitive-behavioral approach to the treatment of bulimia involves:
    a. changing patients' dysfunctional thoughts regarding their weight and previous weight control strategies
    b. helping the patient's family learn new ways of interacting with each other and with the patient
    c. changing the type and frequency of reinforcement associated with being an identified patient
    d. making sure that the patient has a lot of quiet time where she can be alone

    ANS: A   DIF: 3   REF: p. 275   OBJ: 5 TYPE: CON/WWW

46. Studies of the effectiveness of cognitive-behavioral treatment for bulimia have demonstrated:
    a. significant short term gains in reduction of purging, but little change in binge eating behavior
    b. significant short term gains in reduction of binge eating but no long term gains
    c. a few short term gains in reduction of binge eating and purging but no long term gains
    d. significant short and long term gains in reduction of binge eating and purging

    ANS: D   DIF: 1   REF: p. 275   OBJ: 5 TYPE: FACT

47. A comparison of cognitive-behavioral therapy (CBT), behavior therapy (BT) and interpersonal therapy (IPT) for the treatment of bulimia indicates that <u>one year after treatment</u>:
    a. BT was superior to CBT, which was superior to IPT
    b. BT was equivalent to CBT and both were superior to IPT
    c. CBT was equivalent to IPT and both were superior to BT
    d. all therapies had some effectiveness but no therapy was found to be more effective than any other

    ANS: C   DIF: 5   REF: p. 275   OBJ: 5 TYPE: FACT

48. One intriguing result from the studies comparing cognitive behavioral therapy (CBT) and interpersonal therapy (IPT) for bulimia is the finding that:
    a. IPT is more effective in the short term but CBT is more effective when we look at how well patients are doing one year following treatment
    b. IPT and CBT appear to be indistinguishable in terms of their effectiveness in the short and long term, despite their very different approaches
    c. IPT is always more effective than CBT
    d. CBT is more effective in the short term, but IPT patients "catch up" and will do as well as CBT patients one year after treatment

    ANS: D   DIF: 5   REF: p. 275   OBJ: 5 TYPE: FACT

49. Based on the research reported in your text regarding available treatments for bulimia, we can conclude that treatment that focuses on _____ and _____ is most effective in gaining rapid control of bulimia and maintaining these gains over the long term.
    a. dysfunctional thoughts; actual disorder behaviors
    b. family functioning; social relationships
    c. classical conditioning; operant learning
    d. biological processes; genetics

    ANS: A   DIF: 5   REF: p. 275   OBJ: 5 TYPE: CON

50. The following statement is true with regard to the treatment of binge eating disorder:
    a. cognitive-behavioral therapy and self-help appear to be effective
    b. cognitive-behavioral therapy appears to be effective but self-help does not
    c. neither cognitive-behavioral nor self-help appears to be effective
    d. anti-depressant medication is the only proven treatment

    ANS: A   DIF: 3   REF: p. 277   OBJ: 5 TYPE: FACT

51. Recent research (Wilfley, 2002) regarding the treatment of binge eating disorder indicates that interpersonal therapy (IPT) is _____ cognitive behavioral treatment (CBT).
    a. not as effective as
    b. more rapid but not as effective as
    c. more effective than
    d. equally effective as

    ANS: D   DIF: 5   REF: p. 277   OBJ: 5 TYPE: FACT

52. The most important and immediate goal in the treatment of an anorexic patient is:
    a. family acceptance of the problem
    b. weight gain
    c. balanced diet
    d. resolution of family issues

    ANS: B   DIF: 1   REF: p. 277   OBJ: 5 TYPE: FACT

53. Jill has been in treatment for anorexia for the past two months. Over this time she has gained weight to the point where her weight is in the average range for a women of her height. The fact that she gained weight fairly quickly in treatment means:
    a. her prognosis for a full recovery is very good
    b. she is probably in need of little, if any more treatment
    c. she has completed the most difficult part of her treatment
    d. little in terms of how likely she is to be successful in the long-term

    ANS: D   DIF: 3   REF: p. 277   OBJ: 5 TYPE: APP

54. Many clinicians suggest that the most difficult part of treatment for anorexia, and the part of treatment where many anorexics are not successful, is:
    a. initial weight gain
    b. admitting that there is a problem and agreeing to begin treatment
    c. changing their attitudes regarding body and self image
    d. when they become bulimic

    ANS: C   DIF: 3   REF: p. 277   OBJ: 5 TYPE: FACT

55. Outcome research regarding the long-term success of treatment for eating disorders indicates that:
    a. anorexia patients tend to have a better prognosis than bulimia patients
    b. bulimia patients tend to have a better prognosis than anorexia patients
    c. both anorexia and bulimia patients almost always make a full and long term recovery after treatment
    d. neither anorexia nor bulimia patients tend to make long term recoveries, with most patients going through repeated bouts of these disorders throughout their lives

    ANS: B   DIF: 1   REF: p. 277   OBJ: 5 TYPE: FACT

56. Regarding the possibility of developing an eating disorder in the future, it should be a cause for concern when a 10-year-old girl is:
    a. high achieving
    b. competitive
    c. very concerned about her weight
    d. not very popular with the other girls in her class

    ANS: C   DIF: 3   REF: p. 278   OBJ: 4 TYPE: APP

57. In studies of internet based eating disorders prevention programs (Winzelberg et al., 2000) such as the "student bodies program":
   a. the participants showed no beneficial effects
   b. participants reported improvement in body image and decreased drive for thinness
   c. not a single participant has developed symptoms of an eating disorder
   d. the drop-out rate has been extremely high

ANS: A   DIF: 3   REF: p. 279   OBJ: 5 TYPE: FACT

58. As of the year 2000, the percentage of the adult population of the United States with a body mass index in the obese range was:
   a. 10%
   b. 20%
   c. 30%
   d. 40%

ANS: B   DIF: 1   REF: p. 279   OBJ: 3 TYPE: FACT

59. Two forms of maladaptive eating patterns associated with obesity are _____ and _____.
   a. binge eating disorder; night eating syndrome
   b. binge eating disorder; pica
   c. pica; night eating syndrome
   d. night eating syndrome; caloric deregulative disorder

ANS: A   DIF: 1   REF: p. 280   OBJ: 3 TYPE: FACT

60. The most accurate statement regarding the use of self-help diet books in the treatment of obesity is that:
   a. there is a moderate level of long term effectiveness
   b. they are effective only when used in combination with physician counseling
   c. they are more effective then commercial self-help programs such as Jenny Craig
   d. they work for only a very few individuals

ANS: D   DIF: 1   REF: p. 281   OBJ: 5 TYPE: FACT

61. As we grow older, it seems that the amount of sleep that we require:
   a. increases
   b. decreases
   c. stays the same
   d. decreases until early adulthood and then begins to increase again

ANS: B   DIF: 1   REF: p. 286   OBJ: 7 TYPE: FACT

62. Joe has recently started having a great deal of difficulty falling asleep. In addition, he frequently wakes up during the night and has trouble falling back to sleep once awakened. At this point we can conclude that Joe's sleep problems are influenced by
   a. medical conditions
   b. psychological concerns
   c. a diagnosable sleep disorder
   d. either medical or psychological conditions

ANS: D   DIF: 1   REF: p. 286   OBJ: 6 TYPE: CON

63. Individuals who feel tired and cranky all day despite falling asleep at a normal hour and awakening at their usual time are most likely suffering from a(n):
   a. parasomnia
   b. dyssomnia
   c. type of REM sleep deprivation
   d. anxiety problem

   ANS: A   DIF: 3   REF: p. 284   OBJ: 6 TYPE: CON

64. Of the following, the correct pairing is:
   a. dyssomnia - sleepwalking
   b. dyssomnia - inability to fall asleep
   c. parasomnia - waking up after three or four hours of sleep and then being unable to fall back to sleep
   d. parasomnia - lack of REM sleep

   ANS: B   DIF: 1   REF: p. 284   OBJ: 6 TYPE: FACT

65. The most comprehensive evaluation of sleep is performed by a(n):
   a. polysomnographic evaluation
   b. actigraphic evaluation
   c. electromyographic evaluation
   d. electroencephalographic evaluation

   ANS: A   DIF: 3   REF: p. 284   OBJ: 10 TYPE: FACT

66. While a patient sleeps, a polysomnographic evaluation collects data on all of the following characteristics EXCEPT:
   a. respiration
   b. muscle movements
   c. brain waves
   d. metabolic rate

   ANS: D   DIF: 5   REF: p. 284   OBJ: 10 TYPE: FACT/WWW

67. Individuals with a sleep efficiency of 90:
   a. spend more of their "bed time" awake than asleep
   b. have a diagnosable sleep disorder
   c. need to increase the number of hours in bed
   d. spend ten percent of their "bed time" awake

   ANS: D   DIF: 3   REF: p. 284   OBJ: 6 TYPE: APP

68. Individuals suffering from primary insomnia:
   a. do not sleep at all
   b. have difficulty initiating or maintaining sleep
   c. wake up during their sleep cycle with severe nightmares
   d. frequently sleepwalk

   ANS: B   DIF: 1   REF: p. 284   OBJ: 6 TYPE: FACT

69. Sleep disorders are appropriately diagnosed based on the:
   a. quality and quantity of sleep as well as daytime sequelae (how the individual feels when awake)
   b. quality and quantity of sleep only
   c. quantity of sleep plus the amount of sleep time the individual believes is appropriate
   d. subjective judgment of the clinician

   ANS: A   DIF: 1   REF: p. 284   OBJ: 6 TYPE: FACT

70. The term "primary" in the diagnosis of primary insomnia refers to the fact that:
   a. the person has never been diagnosed with insomnia before
   b. the sleep disturbance is not due to another medical or psychiatric condition
   c. the sleep disorder is a primary cause of other medical or psychiatric conditions that the individual is experiencing
   d. other sleep disorders generally follow a diagnosis of primary insomnia

   ANS: B   DIF: 3   REF: p. 285   OBJ: 6 TYPE: FACT/WWW

71. Fred has been having a great deal of trouble initiating and maintaining sleep. He guesses that he is sleeping for an average of about 3 hours each night and complains that he feels terrible during the day. In addition, Fred has always experienced some anxiety but has recently felt a tremendous increase in his overall anxiety level. The existence of both a sleep disorder and anxiety:
   a. makes the diagnosis of primary insomnia incorrect
   b. increases our confidence that primary insomnia is the correct diagnosis
   c. indicates that the insomnia is a result of the anxiety rather than a cause of the anxiety
   d. is extremely common since sleep problems can be both a cause and a result of anxiety

   ANS: D   DIF: 3   REF: p. 285   OBJ: 6 TYPE: CON

72. The percentage of the general population that reports some symptoms of insomnia during any given year is approximately:
   a. 10%
   b. 20%
   c. 33%
   d. 50%

   ANS: C   DIF: 3   REF: p. 285   OBJ: 6 TYPE: FACT

73. Which of the following statements best describes the relationship between alcohol and sleep?
   a. alcohol may help initiate sleep but it interrupts ongoing sleep and can be the cause of a sleep disorder
   b. alcohol may help initiate sleep and enhance ongoing sleep but it leads to addiction if used as a sleep aid
   c. alcohol increases REM sleep
   d. alcohol increases total sleep time in an effective manner but continued use produces tolerance which negates this beneficial effect

   ANS: A   DIF: 3   REF: p. 285   OBJ: 6 TYPE: FACT

74. One biological factor that has been related to individuals who experience insomnia is:
    a. genetics
    b. higher body temperature
    c. low body weight
    d. percentage of body fat

    ANS: B   DIF: 3   REF: p. 286   OBJ: 9 TYPE: FACT

75. The fact that people who have unrealistic expectations such as "I must sleep a full 8 hours every night or I will be unable to function" are more likely to experience insomnia suggests that insomnia is at least partially influenced by:
    a. cognition
    b. early learning
    c. biological predisposition
    d. our current hectic lifestyle

    ANS: A   DIF: 3   REF: p. 286   OBJ: 6 TYPE: CON

76. Samantha started having difficulty falling asleep during final exam week. Although exams are over, she now starts to worry about sleep right after dinner. Even the sight of her bed makes her very anxious. The fact that Samantha's insomnia continues long after the stress of exams is over points to the role of _____ in the maintenance of sleep disorders.
    a. biology
    b. other medical conditions
    c. learning
    d. unknown factors

    ANS: C   DIF: 3   REF: p. 286   OBJ: 6 TYPE: CON

77. The integrative model of the causes of sleep disorders would suggest that most individuals develop sleep disorders as a result of the interaction between:
    a. biological and lifestyle factors
    b. learning and family stress
    c. genetics and bedtime habits
    d. learning and cognition

    ANS: A   DIF: 1   REF: p. 287   OBJ: 6 TYPE: CON

78. Rose sleeps about 8 hours each night. She awakens feeling fine and well rested but she tends to fall asleep about 2 or 3 times during the day. We can conclude that:
    a. Rose should be diagnosed with primary hypersomnia
    b. no disorder exists if this behavior does not bother Rose or interfere in her life
    c. Rose should be diagnosed with primary dyssomnia
    d. a medical condition is a more appropriate diagnosis than a sleep disorder

    ANS: B   DIF: 3   REF: p. 288   OBJ: 7 TYPE: APP

79. Before a clinician can diagnose hypersomnia, it is necessary to rule out all of the following EXCEPT:
    a. sleep apnea
    b. insomnia
    c. early life exposure to a viral infection such as mononucleosis
    d. current medical conditions that would account for the symptoms

    ANS: C   DIF: 5   REF: p. 288   OBJ: 7 TYPE: FACT/WWW

80. Of the following, the only symptom that both patients with narcolepsy and patients with hypersomnia experience is:
    a. falling asleep during normal waking hours
    b. sudden loss of muscle tone
    c. sleep paralysis
    d. hypnagogic hallucinations

    ANS: A   DIF: 3   REF: p. 288   OBJ: 7 TYPE: FACT

81. In which of the following situations is Bill, who has narcolepsy, most likely to experience cataplexy?
    a. immediately upon waking up after a long, restful sleep
    b. at any random moment
    c. under hypnosis
    d. while jumping up and cheering for his favorite team

    ANS: D   DIF: 5   REF: p. 288   OBJ: 7 TYPE: APP

82. While suddenly and unexpectedly falling asleep during normal waking hours, Sarah experiences vivid hallucinations of being in a horrible car crash. The experience is so realistic that she actually feels physical sensations as if the hallucination was real. Sarah's most likely diagnosis is:
    a. sleep apnea
    b. hypersomnia
    c. schizophrenia
    d. narcolepsy

    ANS: D   DIF: 1   REF: p. 289   OBJ: 7 TYPE: APP

83. Cataplexy as experienced by patients with narcolepsy can be characterized by:
    a. sudden, minor loss of muscle tone
    b. physical collapse
    c. slight muscle weakness
    d. all of these

    ANS: B   DIF: 3   REF: p. 289   OBJ: 7 TYPE: FACT

84. An individual who wakes up feeling that there are other people in the room but is unable to move or say anything may be experiencing:
    a. cataplexy associated with narcolepsy
    b. hypnagogic hallucinations associated with hypersomnia
    c. sleep paralysis and hypnagogic hallucinations associated with narcolepsy
    d. sleep paralysis and hypnogogic hallucinations associated with hypersomnia

    ANS: C   DIF: 3   REF: p. 289   OBJ: 7 TYPE: APP

85. Sam sleeps for eight or more hours every night but never feels rested. He can't understand why he is always tired despite the fact that he reports no difficulties with the quality or quantity of his sleep. Of the following, Sam's most likely diagnosis is:
    a. hypersomnia
    b. sleep apnea
    c. narcolepsy
    d. non-specific parasomnia

    ANS: B   DIF: 1   REF: p. 290   OBJ: 7 TYPE: APP

86. Obstructive sleep apnea is characterized by:
    a. complete cessation of respiratory activity for brief periods
    b. interruption of air flow and brief cessation of respiratory activity
    c. interruption of air flow without cessation of respiratory activity
    d. central nervous system disorders and trauma

    ANS: C   DIF: 5   REF: p. 290   OBJ: 7 TYPE: FACT

87. A severe difficulty in regulating sleep that is induced by jet lag or by working rotating shifts is an example of:
    a. circadian rhythm disruption
    b. sleep apnea
    c. hypersomnia
    d. narcolepsy

    ANS: A   DIF: 1   REF: p. 290   OBJ: 7 TYPE: FACT

88. Two factors that help regulate our natural sleep/wake cycles are:
    a. melanin and auditory stimulation
    b. melatonin and auditory stimulation
    c. melatonin and light
    d. light and blood sugar levels

    ANS: C   DIF: 3   REF: p. 291   OBJ: 9 TYPE: FACT

89. The most common treatment for insomnia in the United States is:
    a. medication
    b. hypnosis
    c. behavior modification
    d. psychoanalysis

    ANS: A   DIF: 1   REF: p. 292   OBJ: 10 TYPE: FACT

90. Benzodiazepine medication is not recommended as a long-term solution for the treatment of insomnia because of:
    a. the addictive properties of these medications
    b. rebound insomnia that occurs after the medication is discontinued
    c. excessive sleepiness that may persist during the day
    d. all of these

    ANS: D   DIF: 1   REF: p. 292   OBJ: 10 TYPE: FACT/WWW

91. The reason that antidepressant medications are sometimes used to treat narcolepsy is that:
    a. narcolepsy is often caused by depression
    b. the anti-anxiety properties of these medications reduce narcolepsy
    c. these medications suppress REM sleep that can trigger cataplexy
    d. all of these

    ANS: C   DIF: 5   REF: p. 292   OBJ: 10 TYPE: FACT

92. Medical treatments for severe sleep apnea include medication, mechanical devices and:
    a. surgery
    b. exercise of the neck muscles
    c. a high protein diet
    d. changing the patient's sleep schedule

    ANS: A   DIF: 1   REF: p. 292   OBJ: 10 TYPE: FACT

93. When attempting to "reset the biological clock" of an individual with a circadian rhythm sleep disorder, it is generally easier and more effective to:
    a. make the patient's bedtime earlier
    b. leave the patient's bedtime alone and change the duration of sleep
    c. make the patient's bedtime later
    d. keep the person awake for several days in a row

    ANS: C   DIF: 3   REF: p. 293   OBJ: 9 TYPE: FACT

94. One method (Terman & Terman, 2000) that has been used to help sleep disorder patients to "reset" their biological clock (circadian rhythms) is exposure to:
    a. very loud noises   c. very bright lights
    b. strong smells   d. strong magnetic fields

    ANS: C   DIF: 1   REF: p. 293   OBJ: 9 TYPE: FACT

95. Given what we know about classical conditioning and learning through association, sleep experts generally recommend:
    a. at least 8 hours of sleep each night
    b. using the bed for sleep and sex only
    c. spending a bit of time thinking about sleep before going to bed
    d. learning as much as possible about all of the various sleep disorders

    ANS: B   DIF: 3   REF: p. 293   OBJ: 9 TYPE: CON

96. The term "sleep hygiene" refers to:
    a. washing oneself before going to bed
    b. lifestyle behaviors that facilitate sleep
    c. use of medications to induce sleep
    d. the physical environment of the bedroom

    ANS: B   DIF: 3   REF: p. 293   OBJ: 10 TYPE: FACT/WWW

97. All of the following are examples of behaviors that may contribute to sleep problems EXCEPT:
    a. smoking a cigarette before going to bed
    b. getting out of bed if you are unable to fall asleep after a reasonable period
    c. vigorous exercise an hour before bedtime
    d. keeping the bedroom cold

    ANS: B   DIF: 1   REF: p. 294   OBJ: 10 TYPE: APP

98. Abnormal events such as nightmares, sleep terrors and sleepwalking that occur during sleep or during the twilight time between sleep and waking are classified as:
    a. parasomnias
    b. dyssomnias
    c. narcolepsy
    d. REM disorders

    ANS: A   DIF: 1   REF: p. 294   OBJ: 6 TYPE: FACT

99. Sleep terrors and sleepwalking generally occur:
    a. during REM sleep
    b. during twilight stages between sleep and waking
    c. during NREM sleep
    d. after some severe daytime stressor

    ANS: C   DIF: 3   REF: p. 295   OBJ: 7 TYPE: FACT

100. Joan is a six-year-old child who cries out in the middle of the night appearing frightened and inconsolable. Her parents are unable to comfort her during these episodes and Joan has no memory of the event in the morning. Joan appears to be experiencing:
    a. dyssomnia
    b. hypersomnia
    c. nightmares
    d. sleep terrors

    ANS: D   DIF: 1   REF: p. 295   OBJ: 6 TYPE: APP

101. One approach to successfully reducing the frequency of sleep terrors has been to:
    a. wake the child up during the attack
    b. make sure that the child is very tired before going to bed
    c. use scheduled awakenings to briefly awaken the child before an attack occurs
    d. all of these have been demonstrated to reduce the frequency and duration of sleep terrors

    ANS: C   DIF: 1   REF: p. 295   OBJ: 10 TYPE: APP

102. Sleepwalking is characterized by all of the following EXCEPT:
    a. acting out a dream
    b. occurrence during the deepest stage of sleep
    c. no memory of the sleepwalking event
    d. occurrence primarily in children

    ANS: A   DIF: 3   REF: p. 295   OBJ: 6 TYPE: FACT

103. Susan, who described her experience of anorexia on the "Abnormal Psychology Live" CD for Chapter 8, said that as soon as she eats, she:
   a. becomes anxious
   b. feels disgusting
   c. becomes depressed
   d. gains weight

   ANS: D   DIF: 3   REF: CD

104. On the "Abnormal Psychology Live" CD for Chapter 8, Susan mentioned that she often compensated for eating by purging. She indicated that her weight has been as low as 87 pounds. Her diagnosis is:
   a. anorexia
   b. bulimia
   c. pica
   d. ruminaiton disorder

   ANS: A   DIF: 3   REF: CD

105. Based on Susan's comments regarding her menstrual cycle on the "Abnormal Psychology Live" CD for Chapter 8, it seems reasonable to conclude that when she stops getting her period she is:
   a. afraid that she has hurt her health
   b. unable to deny that she has an eating disorder
   c. surprised at the effect she has on her body
   d. pleased because it means she has lost weight

   ANS: D   DIF: 3   REF: CD

106. According to the presentation regarding the stages of sleep on the "Abnormal Psychology Live" CD for Chapter 8, deepest sleep occurs in stage _____.
   a. 1
   b. 2
   c. 3
   d. 4

   ANS: D   DIF: 1   REF: CD

107. According to the presentation regarding the stages of sleep on the"Abnormal Psychology Live" CD for Chapter 8, a typical and average sleep pattern consists of a ____ minute REM and NREM cycle that repeats throughout the night.
   a. 30
   b. 60
   c. 90
   d. 120

   ANS: C   DIF: 3   REF: CD

ESSAY

1. Discuss the evidence that eating disorders like anorexia and bulimia are largely the result of culture and society.

2. Eating disorders such as anorexia and bulimia are generally "blamed" on culture and society. At the same time, there appears to be a genetic influence as well. Explain how culture and genetics may interact in the development of anorexia and bulimia.

3. In what ways do anorexia and bulimia patients tend to be similar and in what ways do they differ? Make certain to include similarities and differences in the symptoms of the disorders as well as the dysfunctional thoughts typically associated with each disorder.

4. The incidence of eating disorders such as anorexia and bulimia has been increasing over the past thirty years. What factors are believed to be responsible for this increase?

5. Describe the typical treatment goals and treatment methods implemented for bulimia patients.

6. Describe the typical treatment goals and treatment methods implemented for anorexia patients.

7. Anxiety and primary insomnia often co-exist in a "chicken and egg" cycle where it seems impossible to determine whether the anxiety is causing the sleep disorder or the sleep disorder is causing the anxiety. Describe the process of how anxiety and primary insomnia might interact within a patient. Why would it be difficult to determine which came first?   **WWW**

8. Describe the problems associated with using medications such as benzodiazepines as a treatment for primary insomnia.

9. Describe the psychological treatments that are generally used for the treatment of primary insomnia. List at least five "sleep hygiene" behaviors that are associated with improved sleep.

10. What are the differences between nightmares and sleep terrors? Describe what we know about sleep terrors, including the ages at which it generally occurs and how it has been treated.

11. Describe four approaches to the treatment of obesity. Explain the relationship of body mass index (BMI) to the appropriateness of each treatment approach. Describe the risks, benefits and effectiveness of each approach.

MULTIPLE CHOICE

1. What appears to be the main cause of anorexia and bulimia?
   a. perfectionistic mothers
   b. sociocultural factors
   c. genetic predisposition
   d. malnutrition

   ANS: B

2. _____ are disturbances in arousal and sleep stage transition while _____ are disturbances in the amount, timing, or quality of sleep.
   a. dyssomnias; parasomnias
   b. parasomnias; hypersomnia
   c. hypersomnia; dyssomnias
   d. parasomnias; dyssomnias

   ANS: D

3. _____ type anorexics rely on diets to lose weight; _____ type anorexics use vomiting or laxatives for this purpose.
   a. Non-purging; purging
   b. Non-purging; binge-eating/purging
   c. Restricting; purging
   d. Restricting; binge-eating/purging

   ANS: C

4. The most common sleep disorder is
   a. insomnia
   b. hypersomnia
   c. Nightmare Disorder
   d. Sleepwalking Disorder

   ANS: A

5. _____ has many specific types including delayed sleep phase, jet lag, and shift work types.
   a. Primary insomnia
   b. Secondary insomnia
   c. Sleeping Disorder
   d. Circadian Rhythm Sleep Disorder

   ANS: D

6. Biological treatments for dyssomnia include the use of
   a. benzodiazepine medications.
   b. tricyclic antidepressants.
   c. bright light to "trick" the brain into resetting the biological clock.
   d. all of the above

   ANS: D

7. The incidence of eating disorders
   a. has decreased since the 1960s.
   b. has increased dramatically since the 1950s.
   c. has not been determined.
   d. has remained constant for the past 50 years.

   ANS: B

8. Unlike most other disorders, the strongest contribution to the etiology of eating disorders seems to come from:
   a. personality factors
   b. psychological factors
   c. biological factors
   d. sociocultural factors

   ANS: D

9. One major difference between anorexia nervosa and bulimia nervosa is
   a. bulimics do not use exercise as a way to burn calories.
   b. anorexics actually lose too much weight.
   c. bulimics tend to be overweight.
   d. anorexics do not have psychological or medical consequences to their dieting.

   ANS: B

10. Individuals who experience marked distress due to binge eating, but do not engage in extreme compensatory behaviors, would meet the diagnostic criteria for _____.
    a. bulimia
    b. binge-eating disorder (BED)
    c. anorexia
    d. rumination disorder

    ANS: B

MULTIPLE CHOICE

1. At the beginning of the 20th century, the leading cause of death in the U.S. was:
   a. automobile accidents
   b. infectious diseases
   c. heart attacks
   d. suicides

   ANS: B   DIF: 3   REF: p. 303   OBJ: 1 TYPE: FACT

2. Currently, in the United States, some of the major contributing factors to illness and death are:
   a. viral and bacterial
   b. behavioral and psychological
   c. neurological and endocrinological
   d. pharmacological and hormonal

   ANS: B   DIF: 3   REF: p. 303   OBJ: 1 TYPE: FACT

3. In regard to infection by the herpes simplex virus I or II (which causes genital herpes), which of the following statements is incorrect?
   a. More than 50 million Americans have been infected by this virus.
   b. The increase in the number of cases of genital herpes is due solely to biological factors.
   c. Psychological and behavioral factors have contributed to the increased number of cases of genital herpes.
   d. According to research studies, stress plays a role in triggering recurrences of genital herpes.

   ANS: B   DIF: 3   REF: p. 303   OBJ: 1 TYPE: CON

4. Using the word psychosomatic to describe a disorder with an obvious physical component is considered misleading because:
   a. it gives the impression that psychological disorders like anxiety or depression do not have a biological component
   b. it assumes that the physical aspects of a disorder are less important than the psychological aspects
   c. it emphasizes the psychological symptoms of a disorder instead of the physical symptoms
   d. it gives the impression that biological disorders are not influenced by psychological factors

   ANS: A   DIF: 5   REF: p. 304   OBJ: 1 TYPE: APP

5. Which of the following factors are implicated in the cause of all disorders?
   a. biological only
   b. psychological only
   c. biological and psychological, but not social
   d. biological, psychological and social

   ANS: D   DIF: 3   REF: p. 304   OBJ: 1 TYPE: APP

6. What is the name of the new field of study that reflects the shift in focus from infectious disease to psychological/behavioral factors as causes of illness and death?
   a. behavioral medicine
   b. abnormal psychology
   c. medical psychology
   d. physical medicine

   ANS: A   DIF: 1   REF: p. 305   OBJ: 1 TYPE: FACT

7. Health psychology, a subfield of behavioral medicine, focuses on all of the following EXCEPT:
   a. psychological factors affecting health
   b. health policy
   c. health care systems
   d. psychosomatic effects on health

   ANS: D   DIF: 3   REF: p. 305   OBJ: 1 TYPE: CON

8. In which of the following ways do psychological and social factors influence health?
   a. they can affect basic biological processes resulting in illness and disease
   b. unhealthy lifestyles can increase the risk of developing physical disorders
   c. both of these
   d. neither of these

   ANS: C   DIF: 5   REF: p. 305   OBJ: 1 TYPE: CON

9. "AIDS, a disease of the immune system, is directly affected by stress. Stress may then promote the deadly progression of the disease." These two statements are an example of:
   a. psychological factors influencing biological processes
   b. biological factors influencing psychological processes
   c. both of these
   d. neither of these

   ANS: A   DIF: 3   REF: p. 305   OBJ: 1 TYPE: APP

10. According to the principles of health psychology, which of the following is the best protection against acquiring AIDS?
    a. getting an injection of the AIDS vaccine
    b. being treated for HIV before it develops into AIDS
    c. changing risky behaviors that can lead to disease acquisition
    d. deciding to be sexually abstinent after years of being sexually active

    ANS: C   DIF: 3   REF: p. 305   OBJ: 1 TYPE: APP/WWW

11. As an example of a behavioral pattern that leads to illness and death, smoking has been estimated to cause approximately _____ of all deaths.
    a. 2%
    b. 12%
    c. 19%
    d. 32%

    ANS: C   DIF: 1   REF: p. 305   OBJ: 1 TYPE: FACT

12. In 1936 Canadian researcher Hans Selye discovered that giving injections to laboratory rats caused them to develop ulcers. His finding led to a new area of study called:
   a. stress physiology
   b. stress psychology
   c. animal psychology
   d. psychosomatic pathology

   ANS: A   DIF: 3   REF: p. 306   OBJ: 2 TYPE: APP

13. In response to sustained stress, the body goes through several stages that together constitute the General Adaptation Syndrome, a concept proposed by researcher Hans Selye. This GAS consists of all the following stages EXCEPT:
   a. alarm
   b. resistance
   c. exhaustion
   d. death

   ANS: D   DIF: 1   REF: p. 306   OBJ: 2 TYPE: CON

14. According to the textbook, the physiological response of an individual to a stressor is called:
   a. adaptation
   b. fight or flight reaction
   c. stress
   d. a syndrome

   ANS: C   DIF: 1   REF: p. 306   OBJ: 2 TYPE: CON

15. Research has shown that increased levels of cortisol in response to stress may cause damage to parts of the:
   a. skeletal system
   b. brain
   c. lungs
   d. stomach

   ANS: B   DIF: 3   REF: p. 306   OBJ: 3 TYPE: FACT

16. Which of the following statements accurately describes a process in the activation of the HYPAC (hormonal) axis?
   a. The hippocampus secretes corticotropin releasing factor (CRF).
   b. CRF stimulates the thyroid gland.
   c. The pituitary gland (via the parasympathetic nervous system) activates the adrenal glands.
   d. The adrenal glands secrete the stress hormone cortisol.

   ANS: D   DIF: 5   REF: p. 306   OBJ: 3 TYPE: APP

17. Research has shown that excessive secretion of the stress hormone cortisol can result in cell death in the hippocampal region of the brain in cases of:
   a. substance abuse
   b. mania
   c. posttraumatic stress disorder
   d. AIDS

   ANS: C   DIF: 5   REF: p. 306   OBJ: 3 TYPE: APP

18. The final process in the activation of the HYPAC (hormonal) axis is:
    a. secretion of CRF by the hypothalamus
    b. stimulation of the pituitary gland by CRF
    c. activation of the adrenal gland by the pituitary gland
    d. secretion of cortisol by the adrenal gland

    ANS: D   DIF: 5   REF: p. 306   OBJ: 3 TYPE: CON

19. Continuous secretion of the stress hormone cortisol by the adrenal glands can lead to all of the following EXCEPT:
    a. damage to the hippocampus
    b. impaired functioning of the immune system
    c. muscle atrophy
    d. low blood pressure in the cardiovascular system

    ANS: D   DIF: 3   REF: p. 307   OBJ: 3 TYPE: APP

20. A longitudinal research study of 200 men (Vaillant, 1979) showed that those individuals who developed psychological disorders or who were highly stressed:
    a. became chronically ill at a higher rate that those who remained relatively well adjusted
    b. died at a significantly higher rate than men who remained free from psychological disorders
    c. both of these
    d. neither of these

    ANS: C   DIF: 5   REF: p. 307   OBJ: 4 TYPE: APP

21. Whether or not stress and/or anxiety develop in a stressful situation appears to be related to one's perceived sense of:
    a. happiness
    b. excitement
    c. control
    d. acceptance

    ANS: C   DIF: 3   REF: p. 308   OBJ: 4 TYPE: CON

22. Based on your knowledge of recent research studies, which of the following people would you predict is least likely to "catch" a cold following exposure to the virus?
    a. Karen, a very sociable woman, who has many good friends
    b. Mike, a very intelligent student, who understands complex information and concepts
    c. Judy, a very assertive individual, who frequently says exactly what's on her mind
    d. Marilyn, a very compulsive person, who likes to point out other people's mistakes

    ANS: A   DIF: 4   REF: p. 309   OBJ: 5 TYPE: APP/WWW

23. All of the following situations have been associated with lowered immune system functioning EXCEPT:
    a. marital conflict or relationship difficulties
    b. job loss
    c. death of a loved one
    d. pregnancy

    ANS: D   DIF: 1   REF: p. 309   OBJ: 5 TYPE: CON

24. Research findings have suggested that it might not be the stressful event itself that affects immune system functioning but rather the accompanying _____.
    a. dissociation
    b. isolation
    c. depression
    d. anger

    ANS: C   DIF: 3   REF: p. 310   OBJ: 5 TYPE: CON

25. The immune system is weakened in AIDS patients because the human immunodeficiency virus directly attacks the lymphocytes called:
    a. killer T cells
    b. T4 (helper cells)
    c. suppressor T cells
    d. B cells

    ANS: B   DIF: 3   REF: p. 311   OBJ: 5 TYPE: FACT

26. Contrary to the earlier belief that the brain and immune system operate independently of each other, scientists now know that there are nerve endings in many immune system tissues such as:
    a. bone marrow
    b. mucous membranes
    c. blood vessels
    d. muscles

    ANS: A   DIF: 1   REF: p. 311   OBJ: 5 TYPE: FACT

27. In 2003 it was estimated that the total number of people afflicted with HIV, the human immunodeficiency virus, was more than:
    a. 13 million
    b. 23 million
    c. 40 million
    d. 43 million

    ANS: C   DIF: 1   REF: p. 312   OBJ: 5 TYPE: FACT

28. Estimates from the United Nations regarding the prevalence of AIDS in southern Africa indicate that at least _____ of all 15 year-old children will eventually die of the disease.
    a. 10%
    b. 20%
    c. 30%
    d. 40%

    ANS: D   DIF: 3   REF: p. 312   OBJ: 8 TYPE: APP

29. AIDS is now treated with new combinations of drugs called "highly active antiretroviral therapy" (HAART), which:
   a. suppress the virus in people who are HIV positive
   b. cure AIDS by eliminating the virus from the body
   c. suppress immune system functioning
   d. are well tolerated and cause minimal side effects

   ANS: A   DIF: 4   REF: p. 312   OBJ: 5 TYPE: CON

30. Psychosocial interventions such as stress reduction techniques for chronically ill individuals are thought to affect the disease process via the immune system in all of the following ways EXCEPT:
   a. giving patients a greater sense of control
   b. helping patients utilize social support networks
   c. changing patients' negative cognitions
   d. helping patients realize that their sense of hopelessness is realistic

   ANS: D   DIF: 5   REF: p. 313   OBJ: 5 TYPE: CON

31. Brief psychosocial treatments aimed at reducing stress while increasing coping and control leads to improved immune system and prolonged life in:
   a. cancer patients
   b. AIDS patients
   c. both cancer and HIV/AIDS patients
   d. neither cancer nor HIV/AIDS patients

   ANS: C   DIF: 3   REF: p. 313   OBJ: 5 TYPE: APP

32. Which of the following does NOT describe an effective psychosocial intervention that has been reported in oncology research studies?
   a. use of psychological treatments that reduced pain and depression and enhanced feelings of well being
   b. use of videotapes and dolls that reduced children's stress and anxiety during medical procedures
   c. use of therapy sessions that temporarily prolonged life for breast cancer patients both during and after the intervention
   d. use of cognitive imaging techniques that temporarily rendered the AIDS virus inactive for brief periods

   ANS: D   DIF: 1   REF: p. 313-314   OBJ: 4 TYPE: APP

33. Unhealthy and/or risky behaviors that impact directly on the cardiovascular system may contribute to:
   a. strokes and high blood pressure only
   b. coronary heart disease only
   c. strokes, high blood pressure, and coronary heart disease
   d. reduced immunity to autoimmune diseases

   ANS: C   DIF: 1   REF: p. 316-317   OBJ: 5 TYPE: FACT

34. Various psychological factors have been used to explain individual variations in blood pressure including all of the following EXCEPT:
    a. coping style
    b. personality
    c. level of stress
    d. cognitive skills

    ANS: D   DIF: 1   REF: p. 317   OBJ: 6 TYPE: CON

35. During laboratory stress tests, which of the following individuals have been shown to have greater reactivity in their blood pressure?
    a. those with normal blood pressure whose parents had normal blood pressure
    b. those with normal blood presure whose parents had high blood pressure
    c. those with very low blood pressure whose parents had low blood pressure
    d. those with very low blood pressure whose parents had normal blood pressure

    ANS: C   DIF: 4   REF: p. 317   OBJ: 5 TYPE: APP

36. Since heart disease is the number one cause of death in the United States, it would be very important, in terms of prevention, to determine if:
    a. better medications can be found to treat heart disease
    b. changes in behavior, lifestyle and attitude can prevent heart attacks
    c. psychotherapy can help people adjust to having an artificial heart
    d. heart transplants can be made available to more patients

    ANS: B   DIF: 3   REF: p. 317   OBJ: 6 TYPE: APP/WWW

37. In reference to the clinical research studies focusing on factors that are implicated in heart disease, which of the following is an accurate statement?
    a. Males who displayed a Type A behavior pattern were less likely to develop coronary heart disease than females in the Type A group.
    b. Younger males in the Type A group were much less likely to develop coronary heart disease than older males in the Type A group.
    c. Both men and women with the Type A behavioral pattern were more likely to develop coronary heart disease than were non-Type A individuals.
    d. In comparison to "white collar" workers, men in lower socioeconomic positions were more likely to develop coronary heart disease.

    ANS: C   DIF: 5   REF: p. 318   OBJ: 6 TYPE: APP

38. In trying to determine if the Type A/Type B classifications are reliable and valid as predictors of heart disease, it becomes apparent that:
    a. not every individual shows distinctively Type A or Type B characteristics
    b. women are usually Type A and men are usually Type B
    c. interviews to assess people's personality characteristics are more reliable than questionnaires
    d. medical tests are the only valid predictors of heart disease

    ANS: A   DIF: 5   REF: p. 318   OBJ: 6 TYPE: APP/WWW

39. Which of the following is a correct match of medical condition and its definition?
    a. angina -- obstruction caused by build up of plaque in the arteries
    b. atherosclerosis -- deficiency of blood to a body part caused by narrowing of the arteries
    c. mycardial infarction -- death of heart tissue due to a completely clogged artery
    d. ischemia -- chest pain caused by partial obstruction of the arteries

    ANS: C   DIF: 1   REF: p. 317   OBJ: 6 TYPE: CON

40. Mr. V. is participating in a clinical research study that is investigating psychological factors that may influence the development of heart disease. When he is instructed to imagine a situation in which he was very angry, the sensors monitoring his heart reveal that:
    a. his heartbeat has slowed significantly
    b. his heart is pumping less efficiently
    c. the area around his heart has become swollen and inflamed
    d. he is having a "painless" heart attack

    ANS: B   DIF: 5   REF: p. 319   OBJ: 6 TYPE: APP

41. In regard to the condition termed "chronic pain," most researchers now agree that the cause of chronic pain and resulting high costs to our health care system are primarily:
    a. psychological
    b. social
    c. both psychological and social
    d. neither psychological nor social

    ANS: C   DIF: 3   REF: p. 320   OBJ: 7 TYPE: CON

42. All of the following are examples of "pain behaviors" EXCEPT:
    a. complaining about pain to others
    b. grimacing
    c. positional changes (while sitting or walking)
    d. suffering in silence

    ANS: D   DIF: 1   REF: p. 320   OBJ: 7 TYPE: CON

43. Miss T. was slightly injured in an accident but has fully recovered. Although she has been given medical clearance to go back to work and resume her normal activities, she maintains that she is still suffering from pain. You would correctly assess Miss T. as someone who probably has:
    a. adequate coping skills
    b. strong family and social support
    c. no history of anxiety and/or depression
    d. a disability claim pending

    ANS: D   DIF: 3   REF: p. 320   OBJ: 7 TYPE: APP

44. Based on findings from clinical research, treatment programs for chronic pain focus primarily on:
    a. surgical procedures
    b. herbal remedies
    c. psychological factors
    d. experimental procedures for pain relief

    ANS: C   DIF: 1   REF: p. 321   OBJ: 7 TYPE: FACT

45. Which of the following is an example of the phenomenon known as "operant" control of pain behavior?
    a. Kate's family has always been critical and demanding. Since her accident, though, family members have become caring and sympathetic.
    b. Kim is recovering from a broken leg. Although she is walking on crutches, she has been trying to be as independent as possible.
    c. Kinesha had to have a finger amputated after it was partially severed in a slicing accident. Since she feels discomfort in the missing finger, she has been diagnosed with "phantom limb" pain.
    d. Kyomi suffers from chronic back pain. However, she rarely complains about the pain to others and tries to keep her facial expressions from showing that she is in pain.

    ANS: A   DIF: 5   REF: p. 321   OBJ: 7 TYPE: APP

46. In the phenomenon known as "operant" control of pain, the pain behaviors manifested by an individual are determined by:
    a. the type of injury
    b. social consequences
    c. the side effects of medications
    d. the patient's reaction to treatment

    ANS: B   DIF: 3   REF: p. 321   OBJ: 7 TYPE: CON

47. Researchers who study the clinical experience of pain have determined that pain is:
    a. entirely due to physical causes
    b. entirely due to psychological causes
    c. neither entirely physical, nor entirely psychological
    d. always due to unknown and unpredictable factors

    ANS: C   DIF: 3   REF: p. 321   OBJ: 7 TYPE: APP

48. Which of the following is NOT an example of the complex interaction of physical and psychological factors in the experience of pain?
    a. the gate control theory of pain
    b. phantom limb pain
    c. chronic pain
    d. delusional pain

    ANS: D   DIF: 3   REF: p. 320-321   OBJ: 7 TYPE: CON

49. The "natural" opioids called endorphins or enkephalins act like neurotransmitters to:
    a. increase awareness of pain
    b. shut down the sensation of pain
    c. cause a "natural" addiction
    d. relieve the pain caused by a heroin overdose

    ANS: B   DIF: 1   REF: p. 321   OBJ: 7 TYPE: FACT

50. Endogenous opioids have been implicated in a variety of psychopathological conditions including:
    a. eating disorders
    b. phobias
    c. obsessive-compulsive disorder
    d. personality disorders

    ANS: A   DIF: 3   REF: p. 321   OBJ: 7 TYPE: CON

51. Regarding gender differences in the experience of pain, women suffer more frequently than men from all of the following EXCEPT:
    a. migraine headaches
    b. arthritis
    c. menstrual cramps
    d. backache

    ANS: D   DIF: 1   REF: p. 322   OBJ: 7 TYPE: FACT

52. Females may have an "extra" pain-regulating pathway focused on relieving pain associated with the reproductive system. One implication of this biological gender difference is that:
    a. men need more pain relief than women following surgical procedures
    b. women do not need pain relief during childbirth
    c. males and females may benefit from different kinds of medications and different kinds of pain management
    d. the psychological experience of pain is the same for men and women

    ANS: C   DIF: 5   REF: p. 322   OBJ: 7 TYPE: APP

53. In the mid-19th century, symptoms of fatigue, vague aches and pains, low-grade fever, and lack of energy were attributed to a disorder called:
    a. neurasthenia
    b. neurosis
    c. hysteria
    d. somatic syndrome

    ANS: A   DIF: 1   REF: p. 322   OBJ: 8 TYPE: FACT/WWW

54. The same symptoms that were diagnosed in the 19th century as a condition called neurasthenia are currently referred to as:
    a. somatization disorder
    b. chronic fatigue syndrome
    c. wasting disease
    d. psychogenic pain disorder

    ANS: B   DIF: 1   REF: p. 322   OBJ: 8 TYPE: CON

55. At various times the symptoms of the disorder known as chronic fatigue syndrome were attributed to all of the following EXCEPT:
    a. viral infection
    b. environmental toxins
    c. stress
    d. brain atrophy

    ANS: D   DIF: 3   REF: p. 322   OBJ: 8 TYPE: FACT

56. In regard to the gender ratio of neurasthenia, a 19th century ailment, and chronic fatigue syndrome, a 20th century condition, it is accurate to state that:
    a. both conditions are/were diagnosed more frequently in women
    b. both conditions are/were diagnosed more frequently in men
    c. the conditions are/were diagnosed with equal frequency in men and women
    d. more females were diagnosed with neurasthenia, but more men are diagnosed with chronic fatigue syndrome

    ANS: A   DIF: 3   REF: p. 322   OBJ: 8 TYPE: FACT

57. A treatment for chronic fatigue syndrome developed by Michael Sharpe includes all of the following EXCEPT:
    a. medication
    b. increased activity
    c. regulated rest periods
    d. breathing exercises

    ANS: A   DIF: 1   REF: p. 322   OBJ: 8 TYPE: CON

58. A controlled research study investigating the effects of a cognitive-behavioral treatment for chronic fatigue syndrome resulted in improvement on:
    a. measures of fatigue
    b. measures of illness belief
    c. both measures of fatigue and measures of illness belief
    d. neither measures of fatigue nor measures of illness belief

    ANS: C   DIF: 3   REF: p. 323   OBJ: 8 TYPE: APP

59. All of the following are psychosocial treatments that have been developed for physical disorders and pain EXCEPT:
    a. biofeedback
    b. hypnosis
    c. relaxation procedures
    d. acupuncture

    ANS: D   DIF: 3   REF: p. 324   OBJ: 9 TYPE: CON

60. The procedure known as biofeedback involves a process by which a person is first helped to become aware of his/her:
    a. physiological functions
    b. psychological state of mind
    c. negative thoughts
    d. level of pain

    ANS: A   DIF: 3   REF: p. 324   OBJ: 9 TYPE: CON

61. Physiological functions that are a focus of biofeedback procedures include all of the following EXCEPT:
    a. EEG rhythms ("brainwaves")
    b. heart rate
    c. swallowing
    d. muscle tension

    ANS: C   DIF: 3   REF: p. 324   OBJ: 9 TYPE: CON

62. In the 1960s, Neal Miller, using _____ with animals, discovered the first experimental evidence that physiological functions were subject to voluntary control.
    a. classical conditioning
    b. physical retraining
    c. operant conditioning
    d. obedience training

    ANS: C   DIF: 3   REF: p. 324   OBJ: 9 TYPE: APP

63. In biofeedback procedures clinicians use physiological monitoring equipment to make the responses _____ to the patient.
    a. visible
    b. audible
    c. visible and/or audible
    d. tactile

    ANS: C   DIF: 1   REF: p. 324   OBJ: 9 TYPE: CON

64. It has been suggested that biofeedback relieves the pain of tension headaches because it "teaches people to relax," but it is more likely that:
    a. the patients whose pain is seemingly relieved by biofeedback are probably also taking aspirin or Tylenol
    b. the biofeedback training gives patients a sense of control over their headache pain
    c. biofeedback has a "numbing effect" because it affects the nerve endings in the somatic nervous system
    d. patients experience a placebo effect because the headache pain returns once the biofeedback sessions are completed

    ANS: B   DIF: 5   REF: p. 325   OBJ: 9 TYPE: APP/WWW

65. Recent clinical studies indicate that it is a good pain relieving strategy to use biofeedback in conjunction with:
    a. medication
    b. relaxation procedures
    c. a placebo
    d. psychotherapy

ANS: B   DIF: 1   REF: p. 325   OBJ: 9 TYPE: APP

66. In the 1970s Herbert Benson developed a brief relaxation procedure that involved focusing on a:
    a. word
    b. photo
    c. person
    d. musical note

ANS: A   DIF: 1   REF: p. 325   OBJ: 9 TYPE: FACT

67. Comprehensive pain management programs usually include programs for teaching patients about:
    a. relaxation
    b. meditation
    c. both meditation and relaxation
    d. neither meditation nor relaxation

ANS: C   DIF: 3   REF: p. 325   OBJ: 9 TYPE: CON

68. A decrease in the activity of stress hormones and certain neurotransmitters appears to occur during:
    a. sleep
    b. meditation
    c. biofeedback
    d. psychotherapy

ANS: B   DIF: 3   REF: p. 325   OBJ: 9 TYPE: CON

69. Although the improvement is only moderate, relaxation techniques have been shown to have a positive effect on:
    a. headaches
    b. hypertension (high blood pressure)
    c. pain
    d. all of these

ANS: D   DIF: 1   REF: p. 325   OBJ: 9 TYPE: CON

70. In keeping daily records of the stressful events in their lives, patients in pain management programs are taught to be very specific about all of the following EXCEPT:
    a. the actual time of day that they experience stress
    b. what seems to "trigger the stress"
    c. how they attempted to control the stress
    d. the level of intensity of the stress

ANS: C   DIF: 3   REF: p. 325   OBJ: 10 TYPE: APP

71. In a stressful events record, clients in a pain management program are asked to record:
    a. somatic symptoms only
    b. thoughts that occur during stress but not somatic symptoms
    c. thoughts that occur during stress as well as somatic symptoms
    d. intensity of the stress, but not thoughts or somatic symptoms

    ANS: C   DIF: 1   REF: p. 325   OBJ: 10 TYPE: CON

72. Cognitive therapy is used in stress management programs to help clients learn to do all of the following EXCEPT:
    a. develop more realistic appraisals and attitudes
    b. identify unrealistic negative thoughts
    c. tell off people they don't like as a way of reducing stress
    d. assert themselves in an appropriate way in stressful situations

    ANS: C   DIF: 3   REF: p. 327   OBJ: 10 TYPE: CON

73. For coping with chronic pain, chronic fatigue syndrome, and hypertension, _____ is considered generally more effective than either _____ or _____.
    a. a stress management program; biofeedback; relaxation techniques
    b. biofeedback; relaxation techniques; a stress management program
    c. relaxation techniques; biofeedback; a stress management program
    d. relaxation, biofeedback and stress management programs are all considered equally effective

    ANS: A   DIF: 5   REF: p. 327   OBJ: 10 TYPE: APP

74. Individuals who are high users of pain relieving medications are _____ to benefit from pain management programs than less frequent users.
    a. more likely
    b. less likely
    c. equally likely
    d. unable

    ANS: B   DIF: 3   REF: p. 327   OBJ: 10 TYPE: APP

75. In a comprehensive headache treatment program, people who were low users of analgesic medications achieved at least a _____ reduction in headache pain.
    a. 25%
    b. 50%
    c. 75%
    d. 99%

    ANS: B   DIF: 1   REF: p. 327   OBJ: 10 TYPE: FACT

76. Jon W. has just been diagnosed with cancer. His initial response is to deny the seriousness of his condition. This type of coping mechanism:
    a. will enable him to develop better coping mechanisms later
    b. is never psychologically helpful
    c. doesn't really help him endure the initial shock any more easily
    d. results in higher levels of corticosteroids (stress hormones)

    ANS: A   DIF: 3   REF: p. 328   OBJ: 8 TYPE: APP/WWW

77. Which of the following is NOT one of the three of the most common behaviors that put us at risk for physical disorders?
    a. unhealthy eating habits
    b. lack of exercise
    c. smoking
    d. watching too much TV

    ANS: D   DIF: 1   REF: p. 328   OBJ: 1 TYPE: CON

78. According to the textbook, the leading cause of death for children and adults (under age 45) is:
    a. cancer
    b. injuries
    c. infectious diseases
    d. genetic defects

    ANS: B   DIF: 1   REF: p. 328   OBJ: 10 TYPE: FACT

79. In comparison to all the other causes combined, injuries are _____ as likely to cause death in children.
    a. twice
    b. six times
    c. not
    d. equally

    ANS: B   DIF: 1   REF: p. 328   OBJ: 10 TYPE: FACT

80. Injury prevention programs have proven effective in teaching children about all of the following EXCEPT:
    a. escaping fires
    b. crossing streets
    c. riding bikes safely
    d. properly extinguishing cigarettes

    ANS: D   DIF: 1   REF: p. 329   OBJ: 10 TYPE: CON

81. Which is an accurate statement regarding injury prevention programs for children?
    a. most communities have injury prevention programs
    b. repeated warnings have been effective in preventing or reducing the number of injuries
    c. children who participated in safety skills programs remembered what they had learned even after the programs were over
    d. injury prevention programs have been ineffective in changing children's behavior

    ANS: C   DIF: 5   REF: p. 329   OBJ: 10 TYPE: APP/WWW

82. The only effective prevention strategy currently available for reducing the spread of AIDS appears to be:
    a. a vaccine
    b. medications
    c. changing high-risk behavior
    d. educating people about the risk of the disease

    ANS: C   DIF: 3   REF: p. 329   OBJ: 10 TYPE: APP

83. In regard to the epidemic of AIDS in Africa, an individual is most likely to become HIV positive following:
   a. heterosexual sex with an infected partner
   b. homosexual sex with an infected partner
   c. repeated injections with unsterilized needles
   d. close non-sexual contact with an infected person

   ANS: A   DIF: 5   REF: p. 329   OBJ: TYPE: APP

84. Steven and Diane, two young adults who live in different cities and do not know each other, have learned recently that they are HIV positive following sexual intercourse with an infected partner. What changes in their behavior are most likely to occur in the future?
   a. Both Steven and Diane will now abstain from sex completely.
   b. Steven will abstain from sex, but Diane will continue to have sex.
   c. Both Steven and Diane will continue to have unprotected sex.
   d. Both Steven and Diane will be sure to tell future sexual partners that they are HIV positive.

   ANS: C   DIF: 5   REF: p. 329   OBJ: 10 TYPE: APP

85. Carla and Carlos have recently learned that they are HIV positive. According to research studies involving people who are HIV positive, what is most likely to occur?
   a. Carla will now have sex only if her partner uses a condom.
   b. Carlos will abstain from sex completely.
   c. Both Carla and Carlos will stop sharing needles with other drug users.
   d. Neither Carlos nor Carla is likely to change any of their previous behaviors.

   ANS: D   DIF: 3   REF: p. 329   OBJ: 10 TYPE: APP

86. When high-risk individuals are given educational and informational pamphlets about ways to reduce their chances of becoming HIV positive, they typically:
   a. change their high risk behaviors
   b. do not change their high risk behaviors
   c. abstain from unprotected sex
   d. notify previous sex partners of their HIV condition

   ANS: B   DIF: 5   REF: p. 329   OBJ: 10 TYPE: APP/WWW

87. In four cities where community based behavior change programs were carried out for individuals at high risk for HIV/AIDS, results indicated that:
   a. risky sexual practices were substantially reduced
   b. risky sexual practices actually increased
   c. drug addicts stopped sharing needles
   d. providing information and education about HIV/AIDS was just as effective as a behavior change program

   ANS: A   DIF: 3   REF: p. 329   OBJ: 10 TYPE: APP

88. Which of the following is <u>least</u> likely to bring about changes in "risky" behaviors for individuals who are at risk for HIV/AIDS?
   a. a comprehensive behavior change program
   b. cognitive-behavioral self-management training
   c. the development of an effective social support network
   d. distribution of educational and informational pamphlets about the disease

   ANS: D   DIF: 5   REF: p. 329   OBJ: 10 TYPE: CON

89. Which of the following was NOT one of the procedures or types of information used as part of San Francisco's 1990 community-level program to reduce new cases of HIV infection?
   a. personal detailed assessment of HIV risk for each individual
   b. instructions on how to clean needles
   c. classes and videos to demonstrate safe sex skills
   d. discussions of the moral and religious consequences of being HIV positive

   ANS: D   DIF: 3   REF: p. 330   OBJ: 8 TYPE: APP

90. Which of the following factors does NOT accurately represent the circumstances regarding women and HIV/AIDS?
   a. Women frequently do not consider themselves at risk because most media coverage of the AIDS epidemic has focused on gay white males.
   b. Most research on the spread of AIDS has ignored the disease in women.
   c. Women are contracting AIDS approximately four times faster than men.
   d. The highest age of risk for women is after age 25.

   ANS: D   DIF: 5   REF: p. 330   OBJ: 10 TYPE: APP

91. Regarding the age ranges for the risk of HIV/AIDS, which of the following statements is accurate?
   a. For women the highest risk is between 15 and 25.
   b. For women the highest risk is during their late 20s and early 30s.
   c. The age range for risk is younger for men than for women.
   d. The age ranges for risk are the same for both males and females.

   ANS: A   DIF: 3   REF: p. 330   OBJ: 8 TYPE: FACT

92. In regard to setting up behavior change programs that address the HIV/AIDS epidemic, which of the following is an accurate statement?
   a. The same kinds of programs can be set up for both females and males.
   b. Women and men need different types of programs because their risk factors are different.
   c. Women are not acquiring HIV/AIDS as fast as men are.
   d. Media attention and even research has focused on women with AIDS and largely ignored men.

   ANS: B   DIF: 3   REF: p. 330   OBJ: 10 TYPE: APP

93. Which is a type of circumstance in which women put themselves at risk for HIV/AIDS infection differently from men?
    a. having unprotected sex with partners whose sexual history is unknown
    b. using contaminated needles when injecting illegal drugs
    c. becoming prostitutes in response to economic deprivation
    d. having sex with multiple partners

    ANS: C   DIF: 3   REF: p. 330   OBJ: 10 TYPE: APP/WWW

94. Your textbook reports on a behavioral change program to address the high rate of smoking in China. This was an important study for several reasons including the fact that:
    a. the number of people who smoke in China equals the entire population of the United States
    b. almost 100% of the women in China smoke
    c. males and females in China have equally high rates of smoking
    d. the types of cigarettes smoked in China are more potent than in the U.S.

    ANS: A   DIF: 1   REF: p. 330   OBJ: 10 TYPE: FACT

95. A massive antismoking campaign in China in 1989 involved:
    a. bonuses to employees who quit smoking
    b. wives threatening divorce of their husbands didn't stop smoking
    c. children reporting to their schools on their fathers' smoking habits
    d. married couples' written agreements to stop smoking

    ANS: C   DIF: 3   REF: p. 330-331   OBJ: 10 TYPE: FACT

96. In 1989 health professionals in China began a massive antismoking effort in several cities that involved children whose fathers smoked. As part of this effort, all of the following are accurate statements EXCEPT:
    a. schoolchildren were given antismoking literature and questionnaires to take home to their fathers
    b. children wrote letters to their fathers asking them to quit smoking
    c. children submitted monthly reports on their fathers' smoking habits to their schools
    d. photos of the fathers who continued smoking were published in the school newspapers

    ANS: D   DIF: 3   REF: p. 330-331   OBJ: 10 TYPE: APP

97. In the massive antismoking campaign in China in 1989, the results indicated that _____ of the 10,000 fathers in the intervention group quit smoking for at least six months in comparison to a control group of 10,000 in which only _____ quit smoking.
    a. 1%; 0.1%
    b. 12%; 0.2%
    c. 22%; 2.2%
    d. 50%; 25%

    ANS: B   DIF: 1   REF: p. 331   OBJ: 10 TYPE: FACT

98. One of the most successful efforts to reduce risk factors for a medical condition involved three entire communities in California in which residents received different types of interventions or no intervention at all (for the community that served as the control group). The targeted condition in this effort was:
a. diabetes
b. cancer
c. heart disease
d. obesity

ANS: C   DIF: 1   REF: p. 331   OBJ: 10 TYPE: APP

99. A new medical subspecialty called **psychoncology** reflects the influence of psychological factors in the development and progression of:
a. cancer
b. coronary heart disease
c. eating disorders
d. high blood pressure

ANS: A   DIF: 1   REF: p. 313   OBJ: 8 TYPE: CON

100. A new medical specialty called **psychoneuroimmunology** reflects the relationship among:
a. psychological factors including stress
b. the immune system
c. the nervous system
d. all of these

ANS: D   DIF: 1   REF: p. 311   OBJ: 5 TYPE: CON

101. In the "Abnormal Psychology Live CD" for Chapter 9, a young man who is HIV positive talks about his own personal coping mechanisms including:
a. being inspired by a friend who was also   c. maintaining full-time employment
   HIV positive
b. discontinuing medication during the times   d. keeping busy with artwork
   that he feels better

ANS: D   REF: CD

102. In the "Abnormal Psychology Live" CD for Chapter 9, the man with HIV is no longer able to:

a. walk without a cane   c. write (cannot hold a pen or pencil)
b. read without a magnifying glass   d. speak intelligibly

ANS: A   REF: CD

ESSAY

1. Define and describe the new fields of behavioral medicine and health psychology. What are the differences between them? Why did these specialties not exist previously?

2. The field of stress physiology began with the research of Hans Selye. Explain how his findings developed into an understanding of the physical impact of stress.

3. Explore the relationship between stress and the immune system. What is the HYPAC axis? What are stress hormones? Is there a "lab" test to measure stress levels in human beings?

4. Discuss how psychological factors, including negative cognitions, affect immune system functioning. Give examples of physical conditions that are considered stress-related.

5. Discuss the role that stress plays in the progression of AIDS and cancer. Give examples of research studies that demonstrate the positive impact of reduced stress levels on these very serious conditions.

6. Discuss why stress is often implicated as a factor in cardiovascular disease. Define Type A personality; discuss research regarding its validity.   **WWW**

7. Explore how changes in attitudes and life style behaviors impact on illness and death. Give examples of behaviors that are known to impact negatively on health. Why are individuals resistant to behavioral change?

8. Discuss chronic fatigue syndrome and chronic pain. Relate CFS to the condition known as neurasthenia. What psychological factors are thought to maintain chronic pain?

9. Describe the use of biofeedback, meditation and relaxation techniques in the management of stress-related disorders. How effective are these treatments for stress management and pain relief?

10. Discuss prevention and intervention programs. What medical conditions and/or behaviors are targeted? Compare injury prevention programs with the more typical information and warnings.

11. Discuss how Orel, the man with HIV on the "Abnormal Psych Live" CD, developed strategies to enable him to cope with his condition. Compare and contrast coping with HIV to coping with other chronic conditions.

REF: CD

MULTIPLE CHOICE

1. It was initially assumed that emotional disorders seemed to make us more susceptible to developing physiological disorders. Current evidence has
   a. supported this initial assumption.
   b. been inconclusive.
   c. suggested that depression lowers immune system functioning.
   d. suggested that depression raises immune system functioning.

   ANS: C

2. Biofeedback is
   a. a process of stress reduction requiring subjects to tense muscles in order to facilitate better relaxation.
   b. used by farm animals to store and recycle unused food for later consumption.
   c. a process through which patients monitor their own physiological functions.
   d. the process through which neurotransmitters are released into synaptic clefts.

   ANS: C

3. Studies of links between Type A behavior patterns and coronary heart disease (CHD) have revealed which of the following?
   a. a positive relationship between Type A behavior and CHD
   b. no relationship between Type A behavior and CHD
   c. a negative relationship between Type A behavior and CHD
   d. all of the above

   ANS: A

4. What are the potential effects of increased levels of stress hormones in the stress response?
   a. among the aged, deficits in problem-solving skills and dementia may develop
   b. the ability of the hippocampus to "turn off" the body's stress response may be compromised
   c. the high level of stress hormones will cause the stress response to stop
   d. both a and b

   ANS: D

5. Studies involving group therapy and cancer suggest that
   a. social support within groups has had little effect in increasing the life span of terminally ill cancer patients in the groups.
   b. patients in group therapy may be more compliant with medical treatment.
   c. social support within the group may result in a high sense of self-efficacy among the members.
   d. both b and c are true.

   ANS: D

6. Every year during finals week in December, Judy came down with a severe cold. It was the only cold she got each year. Which is the most likely explanation for this pattern of colds?
   a. Cold viruses are present only in December.
   b. The stress of final exams left Judy more susceptible to colds.
   c. Judy's roommate caught a cold every December and gave it to Judy.
   d. There is no rational explanation. It is just a random pattern of colds.

   ANS: B

7. The main branches of the immune system are the
   a. B cells and the leukocytes.
   b. humoral and the macrophages.
   c. humoral and the cellular.
   d. bacteria, viruses, and parasites.
   e. cellular and the digital.

   ANS: C

8. Psychoneuroimmunology is
   a. the study of psychological influences on the neurological responding implicated in the immune response.
   b. the study of the effects of immune-suppressing drugs on psychological functioning and behavior.
   c. feelings of stress arising from relationships with other people.
   d. an immune disorder associated with decreased activity of macrophages.

   ANS: A

9. The term "psychosomatic medicine" is no longer in favor because
   a. it implies that the other disorders that are studied (those without a more obvious physical component) do not have a strong biological component.
   b. it is hard to spell.
   c. it implies a strong psychological component for somatic illnesses.
   d. "neurasthenia" is the preferred term.

   ANS: A

10. Reports from war veterans wounded in combat that they did not feel pain at the time of injury are evidence that
    a. there is a significant psychological component to the experience of pain.
    b. war veterans are reluctant to report feeling pain for fear that they won't appear brave.
    c. they probably were not injured very badly.
    d. both b and c

    ANS: A

MULTIPLE CHOICE

1. Recent surveys of sexual practices in Western countries have suggested that the percentage of men engaging in homosexual activity is:
    a. about 10%, which is the same as estimated by the 1953 Kinsey surveys
    b. about 10%, which is higher than estimated by the 1953 Kinsey surveys
    c. under 5%, which is significantly lower that the estimates of the 1953 Kinsey surveys
    d. between 5% and 10%, which is the same as estimated by the 1953 Kinsey surveys

    ANS: C   DIF: 3   REF: p. 338   OBJ: 2 TYPE: FACT

2. According to a 1989 survey conducted with college age women (DeBuono, et al., 1990) the percentage of sexually active college age women who reported regular use of condoms was:
    a. almost 100%
    b. just over 40%
    c. approximately 75%
    d. about 12%

    ANS: B   DIF: 1   REF: p. 338   OBJ: 1 TYPE: FACT

3. According to recent surveys (Diokno et al., 1990), the following statement is true regarding sexual activity of the elderly:
    a. very few individuals remain sexually active beyond age 70
    b. more than half of the individuals over age 70 remain sexually active
    c. 80% of males and 50% of women aged 75 - 79 remained sexually active
    d. 50% of males and 36% of women aged 75 - 79 remained sexually active

    ANS: D   DIF: 3   REF: p. 338   OBJ: 3 TYPE: FACT

4. The largest difference in sexual behavior for men versus women is that:
    a. men are more likely to engage in premarital sex
    b. women are more likely to engage in premarital sex
    c. men are more likely to masturbate
    d. women are more likely to masturbate

    ANS: C   DIF: 1   REF: p. 339   OBJ: 1 TYPE: FACT/WWW

5. Differences in male and female attitudes toward sexuality have generally _____ over the past 40 years.
    a. decreased
    b. increased
    c. remained the same
    d. disappeared completely

    ANS: A   DIF: 1   REF: p. 339   OBJ: 1 TYPE: FACT

6. Data from research studies on gender differences in human sexuality (Peplau, 2003) reflect all of the following themes EXCEPT:
   a. men show more sexual desire and arousal than women
   b. men emphasize committed relationships more than women
   c. men's self-concept is characterized in part by power, aggression and independence
   d. women's sexual beliefs are more influenced by cultural, social and situational factors

   ANS: B   DIF: 3   REF: p. 340   OBJ: 1 TYPE: CON/WWW

7. In Sweden, where attitudes toward sexuality are somewhat more permissive than they are in the United States, the percentage of Swedish women reporting use of contraception during their first sexual intercourse was:
   a. significantly higher than it was for American women
   b. significantly lower than it was for American women
   c. approximately the same as it was for American women
   d. just about 100%

   ANS: A   DIF: 3   REF: p. 341   OBJ: 1 TYPE: FACT

8. Research regarding sexual orientation suggests that homosexuality is:
   a. purely genetic
   b. completely caused by biological factors
   c. based on learning and choice only
   d. influenced by biological/genetic, psychological and social factors

   ANS: D   DIF: 1   REF: p. 342   OBJ: 2 TYPE: CON

9. Joe is homosexual and has an identical (monozgyotic) twin named Sam. The following statement is true:
   a. Sam is more likely than the general population to be homosexual
   b. Sam is no more likely than the general population to be homosexual
   c. Sam is homosexual also
   d. Sam is only likely to become homosexual if Joe is a positive role model

   ANS: A   DIF: 1   REF: p. 342   OBJ: 2 TYPE: APP

10. The percentage of identical (monozygotic) twins in which both twins are homosexual is 50%. This means:
    a. homosexuality is determined by genetics
    b. genes are only one influence for sexual orientation
    c. the environment determines sexual orientation
    d. genes are not an influence for sexual orientation

    ANS: B   DIF: 1   REF: p. 341   OBJ: 2 TYPE: CON

11. Gender identity disorder is diagnosed when:
    a. a person's physical gender is inconsistent with the person's gender identity
    b. an individual receives sexual pleasure from cross-dressing
    c. an individual is born with ambiguous genitalia
    d. all of these are correct

    ANS: A   DIF: 1   REF: p. 342   OBJ: 4 TYPE: FACT

12. Of the following, the individual who should be diagnosed with gender identity disorder is:
    a. Joe, who gets sexually aroused by wearing women's bras
    b. Lisa, who is gay and has many traditional masculine traits
    c. Mark, who feels like a woman trapped in a man's body
    d. Sid, who can only become sexually aroused while dressed like a woman

    ANS: C   DIF: 1   REF: p. 342   OBJ: 4 TYPE: APP/WWW

13. The incidence of gender identity disorder is:
    a. very low, with far less than 1% of the population affected
    b. very low, with approximately 1% of the population affected
    c. moderately low, with approximately 1% to 5% of the population affected
    d. moderate, with about 5% or more of the population affected

    ANS: A   DIF: 1   REF: p. 343   OBJ: 4 TYPE: FACT

14. The new approaches to understanding and treating intersexed individuals that have been proposed recently (Fausto-Sterling, 2000) are based on the concept of "five sexes" which include all of the following EXCEPT:
    a. "herms"
    b. "merms" and "ferms"
    c. males and females
    d. "andros" and "estros"

    ANS: D   DIF: 1   REF: p. 345   OBJ: 4 TYPE: CON

15. The psychosocial treatment of Joe, a young man with gender identity disorder, described in your textbook suggests that:
    a. gender identity can be influenced with therapy but sexual orientation will not change
    b. sexual orientation can be influenced by therapy but gender identity will not change
    c. both gender identity and sexual orientation can be influenced by therapy
    d. sex reassignment surgery is the only treatment option for gender identity disorder

    ANS: C   DIF: 3   REF: p. 346   OBJ: 4 TYPE: CON

16. Sexual dysfunctions are:
    a. more common in heterosexuals than homosexuals
    b. more common in homosexuals than heterosexuals
    c. equally common in heterosexuals and homosexuals
    d. generally not reported, so little is known about their incidence

    ANS: C   DIF: 5   REF: p. 346   OBJ: 5 TYPE: FACT

17. The incidence of sexual dysfunctions in the United States is approximately:
    a. 43% of women and 31% of men
    b. under 10% for both men and women
    c. 43% of men and 31% of women
    d. 31% for both men and women

    ANS: A   DIF: 3   REF: p. 347   OBJ: 5 TYPE: FACT

18. Of the following, the individual most likely to receive an appropriate diagnosis of hypoactive sexual desire disorder is:
    a. Sue, who fantasizes about sex often but is so exhausted when she gets home that she only has sex about twice a month
    b. John, who thinks about sex, but does not have sexual relations because he thinks it is morally wrong to do so unless the goal is procreation
    c. Mary, whose husband wishes she thought about sex more often because she seems satisfied having sex a few times a month
    d. Fred, who has sex at least once a week to satisfy his wife, but would prefer to be left alone since he is rarely interested in sex

    ANS: D   DIF: 5   REF: p. 348   OBJ: 6 TYPE: APP

19. The individual with the greatest likelihood of hypoactive sexual desire disorder is a(n):
    a. 18-year-old male
    b. 30-year-old male
    c. 30-year-old female
    d. 45-year-old female

    ANS: C   DIF: 5   REF: p. 348   OBJ: 6 TYPE: APP

20. Just the thought of sex makes Harry anxious. When exposed to sexual images, he reports feeling disgust. Harry would most likely be diagnosed with:
    a. hypoactive sexual desire disorder
    b. hyperactive sexual desire disorder
    c. sexual aversion disorder
    d. gender identity disorder

    ANS: C   DIF: 3   REF: p. 349   OBJ: 6 TYPE: APP

21. Approximately 25% of the patients with sexual aversion disorder also suffer from associated:
    a. panic attacks
    b. paraphilias
    c. hypoactive sexual desire disorder
    d. gender identity disorder

    ANS: A   DIF: 5   REF: p. 349   OBJ: 6 TYPE: FACT

22. The main feature of sexual arousal disorders is:
    a. lack of desire for sex despite normal physical sexual response
    b. sexual arousal to inappropriate stimuli
    c. the experience of pain during sex
    d. lack of physical sexual response despite desire for sex

    ANS: D   DIF: 1   REF: p. 349   OBJ: 6 TYPE: CON/WWW

23. Sexual arousal disorders are diagnosed when there is an:
    a. inability to achieve or maintain an erection in males and a lack of desire for sex in females
    b. inability to achieve or maintain an erection in males and a lack of orgasm in females
    c. inability to achieve orgasm for either gender despite erection in males and lubrication in females
    d. inability to achieve or maintain an erection in males and a lack of lubrication in females

    ANS: D   DIF: 1   REF: p. 350   OBJ: 6 TYPE: FACT

24. Based on stringent criteria, research data indicate that the percentage of men between the ages of 18 and 59 with erectile dysfunction is:
    a. 1%
    b. 3%
    c. 5%
    d. 10%

    ANS: C   DIF: 3   REF: p. 350   OBJ: 6 TYPE: FACT

25. What is the percentage of men in their 70s with at least some impairment of erectile function?
    a. 3%
    b. 5%
    c. 20%
    d. 70%

    ANS: D   DIF: 3   REF: p. 350   OBJ: 6 TYPE: FACT

26. The prevalence of sexual arousal disorders for men is:
    a. much higher than it is for women
    b. much lower than it is for women
    c. about the same in both sexes
    d. slightly lower than it is for women

    ANS: A   DIF: 1   REF: p. 350-351   OBJ: 6 TYPE: FACT

27. The percentage of women reporting significant difficulty reaching orgasm is:
    a. 5%
    b. 10%
    c. 25%
    d. 40%

    ANS: C   DIF: 3   REF: p. 351   OBJ: 6 TYPE: FACT

28. One reason that different diagnostic criteria are used for males and females with inhibited orgasm disorder is that:
    a. the disorder is relatively rare in men
    b. only about 50% of women regularly experience orgasm from intercourse
    c. both a and b are correct
    d. neither a nor b is correct

    ANS: C   DIF: 1   REF: p. 351   OBJ: 6 TYPE: CON

29. Sandra and Jim have been happily married for several years. Sandra reports that she reaches orgasm from intercourse only about half of the time and she wonders if something is "wrong" with her. Sandra should:
    a. seek treatment for inhibited orgasm disorder
    b. realize that her inhibited orgasm problem means that she doesn't really love Jim
    c. relax and realize that this is not unusual for women
    d. have a medical exam before assuming that she has a diagnosable psychological disorder

    ANS: C   DIF: 3   REF: p. 351   OBJ: 6 TYPE: APP/WWW

30. Jody and Howard have been happily married for several years. Howard reports that in spite of being sexually aroused and having an erection, he only reaches orgasm from intercourse about half of the time. Howard wonders if something is "wrong" with him. Howard should:
    a. seek treatment for inhibited orgasm disorder
    b. realize that this problem means that he does not really love his wife
    c. relax and realize that this is normal
    d. seek treatment for sexual aversion disorder

    ANS: A   DIF: 3   REF: p. 351   OBJ: 6 TYPE: APP

31. The most common of all the male sexual dysfunctions is:
    a. erectile dysfunction
    b. inhibited orgasm
    c. premature ejaculation
    d. sexual aversion

    ANS: C   DIF: 3   REF: p. 352   OBJ: 6 TYPE: FACT

32. The following paring is correct based on the ages most affected by the disorders:
    a. young men - premature ejaculation; older men - sexual aversion
    b. young men - premature ejaculation; older men - erectile dysfunction
    c. young men - inhibited orgasm; older men - erectile dysfunction
    d. young men - erectile dysfunction; older men - sexual aversion

    ANS: B   DIF: 1   REF: p. 350, 352   OBJ: 6 TYPE: FACT

33. One reason that it is difficult to provide a precise diagnosis of premature ejaculation is that:
    a. the concept of "too soon" is dependent on the individual and the couple
    b. most men are too ashamed to admit the problem
    c. women generally are reluctant to tell their partners of the problem
    d. men are often unaware of what is considered "normal"

    ANS: A   DIF: 1   REF: p. 352   OBJ: 6 TYPE: CON

34. Before diagnosing a sexual pain disorder, it is necessary to rule out:
    a. relationship issues that could be the cause of the dysfunction
    b. other sexual dysfunction such as sexual aversion disorder that has almost identical symptoms
    c. a medical cause of the pain
    d. vaginismus

    ANS: C   DIF: 1   REF: p. 353   OBJ: 6 TYPE: FACT

35. The condition called "dyspareunia" is diagnosed:
    a. when intercourse is uncomfortable or painful
    b. when medical conditions are ruled out as a cause of painful intercourse
    c. only when vaginismus is also present
    d. only when pain is present in the genital area

    ANS: B   DIF: 3   REF: p. 353   OBJ: 6 TYPE: APP

36. One reason that your text suggests questionnaires be used when assessing sexual behavior is that:
    a. people may provide more sexual information in writing than during an interview
    b. written information regarding sexuality has been shown to be more accurate than verbal report
    c. therapists are often uncomfortable asking questions regarding sexual behavior
    d. the therapist needs a written record in the patient's own words to demonstrate progress as the patient improves

    ANS: A   DIF: 3   REF: p. 354   OBJ: 7 TYPE: FACT

37. One of the most important skills that therapists must possess when conducting an interview regarding sexual behavior is:
    a. communicating their own sexual values
    b. using only the proper clinical terms for sexual behavior
    c. demonstrating that they are comfortable talking about sexual issues
    d. being able to diagnose medical causes of sexual dysfunction

    ANS: C   DIF: 1   REF: p. 354   OBJ: 7 TYPE: FACT

38. Psychophysiological assessment of sexual dysfunction is generally conducted by:
    a. using a device that measures physical arousal during exposure to an erotic video or audio tape
    b. asking patients to keep a diary of their sexual activities
    c. a physician during a medical exam
    d. using a device that measures brain waves during exposure to an erotic video or audio tape

    ANS: A   DIF: 1   REF: p. 355   OBJ: 7 TYPE: FACT

39. A male patient complaining of erectile dysfunction is observed to have a complete lack of nocturnal penile erections while sleeping. We can conclude that:
    a. more information is needed to diagnose his problem
    b. his erectile dysfunction is caused by a medication side effect
    c. his erectile dysfunction is due to psychological difficulties
    d. his erectile dysfunction is caused by a medical problem

    ANS: A   DIF: 1   REF: p. 355   OBJ: 7 TYPE: FACT

40. A situation in which a patient experiences more than one sexual disorder at the same time (for example, erectile dysfunction and premature ejaculation) is:
    a. very uncommon
    b. impossible in many cases (i.e., erectile dysfunction and premature ejaculation)
    c. common
    d. almost always due to a medical condition

    ANS: C   DIF: 3   REF: p. 356   OBJ: 6 TYPE: FACT

41. Two extremely common medical causes of erectile dysfunction are:
    a. asthma and diabetes
    b. vascular disease and diabetes
    c. vascular disease and asthma
    d. arthritis and diabetes

    ANS: B   DIF: 1   REF: p. 356   OBJ: 6 TYPE: FACT

42. Approximately 75% of individuals taking _____ medication experience some degree of sexual dysfunction.
    a. SSRI
    b. beta blocker
    c. tricyclic antidepressant
    d. anti-hypertensive

    ANS: A   DIF: 3   REF: p. 356   OBJ: 6 TYPE: FACT

43. Sherri and Leo have been having some sexual difficulties lately. Both have experienced some symptoms of sexual arousal disorders. They decide to have a few glasses of wine before engaging in sex tonight. Is this a good idea or a bad idea?
    a. It's a good idea since wine could increase desire.
    b. It's a good idea since wine could help performance.
    c. It's a bad idea since wine could further impair arousal.
    d. It's a bad idea since wine tends to decrease desire.

    ANS: C   DIF: 3   REF: p. 356   OBJ: 6 TYPE: APP/WWW

44. The effects of alcohol on sexual behavior were well noted by William Shakespeare and can be summarized as:
    a. alcohol decreases desire and performance
    b. alcohol increases desire and performance
    c. alcohol may increase desire but it decreases performance
    d. alcohol may increase performance but it decreases desire
    e. alcohol may increase desire, but nobody wants to sleep with a drunk!

    ANS: C   DIF: 3   REF: p. 356   OBJ: 6 TYPE: CON

45. Our current understanding of the psychological causes of sexual dysfunction suggests that the primary psychological factor in sexual dysfunction is:
    a. anxiety
    b. distraction
    c. relationship issues
    d. unreasonable expectations

    ANS: B   DIF: 3   REF: p. 357   OBJ: 6 TYPE: FACT

46. As a typical male with erectile dysfunction, we can expect Bill to show:
   a. decreased arousal during performance demand and an inaccurate sense of how aroused he is
   b. decreased arousal during performance demand and an accurate sense of how aroused he is
   c. increased arousal during performance demand and an inaccurate sense of how aroused he is
   d. increased arousal during performance demand and an accurate sense of how aroused he is

   ANS: A   DIF: 5   REF: p. 358   OBJ: 6 TYPE: APP

47. The original concept of performance anxiety as a cause of sexual dysfunction has been replaced with a more modern view that performance anxiety is comprised of:
   a. distraction, cognition and depression
   b. arousal, anxiety and distraction
   c. cognition, arousal and distraction
   d. arousal, cognitive processes and negative affect

   ANS: D   DIF: 5   REF: p. 358   OBJ: 6 TYPE: FACT

48. Greg often has problems with premature ejaculation. As he becomes more anxious about his problem, the amount of time between initiating intercourse and ejaculation will most likely:
   a. increase
   b. decrease
   c. remain the same
   d. depend upon what is making him anxious

   ANS: B   DIF: 3   REF: p. 358   OBJ: 6 TYPE: FACT

49. The most accurate description for the condition called erotophobia is:
   a. negative feelings toward sexuality
   b. negative feelings about other people
   c. fear of sex
   d. fear of being raped

   ANS: A   DIF: 3   REF: p. 358   OBJ: 6 TYPE: CON

50. Children or young adults who experience sexual victimization are:
   a. no more likely to experience sexual dysfunction as adults than anyone else
   b. more likely to experience sexual dysfunction as adults if they are females
   c. more likely to experience sexual dysfunction as adults if they are males
   d. more likely to experience sexual dysfunction as adults

   ANS: D   DIF: 3   REF: p. 358   OBJ: 6 TYPE: FACT

51. An unusuallyhigh concern with nocturnal emissions has been reported in _____ where there is a strong culturally held belief that loss of semen causes depletion of physical and mental energy.
   a. Ireland
   b. Indonesia
   c. India
   d. Iceland

   ANS: C   DIF: 3   REF: p. 359   OBJ: 1 TYPE: CON/WWW

52. Belief in common sexual myths such as "women normally reach orgasm every time they have intercourse" are more commonly held by men:
    a. who do not have sexual disorders
    b. with conservative sexual attitudes
    c. who have sexual disorders
    d. who are homosexual

    ANS: C   DIF: 3   REF: p. 360   OBJ: 6 TYPE: FACT

53. Development of sexual dysfunction can be viewed as a "vicious circle" since the typical case progresses in the following manner:
    a. initial dysfunction may be triggered by an event such as substance use; concern about the dysfunction then leads to more dysfunction and sex itself becomes associated with negative feelings
    b. initial dysfunction may be triggered by an event such as substance use; this causes a strain on the relationship and reduces the intimacy in the relationship, which then leads to anxiety about one's desirability
    c. initial dysfunction occurs through slow and gradual deterioration, possibly due to a medical condition; as the medical condition develops, the individual's concern with failing sexuality increases, resulting in relationship problems
    d. a general medical condition triggers the first dysfunction, which is followed by increased anxiety; as the anxiety increases, the sexual dysfunction becomes more severe over time and causes loss of interest in sex

    ANS: A   DIF: 5   REF: p. 359   OBJ: 6 TYPE: CON

54. The authors of your textbook suggest that one of the most effective treatments for many sexual dysfunctions is:
    a. exploration of the patient's sexual orientation
    b. improving the relationship with the patient's partner
    c. education regarding normal sexuality
    d. anti-anxiety medication

    ANS: C   DIF: 1   REF: p. 360   OBJ: 7 TYPE: FACT

55. Sensate focus and non-demand pleasuring were designed by Masters and Johnson to treat sexual dysfunctions primarily through:
    a. improving a couple's sexual skills
    b. identifying medical conditions that contribute to sexual dysfunction
    c. involving an objective third party
    d. elimination of psychologically based performance anxiety

    ANS: D   DIF: 1   REF: p. 361   OBJ: 7 TYPE: FACT

56. Maggie and Jim have started sex therapy to deal with Jim's recent erectile dysfunction. The therapist has instructed them to refrain from intercourse or genital touching but to spend the next several days enjoying each other through hugging, kissing and mutual massage. This is an example of:
    a. stage one of sensate focus treatment
    b. stage two of sensate focus treatment
    c. a strict behavioral treatment for erectile dysfunction
    d. the first step in cognitive therapy for erectile dysfunction

    ANS: A   DIF: 1   REF: p. 361   OBJ: 7 TYPE: APP

57. Stage two of sensate focus involves "genital pleasuring" but prohibits intercourse or orgasm. The main purpose of this stage is to:
    a. allow an individual to communicate his or her desires to the partner
    b. change the usual ways that the couple has tried to have sex
    c. allow sexual experience without the anxiety of performance
    d. provide increased anticipation of intercourse

    ANS: C   DIF: 1   REF: p. 361   OBJ: 7 TYPE: FACT/WWW

58. As a couple completes stage two of sensate focus therapy, they are instructed to:
    a. return to full, prior sexual activity
    b. slowly begin sexual activity, continuing non-demand pleasuring as they progress
    c. take a break from sexual activity for several weeks and then slowly return to normal sexuality
    d. begin the "genital pleasuring" stage of the treatment

    ANS: B   DIF: 3   REF: p. 361   OBJ: 7 TYPE: FACT

59. Masters and Johnson reported that the use of sensate focus therapy for the treatment of premature ejaculation was effective in _____ of cases treated.
    a. 50%
    b. 65%
    c. 75%
    d. almost 100%

    ANS: D   DIF: 3   REF: p. 361   OBJ: 7 TYPE: FACT

60. Treatment effectiveness studies of Masters and Johnson's sensate focus therapy have indicated that:
    a. certain aspects of the treatment such as two therapists and daily therapy are not necessary
    b. many therapists using Masters and Johnson's techniques are able to demonstrate even greater treatment effectiveness than Masters and Johnson did
    c. daily treatment is a critical component of the method
    d. sensate focus is generally only effective when administered by Masters and Johnson

    ANS: A   DIF: 3   REF: p. 361   OBJ: 7 TYPE: FACT

61. Sex therapy for erectile dysfunction has produced a positive treatment outcome in approximately _____ of the cases treated.
   a. 25%
   b. 45%
   c. 65%
   d. 85%

   ANS: C   DIF: 3   REF: p. 361   OBJ: 7 TYPE: FACT

62. The sex therapy technique designed specifically to treat premature ejaculation is:
   a. the squeeze technique
   b. sensate focus
   c. non-demand pleasuring
   d. cognitive restructuring

   ANS: A   DIF: 1   REF: p. 361   OBJ: 7 TYPE: FACT

63. The specific treatment found effective in the treatment of female orgasmic disorder is:
   a. anti-anxiety medication
   b. sensate focus
   c. explicit training in masturbation procedures
   d. increased sexual relations

   ANS: C   DIF: 1   REF: p. 362   OBJ: 7 TYPE: FACT

64. A woman is sent home from sex therapy with an assignment to purchase a vibrator and practice masturbating. She is likely being treated:
   a. for vaginismus
   b. for hypoactive sexual desire disorder
   c. for female orgasmic disorder
   d. by a sex therapist with little or no formal training in psychology

   ANS: C   DIF: 1   REF: p. 362   OBJ: 7 TYPE: FACT

65. Dilators of gradually increasing sizes are used in the treatment of:
   a. female orgasmic disorder
   b. vaginismus
   c. hypoactive sexual desire disorder
   d. all of these

   ANS: B   DIF: 3   REF: p. 362   OBJ: 7 TYPE: FACT

66. According to your textbook, what is the percentage of women who successfully overcome vaginismus?
   a. less than 30%
   b. 30% to 45%
   c. 50% to 75%
   d. 80% to 100%

   ANS: D   DIF: 3   REF: p. 362   OBJ: 7 TYPE: FACT

67. The percentage of men with erectile dysfunction who take Viagra and are then able to maintain an erection sufficient for intercourse is between:
a. 5% and 40%
b. 50% and 80%
c. 80% and 90%
d. 90% and 100%

ANS: B   DIF: 1   REF: p. 363   OBJ: 7 TYPE: FACT

68. What significant side effect is experienced by as many as 30% of Viagra users?
a. severe headache
b. addiction
c. groin pain
d. dizziness

ANS: A   DIF: 3   REF: p. 363   OBJ: 7 TYPE: FACT

69. Research studies on Viagra users indicate that:
a. most users are able to engage in intercourse and are very satisfied with the results
b. approximately half of the users are able to engage in intercourse and are highly satisfied with results
c. most users are able to engage in intercourse but only 32% rated the results as "good" or better
d. most users were unable to engage in intercourse and were not satisfied with results

ANS: C   DIF: 3   REF: p. 363   OBJ: 7 TYPE: FACT

70. Papaverine and prostaglandin, vasodilating drugs used in the treatment of erectile dysfunction, are delivered to the patient:
a. in a capsule taken orally
b. as a dietary supplement
c. by injection directly into the penis
d. by injection into the arm or hip

ANS: C   DIF: 5   REF: p. 363   OBJ: 7 TYPE: FACT

71. Although vasodilating drugs such as papaverine and prostaglandin are effective in producing an erection for patients with erectile dysfunction, many patients discontinue use of the drugs because of:
a. painful side effects
b. the fact that these drugs eventually cure the disorder
c. the expense of the drug
d. the fact that the effectiveness of the drug decreases with continued use

ANS: A   DIF: 3   REF: p. 363   OBJ: 7 TYPE: FACT

72. Which of the following treatments is NOT currently used in the treatment of erectile dysfunction?
a. vasodilating drugs
b. anti-anxiety medication
c. surgical prosthetic implant
d. vacuum device therapy

ANS: B   DIF: 1   REF: p. 363   OBJ: 7 TYPE: FACT

73. One of the reasons that Viagra has become so widely accepted as a treatment for erectile dysfunction is that:
   a. it is more effective than the other available treatments
   b. it is less expensive than other medications such as vasodilators
   c. people are unaware of the other options
   d. an oral medication is less awkward and intrusive than other treatments

   ANS: D   DIF: 3   REF: p. 363   OBJ: 7 TYPE: CON

74. Therapy for sexual dysfunctions such as hypoactive sexual desire disorder can best be described as:
   a. well studied and widely available
   b. well studied but only available in specialty clinics
   c. not well studied and not available in all locations
   d. not well studied but generally available everywhere

   ANS: C   DIF: 1   REF: p. 363   OBJ: 7 TYPE: CON/WWW

75. Paraphilia is defined as:
   a. a dysfunction
   b. an attraction to inappropriate individuals or objects
   c. an attraction to machines
   d. a desire that dominates the personality

   ANS: B   DIF: 1   REF: p. 364   OBJ: 8 TYPE: FACT

76. The definition of a fetish is sexual:
   a. dysfunction
   b. attraction to inappropriate individuals
   c. attraction to nonliving objects
   d. desire that dominates the personality

   ANS: C   DIF: 1   REF: p. 364   OBJ: 8 TYPE: FACT

77. Charles gets very sexually excited by women's shoes. While he used to fantasize about women wearing particular shoes, he now focuses almost exclusively on the shoes themselves. Charles has a(n):
   a. sexual dysfunction
   b. unusual interest but does not have a diagnosable disorder
   c. fetish
   d. frotteuristic obsession

   ANS: C   DIF: 1   REF: p. 364   OBJ: 8 TYPE: APP

78. Greg and Diana often begin their sexual activity with Greg putting on a striptease show for Diana. They both report great satisfaction and excitement with this activity. In fact, Greg says that he gets aroused by exposing himself and Diana reports getting aroused when she watches him undress. Which of the following statements is true?
    a. Greg is an exhibitionist and Diana is a voyeur.
    b. Greg is a voyeur and Diana is an exhibitionist.
    c. Both Diana and Greg have nonspecific fetishes because they admit to getting sexually excited by their atypical behaviors.
    d. Neither Greg nor Diana should be diagnosed with a fetish because these behaviors involve consenting individuals.

    ANS: D   DIF: 5   REF: p. 365   OBJ: 8 TYPE: APP

79. One psychological aspect of voyeurism and exhibitionism that seems to maintain the disordered behavior is:
    a. some anxiety about getting caught
    b. the fact that these individuals are rarely caught
    c. the desire to hurt their victims
    d. some sense that their victims really enjoy being subjected to their fetish

    ANS: A   DIF: 3   REF: p. 365   OBJ: 8 TYPE: CON

80. All of the following are true statements regarding transvestic fetishism EXCEPT:
    a. transvestic fetishists are either homosexual or transsexual
    b. a significant percentage of individuals with this disorder are married
    c. there are cross-dressing clubs and newsletters for individuals with this fetish
    d. some transvestic fetishists compensate by joining macho or paramilitary organizations

    ANS: A   DIF: 5   REF: p. 366   OBJ: 8 TYPE: FACT

81. _____ are individuals who receive a sexual thrill from inflicting pain on others and _____ are individuals who receive a sexual thrill from receiving physical pain.
    a. Sadists; masochists
    b. Masochists; sadists
    c. Transvestites; paraphiliacs
    d. Paraphiliacs; transvestites

    ANS: A   DIF: 1   REF: p. 366   OBJ: 8 TYPE: FACT

82. According to the authors of your textbook, the concurrent existence of masochistic and sadistic fetish within the same individual is:
    a. very rare
    b. impossible because the behaviors are opposite
    c. always present
    d. common

    ANS: D   DIF: 3   REF: p. 366   OBJ: 8 TYPE: FACT

83. "Opportunistic" rape differs from sadistic rape in that the rape in the latter is committed by an individual
   a. who meets the criteria for antisocial personality disorder
   b. with a particular pattern of sexual arousal
   c. who rarely masturbates
   d. during an unplanned assault

   ANS: B   DIF: 3   REF: p. 367, 370   OBJ: 9 TYPE: CON/WWW

84. When the term paraphilia is used to describe the behavior of a rapist, it means that the rapist is aroused by:
   a. images of forced sex
   b. any sexual image
   c. consensual sex
   d. nonviolent sexual imagery

   ANS: A   DIF: 5   REF: p. 367   OBJ: 9 TYPE: CON

85. Which of the following is true about most rapists?
   a. they are sexually aroused only by violence
   b. they are aggressive and have little regard for others
   c. they are either hyposexual or asexual
   d. they are hypersexual and generally obsessed with sex

   ANS: B   DIF: 3   REF: p. 367   OBJ: 9 TYPE: FACT

86. Victims of incest tend to be _____ and victims of pedophilia (who are not also incest victims) tend to be _____.
   a. male; female
   b. young children; girls who are beginning to mature physically
   c. girls who are beginning to mature physically; young children
   d. female; male

   ANS: C   DIF: 3   REF: p. 368   OBJ: 9 TYPE: FACT

87. Research with both non-incestuous pedophiles and perpetrators of incest (Marshall, et al., 1986 and Marshall, 1997) suggests that:
   a. non-incestuous pedophilia is generally influenced by paraphilia where incest may be more opportunistic
   b. incest is generally influenced by paraphilia where non-incestuous pedophilia may be more opportunistic
   c. both behaviors tend to be motivated by paraphilia
   d. both behaviors tend to be motivated by opportunistic individuals rather than by paraphilia

   ANS: A   DIF: 5   REF: p. 368   OBJ: 9 TYPE: FACT

88. The typical adult who molests a child:
   a. is violent and aggressive
   b. threatens the child physically but is not violent
   c. does not use physical force
   d. is fully aware of the psychological damage that he is causing the child

   ANS: C   DIF: 1   REF: p. 369   OBJ: 9 TYPE: FACT

89. Inappropriate sexual arousal, e.g., fetishism, appears to be learned through:
    a. exposure to pornography
    b. masturbatory fantasies about the object
    c. social "scripts" that are transferred from one generation to the next
    d. poor social skills

    ANS: B   DIF: 1   REF: p. 370   OBJ: 8 TYPE: FACT

90. The classical conditioning model of learning predicts that the following boy might grow up to be a voyeur:
    a. Tim whose father is a voyeur
    b. Joe who watches a lot of pornography
    c. Sid who masturbates while peeping at his neighbor
    d. Jim who thinks it's funny to spy on people

    ANS: C   DIF: 3   REF: p. 370   OBJ: 8 TYPE: APP

91. Of the various hypothesized influences of paraphilia, the ones that we know the least about involve:
    a. biological influences such as genetics and neurotransmitters
    b. reinforced but inappropriate masturbatory fantasies
    c. social influences such as inadequate development of social skills
    d. paradoxical effects of repeated attempts to suppress unwanted arousal

    ANS: A   DIF: 5   REF: p. 371   OBJ: 8 TYPE: FACT

92. The procedure that is carried out entirely in the patient's imagination and used to reduce the inappropriate sexual arousal that exists in fetishistic behavior is called:
    a. classical conditioning
    b. sexual re-training
    c. sensate focus
    d. covert sensitization

    ANS: D   DIF: 1   REF: p. 371   OBJ: 10 TYPE: FACT/WWW

93. The basic concept behind the covert sensitization method of treating unwanted sexual arousal is to:
    a. create empathy for the victim of the behavior
    b. replace the immediate reinforcement of the behavior with the unpleasant consequences that ordinarily take longer to be experienced
    c. create a physically painful experience to replace the immediate reinforcement that the unwanted behavior has previously produced
    d. improve family functioning, social skills, and overall effectiveness of appropriate adult relations

    ANS: B   DIF: 5   REF: p. 371   OBJ: 10 TYPE: CON

94. Patients undergoing the procedure called orgasmic reconditioning are instructed to:
    a. masturbate to their usual fantasies but to substitute more desirable ones just before ejaculation
    b. masturbate to their usual fantasies but substitute images of the consequences associated with their behavior (such as getting caught, hurting someone else, etc.) just before ejaculation
    c. substitute images of the consequences associated with their behavior (such as getting caught, hurting someone else, etc.) every time they feel aroused by thoughts of their inappropriate desires
    d. watch video tapes of normal adult sexuality repeatedly until such images result in arousal

    ANS: A   DIF: 3   REF: p. 372   OBJ: 10 TYPE: FACT

95. The procedure called orgasmic reconditioning works according to the principle of:
    a. punishment of inappropriate arousal
    b. extinction of inappropriate arousal
    c. reinforcement of appropriate arousal
    d. reinforcement of self control

    ANS: C   DIF: 3   REF: p. 372   OBJ: 10 TYPE: CON

96. Research regarding the success of treating paraphilias with procedures such as orgasmic reconditioning and covert sensitization indicates that:
    a. treatment is generally not successful
    b. treatment is successful in only the small number of cases where the patient completes all treatment sessions
    c. the number of cases in the research studies is too small to make conclusions at this point
    d. treatment is generally effective

    ANS: D   DIF: 1   REF: p. 371-372   OBJ: 10 TYPE: FACT

97. A poor prognosis associated with the treatment of paraphilia is related to all of the following factors EXCEPT:
    a. having multiple paraphilias
    b. having had the paraphilia for more than 10 years
    c. a history of unstable social relationships
    d. continuing to live with the victim (an incestuous situation, for example)

    ANS: B   DIF: 3   REF: p. 373   OBJ: 10 TYPE: FACT

98. Which of the following is true regarding drugs currently available for the treatment of paraphilias?
    a. the drugs eliminate sexual desire but are only effective while they are being taken
    b. the drugs reduce sex drive and continue to be effective long after the patient stops the medication
    c. the drugs dramatically reduce sex drive but have side effects that make them harmful to many patients
    d. they produce a "chemical castration" that effectively eliminates all sex drive permanently so that the patient will never desire sex even after discontinuing the medication

    ANS: A   DIF: 1   REF: p. 373   OBJ: 10 TYPE: FACT

99. In the study reported by Federoff, et al.,1999, the women had all the following types of paraphilias EXCEPT:
a. fetishism
b. pedophilia
c. exhibitionism
d. sadomasochism

ANS: A   DIF: 2   REF: p. 369   OBJ: 10 TYPE:FACT

100. The scandal in the Catholic Church that came to widespread public awareness in the late 20th and early 21st centuries focused on priests who met the criteria for:
a. voyeurism
b. exhibitionism
c. pedophilia
d. incest

ANS: C   DIF: 2   REF: p. 368   OBJ: 10 TYPE:CON

101. On the "Abnormal Psychology Live" CD for Chapter 10, Clark describes several problems related to his diagnosis of:
a. erectile dysfunction
b. premature ejaculation
c. dyspareunia
d. inhibited male orgasm

ANS: A   REF: CD

102. On the "Abnormal Psychology Live" CD for Chapter 10, Clark is diagnosed not only with a sexual dysfunction but also with:
a. obsessive compulsive disorder
b. bipolar disorder
c. depression
d. social phobia

ANS: C   REF: CD

103. In describing her early years as a child with gender identity disorder ("Abnormal Psychology Live" CD for Chapter 10), Jessica notes especially her attachment to a particular item of female clothing, a _____.
a. blouse
b. bra
c. skirt
d. nightgown

ANS: C   REF: CD

ESSAY

1. Explain the modern definition of the term "disorder" as it relates to sexual behavior. Why is the determination of a sexual disorder a somewhat subjective decision?

2. Describe the impact of culture on the definition of a sexual disorder. What cross-cultural evidence suggests that "normal" sexual behavior is culturally defined?

3. Describe the evidence for the genetic and/or biological basis for homosexuality as well as the evidence for the environmental influences on sexual preference.

4. Explain the features of the treatment options (psychosocial and surgical sex reassignment) for gender identity disorder. Why is it so important for the patient to consider treatment options very carefully?

5. Describe the symptoms and diagnostic criteria for inhibited orgasm disorder in men and women. Explain any differences in the diagnostic criteria for men and women and the rationale for these differences.

6. Describe the development of a typical sexual dysfunction. Explain how the various influences (genetic, psychosocial or substance use) might interact in the following situation: an occasional dysfunction (e.g., first time failure to maintain an erection) develops into a disorder that interferes with the individual's ability to function sexually (e.g., erectile dysfunction).   **WWW**

7. List ten questions that should be asked in an interview to assess sexual behavior. What additional assessment methods are necessary beyond the interview? What is the importance of each assessment method?

8. Describe the symptoms of three different forms of paraphilia. What do all paraphilias have in common?

9. Your text describes a process in which paraphilias may develop through classical conditioning of an inappropriate fantasy or through actual behavior. Using this model, describe how one individual might become a voyeur and another might develop a shoe fetish.

10. Explain the treatment methods of covert sensitization and orgasmic reconditioning. What do these two methods have in common?

11. After watching the "Abnormal Psychology Live" CD for Chapter 10, describe how Clark relates his sexual dysfunction to his feelings of depression. Explain how Clark's masculine self concept has been affected by his erectile dysfunction. Discuss the cultural and interpersonal factors involved in this particular sexual dysfunction.

    REF: CD

12. After viewing the "Abnormal Psychology Live" CD for Chapter 10, discuss the different ways that Jessica's parents coped with their daughter's gender identity disorder. During her "year of transition," how did Jessica come to realize that people were seeing her as woman? Describe some of Jessica's thoughts and feelings as a post-operative transsexual.

    REF: CD

MULTIPLE CHOICE

1. The difference between hypoactive sexual desire disorder and sexual aversion disorder is that
   a. hypoactive sexual desire disorder involves excessive sexual desire.
   b. sexual aversion disorder involves excessive sexual desire.
   c. hypoactive sexual desire disorder involves fear, panic, or disgust brought about by the thought of sex or a brief touch.
   d. sexual aversion disorder involves fear, panic, or disgust brought about by the thought of sex or a brief touch.

   ANS: D

2. _____ refers to psychological dissatisfaction with one's biological gender.
   a. Paraphilia
   b. Gender identity disorder
   c. Transvestic fetishism
   d. Dyspareunia

   ANS: B

3. The incidence of _____ shows the largest difference between the genders in sexual behaviors.
   a. oral sex
   b. casual sex
   c. masturbation
   d. unprotected sex

   ANS: C

4. Research reports have suggested that homosexuality is
   a. more likely concordant among monozygotic twins than among dizygotic twins or non-twin siblings.
   b. associated with exposure to hormones before birth.
   c. dependent upon certain environmental contributions.
   d. all of the above

   ANS: D

5. The development of deviant patterns of sexual arousal may be associated with
   a. levels of "desired" arousal in consenting adults.
   b. deficiencies in consensual adult social skills.
   c. early sexual fantasies that are reinforced through masturbation.
   d. all of the above

   ANS: D

6. Which of the following is true about sexual practices in the United States?
   a. There are more females than males engaged in exclusively homosexual activity.
   b. The regular use of condoms during sexual intercourse has not increased over the last 20 years.
   c. Sexual practices in the United States are very similar to those in Britain and France.
   d. Masturbation is positively correlated with better sexual functioning in older age.

   ANS: C

7. What is considered to be "normal" sexual behavior
   a. is remarkably similar across cultures.
   b. is culture-dependent.
   c. is determined by the dominant religious organizations.
   d. will vary greatly depending on gender.
   e. should be determined by the legislature or ruling group.

   ANS: B

8. Tom thinks he shows his love and worthiness as a sex partner by working hard at the office and keeping the house in good repair. His wife Maria can't feel sexy unless he woos her with gifts and loving words. Theorist John Gagnon would say they differ in their
   a. cognitive restructuring.
   b. irrational beliefs.
   c. texts.
   d. scripts.
   e. proposals.

   ANS: D

9. Roderick and his partner are seeking treatment for Roderick's premature ejaculation. The therapist encourages the couple to stimulate Roderick's penis to nearly full erection and then to squeeze the penis firmly to quickly reduce arousal. After repeating this process, insertion is to be attempted without thrusting and the penis removed if arousal proceeds too quickly. This treatment is called
   a. torture.
   b. erotic desensitization.
   c. stimulus removal.
   d. the squeeze technique.
   e. retarded ejaculation.

   ANS: D

10. About 50% of patients who seek treatment at sexuality clinics complain of
    a. sexual aversion.
    b. loss of appetite.
    c. premature ejaculation.
    d. vaginismus.
    e. hypoactive sexual desire.

    ANS: E

Chapter 11—Substance-Related and Impulse-Control Disorders

MULTIPLE CHOICE

1. In the United States, the annual death rate related to cigarette smoking and the use of alcohol and illegal drugs is estimated to be:
   a. 25,000
   b. 50,000
   c. 250,000
   d. 500,000

   ANS: D   DIF: 1   REF: p. 379   OBJ: 1 TYPE: FACT

2. Which of the following would NOT be an example of substance use?
   a. smoking a cigarette
   b. drinking a cup of coffee
   c. taking a sleeping pill
   d. getting drunk

   ANS: D   DIF: 1   REF: p. 380   OBJ: 1 TYPE: CON

3. The American Psychiatric Association defines substance abuse in terms of:
   a. how drunk or intoxicated a person gets after ingesting a psychoactive substance
   b. whether or not the substance interferes with the person's life
   c. the type and intensity of the substance abuser's biological reaction
   d. which drug is used and whether it is legal or illegal

   ANS: B   DIF: 3   REF: p. 381   OBJ: 1 TYPE: CON

4. Substance intoxication includes all of the following EXCEPT:
   a. the specific drug that is used
   b. how much of a drug is used or ingested
   c. the drug user's individual biological reaction
   d. physiological dependence on the drug

   ANS: D   DIF: 3   REF: p. 381   OBJ: 1 TYPE: CON

5. In terms of substance-related disorders, the word addiction is most closely associated with:
   a. substance use
   b. intoxication
   c. substance dependence
   d. polysubstance abuse

   ANS: C   DIF: 1   REF: p. 381   OBJ: 1 TYPE: CON

6. A person who is physiologically dependent on a drug will experience:
   a. tolerance to the effects of the drug
   b. withdrawal symptoms if the drug is withdrawn
   c. both tolerance and withdrawal
   d. neither tolerance nor withdrawal

   ANS: C   DIF: 3   REF: p. 381   OBJ: 2 TYPE: APP

7. Carol has been addicted to narcotics for many years. Recently she has been trying to quit and has not used any drugs for the last week. We can expect that Carol will be experiencing:
   a. fever and chills
   b. nausea, vomiting and diarrhea
   c. aches and pains
   d. all of these

   ANS: D   DIF: 3   REF: p. 381   OBJ: 2 TYPE: APP

8. The condition called delirium tremens, also known as the "DTs," involves hallucinations and body tremors during withdrawal from:
   a. heroin
   b. cocaine
   c. alcohol
   d. marijuana

   ANS: C   DIF: 1   REF: p. 381   OBJ: 2 TYPE: CON

9. A perspective of substance dependence that involves "drug-seeking behaviors" includes all of the following EXCEPT:
   a. repeated use of the drug
   b. a desperate need to ingest more of the drug
   c. resuming drug use after a period of abstinence
   d. physical symptoms when the drug is no longer used

   ANS: D   DIF: 3   REF: p. 381   OBJ: 2 TYPE: CON

10. The DSM-IV-TR definition of substance dependence includes both physiological and psychological aspects, specifically:
    a. tolerance and withdrawal only
    b. drug seeking behaviors only
    c. both of these
    d. neither of these

    ANS: C   DIF: 3   REF: p. 381   OBJ: 2 TYPE: CON

11. Experts in the field of substance abuse were asked about the relative addictiveness of various drugs. At the top of the list, as most addictive, was:
    a. crack cocaine
    b. heroin
    c. nicotine
    d. methamphetamine

    ANS: C   DIF: 1   REF: p. 383   OBJ: 3 TYPE: FACT

12. In early DSM editions, alcoholism and drug abuse were classified as sociopathic personality disorders because they were considered to be:
    a. criminal behaviors
    b. morally deficient behaviors
    c. signs of mental illness
    d. symptoms of psychosis

    ANS: B   DIF: 3   REF: p. 384   OBJ: 4 TYPE: CON

13. Alcoholism, previously considered a _____, is now conceptualized by many as a disease.
    a. sociopathic personality disturbance
    b. schizophrenic-like behavioral pattern
    c. type of dependent personality disorder
    d. hysterical conversion syndrome

    ANS: A   DIF: 1   REF: p. 384   OBJ: 4 TYPE: CON

14. Nicolai has been an alcoholic for many years. He has also experienced major depression and manic episodes. According to Compton, et al., (2003), about _____ of alcoholics, also have an additional psychiatric disorder.
    a. 25%
    b. 50%
    c. 75%
    d. 99%

    ANS: C   DIF: 3   REF: p. 384   OBJ: 4 TYPE: FACT

15. Alcohol and the drugs Seconal, Halcion, and Valium are all classified as:
    a. stimulants
    b. opiates
    c. depressants
    d. narcotics

    ANS: C   DIF: 1   REF: p. 384-385   OBJ: 3 TYPE: FACT

16. All of the following analgesic substances are classified as opiates EXCEPT:
    a. cocaine
    b. codeine
    c. heroin
    d. morphine

    ANS: A   DIF: 1   REF: p. 385   OBJ: 3 TYPE: FACT

17. Both morphine and codeine are analgesics, which means that they:
    a. activate the central nervous system
    b. relieve pain and produce euphoria
    c. increase alertness
    d. cause delusions and dissociative experiences

    ANS: B   DIF: 1   REF: p. 385   OBJ: 3 TYPE: CON

18. Which of the following is an example of alcohol's effects on brain functioning?
    a. faster reaction time
    b. improved judgment
    c. impaired motor coordination
    d. clear speech

    ANS: C   DIF: 1   REF: p. 385   OBJ: 4 TYPE: CON/WWW

19. What explains the apparent stimulation, feeling of well being, and outgoing behavior that occur as the initial effects of alcohol ingestion?
    a. depression of the inhibitory centers in the brain
    b. activation of the inhibitory centers in the brain
    c. depression of the autonomic nervous system
    d. stimulation of the autonomic nervous system

    ANS: A   DIF: 5   REF: p. 385   OBJ: 4 TYPE: CON

20. Although most psychoactive substances interact with specific substances in the brain cells, the effects of _____ are much more complex because several different neurotransmitter systems are affected.
    a. the opiates
    b. tranquilizers
    c. alcohol
    d. marijuana

    ANS: C   DIF: 5   REF: p. 385   OBJ: 4 TYPE: APP

21. Which of the following does NOT describe the specific effect of alcohol on a particular neurotransmitter system?
    a. serotonin - alcoholic cravings
    b. glutamate - alcoholic blackouts
    c. dopamine - slurred speech
    d. GABA - anti-anxiety effect

    ANS: C   DIF: 5   REF: p. 386   OBJ: 4 TYPE: APP

22. All of the following are symptoms of withdrawal from alcohol EXCEPT:
    a. nausea and/or vomiting
    b. hypersomnia
    c. hallucinations
    d. delirium tremens

    ANS: B   DIF: 1   REF: p. 386   OBJ: 4 TYPE: FACT

23. In some individuals chronic alcohol use causes physical damage to the body. Whether this occurs depends on all of the following factors EXCEPT:
    a. blood alcohol levels during drinking periods
    b. type of alcohol consumed (e.g., beer, wine, liquor)
    c. genetic vulnerability
    d. how frequently drinking binges occur, how long they last, and how much time elapses between binges

    ANS: B   DIF: 5   REF: p. 387   OBJ: 4 TYPE: APP

24. Consequences of long-term excessive drinking include:
    a. liver disease and/or pancreatitis
    b. cardiovascular disorders
    c. brain damage
    d. all of these

    ANS: D   DIF: 1   REF: p. 387   OBJ: 4 TYPE: FACT

25. All of the following occur in persons who are alcohol dependent for even short periods of time EXCEPT:
    a. blackouts and/or seizures
    b. hallucinations
    c. memory loss
    d. dementia

    ANS: D   DIF: 3   REF: p. 387   OBJ: 4 TYPE: FACT

26. The correct pairing of the names, causes, and symptoms of two types of organic brain syndromes that may result from chronic, long-term alcohol abuse are:
    a. dementia - loss of intellectual abilities caused by a deficiency of the vitamin called thiamine
    b. Wernicke's disease - confusion, loss of muscle coordination, and unintelligible speech caused by a deficiency of the vitamin called thiamine
    c. dementia - confusion, loss of muscle coordination, and unintelligible speech caused by the toxic effects of alcohol on the brain
    d. Wernicke's disease - loss of intellectual abilities caused by the toxic effects of alcohol on the brain

    ANS: B   DIF: 5   REF: p. 387   OBJ: 4 TYPE: APP

27. The possibility that a heavy drinker's cognitive ability might improve if the person stops drinking is based on research findings showing that:
    a. alcohol damages neurons in the brain but not the neurotransmitters
    b. alcohol damages the connections between the neurons but not the neurons themselves
    c. alcohol damages the neurons in the brain but not the connections between them
    d. alcohol damages the neurotransmitters but not the neuronal connections

    ANS: B   DIF: 5   REF: p. 387   OBJ: 4 TYPE: APP

28. Fetal alcohol syndrome (FAS) is a combination of problems that can occur in a child whose mother drank alcohol while pregnant. Symptoms of FAS include all of the following EXCEPT:
    a. cognitive deficits and behavior problems
    b. distorted facial features
    c. learning difficulties
    d. excessive fetal growth

    ANS: D   DIF: 3   REF: p. 387   OBJ: 4 TYPE: FACT

29. Research that asks individuals to indicate alcohol use during the previous one month period has found that alcohol use is highest among:
    a. Hispanics
    b. Asian Americans
    c. Caucasian Americans
    d. persons with multiracial backgrounds

    ANS: C   DIF: 1   REF: p. 388   OBJ: 4 TYPE: APP

30. Which of the following is an accurate statement about alcohol use?
    a. Education is negatively correlated with recent alcohol use.
    b. Half of all Americans over the age of 12 report being current drinkers of alcohol.
    c. Female college students were more likely than male college students to report several episodes of binge drinking in a two week period.
    d. Alcohol use in the elderly population is typically high.

    ANS: B   DIF: 3   REF: p. 388   OBJ: 4 TYPE: FACT/WWW

31. In a large survey among college-age men and women, it was found that:
    a. about 75% of the respondents said that they had gone on a binge of heavy drinking once in the preceding two weeks
    b. there was no relationship between frequency of drinking and grades
    c. students with a grade-point average of "A" had no more than one drink per week.
    d. "D" and "F" students averaged 11 alcoholic drinks per week.

    ANS: D   DIF: 3   REF: p. 388   OBJ: 4 TYPE: APP

32. In 2003, researchers at the Substance Abuse and Mental Health Services Administration estimated that about _____ Americans are probably dependent on alcohol.
    a. 1.5 million
    b. 10 million
    c. 15 million
    d. 25 million

    ANS: B   DIF: 1   REF: p. 388   OBJ: 4 TYPE: APP

33. A report from the Substance Abuse and Health Services Administration (2003) indicates that about _____ of Americans reported binge drinking in the month preceding the report.
    a. 2%
    b. 23%
    c. 51%
    d. 65%

    ANS: C   DIF: 1   REF: p. 388   OBJ: 4 TYPE: APP

34. The prevailing view that alcohol abuse usually follows a predictable downward spiral was based on Jellinek's mid 20th century survey of AA (Alcoholics Anonymous) members that asked them how alcohol had affected them physically and psychologically. Data from this survey are now considered inaccurate because:
    a. respondents faked their answers to the questions on the survey
    b. too few AA members answered the survey questions
    c. since the survey was only sent to older members of AA, information on the progression of alcohol use was not available
    d. Jellinek himself became an alcoholic and never finished the research

    ANS: B   DIF: 3   REF: p. 388   OBJ: 4 TYPE: APP

35. According to Jellinek's model of alcoholism (no longer considered accurate but still of scientific interest), an individual progresses through four stages. Which of the following incorrectly describes the characteristic behaviors associated with each of Jellinek's stages?
    a. prealcoholic stage - hangovers, DWI or DUI charges, blackouts
    b. prodromal stage - drinking heavily but few outward signs of problems
    c. chronic stage - loss of control accompanied by occasional binges
    d. crucial stage - primary activities focused on getting and drinking alcohol

    ANS: A   DIF: 3   REF: p. 388   OBJ: 4 TYPE: APP

36. A research study of 6,000 lifetime drinkers (DeWitt et al., 2000) found that drinking at an early age (ages 11-14):
    a. was predictive of later alcohol use disorders
    b. had no relationship to alcohol use later in life
    c. caused more frequent blackouts than drinking at later ages
    d. resulted in more severe withdrawal symptoms than drinking at later ages

    ANS: A   DIF: 3   REF: p. 388   OBJ: 4 TYPE: APP

37. Which of the following is an accurate statement about alcoholism?
    a. A progressive pattern leading to alcoholism is inevitable for those who drink alcohol.
    b. The factors that determine a drinker's susceptibility to alcoholism are not yet known.
    c. Alcohol use and aggressive behavior are negatively correlated.
    d. Use of alcohol by preteens and young teenagers does not predict later abuse.

    ANS: B   DIF: 5   REF: p. 389   OBJ: 4 TYPE: CON/WWW

38. Although alcohol use and aggression are positively correlated, the factors that actually determine aggressive behavior involve all of the following EXCEPT:
    a. quantity and timing of alcohol consumed
    b. the person's previous history of violence
    c. the circumstances and events related to the person's drinking
    d. the person's level of intelligence

    ANS: D   DIF: 3   REF: p. 389   OBJ: 4 TYPE: CON

39. You have just heard about a situation in which someone who was drunk vandalized a building and assaulted a security guard. From your knowledge of abnormal psychology, you are aware that although alcohol does not cause aggressive behavior, it may:
    a. stimulate the inhibitory center of the brain, causing aggressive behavior
    b. activate the aggressive genes in the person's DNA
    c. impair the ability to consider the consequences of acting impulsively
    d. increase the anxiety associated with being punished for one's actions

    ANS: C   DIF: 5   REF: p. 389   OBJ: 4 TYPE: APP

40. Which of the following terms is the definition of *anxioltytic?*
    a. sleep-inducing
    b. anxiety-reducing
    c. antiseizure
    d. calming

    ANS: B   DIF: 3   REF: p. 389   OBJ: 5 TYPE FACT

41. Which of the following terms is the definition of *sedative?*
    a. sleep-inducing
    b. anxiety reducing
    c. antiseizure
    d. calming

    ANS: D   DIF: 3   REF: p. 389   OBJ: 5 TYPE: FACT

42. Which of the following terms is the definition of *hypnotic*?
    a. sleep-inducing
    b. anxiety reducing
    c. antiseizure
    d. calming

    ANS: A   DIF: 3   REF: p. 389   OBJ: 5 TYPE: FACT

43. Which of the following terms is the definition of *anticonvulsant?*
    a. sleep-inducing
    b. anxiety reducing
    c. antiseizure
    d. calming

    ANS: C   DIF: 3   REF: p. 389   OBJ: 5 TYPE: FACT

44. Which of the following drugs is NOT classified as a barbiturate?
    a. Amytal
    b. Seconal
    c. Rohypnol
    d. Nembutal

    ANS: C   DIF: 1   REF: p. 389   OBJ: 5 TYPE: FACT

45. Which of the following drugs is NOT classified as a benzodiazepine?
   a. Halcion
   b. Valium
   c. Xanax
   d. Seconal

   ANS: D   DIF: 1   REF: p. 389   OBJ: 5 TYPE: FACT

46. The benzodiazepine medications are prescribed primarily to treat:
   a. pain
   b. depression
   c. anxiety
   d. addiction

   ANS: C   DIF: 1   REF: p. 389   OBJ: 5 TYPE: FACT/WWW

47. Misuse of the benzodiazepine _____ has resulted in it being referred to as the "date rape drug."
   a. Amytal
   b. Halcion
   c. Rohypnol
   d. Ritalin

   ANS: C   DIF: 3   REF: p. 389   OBJ: 5 TYPE: FACT

48. Which of the following types of drugs typically is used in large amounts to commit suicide?
   a. benzodiazepines
   b. barbiturates
   c. stimulants
   d. hallucinogens

   ANS: B   DIF: 1   REF: p. 389   OBJ: 5 TYPE: FACT

49. The most commonly consumed of all the psychoactive drugs are the stimulants, which include all of the following EXCEPT:
   a. caffeine
   b. cocaine
   c. nicotine
   d. mescaline

   ANS: D   DIF: 1   REF: p. 390   OBJ: 6 TYPE: FACT

50. Which of the following is an accurate statement about amphetamines and/or amphetamine use disorders?
   a. Amphetamines cause a period of depression and fatigue (called "crashing"), which is followed by feelings of elation and euphoria.
   b. Amphetamines cause an increase in appetite and a decrease in fatigue.
   c. Amphetamines decrease the availability of dopamine and norepinephrine in the nervous system.
   d. Amphetamine overdose can cause hallucinations, panic, agitation, and paranoid delusions.

   ANS: D   DIF: 3   REF: p. 391   OBJ: 6 TYPE: CON/WWW

51. Which of the following effects is associated with cocaine use?
    a. decreased alertness
    b. increased appetite
    c. decreased pulse and blood pressure
    d. rapid and irregular heartbeat

    ANS: D   DIF: 1   REF: p. 392   OBJ: 6 TYPE: FACT

52. "Crack babies," born to mothers who have used cocaine, often develop problems that are
    attributed not only to the effects of cocaine but also to:
    a. inadequate parenting
    b. mother's use of alcohol, nicotine and/or other drugs
    c. disrupted home environments
    d. all of these

    ANS: D   DIF: 1   REF: p. 392   OBJ: 6 TYPE: FACT

53. Stimulation of the _____ neurons in the "pleasure pathway" (the site in the brain that seems
    to be involved in the experience of pleasure) probably causes the "high" associated with cocaine
    use.
    a. dopamine
    b. serotonin
    c. adrenaline
    d. endorphin

    ANS: A   DIF: 1   REF: p. 393   OBJ: 6 TYPE: CON

54. Your shy and introverted friend tells you that she has discovered a wonder drug that produces
    feelings of euphoria and is not addictive. When you realize that she is talking about cocaine, you
    inform her that:
    a. scientists agree that it is wonder drug just as she describes
    b. in the early 20th century cocaine was an ingredient in Pepsi-Cola
    c. cocaine will make her more social and outgoing
    d. dependence on cocaine develops slowly over a period of years

    ANS: D   DIF: 3   REF: p. 393   OBJ: 6 TYPE: APP/WWW

55. Nikki has decided to stop smoking (again). She can expect to experience which of the following
    withdrawal symptoms?
    a. elevated mood
    b. decreased appetite
    c. weight loss
    d. irritability

    ANS: D   DIF: 3   REF: p. 393-394   OBJ: 6 TYPE: APP

56. From a physiological perspective, the reason that a nicotine addict smokes cigarettes frequently throughout the day is to prevent withdrawal symptoms, which include all of the following EXCEPT:
    a. irritability
    b. weight loss
    c. depression
    d. difficulty concentrating

    ANS: B   DIF: 3   REF: p. 393-394   OBJ: 6 TYPE: FACT

57. The most common of the psychoactive substances, used by 90% of Americans, is:
    a. nicotine
    b. caffeine
    c. marijuana
    d. opium

    ANS: B   DIF: 1   REF: p. 395   OBJ: 7 TYPE: FACT

58. Among the opioids are both natural substances (opiates) and the synthetic narcotic called:
    a. morphine
    b. heroin
    c. methadone
    d. codeine

    ANS: C   DIF: 1   REF: p. 396   OBJ: 7 TYPE: FACT

59. Legally available narcotic medications, including morphine and codeine, are used primarily as:
    a. antagonists
    b. analgesics
    c. antibiotics
    d. antidotes

    ANS: B   DIF: 3   REF: p. 396   OBJ: 7 TYPE: FACT

60. Which of the following is an accurate statement about opiate (narcotic) addiction?
    a. Discontinuing narcotic use brings on withdrawal symptoms in 1-2 hours.
    b. Since opiates (narcotics) are usually injected, users are at increased risk for HIV/AIDS.
    c. The withdrawal process for narcotic addiction takes about 1 to 3 weeks.
    d. Most addicts die before the age of 50 from a drug overdose.

    ANS: B   DIF: 3   REF: p. 397   OBJ: 7 TYPE: FACT/WWW

61. According to a research study in the 1980s of 500 narcotics addicts, the average age at death was about:
    a. 15
    b. 25
    c. 35
    d. 40

    ANS: D   DIF: 1   REF: p. 397   OBJ: 7 TYPE: FACT

62. Enkephalins and endorphins are natural opioids found in:
    a. the brain
    b. the humoral system
    c. DNA
    d. poppy seeds

    ANS: A   DIF: 3   REF: p. 397   OBJ: 7 TYPE: FACT

63. Substances that distort sensory experiences, feelings and perceptions are known as:
    a. opiates
    b. hallucinogens
    c. "roofies"
    d. "benzos"

    ANS: B   DIF: 1   REF: p. 398   OBJ: 7 TYPE: FACT

64. Which of the following is an accurate statement concerning marijuana use and abuse?
    a. Paranoia and hallucinations can occur.
    b. Tolerance develops rapidly.
    c. Psychological dependence can occur with even occasional use.
    d. Marijuana is free of carcinogens.

    ANS: A   DIF: 3   REF: p. 398   OBJ: 7 TYPE: FACT

65. Which of the following hallucinogenic substances is processed synthetically?
    a. marijuana
    b. LSD
    c. psilocybin
    d. mescaline

    ANS: B   DIF: 1   REF: p. 399   OBJ: 7 TYPE: FACT

66. All of the following are informative and accurate statements about inhalants EXCEPT:
    a. Inhalant use is most commonly observed among college students.
    b. Symptoms of inhalant use include slurred speech, dizziness, and euphoria.
    c. Long-term inhalant use can damage bone marrow, the kidneys, the liver, and the brain.
    d. Use of inhalants can cause users to be antisocial and aggressive.

    ANS: A   DIF: 3   REF: p. 400   OBJ: 8 TYPE: FACT

67. Use of the testosterone derived anabolic-androgenic steroids differs from other illicit drug use because:
    a. the "high" produced from steroid use is more intense than that experienced with other drugs
    b. steroids are used to increase body mass and enhance performance
    c. more females than males use anabolic steroids
    d. steroids can be taken orally or by injection

    ANS: B   DIF: 3   REF: p. 400-401   OBJ: 8 TYPE: CON/WWW

68. Among the so-called recreational or illicit "designer drugs" is a dissociative anesthetic that produces a sense of detachment along with a reduced awareness of pain. It is called:
    a. Ecstasy (MDMA)
    b. "K" or "Special K"
    c. Eve
    d. Nexus

    ANS: B   DIF: 1   REF: p. 401   OBJ: 8 TYPE: FACT

69. The drug called Antabuse helps people abstain from drinking alcohol by:
    a. causing alcoholic drinks to taste bitter
    b. interfering with the body's metabolism of alcohol
    c. making people allergic to alcohol
    d. reducing the pleasurable feelings that are associated with alcohol

    ANS: B   DIF: 3   REF: p. 409   OBJ: 13 TYPE: CON

70. A recent research study on alcoholism suggests that *use* of illegal drugs is influenced by environmental factors but *abuse and dependence* are more influenced by:
    a. genetic factors
    b. psychological factors
    c. non-biological factors
    d. cultural factors

    ANS: A   DIF: 3   REF: p. 402   OBJ: 10 TYPE: FACT

71. When an individual who has previously taken Antabuse drinks alcohol, he or she will probably:
    a. become very ill
    b. have a convulsion
    c. develop a skin rash
    d. become feverish

    ANS: A   DIF: 1   REF: p. 409   OBJ: 13 TYPE: FACT

72. The common factor among psychoactive drugs may be:
    a. their ability to activate the "pleasure pathways" of the brain
    b. the ease of obtaining them and the relatively inexpensive cost
    c. the similar way in which they are metabolized in the body
    d. their identical effect on neurotransmitters at the synapse

    ANS: A   DIF: 3   REF: p. 402   OBJ: 9 TYPE: CON/WWW

73. In the 1950s James Olds used electrical stimulation on the brains of rats and discovered:
    a. the aggressive center of the brain
    b. the pleasure center of the brain
    c. that rats did not like to have their brains electrically stimulated
    d. that rats had no brains

    ANS: B   DIF: 1   REF: p. 402   OBJ: 9 TYPE: APP

74. The "pleasure pathways," or internal reward centers, in the human brain are primarily made up of:
   a. dopamine-sensitive neurons
   b. serotonin-sensitive neurons
   c. both of these
   d. neither of these

   ANS: A   DIF: 3   REF: p. 402   OBJ: 9 TYPE: FACT

75. The drugs that directly stimulate the internal reward center or pleasure pathways in the brain include:
   a. amphetamines and cocaine
   b. the opiates
   c. all of these
   d. none of these

   ANS: C   DIF: 3   REF: p. 402   OBJ: 9 TYPE: FACT

76. The field of research called "functional genomics" is concerned with how:
   a. to find the genes that are responsible for alcoholism
   b. alcoholics function in their daily lives
   c. genes work to influence addiction
   d. people recover from alcoholism

   ANS: C   DIF: 1   REF: p. 402   OBJ: 9 TYPE: FACT

77. Yesterday you asked your friend Ray for a couple of aspirin tablets. Ray has been taking a psychology course and informs you that, in behavioral terms, aspirin is a _____ reinforcer. (After listening to this, your headache begins to gets worse.)
   a. positive
   b. negative
   c. neutral
   d. variable

   ANS: B   DIF: 3   REF: p. 402   OBJ: 9 TYPE: APP

78. In behavioral terms drugs like aspirin are considered negative reinforcers because they:
   a. make a person feel good
   b. stop a person from feeling pain
   c. have toxic effects on the nervous system
   d. can cause frequent users to become dependent on them

   ANS: B   DIF: 1   REF: p. 402   OBJ: 9 TYPE: CON

79. In trying to understand why some individuals become addicted to drugs and others do not, it is important to consider the negative reinforcement that is associated with the anxiolytic effect, i.e., a drug's ability to:
   a. produce a "high"
   b. reduce anxiety
   c. metabolize quickly
   d. relieve pain

   ANS: B   DIF: 5   REF: p. 402   OBJ: 9 TYPE: CON/WWW

80. Which of the following drugs is known to have an anxiolytic (anxiety-relieving) effect?
    a. methamphetamine
    b. alcohol
    c. caffeine
    d. LSD

    ANS: B   DIF: 1   REF: p. 402   OBJ: 9 TYPE: FACT

81. In trying to understand why some people continue to use drugs until they become dependent on them and others are able to stop before this happens, it is important to consider:
    a. how sensitive a person is to both the negative effects of alcohol when it is first ingested and to the negative effects of alcohol after a few hours
    b. how sensitive a person is to the positive effects of alcohol when it is first ingested and to the negative effects after a few hours
    c. how sensitive a person is to the negative effects of alcohol when it is first ingested and to the positive effects a few hours later
    d. how sensitive a person is to the positive effects of alcohol when it is first ingested and to the positive effects a few hours later

    ANS: B   DIF: 5   REF: p. 403   OBJ: 9 TYPE: CON

82. In a study involving the sons of alcoholics who were at high risk themselves for developing alcoholism, it was found that:
    a. they were less sensitive to the positive effects of alcohol when it was first ingested
    b. they were more sensitive to the negative effects of alcohol after a few hours
    c. both of these
    d. neither of these

    ANS: D   DIF: 5   REF: p. 403   OBJ: 9 TYPE: APP

83. In a laboratory research study involving "drug addiction" in animals, it was demonstrated that the positive reinforcing effect of drugs was:
    a. biological only
    b. tied to social and cultural influences
    c. free from social and cultural influences
    d. biological, social and cultural

    ANS: C   DIF: 3   REF: p. 403   OBJ: 9 TYPE: APP

84. Many individuals use drugs as negative reinforcement, i.e., to escape from the unpleasantness (pain, stress, anxiety) in their lives. This phenomenon is called all of the following EXCEPT:
    a. self-medication
    b. tension reduction
    c. controlled dosing
    d. negative affect

    ANS: C   DIF: 3   REF: p. 403   OBJ: 9 TYPE: CON

85. The integration of both positive and negative reinforcement in explaining why the "crash" that follows the initial euphoria of drug use is not a deterrent to further drug use is called:
    a. the opponent-process theory
    b. amotivational syndrome
    c. substance induced myopia
    d. an expectancy effect

    ANS: A   DIF: 3   REF: p. 404   OBJ: 9 TYPE: CON

86. Which of the following is an accurate statement about the opponent-process explanation of drug addiction?
    a. an increase in positive feelings will be followed by an increase in negative feelings
    b. an increase in negative feelings will be followed by an increase in positive feelings
    c. both of these
    d. neither of these

    ANS: C   DIF: 5   REF: p. 404   OBJ: 9 TYPE: CON

87. In the 1980s, a research study focusing on seventh and eighth graders' expectations about drinking alcohol revealed that some of the students begin drinking because they think it will have positive effects on their social behavior and cognitive and motor skills, a phenomenon called:
    a. alcoholic myopia
    b. an expectancy effect
    c. opponent-process theory
    d. regressive alcoholism

    ANS: B   DIF: 3   REF: p. 404   OBJ: 9 TYPE: CON

88. The cognitive phenomenon called alcohol myopia occurs when an individual:
    a. finally sees that drinking alcohol has only negative consequences and stops drinking
    b. continues to drink even when he or she knows that excessive drinking has severe negative consequences
    c. continues to drink and denies that there are any negative consequences associated with alcohol
    d. properly evaluates the risks associated with continued abuse of alcohol and decides to enter a treatment program

    ANS: B   DIF: 5   REF: p. 404   OBJ: 9 TYPE: APP

89. A research study suggesting that 20% to 50% of young children (ages 3-6) have already had some exposure to alcohol asked the children to:
    a. taste small amounts of wine, whiskey and beer
    b. describe what wine, whiskey and beer taste like
    c. identify alcoholic and non-alcoholic drinks by smell
    d. talk about family members and other relatives who drink alcohol

    ANS: C   DIF: 3   REF: p. 405   OBJ: 9 TYPE: APP

90. Substance abuse can be seen from either a biological or a psychosocial perspective. For example, the condemnation of drug abuse as an official sin by the Catholic Church is an example of

    _____.
    a. the moral weakness model
    b. the disease model of dependence
    c. the AA model of drug dependency
    d. a 12 step program

    ANS: A   DIF: 3   REF: p. 405   OBJ: 9 TYPE: CON

91. The integrative approach to substance abuse reflects the concept of equifinality, which means that:
    a. a genetic factor alone is the cause of substance abuse
    b. neurobiological factors determine whether substance abuse will develop
    c. psychological factors are the primary determinants of whether or not a person becomes a drug addict
    d. for any particular individual substance abuse may arise from multiple and different causes

    ANS: D   DIF: 3   REF: p. 406   OBJ: 11 TYPE: CON

92. Which of the following are examples of agonist types of treatment for substance abuse?
    a. the use of methadone to treat heroin addiction
    b. a nicotine patch or nicotine gum to treat addiction to cigarette smoking
    c. both of these
    d. neither of these

    ANS: C   DIF: 1   REF: p. 408   OBJ: 13 TYPE: FACT

93. The drug opiate-antagonist naltrexone is a treatment for substance abuse that works by:
    a. substituting a chemically similar drug for the addictive drug
    b. both counteracting the effects of opiates and producing withdrawal symptoms
    c. producing a cross-tolerance effect in a drug user
    d. producing only a temporary euphoric effect if opiates continue to be used

    ANS: B   DIF: 3   REF: p. 408   OBJ: 13 TYPE: FACT

94. An alcoholic who is highly motivated to stop drinking and who understands the possibly severe consequences of treatment may be prescribed the drug called Antabuse. This medication is an example of an _____ treatment for alcoholism.
    a. agonist (substitution)
    b. antagonist
    c. aversive
    d. AA

    ANS: C   DIF: 1   REF: p. 409   OBJ: 13 TYPE: APP

95. Which of the following is NOT an accurate statement about Alcoholics Anonymous?
    a. AA is clearly an effective treatment for some people with alcohol dependence.
    b. More than 3% of the adult population of the United States has attended an AA meeting.
    c. AA advocates controlled drinking in which former alcoholics can become social drinkers.
    d. It is difficult to conduct accurate research on AA because participation is anonymous.

    ANS: C   DIF: 3   REF: p. 409-410   OBJ: 13 TYPE: FACT

96. The community reinforcement approach, a new type of program that has been started to address the problem of substance abuse, includes all of the following components EXCEPT:
    a. a non-substance abusing relative participates with the alcoholic in relationship improvement sessions
    b. the substance abuser is encouraged to accept that his or her friends may continue to be users but associating with them is still OK
    c. assistance with employment, education, finances, or other social service areas is provided to help reduce stress
    d. options are suggested for new recreational activities to replace previous drug related activities

    ANS: B   DIF: 3   REF: p. 411   OBJ: 14 TYPE: CON

97. Of the following types of drug prevention strategies which one has the potential for the most successful outcome (according to the information in your textbook)?
    a. education-based programs (e.g., DARE)
    b. skills training to resist social, media and peer pressure to use drugs
    c. relapse prevention programs focusing on the learned aspects of dependence, i.e., the failure of cognitive and behavioral coping skills
    d. cultural attitude change (e.g., widespread enactment of no-smoking legislation)

    ANS: D   DIF: 3   REF: p. 412   OBJ: 14 TYPE: FACT

98. In the excerpt from Drinking: A Love Story (1996) in your textbook, author Caroline Knapp writes that in addition to being an alcoholic, she also had cross-addictions to:
    a. cigarette smoking
    b. anorexia
    c. both of these
    d. neither of these

    ANS: C   DIF: 3   REF: p. 415   OBJ: 4 TYPE: APP

99. An impulse control disorder involving the recurrent failure to resist urges to steal things for neither personal nor monetary value is called:
    a. pyromania   c. trichotillomania
    b. kleptomania   d. erotomania

    ANS: B   DIF: 2   REF: p. 412   OBJ: 15 TYPE: CON

100. In the impulse control disorders, the individual feels _____ prior to carrying out the act.
    a. relaxed and calm   c. spaced out
    b. tense and aroused   d. angry and aggressive

    ANS: B   DIF: 2   REF: p. 413   OBJ: 15 TYPE: CON

101. Although most impulse control disorders are considered rare, one that affects an increasing number of people is _____.
    a. kleptomania   c. pathological gambling
    b. pyromania   d. intermittent explosive disorder

    ANS: C   DIF: 2   REF: p. 413   OBJ: 15 TYPE: FACT

102. Although AA (Alcoholics Anonymous) programs are considered effective, the drop out rate for GA (Gambler's Anonymous) programs is:
    a. 10-30%
    b. 30-50%
    c. 50-70%
    d. 70-90%

    ANS: D   DIF: 1   REF: p. 414   OBJ: 15 TYPE: FACT

103. Which of the following is an accurate statement about trichotillomania?
    a. More males than females are diagnosed with this problem.
    b. Compulsive hair pulling is confined to the head only.
    c. Between 1% and 5% of college students are diagnosed with this disorder.
    d. Cognitive behavioral interventions have not been effective in treating this disorder.

    ANS: C   DIF: 3   REF: p. 414   OBJ: 15 TYPE: FACT

104. On the "Abnormal Psychology Live" CD for Chapter 11, Tim relates that after a night of heavy drinking, he _____ to get over a hangover.
    a. takes medication
    b. exercises
    c. drinks more alcohol
    d. sleeps all day

    ANS: C   REF: CD

105. On the "Abnormal Psychology Live" CD for Chapter 11, Tim, an alcoholic, relates that his drinking has resulted in:
    a. loss of employment
    b. trouble with the law
    c. a broken marriage
    d. medical problems

    ANS: B   REF: CD

106. On the "Abnormal Psychology Live" CD, Tim's need to increase his alcohol intake to maintain the same effect is called:
    a. tolerance
    b. intoxication
    c. withdrawal
    d. a hangover

    ANS: A   REF: CD

ESSAY

1. Compare and contrast the "levels of involvement" in substance related disorders: use, intoxication, abuse, and dependence. Define the meaning of the word "addiction."

2. Define "psychoactive substance" and give examples of the different categories of psychoactive drugs. Discuss whether these drugs are psychologically or physiologically addictive.

3. Describe the psychological and behavioral effects of alcohol. Discuss both the short term and long term consequences of alcohol abuse.

4. Compare Jellinek's stages of alcoholism with information from the current research on progression of the disorder.

5. Compare and contrast the depressant drugs, including benzodiazepines, barbiturates and anxiolytics. Discuss medical uses for these substances and the potential for abuse and/or addiction.

6. Compare and contrast the stimulant drugs. Discuss the history of cocaine as well as its atypical type of addictive process.   **WWW**

7. Discuss the problems of both steroid and inhalant abuse, noting psychological and physical effects. How do steroid and inhalant abuse differ from abuse of other substances?

8. Discuss current research on the genetic/biological, social and cultural factors related to alcoholism. Which factors appear most strongly related to the development and progression of the disorder?

9. Explain the Alcoholics Anonymous model of treatment for alcoholism and its policy of abstinence. Discuss the reasons for the worldwide support of AA as well as the criticisms of the program.

10. Discuss the issue of substance addiction in terms of consequences for the individual and society. Explore why relapse prevention and intervention programs have had only limited effectiveness in solving the problem of drug addiction.

11. After viewing the "Abnormal Psychology Live" CD for Chapter 11, describe some of the consequences of alcoholism for Tim. What changes in his life occurred as a result of his drinking behavior? Use specific examples to discuss whether Tim understands that alcohol has controlled his life.

REF: CD

MULTIPLE CHOICE

1. _____ are psychoactive substances that are among the most likely to produce physical dependence, tolerance, and withdrawal. These substances include alcohol and anxiolytic drugs.
   a. Opioids
   b. Depressants
   c. Stimulants
   d. Hallucinogens

   ANS: B

2. Two important aspects of a definition of substance dependence are _____ and _____.
   a. tolerance; withdrawal
   b. withdrawal; relapse
   c. relapse; tolerance
   d. alcohol delirium; tolerance

   ANS: A

3. Nicotine is a _____, alcohol is a _____, and morphine is a _____.
   a. stimulant; depressant; opioid
   b. stimulant; depressant; hallucinogenic
   c. depressant; stimulant; opioid
   d. opioid; hallucinogenic; stimulant

   ANS: A

4. Relapse prevention is a treatment method that
   a. looks at the learned aspect of dependence.
   b. sees relapse as a failure of cognitive and behavioral coping skills.
   c. looks at relapse as inevitably leading to more drug use.
   d. both a and b

   ANS: D

5. _____ refers to the physiological reaction called drunkenness or high.
   a. Substance use
   b. Substance abuse
   c. Substance dependence
   d. none of the above

   ANS: D

6. Which of the following is the most routinely used illegal substance in the United States?
   a. opioids
   b. heroin
   c. cocaine
   d. marijuana

   ANS: D

7. A person with a genetic vulnerability to substance dependence
   a. will inevitably develop that dependence.
   b. may choose not to use the substance in order to avoid becoming dependent.
   c. will be more likely to try the substance.
   d. has no control over whether he or she initiates use of the substance.

   ANS: B

8. Factors that affect whether alcohol will cause organic damage include:
   a. frequency of use
   b. whether the body has time to recover between binges
   c. blood alcohol levels attained while drinking
   d. all of the above

   ANS: D

9. Which of the following is true of substance-related disorders?
   a. They kill 500,000 Americans every year.
   b. They cost hundreds of billions of dollars each year.
   c. They play a role in homelessness.
   d. all of the above

   ANS: D

10. The liver of an average-size person can metabolize how much alcohol per hour?
    a. 7 to 10 grams (one glass of beer)
    b. 12 to 16 grams (two glasses of beer)
    c. 3 to 4 grams (a half glass of beer)
    d. The liver does not metabolize alcohol.

    ANS: A

MULTIPLE CHOICE

1. According to the definition of personality disorder, only individuals who show _____
   patterns of maladaptive behavior should be diagnosed with a personality disorder.
   a. suicidal
   b. the most severe
   c. relatively permanent
   d. highly variable

   ANS: C   DIF: 1   REF: p. 421   OBJ: 1 TYPE: FACT/WWW

2. All of the following are necessary conditions for the diagnosis of a personality disorder EXCEPT:
   a. patient feelings of distress
   b. pervasive pattern of behavior
   c. maladaptive functioning
   d. chronic

   ANS: A   DIF: 3   REF: p. 421   OBJ: 1 TYPE: FACT

3. On which axis of DSM-IV are personality disorders coded?
   a. I
   b. II
   c. III
   d. IV

   ANS: B   DIF: 1   REF: p. 421   OBJ: 1 TYPE: FACT

4. The reason that personality disorders are coded on Axis II of DSM-IV-TR is that:
   a. they relate to extreme deficits in functioning
   b. there is a relationship between personality disorder and mental retardation
   c. they are biological in nature
   d. they relate to more ingrained and permanent features than other disorders

   ANS: D   DIF: 1   REF: p. 421   OBJ: 1 TYPE: FACT

5. Unlike schizophrenia or an eating disorder, personality disorders can be viewed as disorders of:
   a. biology rather than learning
   b. learning rather than disease
   c. degree rather than kind
   d. functioning rather than disease

   ANS: C   DIF: 3   REF: p. 422   OBJ: 2 TYPE: CON

6. Clinicians who view personality disorders as extremes of normal personality rather than as
   _____ have criticized the way DSM-IV-TR classifies personality disorders.
   a. medical conditions
   b. biologically based traits
   c. separate categories of disorders
   d. impaired functioning

   ANS: C   DIF: 3   REF: p. 422   OBJ: 2 TYPE: CON

7. Both John and Fred meet the diagnostic criteria for paranoid personality disorder. John's friends
   are aware of his paranoia although he continues to live a meaningful life. Fred's paranoia is so
   extreme that he finds it hard to function in society. The DSM-IV-TR, Axis II diagnosis for these
   individuals would be:
   a. exactly the same
   b. categorically different
   c. in the same category but reflect the different levels of pathology
   d. in the same category with different specifiers

   ANS: A   DIF: 3   REF: p. 422   OBJ: 2 TYPE: APP

8. The five factor model of personality includes all of the following as personality dimensions
   EXCEPT:
   a. extroversion
   b. conscientiousness
   c. expressiveness
   d. emotional stability

   ANS: C   DIF: 3   REF: p. 422   OBJ: 2 TYPE: FACT

9. Cross-cultural research on the five factor model of personality suggests that:
   a. there is no such thing as a universal human personality structure
   b. the five dimensions are fairly universal
   c. only two dimensions are universal
   d. Western type personality structure differs from the non-Western type

   ANS: B   DIF: 5   REF: p. 422   OBJ: 2 TYPE: FACT

10. DSM-IV-TR divides personality disorders into ___ distinct clusters.
    a. 1
    b. 2
    c. 3
    d. 4

    ANS: C   DIF: 1   REF: p. 422   OBJ: 1 TYPE: FACT

11. Which set of adjective pairs correctly describes the clusters into which DSM-IV-TR personality
    disorders are grouped?
    a. odd/eccentric, dangerous/inconsistent, and shy/withdrawn
    b. shy/withdrawn, anxious/fearful, and dangerous/inconsistent
    c. shy/withdrawn, dramatic/emotional, and bizarre/thought disordered
    d. odd/eccentric, dramatic/emotional, and anxious/fearful

    ANS: D   DIF: 1   REF: p. 423   OBJ: 1 TYPE: FACT

12. In the U.S. the prevalence of personality disorders is estimated to be between:
    a. .1 and .5%
    b. .5 and 2.5%
    c. 2.5 and 5%
    d. 5 and 10%

    ANS: B   DIF: 1   REF: p. 424   OBJ: 1 TYPE: FACT

13. The characteristic features of personality disorders tend to develop with:
    a. rapid onset in late adolescence
    b. gradual onset in adulthood
    c. rapid onset in adulthood
    d. onset in childhood that is difficult to pinpoint

    ANS: D   DIF: 3   REF: p. 424   OBJ: 1 TYPE: FACT/WWW

14. According to your textbook, the main reason that we do not have sufficient research examining the development of personality disorders is that:
    a. many individuals do not seek treatment in the early phases of these disorders
    b. there is insufficient research funding for these disorders due to relative lack of public awareness
    c. sophisticated research methods are necessary to study disorders that are so ingrained in personality
    d. all of these are correct

    ANS: A   DIF: 3   REF: p. 424   OBJ: 7 TYPE: FACT

15. A study by Ford and Widiger (1989) suggests that the gender differences observed in the prevalence of many personality disorders (i.e., histrionic, dependent, antisocial) may be due to:
    a. genetic differences
    b. gender specific learned behavior patterns
    c. gender bias on the part of the diagnosing clinician
    d. cultural scripts that dictate the type of disordered behavior appropriate for each gender

    ANS: C   DIF: 3   REF: p. 425   OBJ: 7 TYPE: FACT

16. A woman demonstrating very stereotypical female traits probably would be diagnosed with histrionic personality disorder. Which of the following would probably occur if a man demonstrated very stereotypical masculine traits?
    a. He would be given a diagnosis of antisocial personality disorder.
    b. He would be given a diagnosis of avoidant personality disorder.
    c. He would be given a diagnosis of narcissistic personality disorder.
    d. He would not be diagnosed with a personality disorder.

    ANS: D   DIF: 5   REF: p. 425   OBJ: 7 TYPE: CON

17. The diagnosis of more than one personality disorder in an individual patient is:
    a. common
    b. impossible unless the person suffers from dissociative identity disorder
    c. rare
    d. only possible for personality disorders in the same DSM-IV cluster

    ANS: A   DIF: 1   REF: p. 426   OBJ: 7 TYPE: FACT

18. Max is always sure that others are trying to harm him. His perception that the world is a threatening place impacts most of his life. Most likely Max would be diagnosed with the personality disorder called:
    a. histrionic
    b. avoidant
    c. paranoid
    d. antisocial

    ANS: C   DIF: 1   REF: p. 427   OBJ: 3 TYPE: APP

19. An individual presents for treatment and keeps talking about how gangsters are "out to get him." Before diagnosing paranoid personality disorder, we must determine whether:
    a. his fears are justified
    b. his family life is stable
    c. he has ever been in trouble with the law
    d. he avoids socialization

    ANS: A   DIF: 1   REF: p. 427   OBJ: 3 TYPE: CON

20. The language barrier of refugees from other countries and people with hearing impairments may make these individuals particularly susceptible to:
    a. histrionic personality disorder
    b. paranoid personality disorder
    c. schizotypal personality disorder
    d. schizoid personality disorder

    ANS: B   DIF: 3   REF: p. 428   OBJ: 3 TYPE: APP

21. You are waiting to board a plane when you hear that the flight has been delayed due to a passing thunderstorm. The man sitting next to you says, "passing thunder storm, sure! That's Jim again, he's been doing everything to make me miss this meeting because he's trying to get me fired!" Of the following, this statement would be most consistent with _____ personality disorder.
    a. avoidant
    b. histrionic
    c. borderline
    d. paranoid

    ANS: D   DIF: 3   REF: p. 428   OBJ: 3 TYPE: APP

22. One of the greatest challenges for any therapist treating an individual with paranoid personality disorder is:
    a. understanding the patient's belief system
    b. getting the patient to trust the therapist
    c. convincing the patient to talk about his beliefs
    d. getting the patient to speak clearly

    ANS: B   DIF: 1   REF: p. 428   OBJ: 3 TYPE: CON

23. The data regarding treatment outcome for individuals with paranoid personality disorder:
    a. indicate no evidence for treatment success
    b. suggest that treatment can only be successful if the patient remains in therapy for a minimum of one year
    c. indicate that cognitive therapy is effective in most cases
    d. demonstrate that strict behavioral approaches are effective

    ANS: A   DIF: 1   REF: p. 429   OBJ: 3 TYPE: FACT

24. Theo is quite a loner. He walks to class by himself, does not talk to anyone and appears indifferent to other people. It is clear that Theo neither desires nor enjoys closeness with others. He does not act in any obviously unusual ways nor does he appear to possess strange beliefs about the world. Of the following personality disorders, Theo appears to be:
    a. avoidant
    b. antisocial
    c. schizoid
    d. schizotypal

    ANS: C   DIF: 5   REF: p. 429   OBJ: 3 TYPE: APP/WWW

25. An individual who goes through life as a loner with no motivation to interact with others but with relatively normal behavior and beliefs is likely to be diagnosed with _____ personality disorder:
    a. histrionic
    b. narcissistic
    c. schizoid
    d. paranoid

    ANS: C   DIF: 1   REF: p. 429   OBJ: 3 TYPE: FACT

26. One prevelant outcome for individuals with schizoid personality disorder is:
    a. homelessness   c. eating disorders
    b. drug abuse   d. anxiety

    ANS: A   DIF: 3   REF: p. 429   OBJ: 3 TYPE: FACT

27. The cause of schizoid personality disorder is:
    a. unknown
    b. biological
    c. genetic
    d. learned

    ANS: A   DIF: 1   REF: p. 430   OBJ: 3 TYPE: FACT

28. Patients diagnosed with schizoid personality disorder are usually:
   a. motivated to begin therapy and generally make progress quickly
   b. motivated to begin therapy but generally make little progress
   c. not motivated to begin therapy and generally make little progress while in therapy
   d. not motivated to begin therapy but generally make progress quickly while in therapy

   ANS: C   DIF: 1   REF: p. 430   OBJ: 3 TYPE: FACT

29. Individuals who are socially isolated, behave in ways that seem unusual, tend to be suspicious and have odd beliefs are generally diagnosed with _____ personality disorder.
   a. schizotypal
   b. schizoid
   c. paranoid
   d. multiple

   ANS: A   DIF: 3   REF: p. 430   OBJ: 3 TYPE: FACT

30. Individuals who have "ideas of reference" but who sense that these beliefs are probably unrealistic are generally diagnosed with _____ personality disorder.
   a. schizotypal
   b. paranoid
   c. antisocial
   d. histrionic

   ANS: A   DIF: 5   REF: p. 431   OBJ: 3 TYPE: FACT

31. The personality disorder that shares many similar symptoms with schizophrenia is:
   a. schizoid
   b. paranoid
   c. borderline
   d. schizotypal

   ANS: D   DIF: 1   REF: p. 431   OBJ: 3 TYPE: FACT

32. According to the textbook the most likely cause of schizotypal personality disorder is:
   a. poor parenting
   b. social modeling
   c. biological
   d. isolation during childhood

   ANS: C   DIF: 3   REF: p. 431   OBJ: 3 TYPE: FACT

33. As many as 30% to 50% of the individuals with schizotypal personality disorder who request clinical help also meet the criteria for:
   a. obsessive compulsive disorder   c. anorexia
   b. substance disorder   d. major depressive disorder

   ANS: D   DIF: 3   REF: p. 432   OBJ: 3 TYPE: FACT

34. Alan has been diagnosed with schizotypal personality disorder and has begun psychotherapy. Since he is willing to attend therapy sessions, his prognosis for success in treatment is:
   a. excellent since most patients seeking treatment eventually are symptom free
   b. at best moderate since research shows only modest treatment gains for this diagnosis
   c. excellent only if he is willing to take medication
   d. poor since most patients go on to develop schizophrenia

   ANS: B   DIF: 3   REF: p. 432   OBJ: 3 TYPE: APP

35. Steve steals money from his friends and family, lies to get what he wants and often hurts others with no sign of guilt or remorse. Steve should probably be diagnosed with _____ personality disorder.
   a. paranoid
   b. histrionic
   c. antisocial
   d. narcissistic

   ANS: C   DIF: 1   REF: p. 434   OBJ: 4 TYPE: APP

36. The most accurate statement regarding antisocial personality disorder and psychopathy is that they:
   a. are similar in almost every way except that psychopaths are criminals
   b. completely different populations
   c. overlap in some features but not all
   d. just different names for the same features

   ANS: C   DIF: 3   REF: p. 434   OBJ: 4 TYPE: FACT

37. With which of the following personality disorders is the term psychopath closely associated?
   a. schizotypal
   b. schizoid
   c. paranoid
   d. antisocial

   ANS: D   DIF: 1   REF: p. 434   OBJ: 5 TYPE: FACT

38. One difference between a psychopath and a person with antisocial personality disorder is that _____ are used in diagnosing the psychopath but _____ are used to diagnose antisocial personality disorder.
   a. personality traits; observable behaviors
   b. observable behaviors; personality traits
   c. clinical judgments; objective test scores
   d. medical criteria; psychological assessments

   ANS: A   DIF: 5   REF: p. 434   OBJ: 5 TYPE: CON

39. An adult diagnosed with antisocial personality disorder is most likely to have met the criteria for
    _____ as a child.
    a. autism
    b. conduct disorder
    c. learning disabled
    d. mental retardation

    ANS: B   DIF: 1   REF: p. 435   OBJ: 4 TYPE: FACT/WWW

40. Rob is a 15-year-old boy who has been repeatedly arrested for theft and assault. In addition to
    shoplifting and other theft, he has been caught stealing money from his parent's wallets and his
    young sister's piggy bank. Rob shows no guilt or remorse for the many ways that he hurts others.
    Rob's current diagnosis is most likely:
    a. antisocial personality disorder
    b. attention deficit hyperactivity disorder
    c. conduct disorder
    d. narcissistic personality disorder

    ANS: C   DIF: 3   REF: p. 435   OBJ: 4 TYPE: APP

41. The research examining the cause of antisocial personality disorder suggests that:
    a. the primary cause is genetics
    b. genetics and environment interact to cause the disorder
    c. the primary cause is poor parenting
    d. there is no evidence of either a genetic or environmental cause

    ANS: B   DIF: 1   REF: p. 436   OBJ: 5 TYPE: FACT

42. Most of the research examining the causes of antisocial personality disorder has been conducted
    with:
    a. hospital inpatients
    b. criminals
    c. outpatient volunteers
    d. orphans

    ANS: B   DIF: 3   REF: p. 436   OBJ: 5 TYPE: FACT

43. Which of the following are the two major theories that have been proposed to explain antisocial
    personality disorder?
    a. underarousal and fearlessness
    b. underarousal and shamelessness
    c. Yerkes-Dodson and underarousal
    d. Yerkes-Dodson and shamelessness

    ANS: A   DIF: 1   REF: p. 437   OBJ: 5 TYPE: FACT

44. The presence of low frequency theta waves in the brains of psychopaths led to the development of the:
    a. underarousal hypothesis
    b. fearlessness hypothesis
    c. shamelessness hypothesis
    d. cortical-immaturity hypothesis

    ANS: D   DIF: 5   REF: p. 437   OBJ: 5 TYPE: CON

45. According to the underarousal hypothesis, individuals with antisocial personality disorder may engage in their characteristic behaviors as a way to:
    a. deal with their fears
    b. provide a level of stimulation that most of us receive from more typical behaviors
    c. provide a sense of relief from the feelings of depression that they experience when they are not highly aroused
    d. reduce the generally high level of arousal that they feel

    ANS: B   DIF: 3   REF: p. 437   OBJ: 5 TYPE: CON

46. The concept of the fearlessness hypothesis of antisocial personality disorder is that individuals with this disorder:
    a. learn to avoid punishment
    b. have an under-active cortex
    c. under react to the threat of punishment
    d. have brain damage that inhibits their ability to understand the implications of their actions

    ANS: C   DIF: 3   REF: p. 437   OBJ: 5 TYPE: CON

47. One prominent theory of antisocial personality disorder suggests that the behaviors are caused by an imbalance between the brain's:
    a. behavioral inhibition system and fight/flight system
    b. fight/flight system and reward system
    c. cortical stimulation system and behavioral inhibition system
    d. behavioral inhibition system and reward system

    ANS: D   DIF: 5   REF: p. 438   OBJ: 5 TYPE: FACT

48. If you had absolutely no concept or fear of the consequences of your actions (for yourself or others) and were overly motivated by pleasing yourself, you might behave like a person with _____ personality disorder.
    a. antisocial
    b. narcissistic
    c. histrionic
    d. schizotypal

    ANS: A   DIF: 1   REF: p. 438   OBJ: 5 TYPE: CON

49. Some research with psychopaths suggests that these individuals are:
   a. more likely to quit trying as soon as failure appears imminent
   b. less likely to attempt difficult goals
   c. more likely to keep trying even though failure is certain
   d. less likely to be motivated towards a goal

   ANS: C   DIF: 3   REF: p. 438   OBJ: 5 TYPE: FACT/WWW

50. One of the contributing factors in the developmental history of individuals with antisocial personality disorder appears to be that their parents were more likely to have utilized:
   a. firm discipline
   b. inconsistent discipline
   c. an overly protective parenting style
   d. physical discipline

   ANS: B   DIF: 1   REF: p. 438   OBJ: 5 TYPE: FACT

51. The antisocial behavior of those diagnosed with antisocial personality disorder tends to:
   a. continue to increase throughout the life span
   b. increase dramatically at about age 30
   c. decline significantly around age 40
   d. remain stable throughout the lifespan

   ANS: C   DIF: 3   REF: p. 439   OBJ: 5 TYPE: FACT

52. Criminal behavior by individuals with antisocial personality disorder tends to _____ after the age of 40.
   a. decrease
   b. increase
   c. decrease in frequency but increase in severity
   d. increase in frequency but decrease in severity

   ANS: A   DIF: 1   REF: p. 439   OBJ: 5 TYPE: FACT

53. Regarding the likelihood of successful treatment outcome for individuals with antisocial personality disorder, most clinicians are:
   a. optimistic
   b. optimistic only if the patient is willing to work in therapy
   c. pessimistic only if the patient is mandated to therapy by the legal system
   d. pessimistic

   ANS: D   DIF: 1   REF: p. 439   OBJ: 5 TYPE: FACT

54. Given what we know about the treatment of antisocial personality disorder, the best way to ensure that a person with this disorder and a history of violence is not a threat to society is:
   a. intensive psychotherapy
   b. medication
   c. behavioral treatment
   d. incarceration

   ANS: D   DIF: 1   REF: p. 439   OBJ: 5 TYPE: FACT

55. Which of the following is an accurate statement regarding the treatment of antisocial personality disorder and related antisocial behaviors?
    a. patients are generally willing participants in their therapy
    b. most patients refer themselves for treatment because they recognize that they have a problem
    c. there has been greater success in reducing antisocial behavior in children than adults
    d. therapy is successful in about half of the cases treated

    ANS: C   DIF: 1   REF: p. 440   OBJ: 4 TYPE: FACT

56. Recent research (Flannery et al., 2003) suggests that one possible way to reduce the level of antisocial personality disorder in society may be:
    a. group therapy for individuals with antisocial personality disorder
    b. intensive individual therapy for individuals with antisocial personality disorder
    c. behavioral programs and social skills training for aggressive young children
    d. very strict behavioral programs of powerful reinforcers and strict punishers for "at risk" children

    ANS: A   DIF: 3   REF: p. 440   OBJ: 4 TYPE: FACT

57. Lenny is 25 years old and has had multiple arrests for assaults, theft and drug use. He has hurt strangers, friends and family and has never shown any remorse or regret. Following his last arrest, Lenny met with a social worker who told him about antisocial personality disorder; he is now convinced that that is "what's wrong" with him. Lenny recently went to a local community mental health center and asked to be treated by a psychotherapist. The problem with this story is that:
    a. individuals with antisocial personality disorder do not generally seek treatment
    b. Lenny has misdiagnosed himself since his behaviors are more typical of conduct disorder
    c. the drug use does not fit the pattern of antisocial personality disorder
    d. the description does not fit any known personality disorder

    ANS: A   DIF: 3   REF: p. 439   OBJ: 4 TYPE: APP

58. The personality disorder characterized by extreme instability in behavior and emotion, impulsivity, depression and self-injurious behaviors is _____ personality disorder.
    a. narcissistic
    b. borderline
    c. dependent
    d. histrionic

    ANS: B   DIF: 1   REF: p. 440   OBJ: 4 TYPE: FACT

59. Nicole has difficulty maintaining relationships because she goes back and forth from being a best friend to hating people in her life quite often. Her romantic relationships are always characterized by incredible loving passion alternating with episodes of horrible fighting and sometimes she becomes violent. At times Nicole becomes so upset that she cuts herself and reports that this makes her feel better emotionally. Nicole suffers from _____ personality disorder.
    a. dependent
    b. histrionic
    c. borderline
    d. narcissistic

    ANS: C   DIF: 1   REF: p. 441   OBJ: 4 TYPE: APP

60. All of the following are common disorders that tend to be comorbid, i.e., to coexist, with borderline personality disorder EXCEPT:
   a. depression
   b. substance abuse
   c. bulimia
   d. obsessive-compulsive disorder

   ANS: D   DIF: 3   REF: p. 441   OBJ: 4 TYPE: FACT

61. The approximate percentage of individuals diagnosed with borderline personality disorder who also have a substance related disorder is:
   a. 10%
   b. 40%
   c. 70%
   d. almost 100%

   ANS: C   DIF: 5   REF: p. 441   OBJ: 4 TYPE: FACT

62. One of the influences that has been associated with the development of borderline personality disorder is:
   a. history of child abuse or neglect
   b. developmental delay for major milestones (i.e., walking, talking)
   c. parental alcoholism
   d. deficits in neurotransmitter circuits involving dopamine

   ANS: A   DIF: 3   REF: p. 442   OBJ: 4 TYPE: FACT

63. When presented with words projected on a computer screen, individuals with borderline personality disorder are more likely than individuals without the disorder to remember the word:
   a. celebrate   c. full
   b. abandon   d. charming

   ANS: B   DIF: 3   REF: p. 441   OBJ: 4 TYPE: FACT

64. Childhood trauma as a cause of borderline personality disorder may be too simplistic an explanation because:
   a. there are too many neurological deficits that are noted in borderline personality disorder patients
   b. individuals with borderline personality disorder tend to respond to SSRI medications
   c. most individuals diagnosed with borderline personality disorder are female
   d. a significant percentage of individuals diagnosed with borderline personality disorder do not have a history of childhood trauma

   ANS: D   DIF: 3   REF: p. 442   OBJ: 4 TYPE: FACT

65. Which of the following is the most likely model to explain the cause of borderline personality disorder?
    a. biological
    b. early trauma resulting in post traumatic stress disorder symptoms that are not recognized or dealt with during childhood
    c. stressful life events
    d. biological predisposition interacting with life events such as childhood trauma and later life stressors

    ANS: D   DIF: 1   REF: p. 442   OBJ: 4 TYPE: CON

66. Research regarding psychological treatment for borderline personality disorder suggests that _____ appears to be helpful in improving mood and reducing suicidal and self-injurious behaviors.
    a. dialectical behavior therapy
    b. cognitive therapy
    c. operant conditioning
    d. nothing

    ANS: A   DIF: 3   REF: p. 443   OBJ: 4 TYPE: FACT

67. The psychological treatment that has been found to have significant effectiveness in helping patients with borderline personality disorder centers around:
    a. regressing patients to the time in their lives when they experienced trauma
    b. removing the reinforcing attention that they have received for their disordered behavior in the past
    c. joining a 12 step program such as Alcoholics Anonymous
    d. learning to cope with life stressors in a more effective manner

    ANS: D   DIF: 5   REF: p. 443   OBJ: 4 TYPE: CON

68. Individuals who overreact to everything, are overly dramatic and vain are most likely to be diagnosed with _____ personality disorder.
    a. borderline
    b. histrionic
    c. narcissistic
    d. dependent

    ANS: B   DIF: 1   REF: p. 443   OBJ: 4 TYPE: FACT

69. Amy quickly becomes the center of attention when she enters a room. She is a tall and attractive young woman who generally wears something striking. Amy is known as a flirt and acts in a seductive manner around men. When Amy speaks, she uses very exaggerated terms, even when describing relatively ordinary situations. Amy's diagnosis is most likely _____ personality disorder.
    a. histrionic
    b. narcissistic
    c. borderline
    d. dependent

    ANS: A   DIF: 1   REF: p. 443   OBJ: 4 TYPE: APP/WWW

70. There appears to be a relationship between _____ personality disorder and _____ personality disorder with some evidence that each may be gender-typed alternative ways of expressing the same underlying condition.
    a. histrionic; narcissistic
    b. dependent; histrionic
    c. antisocial; histrionic
    d. antisocial; dependent

    ANS: C   DIF: 3   REF: p. 444   OBJ: 4 TYPE: FACT

71. According to your text, the most accurate statement regarding the treatment of histrionic personality disorder is that:
    a. there are no scientific studies demonstrating success
    b. patients who voluntarily attend therapy tend to get better
    c. strict behavioral programs have been shown to be effective in scientific research
    d. cognitive therapy is most effective

    ANS: A   DIF: 3   REF: p. 444   OBJ: 4 TYPE: FACT

72. One of the likely problems a therapist may encounter while trying to help a patient with histrionic personality disorder is the patient's:
    a. unwillingness to admit there is a problem
    b. use of threatenting language
    c. lack of intellectual ability necessary to succeed in therapy
    d. manipulative use of crying, charm, or seductive behavior

    ANS: D   DIF: 5   REF: p. 444   OBJ: 4 TYPE: CON

73. Narcissistic personality disorder is characterized by:
    a. preoccupation with other people
    b. obsession with keeping things neat and orderly
    c. thinking of oneself as deserving of special treatment
    d. pathological dishonesty

    ANS: C   DIF: 1   REF: p. 444   OBJ: 4 TYPE: FACT

74. Vince is extremely impressed with himself. Although he has only achieved a moderate amount of success, he thinks of himself as being uniquely special and deserving of the best of everything. Vince fantasizes frequently about great wealth and fame and does not really pay much attention to other people except to note how they react to him. Vince should be diagnosed with _____ personality disorder.
    a. antisocial
    b. histrionic
    c. narcissistic
    d. dependent

    ANS: C   DIF: 1   REF: p. 445   OBJ: 4 TYPE: APP

75. One reason why individuals with narcissistic personality disorder tend to become depressed at times is that they:
   a. become upset when their intimate relationships fail
   b. seldom live up to their unrealistic expectations of themselves
   c. are overly sensitive to the pain of others
   d. have faulty serotonin circuits

   ANS: B   DIF: 3   REF: p. 445   OBJ: 4 TYPE: CON

76. The personality disorder that sociologists have associated with the increased attention to individualism, competitiveness, success and the short-term pleasure seeking of the "me generation" is _____ personality disorder.
   a. antisocial
   b. dependent
   c. histrionic
   d. narcissistic

   ANS: D   DIF: 1   REF: p. 446   OBJ: 4 TYPE: CON

77. The most accurate statement with regard to treatment research for narcissistic personality disorder (Groopman & Cooper, 2001) is that the research is:
   a. extremely limited in both number of studies and reports of successes
   b. extremely limited in number of studies, though some promising results have been reported
   c. extensive, though few positive results are reported
   d. extensive, though the studies are not scientific

   ANS: A   DIF: 3   REF: p. 446   OBJ: 4 TYPE: CON/WWW

78. All of the following are mentioned in your text as appropriate treatment strategies for narcissistic personality disorder EXCEPT:
   a. cognitive therapy to replace grandiose fantasies with more realistic goals
   b. coping strategies to help accept criticism
   c. exploration of early life trauma that led to the disorder
   d. being helped to focus on the feelings of others

   ANS: C   DIF: 1   REF: p. 446   OBJ: 4 TYPE: FACT/WWW

79. The reason that individuals with avoidant personality disorder avoid most relationships is that they:
   a. are extremely sensitive to the opinions of others and fear rejection
   b. generally dislike other people and prefer to be alone
   c. are so stimulated by the fantasy life in their own minds that they have little need for the company of others
   d. experience bizarre thoughts and beliefs that distance them from others

   ANS: A   DIF: 1   REF: p. 446   OBJ: 6 TYPE: FACT

80. Without understanding the thought process motivating the patient's behavior, it would probably be impossible to determine whether a patient had _____ personality disorder or _____ personality disorder.
    a. narcissistic; antisocial
    b. dependent; narcissistic
    c. schizoid; avoidant
    d. borderline; histrionic

    ANS: C   DIF: 5   REF: p. 446   OBJ: 6 TYPE: CON

81. Individuals who keep to themselves because they are anxious and fearful of rejection are likely to be diagnosed with _____ personality disorder.
    a. avoidant
    b. schizoid
    c. schizotypal
    d. antisocial

    ANS: A   DIF: 3   REF: p. 446   OBJ: 6 TYPE: CON

82. When asked about their childhood, individuals diagnosed with avoidant personality disorder tend to remember their parents as:
    a. warm and loving
    b. substance abusing
    c. rejecting
    d. depressed

    ANS: C   DIF: 1   REF: p. 446   OBJ: 6 TYPE: FACT

83. Of the following, the most accurate statement with regard to the treatment of avoidant personality disorder is:
    a. no well controlled studies of treatment outcomes have been conducted
    b. there are well controlled studies though none show any treatment success
    c. individuals with this disorder are seldom sufficiently motivated to succeed in treatment
    d. behavioral intervention programs for anxiety and social skills have had some success

    ANS: D   DIF: 3   REF: p. 446   OBJ: 6 TYPE: FACT

84. In Jill's psychotherapy sessions the therapist has been using systematic desensitization to gradually make her more comfortable with social situations. Similar to the treatments used for individuals with social phobia, the therapist has given Jill homework assignments that require her to practice talking to strangers, join informal groups and speak in front of small groups. Most likely she is being treated for _____ personality disorder.
    a. antisocial
    b. dependent
    c. avoidant
    d. histrionic

    ANS: C   DIF: 1   REF: p. 447   OBJ: 6 TYPE: APP/WWW

85. The personality disorder characterized by unreasonable fear of abandonment, fear of being rejected, avoidance of disagreement, inability to make decisions for oneself and clinging behavior is _____ personality disorder.
    a. dependent
    b. avoidant
    c. schizoid
    d. histrionic

    ANS: A   DIF: 1   REF: p. 447   OBJ: 6 TYPE: FACT

86. Mary has been married for 20 years and describes how her husband has been verbally abusive toward her for most of that time. She indicates that her husband has had multiple affairs with other women but she can't leave him because she "loves and needs him." When challenged by the interviewer regarding the wisdom of staying with such a man, Mary agrees with the interviewer although she later confides that she always agrees with everyone to avoid conflict and disapproval. Mary should be diagnosed with _____ personality disorder.
    a. avoidant
    b. histrionic
    c. dependent
    d. borderline

    ANS: C   DIF: 1   REF: p. 447   OBJ: 6 TYPE: APP

87. In terms of feelings of inadequacy, sensitivity to criticism and need for reassurance, individuals with _____ personality disorder and _____ personality disorder are quite similar.
    a. dependent; avoidant
    b. dependent; schizoid
    c. schizoid; avoidant
    d. histrionic; antisocial

    ANS: A   DIF: 5   REF: p. 447   OBJ: 6 TYPE: CON

88. Individuals who have excessive feelings of social inadequacy, sensitivity to criticism and a need for reassurance are likely to develop either _____ personality disorder or _____ personality disorder.
    a. narcissistic; antisocial
    b. dependent; narcissistic
    c. avoidant; dependent
    d. antisocial; histrionic

    ANS: C   DIF: 5   REF: p. 447   OBJ: 6 TYPE: CON

89. According to your text, treatment of dependent personality disorder is:
    a. generally successful with a cognitive-behavioral approach
    b. well researched, though no effective treatments have been established
    c. not well researched
    d. successful when based on systematic desensitization and social skills training

    ANS: C   DIF: 3   REF: p. 448   OBJ: 6 TYPE: FACT

90. When individuals with dependent personality disorder are in therapy, they are:
    a. seemingly "model" patients
    b. resistant to the therapeutic process
    c. too unstable to do the intellectual work that therapy requires
    d. demanding and impulsive

    ANS: A   DIF: 3   REF: p. 448   OBJ: 6 TYPE: FACT

91. When working with a patient diagnosed with dependent personality disorder, the therapist must be particularly careful that the patient does not:
    a. take over the agenda of the sessions
    b. become inconsistent in attending sessions
    c. manipulate the therapist by being overly dramatic
    d. become overly dependent on the therapist

    ANS: D   DIF: 3   REF: p. 448   OBJ: 6 TYPE: CON

92. Helen has been in therapy with Dr. Block for dependent personality disorder during the past 3 years. When she first came to therapy she was in an abusive marriage, complained that her adult children treated her poorly and that people in her life "walked all over her." Helen has attended therapy religiously, been a "model" patient and generally done everything that Dr. Block has suggested. At this time in her life, she is divorced, more assertive with her children and generally feeling better about herself. Her current therapy sessions are often centered on everyday decisions for which she anxiously seeks Dr. Blocks's advice. The most appropriate next therapy step is:
    a. immediate termination
    b. working to reduce Helen's reliance on Dr. Block
    c. a behavioral plan to increase Helen's socialization
    d. exploration of the issues that made Helen seek therapy initially

    ANS: B   DIF: 5   REF: p. 448   OBJ: 6 TYPE: APP

93. Your text shows the very fictitious criteria for a made-up diagnostic category called "independent" personality disorder (Kaplan, 1983) to point out the:
    a. lack of reliability for personality disorder criteria
    c. possibility that sexism is relevant to several personality disorders
    b. need for a dimensional system for personality disorders
    d. show the need for new diagnostic categories

    ANS: C   DIF: 3   REF: p. 448   OBJ: 6 TYPE: FACT

94. The personality disorder that is characterized by an insistence that things have to be done "the right way" is _____ personality disorder.
    a. antisocial
    b. avoidant
    c. paranoid
    d. obsessive-compulsive

    ANS: D   DIF: 1   REF: p. 448   OBJ: 6 TYPE: FACT

95. Henry is viewed by many as a workaholic and not very social. He is at his desk every morning at 7:30 and takes few breaks (although these breaks are always at the same time every day). Henry is known to be a perfectionist. The problem is that he does not seem to get much accomplished since he spends so much time making sure that everything is perfect before moving on to the next task. Henry appears to suffer from _____ personality disorder.
    a. avoidant
    b. obsessive-compulsive
    c. schizoid
    d. antisocial

    ANS: B   DIF: 1   REF: p. 448   OBJ: 6 TYPE: APP

96. One of the major differences between individuals with obsessive-compulsive <u>personality</u> disorder and obsessive-compulsive disorder (OCD) is that patients with the personality disorder generally:
    a. have more obsessive thoughts
    b. show more compulsive and ritualistic behaviors
    c. do not have obsessive thoughts and compulsive behaviors
    d. have multiple diagnoses

    ANS: C   DIF: 3   REF: p. 449   OBJ: 6 TYPE: CON/WWW

97. One of the major differences between individuals with obsessive-compulsive <u>personality</u> disorder and obsessive-compulsive disorder (OCD) is that OCD is a disorder of:
    a. anxiety
    b. dopamine imbalances
    c. modeled behavior
    d. achievement related fears

    ANS: A   DIF: 5   REF: p. 449   OBJ: 6 TYPE: CON

98. One unusual finding discussed in your text is that _____ personality disorder may have played a role in the behavior of several serial killers.
    a. narcissistic
    b. histrionic
    c. obsessive-compulsive
    d. schizotypal

    ANS: C   DIF: 3   REF: p. 449   OBJ: 6 TYPE: FACT

99. Of the following, the most accurate statement regarding the cause of obsessive-compulsive personality disorder is that obsessive compulsive personality disorder appears to be:
    a. caused by neurotransmitter imbalances
    b. influenced by an interaction between serotonin deficiencies and early learning
    c. influenced by genetics and early learning
    d. caused by classically conditioned social anxiety

    ANS: C   DIF: 1   REF: p. 449   OBJ: 6 TYPE: FACT

100. Of the following, the most accurate statement regarding the research for treatment of obsessive-compulsive personality disorder is:
   a. well controlled research suggests the use of a highly structured behavioral program can be effective with motivated patients
   b. well controlled research suggests the use of cognitive-behavioral treatment
   c. the great deal of research that has been conducted indicates there are currently no effective treatments
   d. there is little research regarding the successful treatment of this disorder though relaxation and distraction techniques seem to make sense

   ANS: D   DIF: 5   REF: p. 449   OBJ: 6 TYPE: FACT

101. George, the patient with antisocial personality disorder interviewed on the "Abnormal Psychology Live" CD described having threatened and stolen from his:
   a. best friend   c. wife
   b. sister   d. parents

   ANS: D   DIF: 1   REF: CD

102. When George, the patient with antisocial personality disorder interviewed on the "Abnormal Psychology Live" CD described the emotion he has for others that is "inside" of him, he referred to it as:
   a. sorrow   c. love
   b. hate   d. apathy

   ANS: B   DIF: 3   REF: CD

103. During the "Abnormal Psychology Live" CD interview with George (who has antisocial personality disorder) the patient indicated that he grew up with pets and:
   a. hated them   c. would never hurt animals
   b. tortured them   d. was ambivalent towards them

   ANS: C   DIF: 1   REF: CD

104. During the "Abnormal Psychology Live" CD discussion of borderline personality disorder, it was mentioned that it is tough for therapists to treat this disorder because the therapists often feel _____ towards their patients.
   a. anger   c. fear
   b. sorrow   d. deep attachment

   ANS: A   DIF: 3   REF: CD

105. Kim, the patient who had been in treatment for borderline personality disorder ("Abnormal Psychology Live" CD) indicated that her treatment had been successful in teaching her that she:
   a. needs to stay on her medications   c. does not need to cut herself in order to feel better
   b. can experience strong emotion without feeling that she has to act on it   d. can have stable relationships with others if she just learns to tolerate disappointment

   ANS: B   DIF: 3   REF: CD

ESSAY

1. What is the difference between the types of disorders that are listed on Axis I of the DSM-IV and the personality disorders that are listed on Axis II? Why is there more disagreement in the mental health profession regarding the categorization of personality disorders than for the classification of most Axis I disorders?

2. Describe the three clusters of DSM-IV personality disorders and provide an example of at least one personality disorder that belongs to each cluster. How would you characterize each cluster?

3. Explain the reasons that the prognosis for patients treated for personality disorders is generally less optimistic than the prognosis for patients treated for many Axis I disorders. Select any personality disorder and describe a treatment strategy that has had some evidence of success.

4. Describe the basic features of the antisocial personality disorder. Why is psychotherapy with this population so likely to fail?

5. Describe some factors that might influence the development of the antisocial personality disorder. What childhood behaviors/diagnoses have been observed in the histories of individuals who later developed antisocial personality disorders? Describe a typical intervention strategy designed to prevent "at risk" youth from developing antisocial personality disorder.

6. Compare and contrast the behaviors, thoughts and motivations of an individual with avoidant personality disorder versus someone with schizoid personality disorder. Make sure to note similarities and differences.   **WWW**

7. One might say that the thoughts of avoidant and dependent personality disorders are similar but the behaviors are not. We could further note that the behaviors of avoidant and schizoid personality disorders are similar but the thoughts are not. Please explain these two statements.

8. Explain why we might we see a marriage between a man with narcissistic personality disorder and a woman with dependent personality disorder. Assume that the woman enters therapy and successfully becomes more independent. Predict how her narcissistic husband might react to her improvement and growing independence.

9. Explain what differentiates individuals with schizotypal personality disorder from schizophrenia. What are the similarities observed for individuals diagnosed with schizotypal personality disorder and schizophrenia?

10. Describe the similarities and differences between individuals with obsessive-compulsive personality disorder and individuals diagnosed with the anxiety disorder called obsessive-compulsive disorder.

MULTIPLE CHOICE

1. A pervasive pattern of social inhibition, feelings of inadequacy, and hypersensitivity to negative evaluations, part of the Anxious or Fearful disorder cluster, is diagnosed as _____ personality disorder.
    a. narcissistic
    b. schizoid
    c. avoidant
    d. dependent

    ANS: C

2. George lives every day on a strict schedule. He must have everything perfect and organized, and is excessively devoted to his work. However, he has difficulty completing projects. With which personality disorder is he likely to be diagnosed?
    a. paranoid
    b. obsessive-compulsive
    c. dependent
    d. borderline

    ANS: B

3. According to the text, which is NOT true in the treatment of paranoid personality disorder?
    a. Clients often do not remain in therapy long enough to be helped.
    b. Clients usually seek help for problems such as anxiety or depression, rather than for their personality disorder.
    c. Paradoxical intervention is used, i.e., therapists intentionally lie to these clients to create mistrust.
    d. No therapy has been shown to greatly improve the lives of those with the disorder.

    ANS: C

4. Personality disorders involve enduring patterns of perceiving, relating to, and thinking about the environment and oneself that
    a. may cause functional impairment.
    b. may cause subjective distress.
    c. cut across many times and places.
    d. all of the above

    ANS: D

5. In a study described in the text, when a case history of antisocial personality disorder was ascribed to a male client, therapists diagnosed it correctly. When the same behavior was ascribed to a woman
   a. their different diagnosis proved the existence of gender bias.
   b. their different diagnosis probably reflects a belief by therapists, accurate or not, that males are more likely to display antisocial behavior.
   c. the client was more frequently labeled dependent personality disorder.
   d. all of the above

   ANS: B

6. When clinicians use subjective impressions of clients based on interpersonal interactions rather than behavioral observations outlined by DSM criteria, more _____ is likely to enter into diagnostic decisions.
   a. bias
   b. error
   c. accuracy
   d. expert opinion

   ANS: A

7. Deceitful, irresponsible, aggressive, irritable, and lacking remorse are characteristics describing
   a. bipolar disorder.
   b. antisocial personality disorder.
   c. borderline personality disorder.
   d. schizoid personality disorder.
   e. psychology study guide authors.

   ANS: B

8. DSM-IV calls for categorical judgments about the diagnosis for Personality Disorders. Imagine that the new DSM-V appears just as you earn your professional license in a few years, and it calls for dimensional determinations, as many current psychologists suggest. This change would mean
   a. deciding whether to reject the Personality Disorder diagnosis.
   b. deciding whether another diagnosis is more appropriate.
   c. differential diagnosis.
   d. determining the severity of the personality disorder.

   ANS: D

9. Many people have fantasies of unlimited power, brilliance or beauty, but a man who also believes himself grandly unique and entitled to special privileges, who is arrogant, and expects to be admired and recognized as superior while envying others who are successful, might find himself with a psychological diagnosis. Which personality disorder would apply?
   a. the one named for the Greek word for "uterus"
   b. borderline personality disorder
   c. the one named for the mythological Greek character Narcissus
   d. schizotypal personality disorder

   ANS: C

10. A person diagnosed with avoidant personality disorder has just lost a close friend to a rival and is now seeking other friendships as replacements. You know the person
   a. actually is desperate for nurturance.
   b. will assume the worst about other people.
   c. will conclude the original relationship person really wasn't good enough anyway.
   d. has been misdiagnosed.

   ANS: D

MULTIPLE CHOICE

1. Which of the following characterize the disorder known as schizophrenia?
   a. delusions and hallucinations
   b. inappropriate emotions
   c. disorganized speech and behavior
   d. all of these

   ANS: D   DIF: 1   REF: p. 455   OBJ: 1 TYPE: CON

2. Which of the following is accurate in regard to the long-term outlook for schizophrenic patients?
   a. About 50% of persons diagnosed with the disorder eventually recover.
   b. Recovery is possible only if the person stays on medication.
   c. Recovery is possible only if the patient receives psychotherapy.
   d. Complete recovery from schizophrenia is rare.

   ANS: D   DIF: 3   REF: p. 455   OBJ: 1 TYPE: FACT

3. According to statistical data the prevalence of schizophrenia is about:
   a. .01%
   b. 1%
   c. 5%
   d. 10%

   ANS: B   DIF: 1   REF: p. 455   OBJ: 1 TYPE: FACT

4. In the 1850s a French physician named Benedict Morel used the terms *demence* (loss of mind) *precoce* (early, premature) to describe what we now know as schizophrenia because he observed that the onset of symptoms often occurs:
   a. in the early part of the year
   b. during adolescence
   c. in the morning
   d. prior to symptoms of other mental illnesses

   ANS: B   DIF: 1   REF: p. 455   OBJ: 2 TYPE: CON

5. In the 1800s physicians studying the disorder we now call schizophrenia used the term _____ because they observed that the onset of symptoms often occurred before adulthood.
   a. adolescent insanity
   b. folie à deux
   c. catatonia previa
   d. dementia praecox

   ANS: D   DIF: 1   REF: p. 456   OBJ: 2 TYPE: FACT

6. Which of the following is the definition of catatonia?
   a. silly and immature behavior
   b. early madness
   c. immobility or agitated excitement
   d. delusions of grandeur or persecution

   ANS: C   DIF: 1   REF: p. 455   OBJ: 2 TYPE: CON

7. Which of the following is the definition of paranoia?
   a. silly and immature behavior
   b. early madness
   c. alternating immobility and agitated excitement
   d. delusions of grandeur or persecution

   ANS: D   DIF: 1   REF: p. 456   OBJ: 2 TYPE: CON

8. Which of the following is the definition for hebephrenia?
   a. silly and immature behavior
   b. early madness
   c. alternating immobility and agitated excitement
   d. delusions of grandeur or persecution

   ANS: A   DIF: 1   REF: p. 455   OBJ: 2 TYPE: CON

9. Which of the following is the defintion of dementia praecox?
   a. silly and immature behavior
   b. early madness
   c. alternating immobility and agitated excitement
   d. delusions of grandeur or persecution

   ANS: B   DIF: 1   REF: p. 456   OBJ: 2 TYPE: CON

10. In the late 1800s, the German psychiatrist Emil Kraeplin made all of the following contributions to our knowledge of schizophrenia EXCEPT:
    a. distinguished dementia praecox (schizophrenia) from manic-depressive illness
    b. noted that hallucinations, delusions, and negativism were symptoms of dementia praecox (schizophrenia)
    c. combined several symptoms of insanity (catatonia, paranoia, hebephrenia) that had usually been viewed as reflecting separate and distinct disorders
    d. conceptualized a treatment for schizophrenic patients that is still being used today

    ANS: D   DIF: 3   REF: p. 455-456   OBJ: 2 TYPE: APP

11. The term "schizophrenia" was introduced about 1908 by a Swiss psychiatrist named:
    a. Emil Kraepelin
    b. Sigmund Freud
    c. Eugen Bleuler
    d. Phillipe Pinel

    ANS: C   DIF: 1   REF: p. 456   OBJ: 2 TYPE: FACT

12. Eugen Bleuler's concept of schizophrenia as an "associative splitting" of the basic functions of personality led to the incorrect use of the term to mean:
    a. a fugue state
    b. multiple personality
    c. cognitive slippage
    d. folie à deux

    ANS: B   DIF: 1   REF: p. 456   OBJ: 2 TYPE: CON

13. If an individual is diagnosed as psychotic it usually means that the person has:
    a. hallucinations
    b. delusions
    c. both of these
    d. neither of these

    ANS: C   DIF: 1   REF: p. 456   OBJ: 1 TYPE: CON

14. In the textbook case of Arthur, he said that he had a "secret plan to save all the starving children in the world." After Arthur showed other bizarre behavior and also said he was going to climb the fence of a government building, his parents tried to have him admitted to a psychiatric hospital. They were not able to do that because:
    a. he was not considered a danger to himself or others
    b. he was given medication instead to calm him down
    c. the hospital staff didn't believe his parents
    d. his behavior was due to a substance abuse problem

    ANS: A   DIF: 3   REF: p. 457   OBJ: 1 TYPE: APP

15. In working with schizophrenic patients, mental health professionals typically distinguish between _____ symptoms (an excess or distortion of normal behavior) and _____ symptoms (deficits in normal behavior).
    a. positive / negative
    b. negative / positive
    c. manic / depressive
    d. dysmorphic / dysfunctional

    ANS: A   DIF: 3   REF: p. 458,461   OBJ: 3 TYPE: CON

16. Which of the following is the *persecutory* type of psychotic delusion?
    a. a familiar person is actually a double
    b. one is a famous or important person
    c. people are out to get you
    d. a body part has changed in some impossible way

    ANS: C   DIF: 3   REF: p. 458   OBJ: 4 TYPE: CON

17. Which of the following psychotic delusions defines the *Capgras syndrome*?
    a. a familiar person is actually a double
    b. one is a famous or important person
    c. people are out to get you
    d. a body part has changed in some impossible way

    ANS: A   DIF: 3   REF: p. 458   OBJ: 4 TYPE: CON

18. Which of the following describes a *delusion of grandeur?*
    a. a familiar person is actually a double
    b. one is a famous or important person
    c. people are out to get you
    d. a body part has changed in some impossible way

    ANS: B   DIF: 3   REF: p. 458   OBJ: 4 TYPE: CON

19. Which of the following defines *Cotard's syndrome?*
    a. a familiar person is actually a double
    b. one is a famous or important person
    c. people are out to get you
    d. a body part has changed in some impossible way

    ANS: D   DIF: 3   REF: p. 458   OBJ: 4 TYPE: CON

20. The most common type of hallucination experienced by psychotic individuals is:
    a. visual
    b. auditory
    c. tactile
    d. olfactory

    ANS: B   DIF: 1   REF: p. 460   OBJ: 3 TYPE: FACT

21. Research using brain imaging techniques has localized auditory hallucinations in the part of the brain called:
    a. Wernicke's area
    b. Broca's area
    c. the occipital lobe
    d. the limbic system

    ANS. B   DIF. 3   REF: p. 460   OBJ: 3 TYPE: APP/WWW

22. Results of research showing that auditory hallucinations are localized in the expressive speech area of the brain suggest that:
    a. these hallucinations are produced by the auditory nerve in the ear as well as the speech area of the brain
    b. people who are hallucinating think the voices of other people are actually their own
    c. a person who is hallucinating is actually listening to his/her own thoughts
    d. these hallucinations are related to the disorganized speech that occurs in schizophrenia

    ANS: C   DIF: 3   REF: p. 460   OBJ: 3 TYPE: APP

23. The negative schizophrenic symptom called *avolition* is defined as:
    a. inability to initiate and persist in activities
    b. inability to experience pleasure
    c. lack of emotional response, blank facial expression
    d. lack of speech content and/or slowed speech response

    ANS: A   DIF: 3   REF: p. 461   OBJ: 3 TYPE: CON

24. The negative schizophrenic symptom called *alogia* is defined as:
    a. inability to initiate and persist in activities
    b. inability to experience pleasure
    c. lack of emotional response, blank facial expression
    d. lack of speech content and/or slowed speech response

    ANS: D   DIF: 3   REF: p. 461   OBJ: 3 TYPE: CON

25. The negative schizophrenic symptom called *anhedonia* is defined as:
    a. inability to initiate and persist in activities
    b. inability to experience pleasure
    c. lack of emotional response, blank facial expression
    d. lack of speech content and/or slowed speech response

    ANS: B   DIF: 3   REF: p. 461   OBJ: 3 TYPE: CON

26. Match the following negative symptom of schizophrenia with its definition: flat affect
    a. inability to initiate and persist in activities
    b. inability to experience pleasure
    c. lack of emotional response, blank facial expression
    d. lack of speech content and/or slowed speech response

    ANS: C   DIF: 3   REF: p. 461   OBJ: 3 TYPE: CON

27. A research study involving schizophrenic adults looked at their facial expressions in home movies taken when they were children. The researchers were trying to determine if the development of schizophrenia could be predicted by facial expressions showing limited emotional reactions. This research study focused on the negative symptom called:
    a. alogia
    b. affective flattening
    c. associative splitting
    d. emotional effect syndrome

    ANS: B   DIF: 3   REF: p. 462   OBJ: 3 TYPE: APP

28. Mark was diagnosed with schizophrenia many years ago. Most recently he has been exhibiting some bizarre behaviors. For example, he has been standing for hours in unusual postures. Mark's motor dysfunction is called:
    a. cognitive slippage
    b. inappropriate affect
    c. catatonic immobility
    d. hebephrenia

    ANS: C   DIF: 3   REF: p. 462   OBJ: 3 TYPE: APP

29. Marta, a hospitalized schizophrenic patient, shows an unusual form of catatonia. If someone moves one of her arms or legs into a different position, it just stays that way. Marta's bizarre behavior is called:
    a. postural dysfunction
    b. aerobic mobility
    c. waxy flexibility
    d. schizophrenic movement disorder

    ANS: C   DIF: 1   REF: p. 462   OBJ: 3 TYPE: APP

30. Which of the following is most likely to occur in the paranoid type of schizophrenia?
    a. disorganized speech
    b. poor prognosis when compared to the other subtypes of schizophrenia
    c. limited cognitive skills and flat affect
    d. hallucinations and thematic or systematized delusions

    ANS: D   DIF: 3   REF: p. 463   OBJ: 4 TYPE: CON/WWW

31. Which of the following does NOT apply to the disorganized subtype of schizophrenia?
    a. fragmented delusions and hallucinations
    b. inappropriate or flat affect
    c. frequent remissions and improvement of symptoms
    d. self-absorption and mirror gazing

    ANS: C   DIF: 3   REF: p. 463   OBJ: 4 TYPE: CON

32. The DSM-IV criteria for the disorganized type of schizophrenia include all of the following EXCEPT:
    a. disorganized speech
    b. echolalia or echopraxia
    c. disorganized behavior
    d. flat or inappropriate affect

    ANS: B   DIF: 1   REF: p. 463   OBJ: 4 TYPE: FACT

33. One of the subtypes of schizophrenia is termed residual. Which of the following individuals would be diagnosed with this condition?
    a. Mr. S. is actively hallucinating and has delusions of persecution.
    b. Miss L. has had an episode of schizophrenia but has no active symptoms at this time.
    c. Mrs. R. has never had an episode of schizophrenia but acts in a very bizarre manner.
    d. Mr. F. is at risk for developing schizophrenia because of his family history.

    ANS: B   DIF: 3   REF: p. 464   OBJ: 4 TYPE: APP/WWW

34. Which of the following symptoms would NOT constitute criteria for the residual subtype of schizophrenia?
    a. social withdrawal
    b. negative beliefs or bizarre thoughts
    c. flat affect
    d. delusions

    ANS: D   DIF: 1   REF: p. 464   OBJ: 4 TYPE: FACT

35. Callie has been diagnosed with schizoaffective disorder. This means that in addition to schizophrenic symptoms, she also has symptoms of:
    a. an anxiety disorder
    b. a mood disorder
    c. a split personality
    d. obsessive-compulsive disorder

    ANS: B   DIF: 3   REF: p. 464   OBJ: 5 TYPE: APP

36. In which of the following disorders are hallucinations and delusions NOT part of the symptom pattern?
    a. schizotypal personality disorder
    b. schizoaffective disorder
    c. schizophreniform disorder
    d. brief psychotic disorder

    ANS: A   DIF: 3   REF: p. 464,466   OBJ: 3 TYPE: CON

37. At various times individuals have been arrested for stalking celebrities who they believed were in love with them. This condition is called a(n) _____ delusion.
    a. jealous
    b. erotomanic
    c. somatic
    d. persecutory

    ANS: B   DIF: 1   REF: p. 465   OBJ: 5 TYPE: APP/WWW

38. How do the delusions in delusional disorder differ from the delusions in paranoid schizophrenia?
    a. In delusional disorder, the imagined events could really be happening but there is no evidence that they are happening.
    b. In paranoid schizophrenia, the imagined events have actually happened or are now happening.
    c. In delusional disorder, the imagined events are so bizarre that they could never have happened and never will happen.
    d. There is no difference. Delusions are defined similarly for all conditions.

    ANS: A   DIF: 5   REF: p. 465   OBJ: 5 TYPE: CON/WWW

39. A woman diagnosed as schizophrenic announces that she has a plan to end poverty and homelessness in the world and that the Pope has given her secret instructions on how this can be accomplished. Her thinking is indicative of a delusion of _____.
    a. persecution
    b. thought insertion
    c. grandeur
    d. reference

    ANS: C   DIF: 3   REF: p. 458   OBJ: 5 TYPE: APP

40. Which of the following defines the *jealous* type of delusional disorder?
    a. believing that one is loved by an important person or celebrity
    b. falsely believing that one's sexual partner is unfaithful
    c. believing in one's inflated worth, identity or special relationship
    d. believing one is being malevolently treated in some way

    ANS: B   DIF: 3   REF: p. 465   OBJ: 5 TYPE: APP

41. Which of the following defines the *erotomanic* type of delusional disorder?
    a. believing that one is loved by an important person or celebrity
    b. falsely believing that one's sexual partner is unfaithful
    c. believing in one's inflated worth, identity or special relationship
    d. believing one is being malevolently treated in some way

    ANS: A   REF: p. 465   OBJ: 5 TYPE: APP

42. Which of the following defines the *persecutory* type of delusional disorder?
    a. believing that one is loved by an important person or celebrity
    b. falsely believing that one's sexual partner is unfaithful
    c. believing in one's inflated worth, identity or special relationship
    d. believing one is being malevolently treated in some way

    ANS: D   REF: p. 465   OBJ: 5 TYPE: APP

43. Which of the following defines the *grandiose* type of delusional disorder?
    a. believing that one is loved by an important person or celebrity
    b. falsely believing that one's sexual partner is unfaithful
    c. believing in one's inflated worth, identity or special relationship
    d. believing one is being malevolently treated in some way

    ANS: C   REF: p. 465   OBJ: 5 TYPE: APP

44. The case of Arthur (described in your textbook), who suddenly experienced the delusion that he could save all the starving children in the world with a "secret plan," but whose symptoms lasted only a few days, was diagnosed with:
    a. schizotypal personality disorder
    b. folie à deux (shared psychotic disorder)
    c. brief psychotic disorder
    d. cocaine abuse

    ANS: C   DIF: 1   REF: p. 466   OBJ: 5 TYPE: APP/WWW

45. The DSM-IV-TR criteria for brief psychotic disorder indicate that the duration of an episode of the disturbance must be at least one day but not more than:
    a. one week
    b. one month
    c. 6 months
    d. one year

    ANS: B   DIF: 3   REF: p. 466   OBJ: 5 TYPE: CON

46. Which of the following statistical data are NOT accurate regarding schizophrenia?
   a. the lifetime prevalence rate is 1%
   b. life expectancy is less than average due to suicides and accidents
   c. men with schizophrenia have a better prognosis than women with schizophrenia
   d. more women than men develop schizophrenia later in life

   ANS: C   DIF: 3   REF: p. 467   OBJ: 6 TYPE: FACT

47. A classification system introduced in the 1970s dichotomized schizophrenia into two categories based on all of the following EXCEPT:
   a. symptoms and outcome
   b. age of onset
   c. response to medication
   d. degree of intellectual impairment

   ANS: B   DIF: 3   REF: p. 468   OBJ: 8 TYPE: CON

48. Type I schizophrenia is associated with "positive symptoms" including all of the following EXCEPT:
   a. hallucinations and delusions
   b. good response to medication
   c. optimistic prognosis
   d. flat affect

   ANS: D   DIF: 1   REF: p. 468   OBJ: 8 TYPE: CON

49. Type II schizophrenia is associated with "negative symptoms" including all of the following EXCEPT:
   a. poor response to medication
   b. intellectual impairment
   c. poverty of speech (alogia)
   d. hallucinations and delusions

   ANS: D   DIF: 1   REF: p. 468   OBJ: 8 TYPE: CON

50. Which of the following is true in regard to the genetic basis of schizophrenia?
   a. Researchers have discovered the gene responsible for causing schizophrenia.
   b. Genes are responsible for making some individuals vulnerable to schizophrenia.
   c. Both of these statements are true.
   d. Neither of these statements is true.

   ANS: B   DIF: 3   REF: p. 469   OBJ: 6 TYPE: APP

51. Research studies on the genetic basis of schizophrenia have focused on high risk individuals including all of the following EXCEPT:
   a. healthy twins of schizophrenic patients
   b. adopted children of schizophrenic parents
   c. family members or relatives of schizophrenics
   d. children adopted by schizophrenic mothers

   ANS: D   DIF: 3   REF: p. 469-471   OBJ: 6 TYPE: APP

52. Research studies focusing on genetic factors in schizophrenia have found that:
   a. An individual with a schizophrenic identical twin has the highest risk factor (almost 50%) of developing schizophrenia.
   b. In family studies of schizophrenia the genetic influence can be separated from the environmental impact.
   c. If one person in a family has a particular subtype of schizophrenia, e.g., paranoid, the other family members inherit a predisposition for that subtype only.
   d. The more severe a parent's schizophrenic disorder, the less likely the children were to develop it.

   ANS: A   DIF: 5   REF: p. 469   OBJ: 6 TYPE: APP/WWW

53. The famous case of the Genain sisters, identical quadruplets all diagnosed with schizophrenia, points out that siblings raised in the same household may experience their environment very differently, a concept called a(n):
   a. variable home structure
   b. unshared environment
   c. environmental phenomenon
   d. unique perceptive interpretation

   ANS: B   DIF: 3   REF: p. 470   OBJ: 6 TYPE: APP

54. An ongoing research study in Finland is focusing on children of schizophrenic mothers who were adopted into other families. To date, researchers have determined that _____ of these children have developed schizophrenia or other psychotic disorders.
   a. 1%
   b. 10%
   c. 25%
   d. 50%

   ANS: B   DIF: 1   REF: p. 470-471   OBJ: 6 TYPE: FACT

55. In regard to research on schizophrenia involving the offspring of twins, all of the following are accurate statements EXCEPT:
   a. The child of a schizophrenic identical twin has the same risk (17%) of having the disorder as the child of the non-schizophrenic identical twin.
   b. The child of a non-schizophrenic fraternal twin has about a 2% risk of having the disorder.
   c. A mentally healthy individual with a schizophrenic parent cannot pass on a genetic predisposition for the disorder to his or her offspring.
   d. An individual can be free from schizophrenia but still be a "carrier."

   ANS: C   DIF: 5   REF: p. 471   OBJ: 6 TYPE: APP

56. In which of the following situations would the risk of developing schizophrenia be the lowest for a child?
   a. a child's schizophrenic parent has a non-schizophrenic identical twin
   b. a child's non-schizophrenic parent has a schizophrenic identical twin
   c. a child's schizophrenic parent has a non-schizophrenic fraternal twin
   d. a child's non-schizophrenic parent has a schizophrenic fraternal twin

   ANS: D   DIF: 5   REF: p. 471   OBJ: 6 TYPE: APP

57. Of the various genetic linkage and association studies, the one that seems to be a possible "marker" for schizophrenia involves:
   a. eye-tracking
   b. dopamine sites
   c. unusual facial features
   d. blood type

ANS: A   DIF: 3   REF: p. 472   OBJ: 6 TYPE: APP

58. When looking for abnormalities in the brain as clues to the influences of schizophrenia, it is important to keep certain questions in mind when doing correlational research. For example, if a schizophrenic person were found to have an excess of dopamine, a researcher would need to ask all of the following questions EXCEPT:
   a. Does too much dopamine cause schizophrenia?
   b. Does having schizophrenia cause an excess of dopamine?
   c. Is there some factor that causes both schizophrenia and an excess of dopamine?
   d. Why is the dopamine system active in the schizophrenic brain?

ANS: D   DIF: 5   REF: p. 472   OBJ: 6 TYPE: APP

59. Which of the following statements reflects "circumstantial evidence" for the dopamine theory of schizophrenia?
   a. antipsychotic drugs (neuroleptics) act as dopamine agonists, increasing the amount of dopamine in the brain
   b. antipsychotic drugs (neuroleptics) can produce symptoms similar to those of Parkinson's disease (a disorder due to insufficient dopamine)
   c. the drug L-dopa, a dopamine agonist, is used to treat schizophrenic symptoms in patients with Parkinson's disease
   d. amphetamines, which activate dopamine, can lessen psychotic symptoms in persons with schizophrenia

ANS: B   DIF: 5   REF: p. 473   OBJ: 6 TYPE: APP/WWW

60. In regard to the ways that drugs affect neurotransmitters, which of the following is true'?
   a. A drug that is an agonist occupies the receptor sites, blocking the neurotransmitter.
   b. A drug that is an antagonist helps increase the release of the neurotransmitter.
   c. Both of these are correct.
   d. Neither of these is correct.

ANS: D   DIF: 3   REF: p. 472   OBJ: 6 TYPE: CON

61. Which of the following occurs when drugs are administered to schizophrenic patients?
   a. drugs that increase dopamine (agonists) cause an increase in schizophrenic behavior
   b. drugs that decrease dopamine (antagonists) decrease schizophrenic symptoms
   c. both of these statements are accurate
   d. neither of these statements is accurate

ANS: C   DIF: 3   REF: p. 473   OBJ: 6 TYPE: APP

62. Which of the following statements contradicts the dopamine theory of schizophrenia?
    a. Many people with schizophrenia are not helped by dopamine antagonists.
    b. Clozapine, one of the weakest dopamine antagonists, reduces schizophrenic symptoms in those patients who were not helped by stronger dopamine antagonists.
    c. Both of these statements contradict the dopamine theory of schizophrenia.
    d. Neither of these statements contradicts the dopamine theory of schizophrenia.

    ANS: C   DIF: 3   REF: p. 473-474   OBJ: 7 TYPE: APP

63. Recent and highly sophisticated research focusing on neurochemical abnormalities as the cause of schizophrenia involves all of the following EXCEPT:
    a. deficiency in the stimulation of prefrontal dopamine D_1 receptors
    b. excessive stimulation of striatal dopamine D_2 receptors
    c. alterations in prefrontal activity involving glutamate transmissions
    d. changes in temporal lobe function associated with serotonin receptor activity

    ANS: D   DIF: 3   REF: p. 474   OBJ: 7 TYPE: APP

64. Scientists can observe how the newer antipsychotic medications work in the living brain of a schizophrenic patient by using brain-imaging techniques such as:
    a. CT scan   c. X-ray
    b. MRI   d. SPECT

    ANS: D   DIF: 2   REF: p. 474   OBJ: 6 TYPE:FACT

65. What is the evidence for structural damage in the brains of schizophrenic patients?
    a. All schizophrenic patients have smaller ventricles in their brains.
    b. In some schizophrenic patients there is an excess amount of "gray matter" in the cerebral cortex.
    c. The majority of schizophrenic patients have enlarged ventricles in their brains.
    d. Many schizophrenic patients have increased activity in the frontal lobes of the brain.

    ANS: C   DIF: 3   REF: p. 475   OBJ: 7 TYPE: APP

66. In historic records or ancient literature there are descriptions of symptoms that today would lead to a diagnosis of all of the following disorders EXCEPT:
    a. mood disorders (depression and mania)
    b. schizophrenia
    c. mental retardation
    d. senile dementia

    ANS: B   DIF: 1   REF: p. 442   OBJ: 7 TYPE: FACT

67. Recent research into the causes of schizophrenia, including studies of schizophrenic patients who had been exposed prenatally to influenza epidemics, suggests that there might be a _____ cause of schizophrenia.
    a. viral
    b. bacterial
    c. both of these
    d. neither of these

    ANS: A   DIF: 1   REF: p. 475   OBJ: 6 TYPE: APP

68. In contrast to retrospective research studies, those that rely on after-the-fact reports (meaning after a person has already developed symptoms of schizophrenia), prospective research studies:
    a. assess recovery rates in patients who have taken different medications
    b. examine factors that predict the recurrence of schizophrenic symptoms after a period of improvement
    c. compare genetic, biological and social etiological factors to try to determine inheritance patterns in offspring of schizophrenic parents
    d. look at brain imaging diagnostic tests to determine if schizophrenic patients have structural neurological defects

    ANS: B   DIF: 5   REF: p. 476   OBJ: 6 TYPE: APP

69. In regard to the family interactions among schizophrenic patients, the word "schizophrenogenic" (no longer used), was first proposed in the 1940s to describe:
    a. an abusive and alcoholic father whose child became schizophrenic
    b. an emotionally distant mother whose child became schizophrenic
    c. divorced parents who had several psychotic children
    d. a family in which relatives on both sides were psychotic

    ANS: B   DIF: 1   REF: p. 477   OBJ: 6 TYPE: CON

70. In terms of a particular emotional communication style known as expressed emotion (EE), researchers have shown that schizophrenic patients were more likely to relapse if:
    a. they had long periods of contact with their families
    b. they had families who were disapproving and intrusive
    c. both of the these are correct
    d. neither of these is correct

    ANS: C   DIF: 5   REF: p. 477   OBJ: 9 TYPE: APP

71. In regard to cultural differences in "expressed emotion," which is thought to be positively correlated with schizophrenia, research has found that _____ families have the highest percentage of expressed emotion.
    a. Indian
    b. Mexican
    c. British
    d. Anglo-American

    ANS: D   DIF: 1   REF: p. 477   OBJ: 9 TYPE: APP

72. The familial communication style called expressed emotion (EE) sometimes used to predict relapse rates in schizophrenic patients includes all of the following EXCEPT:
    a. overinvolvement
    b. criticism
    c. emotional distance
    d. hostility

    ANS: C   DIF: 1   REF: p. 477   OBJ: 9 TYPE: CON

73. A treatment first used in the 1930s as a treatment for schizophrenia but now used primarily to treat severe depression is:
    a. electroconvulsive therapy (ECT)
    b. prefrontal lobotomy
    c. insulin coma therapy
    d. psychosurgery

ANS: A   DIF: 3   REF: p. 478   OBJ: 10 TYPE: FACT/WWW

74. The neuroleptic drugs introduced in the 1950s affect primarily the positive symptoms of schizophrenia which include all of the following EXCEPT:
    a. hallucinations
    b. delusions
    c. social deficits
    d. agitation

ANS: C   DIF: 1   REF: p. 478   OBJ: 10 TYPE: FACT

75. During the 1990s a new type of antipsychotic medication became available to treat schizophrenic patients who were not helped by conventional antipsychotic medications or who had developed unpleasant side effects. These new anitpsychotic medications include all of the following EXCEPT:
    a. Thorazine (chlorpromazine)
    b. Clozaril (clozapine)
    c. Risperdal (risperidone)
    d. Zyprcxa (olanzapinc)

ANS: A   DIF: 1   REF: p. 479   OBJ: 10 TYPE: FACT

76. Which of the following is NOT one of the typical minor side effects of antipsychotic medications?
    a. grogginess
    b. blurred vision
    c. headaches
    d. dryness of the mouth

ANS: C   DIF: 1   REF: p. 479   OBJ: 10 TYPE: FACT

77. Extrapyramidal symptoms, serious side effects of antipsychotic medications that occur in some schizophrenic patients, are similar to the symptoms of:
    a. Alzheimer's disease
    b. Parkinson's disease
    c. multiple sclerosis
    d. leukemia

ANS: B   DIF: 3   REF: p. 479   OBJ: 10 TYPE: FACT

78. Tardive dyskinesia, a severe side effect of antipsychotic medications, includes all of the following involuntary movements EXCEPT:
   a. involuntary chewing
   b. puffing of the cheeks
   c. tongue protrusion
   d. tooth grinding

   ANS: D   DIF: 3   REF: p. 479-480   OBJ: 10 TYPE: FACT

79. Schizophrenic patients who take antipsychotic medications sometimes develop severe side effects such as akinesia, a parkinsonian-like condition that produces all of the following EXCEPT:
   a. hand tremors
   b. expressionless face
   c. slowed movements
   d. monotonous speech

   ANS: A   DIF: 3   REF: p. 479   OBJ: 10 TYPE: FACT

80. Tardive dyskinesia, a condition that can occur in patients who take antipsychotic medications:
   a. can result from short-term use
   b. can result from low doses
   c. occurs in less than 2% of patients
   d. may often be irreversible

   ANS: D   DIF: 3   REF: p. 480   OBJ: 10 TYPE: FACT

81. One of the ways of improving patient compliance in regard to taking antipsychotic medication involves the use of:
   a. injections
   b. skin patches
   c. pills
   d. liquids

   ANS: A   DIF: 1   REF: p. 480   OBJ: 10 TYPE: FACT

82. An experimental technique called transcranial magnetic stimulation has been used in some schizophrenic patients to try to:
   a. block auditory hallucinations
   b. change delusional content
   c. both of these are correct
   d. neither of these is correct

   ANS: A   DIF: 1   REF: p. 480   OBJ: 10 TYPE: FACT

83. Which of the following is an accurate statement about the role of psychological factors in the etiology of schizophrenia?
   a. Psychological factors cause schizophrenia in about 10% of diagnosed cases.
   b. Psychological factors cause schizophrenia in about 50% of diagnosed cases.
   c. Psychological factors cause schizophrenia more often than biological factors.
   d. Psychological factors do not cause schizophrenia.

   ANS: D   DIF: 3   REF: p. 480   OBJ: 6 TYPE: CON

84. In the 1970s researchers set up a treatment system called a token economy in a mental health center. This type of "milieu" treatment for schizophrenic patients focused on:
    a. language and speech
    b. socialization and self-care skills
    c. educational studies
    d. spiritual and religious development

    ANS: B   DIF: 1   REF: p. 480   OBJ: 10 TYPE: APP

85. A token economy is an incentive system in which hospitalized schizophrenic patients:
    a. earn "tokens" for appropriate behavior
    b. lose "tokens" for disruptive behavior
    c. both of these
    d. neither of these

    ANS: C   DIF: 3   REF: p. 480   OBJ: 10 TYPE: CON

86. The 1970s experiment in which behavioral (or social learning) principles were applied to a traditional inpatient environment in the form of a token economy resulted in:
    a. more patients able to be discharged
    b. fewer patients able to be discharged
    c. more patients recovering from schizophrenia
    d. fewer patients recovering from schizophrenia

    ANS: A   DIF: 1   REF: p. 480-481   OBJ: 10 TYPE: APP

87. In the latter half of the 20th century the routine institutionalization of schizophrenic patients was significantly reduced because of:
    a. the effectiveness of antipsychotic medications
    b. court rulings limiting involuntary hospitalization
    c. both of these
    d. neither of these

    ANS: C   DIF: 3   REF: p. 481   OBJ: 10 TYPE: FACT

88. Since the latter half of the 20th century the policy of deinstitutionalization (time limited hospital stays for psychotic patients) has resulted in:
    a. more patients remaining hospitalized
    b. former patients becoming productive members of the community
    c. many former patients becoming homeless
    d. greater patient compliance regarding medication

    ANS: C   DIF: 3   REF: p. 481   OBJ: 10 TYPE: APP/WWW

89. Some schizophrenic patients are helped to function better in the community in independent living skills programs that teach them all of the following EXCEPT:
    a. medication management
    b. to identify signs that warn of a relapse
    c. to maintain eye contact when interacting with others
    d. how to help others who are mentally ill

    ANS: D   DIF: 3   REF: p. 481   OBJ: 10 TYPE: CON

90. Social skills training programs for schizophrenic patients have been:
    a. very successful
    b. not at all successful
    c. somewhat successful while the program is in effect
    d. only successful when the patient is on medication

    ANS: C   DIF: 3   REF: p. 481   OBJ: 10 TYPE: CON

91. In the Independent Living Skills Program for schizophrenic patients at UCLA, the learning objectives of "medication management" include all of the following EXCEPT:
    a. understanding how antipsychotic drugs work
    b. following the correct procedures for taking the medication
    c. being able to identify side effects of the medication if they occur
    d. increasing the dosage gradually if the desired effect is not occurring

    ANS: D   DIF: 3   REF: p. 481   OBJ: 10 TYPE: APP

92. Which of the following is NOT recommended as a helpful addition to biological treatment for schizophrenia?
    a. social skills training
    b. family intervention
    c. high levels of expressed emotion
    d. programs in vocational rehabilitation

    ANS: C   DIF: 1   REF: p. 481   OBJ: 10 TYPE: CON

93. Psychosocial "clubs" or "clubhouses" for schizophrenic patients have been formed as a part of some rehabilitation programs. Research indicates that participation in these clubs may help prevent relapses. However, it is difficult to interpret the improvement in these patients because:
    a. some patients are on medication and some aren't
    b. only the most psychotic patients participated
    c. patients who participate may be significantly different from those who don't
    d. a significant number of patients dropped out before completing the program

    ANS: C   DIF: 5   REF: p. 482   OBJ: 10 TYPE: APP

94. There are cross-cultural differences in the treatment of schizophrenia. For example, a schizophrenic patient in China would probably receive _____ in addition to antipsychotic medication.
    a. herbal medicine
    b. acupuncture
    c. both of these are correct
    d. neither of these are correct

    ANS: C   DIF: 3   REF: p. 482   OBJ: 10 TYPE: APP

95. In his memoir, <u>When the Music's Over: My Journey into Schizophrenia</u>, Ross David Burke relates that he also had problems with all of the following EXCEPT:
    a. drug abuse
    b. crime
    c. obsessive sex
    d. an eating disorder

    ANS: D   DIF: 1   REF: p. 484   OBJ: 10 TYPE: APP

96. What is the generic name of the antipsychotic medication Risperdal?
    a. haloperidol
    b. chlorpromazine
    c. clozapine
    d. risperidone

    ANS: D   DIF: 3   REF: p. 479   OBJ: 10 TYPE: FACT

97. What is the generic name of the antipsychotic medication Haldol?
    a. haloperidol
    b. chlorpromazine
    c. clozapine
    d. risperidone

    ANS: A   DIF: 3   REF: p. 479   OBJ: 10 TYPE: FACT

98. What is the generic name of the antipsychotic medication Clozaril?
    a. haloperidol
    b. chlorpromazine
    c. clozapine
    d. risperidone

    ANS: C   DIF: 3   REF: p. 479   OBJ: 10 TYPE: FACT

99. What is the generic name of the antipsychotic medication Thorazine?
    a. haloperidol
    b. chlorpromazine
    c. clozapine
    d. risperidone

    ANS: B   DIF: 3   REF: p. 479   OBJ: 10 TYPE: FACT

100. During the interview with Etta on the "Abnormal Psychology Live" CD for Chapter 13, her schizophrenic thought processes are revealed as she talks meaninglessly about all of the following EXCEPT:
    a. clocks   c. animals
    b. eagles   d. numbers

    ANS: C   REF: CD

101. On the "Abnormal Psychology Live" CD, Etta states that Jesus communicates with her through the sounds of barking dogs. This type of schizophrenic symptom is called a(n):
   a. neologism
   b. loose association
   c. delusion
   d. hallucination

   ANS: C   REF: CD

102. As discussed on the "Abnormal Psychology Live" CD for Chapter 13, which of the following would NOT be an example of a negative symptom of schizophrenia?
   a. blunted affect
   b. a delusion
   c. lack of initiative
   d. limited speech

   ANS: B   REF: CD

103. In the discussion of schizophrenia on the "Abnormal Psychology Live" CD for Chapter 13, _____ symptoms refer to experiences that a patient has but that ordinary people don't have.
   a. positive symptoms
   b. negative negative symptoms
   c. both of these
   d. neither of these

   ANS: C   REF: CD

104. Which of the following is NOT a scenario described by one of the three schizophrenic patients presented on the "Abnormal Psychology Live" CD for Chapter 13?
   a. having thoughts taken out of her head by some external force
   b. hearing voices telling the the patient that he was going to be in a James Bond movie
   c. being beheaded and having the head "pop right back up"
   d. feeling bugs crawling under her skin that were put there to punish her

   ANS: D   REF: CD

ESSAY

1. Define what is meant by schizophrenia. Using concepts from the history of schizophrenia show why the common misconception that schizophrenia means split personality is not correct.

2. Describe some of the "positive" and "negative" symptoms of schizophrenia. Explain what is meant by these terms and how they relate to prognosis and outcome.

3. Compare the major subtypes of schizophrenia (paranoid, catatonic, disorganized, undifferentiated, residual) in terms of symptoms, treatment and prognosis.   **WWW**

4. Compare schizophrenia and the "other psychotic disorders" (schizophreniform, schizoaffective, delusional, folie à deux, brief psychotic disorder) in terms of symptoms, duration and outcome.

5. Discuss some of the causative factors of schizophrenia including genetic influences, neurotransmitter imbalances, prenatal viral exposure, and psychological stressors.

6. Discuss treatment of the mentally ill from a historical perspective. Include "shock therapies," psychosurgical procedures and antipsychotic medications.

7. Explore the concept of psychosocial interventions for schizophrenia. Discuss the goals and effectiveness of these treatment programs.

8. Compare the conventional antipsychotic medications with the newer drugs in terms of their biochemical dynamics, side effects, and treatment effectiveness.

9. Discuss the issue of patient compliance with antipsychotic drug regimens. Describe the problems caused by noncompliance and how this situation has been addressed in treatment settings.

10. Discuss several types of research studies (twin, adoptee, family) that focus on etiological factors in schizophrenia. Explain what is meant by "high risk" or "at risk" and how these studies provide information on genetic and/or environmental influences on the disorder.

11. Referring to the "Abnormal Psychology Live" CD for Chapter 13, discuss the difference between postive and negative symptoms of schizophrenia and give examples of each. Mention the effectiveness of treatment for these two types of symptoms.

MULTIPLE CHOICE

1. Which of the following is NOT a negative symptom of schizophrenia?
    a. flat affect
    b. alogia
    c. tangentiality
    d. anhedonia
    e. all of the above are negative symptoms

    ANS: C

2. The subtype of schizophrenia in which delusions and hallucinations have themes is
    a. catatonic type.
    b. disorganized type.
    c. paranoid type.
    d. undifferentiated type.

    ANS: C

3. The behaviors displayed in the _____ of schizophrenia primarily involve motor behavior disruptions.
    a. catatonic type
    b. disorganized type
    c. paranoid type
    d. undifferentiated type

    ANS: A

4. The 48% concordance rate of schizophrenia in identical (monozygotic) twins, who share 100% of their genetic information, tells us that
    a. schizophrenia is not a purely genetic disorder.
    b. schizophrenia is not a purely environmentally controlled disorder.
    c. environmental influences play some role in schizophrenia.
    d. genetic influences play some role in schizophrenia.
    e. all of the above

    ANS: E

5. We need to use caution when drawing conclusions from family and twin studies of schizophrenia, because
    a. researchers study only their own families.
    b. individuals with schizophrenia are often taken away from their families.
    c. when people share environments as well as genes, it is difficult to separate out the influences of each.
    d. none of the above

    ANS: C

6. The most common type of hallucination experienced in schizophrenia is
   a. visual
   b. auditory
   c. olfactory
   d. somatic
   e. none of the above

   ANS: B

7. One characteristic of schizophrenia that differentiates it from other disorders described in DSM-IV is that the concept of schizophrenia
   a. is made up of a number of behaviors or symptoms that aren't necessarily shared by all the people with the disorder.
   b. has been recognized as a serious problem since the early 1800's.
   c. was first identified in the United States.
   d. has a single biological cause that has been identified through the use of PET scan technology.

   ANS: A

8. The effectiveness of antipsychotic medications in those with schizophrenia
   a. suggests an overactive dopamine system in persons with schizophrenia.
   b. suggests an underactive dopamine system in persons with schizophrenia.
   c. does not completely explain the role of dopamine in schizophrenia.
   d. both a and c

   ANS: C

9. Researchers have found that _____ may be related to both the onset of schizophrenia, and to relapse.
   a. stressful life events
   b. alcohol intoxication
   c. excessive studying for psych exams
   d. poor sleeping habits
   e. none of the above

   ANS: A

10. During your volunteer work at a group home for people with schizophrenia, you have a series of conversations with one young man. He seems lucid, coherent, and reasonable on every occasion. You begin to think he has been misdiagnosed and wonder why he is there. Suddenly, he tells you he is the queen of England, working closely with God to rid the world of evil spirits. You realize his schizophrenia subtype is
    a. catatonic.
    b. disorganized.
    c. paranoid.
    d. residual.
    e. undifferentiated.

    ANS: C

MULTIPLE CHOICE

1. Psychological disorders are considered developmental disorders when there is a:
    a. change in symptoms over the lifespan
    b. genetic component to the disorder
    c. significant dysfunction during childhood
    d. general decline in functioning over time

    ANS: C   DIF: 1   REF: p. 489   OBJ: 1 TYPE: FACT

2. Although not classified as developmental disorders, many, if not most, psychological disorders can be considered developmental because they:
    a. appear early in life and change over the lifespan
    b. have a genetic component
    c. lack biological causes and are influenced by learning
    d. are unique to children

    ANS: A   DIF: 3   REF: p. 489   OBJ: 1 TYPE: CON/WWW

3. The major reason that developmental disorders are considered to be so serious in terms of their capacity to disrupt later functioning is:
    a. the fact that medications used in children can have long term effects
    b. the impact that they have on family functioning
    c. that the purely biological nature of developmental disorders leads to subsequent developmental failures
    d. that failure to develop at one level is thought to inhibit later stages of development

    ANS: D   DIF: 1   REF: p. 490   OBJ: 1 TYPE: CON

4. Johnny is a 2-year-old boy who has no motivation to interact with other people. His absence of interest in people may also lead to severe deficits in his ability to:
    a. amuse himself
    b. think
    c. communicate
    d. walk

    ANS: C   DIF: 1   REF: p. 490   OBJ: 1 TYPE: APP

5. The main reason that it is so important to identify children with developmental disorders as early as possible is that:
    a. medications are most effective when administered at an early stage of the disorder
    b. skill deficits can be identified and addressed before they impact later development
    c. family functioning often declines as the developmental disorder progresses
    d. children are more receptive to therapy when they are young

    ANS: B   DIF: 3   REF: p. 490   OBJ: 1 TYPE: CON

6. One of the most common reasons that children are referred for mental health services in the United States is:
   a. ADHD
   b. autism
   c. pervasive developmental disorder
   d. stuttering

   ANS: A   DIF: 1   REF: p. 490   OBJ: 2 TYPE: FACT

7. An individual diagnosed with attention deficit/hyperactivity disorder will always present with:
   a. hyperactive behavior that alternates with periods of distraction
   b. patterns of inattention or hyperactivity/impulsivity
   c. both patterns of inattention and hyperactivity/impulsivity
   d. periods of distraction that lead to hyperactive/impulsive behavior

   ANS: B   DIF: 3   REF: p. 491   OBJ: 2 TYPE: FACT

8. What are the two DSM-IV symptom clusters for attention deficit/hyperactivity disorder?
   a. hyperactivity and impulsivity
   b. inattention and distraction
   c. inattention and hyperactivity/impulsivity
   d. impulsivity and distraction

   ANS: C   DIF: 1   REF: p. 491   OBJ: 2 TYPE: FACT

9. The inattention cluster of attention deficit/hyperactivity disorder symptoms is characterized by:
   a. careless mistakes
   b. fidgeting
   c. not waiting one's turn to answer questions
   d. all of these

   ANS: A   DIF: 1   REF: p. 491   OBJ: 2 TYPE: FACT

10. In order to diagnose an individual with attention deficit/hyperactivity disorder, it is necessary for symptoms to be present in:
    a. both symptom clusters
    b. the hyperactivity cluster
    c. the area of impulsivity
    d. either of the symptom clusters

    ANS: D   DIF: 3   REF: p. 491   OBJ: 2 TYPE: FACT

11. Two alternative reasons that have been proposed to explain why children with attention deficit/hyperactivity disorder (ADHD) have problems with academics are:
    a. ADHD symptoms directly inhibit school performance or a brain deficit associated with ADHD inhibits academic ability
    b. ADHD symptoms directly inhibit school performance or social difficulties make school a negative experience for children with ADHD
    c. social difficulties make school a negative experience for children with ADHD or a brain deficit associated with ADHD inhibits academic ability
    d. dietary factors responsible for ADHD limit school performance or ADHD symptoms directly inhibit school performance

    ANS: A   DIF: 5   REF: p. 491   OBJ: 2 TYPE: CON

12. Children diagnosed with attention deficit/hyperactivity disorder tend to be:
    a. popular with other children because of their "acting out"
    b. no more or less popular than other children
    c. unpopular with other children
    d. uninterested in socialization

    ANS: C   DIF: 1   REF: p. 491   OBJ: 2 TYPE: FACT

13. Children with attention deficit/hyperactivity disorder (ADHD) tend to be unpopular with other children because:
    a. of their ADHD behaviors
    b. brain deficits that lead to ADHD negatively influence the desire to socialize
    c. children with ADHD are uninterested in socialization
    d. teachers tend to stigmatize and isolate children with ADHD

    ANS: A   DIF: 1   REF: p. 491   OBJ: 2 TYPE: FACT

14. Attention deficit/hyperactivity disorder is estimated to occur in about ____ percent of school age children.
    a. 2
    b. 4
    c. 6
    d. 10

    ANS: C   DIF: 3   REF: p. 492   OBJ: 2 TYPE: FACT

15. The ratio of boys to girls for attention deficit/hyperactivity disorder is approximately:
    a. equal or 1:1
    b. 2 boys for every 1 girl
    c. 4 boys for every 1 girl
    d. almost entirely male with more than 10 boys for every girl

    ANS: C   DIF: 3   REF: p. 492   OBJ: 2 TYPE: FACT

16. Which best describes the way attention deficit/hyperactivity disorder (ADHD) develops as children grow into adulthood?
    a. children tend to outgrow ADHD
    b. ADHD tends to evolve into more severe forms of pathology
    c. symptoms remain relatively stable throughout the life-span for most individuals
    d. manifestations of ADHD tend to change over time but many problems often persist

    ANS: D   DIF: 3   REF: p. 492   OBJ: 2 TYPE: CON/WWW

17. When comparing data across countries, the number of diagnosed cases of attention deficit/hyperactivity disorder is:
    a. highest in the United States
    b. highest in all Western cultures
    c. about the same across most countries
    d. highest in Eastern cultures

    ANS: A   DIF: 1   REF: p. 492   OBJ: 2 TYPE: FACT

18. According to your text, the reason that countries previously reporting lower rates of ADHD (than those found in the United States) are now finding rates of the disorder closer to the rate reported in the U.S. is:
    a. improvements in diagnosis   c. the influence of drug companies
    b. better parent education   d. poor parenting

    ANS: A   DIF: 3   REF: p. 492   OBJ: 2 TYPE: FACT

19. Neurotransmitters implicated in the cause of ADHD include all of the following EXCEPT:
    a. dopamine
    b. endorphin
    c. norepinephrine
    d. GABA

    ANS: B   DIF: 1   REF: 492   OBJ: 2 TYPE: FACT

20. The most accurate statement with regard to the genetic influences of attention deficit/hyperactivity disorder is:
    a. there are no known genetic influences
    b. there appears to be a single gene influence
    c. there appear to be multiple genetic influences
    d. defects on the Y chromosome are the major influence

    ANS: C   DIF: 3   REF: p. 492   OBJ: 2 TYPE: FACT

21. ADHD is associated with smaller brain volume in all of the following areas EXCEPT the:
    a. frontal cortex
    b. basal ganglia
    c. brain stem
    d. cerebellar vermis

    ANS: B   DIF: 5   REF: p. 493   OBJ: 2 TYPE: FACT

22. The hypothesis that attention deficit/hyperactivity disorder (ADHD) may be influenced by toxins, food additives, or diet:
    a. is based on well controlled studies
    b. is not well understood or studied, but generally effective as a treatment
    c. appears true for a small subset of individuals diagnosed with ADHD
    d. has no scientific evidence

    ANS: D   DIF: 3   REF: p. 493   OBJ: 2 TYPE: FACT

23. Alicia is pregnant and continues to smoke cigarettes throughout her pregnancy. She is
    _____ more likely to have a child diagnosed with attention deficit/hyperactivity disorder
    (Linnet, Dalsgaard, Obel, et al., 2003) than a mother who does not smoke during pregnancy.
    a. no
    b. 2 times
    c. 3 times
    d. 5 times

    ANS: C   DIF: 3   REF: p. 493   OBJ: 2 TYPE: APP

24. The medications such as Ritalin and Cylert that are generally used to treat attention deficit/hyperactivity disorder have proven particularly helpful to most patients in:
    a. temporarily reducing hyperactivity and impulsivity and/or improving concentration
    b. reducing hyperactivity and impulsivity and/or improving concentration with gains maintained after the medication is discontinued
    c. temporarily increasing academic performance and socialization
    d. increasing academic performance and socialization with gains maintained even after the medication is discontinued

    ANS: A   DIF: 1   REF: p. 494   OBJ: 2 TYPE: FACT

25. The medications such as Ritalin and Cylert that are generally used to treat attention deficit/hyperactivity disorder (ADHD) have proven to be helpful to ___ % of ADHD patients.
    a. 25
    b. 50
    c. 70
    d. 90

    ANS: C   DIF: 3   REF: p. 494   OBJ: 2 TYPE: FACT

26. Ritalin and Cylert, medications generally used to treat attention deficit/hyperactivity disorder, are classified as:
    a. minor sedatives
    b. depressants
    c. stimulants
    d. anti-depressants

    ANS: C   DIF: 3   REF: p. 494   OBJ: 2 TYPE: FACT/WWW

27. All of the following side effects EXCEPT _____ are associated with the medications, Ritalin and Cylert, that are used to treat attention deficit/hyperactivity disorder.
    a. insomnia
    b. drowsiness
    c. irritability
    d. weight gain

    ANS: D   DIF: 3   REF: p. 494   OBJ: 2 TYPE: FACT

28. Current estimates (Volkow & Swanson, 2003) are that approximately _____ children in the United States are being treated with stimulant medications.
    a. one million   c. twenty million
    b. ten million   d. fifty million

    ANS: B   DIF: 3   REF: p. 494   OBJ: 2 TYPE: FACT

29. The drug Strattera (atomoxetine) appears effective for some children with ADHD and according to recent research (Eiland & Guest, 2004) does not cause the same _____ as stimulant medication when used in larger doses.
    a. intolerance   c. "high"
    b. withdrawal symptoms   d. academic disturbance

    ANS: C   DIF: 3   REF: p. 494   OBJ: 2 TYPE: FACT

30. Non-medication treatments for attention deficit/hyperactivity disorder usually involve:
    a. interpersonal therapy
    b. behavioral programs and parent training
    c. brief, inpatient treatment at a specialty hospital
    d. cognitive behavioral therapy and diet control

    ANS: B   DIF: 1   REF: p. 494   OBJ: 2 TYPE: FACT

31. Ron is a 9-year-old boy recently diagnosed with attention deficit/hyperactivity disorder. His parents have chosen a combined approach to treatment which will most likely involve:
    a. new experimental medications and behavior therapy
    b. no medication but a combination of behavioral therapy and parent training
    c. medication such as Ritalin and behavior therapy
    d. medication such as Ritalin and psychoanalysis

    ANS: C   DIF: 3   REF: p. 494   OBJ: 2 TYPE: APP

32. A learning disorder is defined as:
    a. achievement in reading, writing or math below the level predicted by the individual's age, IQ and education
    b. achievement in any academic subject below the level predicted by the individual's age, IQ and education
    c. substandard IQ score in comparison to the individual's family and educational background
    d. the existence of a neurological deficit that interferes with the individual's ability to assimilate new information

    ANS: A   DIF: 1   REF: p. 495   OBJ: 3 TYPE: FACT

33. All of the following are likely signs of a learning disorder EXCEPT:
    a. difficulty with reading and word recognition
    b. inability to comprehend what has been read
    c. standardized math scores that are above grade average but well below the level predicted by the child's IQ and education
    d. poor grades in a foreign language despite straight As in all other subjects

    ANS: D   DIF: 3   REF: p. 495   OBJ: 3 TYPE: APP

34. Why would it be incorrect to say that individuals diagnosed with learning disorders are not intelligent?
    a. it would confuse learning disorders with mental retardation
    b. the concept of learning disorder has absolutely nothing to do with intelligence
    c. learning disorders can be diagnosed in people of below average, average or high intelligence
    d. learning disorders are only diagnosed in people of high intelligence

    ANS: C   DIF: 3   REF: p. 495   OBJ: 3 TYPE: CON

35. Which learning disorder affects approximately 5% to 15% of the population?
    a. written expression
    b. oral communication
    c. mathematics
    d. reading

    ANS: D   DIF: 1   REF: p. 496   OBJ: 3 TYPE: FACT

36. Mathematics learning disorder is estimated to occur in approximately _____ % of the population.
    a. .5
    b. 3
    c. 6
    d. 12

    ANS: C   DIF: 1   REF: p. 496   OBJ: 3 TYPE: FACT

37. All of the following are problems observed to result from learning disorders EXCEPT:
    a. low employment
    b. school drop-out
    c. drug abuse
    d. poor self-esteem

    ANS: C   DIF: 1   REF: p. 496   OBJ: 3 TYPE: FACT

38. Ken is a 12-year-old boy of average intelligence as indicated by his IQ scores. He loves school
    and works hard on his homework. Ken has earned straight As in every subject except math where
    he has been achieving grades in the C range. Which of the following statements is correct?
    a. Ken does not appear to have a learning disorder because his achievement is consistent
       with expectations based on his intelligence.
    b. Ken appears to have a math disorder because his math grade is so far below his other
       grades.
    c. Ken appears to have a math disorder because there is a discrepancy between his
       intelligence and his achievement in many subjects
    d. Ken does not appear to have a learning disorder because he has shown that he can achieve
       when he wants to.

    ANS: A   DIF: 5   REF: p. 495   OBJ: 3 TYPE: APP/WWW

39. Samantha is a 6th grade girl who has great difficulty in school. She pays attention and works hard
    but appears to have trouble remembering facts and concepts that she has read about. Before we
    can determine whether Samantha has a learning disability, it is most important to know her:
    a. family history
    b. social skills
    c. math skills
    d. IQ

    ANS: D   DIF: 1   REF: p. 495   OBJ: 3 TYPE: APP

40. Studies with identical twins have indicated that reading disorders:
    a. have a large genetic component
    b. have a slight genetic component
    c. are influenced more by learning than genetics
    d. have a smaller genetic component that mathematics disorders

    ANS: A   DIF: 3   REF: p. 497   OBJ: 3 TYPE: FACT

41. One intriguing finding from research involving reading disordered individuals who speak multiple languages is that:
    a. reading disorders are independent of culture/language
    b. individuals who speak more than one language rarely have learning disorders
    c. evidence of the reading disorder may exist for one or two languages, while the individual may be completely free of the disorder in another language
    d. complexity of the English language may contribute to the higher rate of reading disorder in English speaking countries

    ANS: D   DIF: 3   REF: p. 498   OBJ: 3 TYPE: FACT

42. Treatment for learning disorders generally involves:
    a. stimulant medication
    b. educational remediation
    c. family therapy
    d. cognitive-behavioral therapy

    ANS: B   DIF: 1   REF: p. 499   OBJ: 3 TYPE: FACT

43. Alvin is a 10-year-old boy diagnosed with a mathematics disorder. His treatment plan will most likely involve:
    a. teaching him different strategies to compensate for areas where he has difficulty
    b. stimulant medication
    c. developing an educational plan that exempts him from mathematics requirements
    d. placing him in a school for learning disordered children

    ANS: A   DIF: 1   REF: p. 499   OBJ: 3 TYPE: APP

44. Given the available intervention strategies for learning disorders, the method that probably has the best chance of actually removing the learning disorder is:
    a. development of better study skills
    b. efforts to develop compensating cognitive skills
    c. remediation of the processing problem
    d. improving overall intelligence

    ANS: C   DIF: 5   REF: p. 499   OBJ: 3 TYPE: CON

45. All of the following are classified as pervasive developmental disorders EXCEPT:
    a. autistic disorder
    b. Rett's disorder
    c. Asperger's disorder
    d. learning disorder

    ANS: D   DIF: 3   REF: p. 499   OBJ: 4 TYPE: FACT

46. The term "pervasive" in the title of pervasive developmental disorders relates to the fact that these disorders:
    a. occur with great frequency
    b. are found in virtually all cultures
    c. significantly affect individuals throughout their lives
    d. are generally terminal

    ANS: C   DIF: 1   REF: p. 499   OBJ: 4 TYPE: CON

47. One of the most characteristic patterns for autistic children is that they are generally:
    a. uninterested in people
    b. very intelligent
    c. extremely talkative
    d. hyperactive

    ANS: A   DIF: 1   REF: p. 499   OBJ: 5 TYPE: FACT

48. Robin is a 3-year-old girl who appears uninterested in people. She generally interacts with her mom only when she needs something. In some ways, Robin seems to be interested in her mother only as a tool to help her get what she wants. Robin would probably be diagnosed with:
    a. autistic disorder
    b. Rett's disorder
    c. Asperger's disorder
    d. a learning disorder

    ANS: A   DIF: 1   REF: p. 499   OBJ: 5 TYPE: APP

49. Four-year-old Susan has just been diagnosed with autism. Research suggests that her chances of ever developing meaningful speech are about:
    a. 10%
    b. 25%
    c. 50%
    d. 75%

    ANS: C   DIF: 3   REF: p. 501   OBJ: 5 TYPE: APP

50. The restricted pattern of behavior generally observed in autism involves:
    a. repetitive movements such as spinning in circles
    b. an intense preference for keeping things the same
    c. inappropriate communication patterns
    d. lack of recognition of significant others

    ANS: B   DIF: 1   REF: p. 501   OBJ: 5 TYPE: FACT

51. Jean is a 14-year-old autistic girl who seems compelled to run around touching each door every time she comes home. If she is prevented from touching each door, Jean has a tantrum. This is an example of:
    a. restricted behavior pattern
    b. social impairment
    c. ritualistic behavior
    d. maintenance of sameness

    ANS: C   DIF: 3   REF: p. 501   OBJ: 5 TYPE: APP/WWW

52. All of the following are typical behaviors for autistic children EXCEPT:
    a. spinning a wheel on a toy truck and starring at it for hours
    b. throwing a loud tantrum when prevented from carrying out a ritual
    c. becoming wildly upset when one toy was removed from the shelf
    d. performing complex math calculations that appear well beyond their abilities

    ANS: D   DIF: 3   REF: p. 502   OBJ: 5 TYPE: APP

53. Cross-cultural research has indicated that autism is:
    a. universal across cultures and countries
    b. predominantly found in the United States
    c. predominantly found in Western cultures and countries
    d. more common in wealthy countries

    ANS: A   DIF: 3   REF: p. 502   OBJ: 5 TYPE: FACT

54. Most autistic individuals develop symptoms of the disorder:
    a. at birth
    b. by age one
    c. by age three
    d. by teen years

    ANS: C   DIF: 1   REF: p. 502   OBJ: 5 TYPE: FACT

55. In terms of the level of support that will be necessary for an autistic child, which factor is used as a predictor to determine the prognosis?
    a. age of onset
    b. severity of initial symptoms
    c. rate of symptom progression
    d. IQ

    ANS: D   DIF: 3   REF: p. 502   OBJ: 5 TYPE: FACT/WWW

56. Monte is a 3-year-old boy recently diagnosed with autism. He appears completely unresponsive to his parents and shows no indication of any language development. Monte seems uninterested in communication of any kind and has significant rituals such as lining up his toys and realigning them every few minutes. He becomes hysterical if anyone interrupts his ritualistic activity. On an IQ assessment designed for very young children, Monte's score was extremely low. His prognosis is poor primarily because of:
    a. lack of language acquisition and low IQ
    b. low IQ and early age of onset
    c. early age of onset and lack of language acquisition
    d. ritualistic behavior and disinterest in his parents

    ANS: A   DIF: 5   REF: p. 502   OBJ: 5 TYPE: APP

57. Research regarding the behavior of the parents of autistic children suggests that autism is:
    a. the result of cold and aloof parenting
    b. the result of a complex interaction of genetics and parenting style
    c. the result of overindulgent parenting style
    d. not the result of parenting behaviors

    ANS: D   DIF: 3   REF: p. 502   OBJ: 5 TYPE: FACT

58. The ability to perform "computer like" mathematical calculations and other incredible skills that are sometimes associated with autistic individuals (such as the character in the movie "Rainman") are:
    a. not typical of the disorder
    b. a defining symptom of the disorder
    c. fairly common but not present in every autistic individual
    d. a complete myth and not possible for any autistic individual

    ANS: A   DIF: 3   REF: p. 503   OBJ: 5 TYPE: FACT

59. While the risk of having an autistic child is approximately .0002 to .0005% for the general population, the risk for parents of an autistic child that another child will be autistic is:
    a. the same .0002 to .0005% since there is no known genetic component
    b. .002% to .005%
    c. about 1%
    d. 3% to 5%

    ANS: D   DIF: 3   REF: p. 503   OBJ: 5 TYPE: FACT

60. What is the convincing evidence that autism involves some form of brain damage?
    a. 75% of the individuals with autism have some level of mental retardation
    b. most autistic children suffered some form of brain trauma at birth
    c. autism runs in families
    d. autism develops fairly quickly and at a young age

    ANS: A   DIF: 3   REF: p. 503   OBJ: 5 TYPE: FACT

61. Brain scans of individuals with autism suggest that one area of the brain that may be involved with the disorder is the:
    a. brain stem
    b. hypothalamus
    c. cerebellum
    d. reticular formation

    ANS: C   DIF: 5   REF: p. 503   OBJ: 5 TYPE: FACT

62. One major distinction between Asperger's disorder and autism is that:
    a. Asperger's disorder is associated with longer language delays and lower IQ
    b. Autism is associated with social impairment and Asperger's disorder is not
    c. Autism develops in early childhood and Asperger's develops during adolescence
    d. Asperger's disorder is not associated with severe language delays

    ANS: D   DIF: 1   REF: p. 503   OBJ: 6 TYPE: FACT

63. Jim is a teen who has no friends. Although he is quite verbal, he speaks in a strange and formal style of speech. Jim is obsessed with airplanes and behaves in a very strange way. All of his activities center around planes and he possesses an almost encyclopedic knowledge of aircraft. Jim's constant verbal display of this knowledge interferes with socialization. Most people consider him "weird" and avoid him. The most likely diagnosis for Jim is:
    a. autism
    b. Asperger's disorder
    c. Rett's disorder
    d. pervasive developmental disorder not otherwise specified

    ANS: B   DIF: 3   REF: p. 504   OBJ: 6 TYPE: APP

64. The authors of the textbook report an interview with a patient named Jim who was originally diagnosed with autism, although today he would probably receive a diagnosis of Asperger's disorder. Jim's lucid description of his internal experiences suggests that the unusual behaviors characteristic of Asperger's might be influenced by:
    a. delusions
    b. limited cognitive abilities
    c. abnormal sensory experiences
    d. anxiety

    ANS: C   DIF: 3   REF: p. 504   OBJ: 6 TYPE: CON

65. An appropriate treatment goal for an autistic child is:
    a. resolution of all autistic symptoms by age 18
    b. immediate cessation of ritualistic behaviors
    c. development of normal social skills by age 18
    d. reduction in tantrums and eventual development of some self-care activities

    ANS: D   DIF: 1   REF: p. 505   OBJ: 5 TYPE: FACT/WWW

66. Modern treatment programs for autism generally involve:
    a. ego development
    b. interpersonal therapy
    c. anxiety reduction
    d. basic skills training

    ANS: D   DIF: 1   REF: p. 505   OBJ: 5 TYPE: FACT

67. Treatment for autism is most similar to the treatment for:
    a. mental retardation
    b. learning disorders
    c. personality disorders
    d. attention deficit hyperactivity disorder

    ANS: A   DIF: 3   REF: p. 505   OBJ: 5 TYPE: CON

68. Some success has been noted in the development of communication skills in autistic children through the use of:
   a. modeling appropriate communication
   b. behavioral procedures involving shaping and discrimination training
   c. intensive therapy where the patient is placed in many social situations
   d. stimulant medications

   ANS: B   DIF: 3   REF: p. 505   OBJ: 5 TYPE: CON

69. The results of behavioral treatment targeting the socialization deficits of individuals with autism have shown:
   a. no improvement
   b. some improvement in quantity of socialization but little improvement in the quality of social contacts
   c. some improvement in the quality of socialization but little improvement in the quantity of social contacts
   d. substantial improvement in both the quantity and quality of social contacts

   ANS: B   DIF: 3   REF: p. 506   OBJ: 5 TYPE: FACT

70. Jane is a fourteen-year-old autistic girl currently participating in a behavioral social skills training program for autistic adolescents. Jane's most likely outcome from this program is:
   a. relatively normal socialization for her age
   b. no progress at all
   c. some increase in the quality of her social skills, although little increase in the quantity of socialization
   d. some increase in the quantity of socialization in which she participates but little improvement in the quality of socialization

   ANS: D   DIF: 3   REF: p. 506   OBJ: 5 TYPE: APP

71. Based on the research of Lovaas (1987), improvements in the intellectual and educational functioning of autistic children have been documented for intervention programs that:
   a. use a group therapy model
   b. provide multiple therapists
   c. meet one-on-one for 40 hours per week
   d. are school based

   ANS: C   DIF: 5   REF: p. 506   OBJ: 5 TYPE: FACT

72. Research by Lovaas (1987) and others suggest that intervention for autism may be most effective when it is provided:
   a. at as young an age as possible
   b. during adolescence
   c. during late childhood/early adolescence
   d. to adults

   ANS: A   DIF: 1   REF: p. 506   OBJ: 5 TYPE: FACT

73. Research by Lovaas (1987) has suggested that autistic children show the greatest intellectual and educational improvement when they are:
    a. placed in special education classrooms
    b. placed in regular classrooms
    c. treated in group therapy
    d. treated with medication

    ANS: B   DIF: 3   REF: p. 506   OBJ: 5 TYPE: FACT

74. Jake is an autistic 8-year-old boy whose parents have just been informed that their son will be placed in a regular classroom and provided with whatever special support he needs. Jake's parents should:
    a. insist on a special education classroom since research suggests this is best for autistic children
    b. consider changing schools because it is obvious that Jake's school knows nothing about the needs of autistic children
    c. be relieved that Jake's autism must be very mild since the school would not place a child with significant autistic deficits in a regular classroom
    d. be pleased since research suggests that regular classroom placement is best for autistic children

    ANS: D   DIF: 3   REF: p. 506   OBJ: 5 TYPE: APP

75. Medication treatment for autism has been found to be:
    a. mildly effective
    b. ineffective
    c. generally effective
    d. highly effective initially, though the benefits of medication decrease over time

    ANS: B   DIF: 1   REF: p. 506   OBJ: 5 TYPE: FACT

76. Your friends Beth and Tim have recently discovered that their 3- year-old girl is autistic. Beth and Tim are both nutrition fanatics and are convinced that they can cure their daughter's autism with vitamins and diet. You should tell Beth and Tim that vitamins and diet:
    a. have been shown to be effective but the gains are not sufficient to be considered a cure
    b. may improve their daughter's symptoms, but it is necessary to consult a professional to determine exactly which dietary deficiencies may be involved
    c. are currently being investigated as a promising treatment for autism, but the results are too preliminary to be applied as a treatment
    d. do not appear to be an effective treatment for autism

    ANS: D   DIF: 1   REF: p. 506   OBJ: 5 TYPE: APP

77. Generally speaking, the treatment for an autistic child should involve:
    a. behavioral therapy, school-based education and a focus on developing as much independence as possible
    b. behavioral therapy, home schooling and a focus on developing as much independence as possible
    c. cognitive therapy, school-based education and a focus on developing as much independence as possible
    d. behavioral therapy and a focus on provisions for long term custodial care

    ANS: A   DIF: 3   REF: p. 506   OBJ: 5 TYPE: CON

78. The goal of most modern therapy for autistic children is to:
    a. have the child and family accept the inherent limitations of the disorder
    b. provide a separate and secure environment for the individual
    c. integrate the autistic child into regular society as much as possible
    d. isolate autistic children in intensive therapy for as long as possible before attempting to introduce them into the larger world

    ANS: C   DIF: 1   REF: p. 507   OBJ: 5 TYPE: CON

79. Mental retardation is defined as:
    a. below-average intellectual ability
    b. below-average intellectual ability and adaptive functioning
    c. significant deficits in self-care abilities
    d. low IQ score

    ANS: B   DIF: 1   REF: p. 507   OBJ: 7 TYPE: FACT

80. Individuals with mental retardation show extremely:
    a. similar types and degree of deficits
    b. similar types of deficits, although the degree of deficit varies greatly
    c. varied types and degree of deficits
    d. varied types of deficits, although the degree of deficit tends to be quite similar

    ANS: C   DIF: 1   REF: p. 508   OBJ: 7 TYPE: FACT

81. Mental retardation is recorded on DSM-IV Axis _____:
    a. I
    b. II
    c. III
    d. IV

    ANS: B   DIF: 1   REF: p. 508   OBJ: 7 TYPE: FACT

82. The reason that mental retardation is recorded on the same DSM-IV axis as personality disorders is because:
    a. this axis relates to relatively chronic conditions
    b. mental retardation and personality disorder generally have similar causes
    c. mental retardation and personality disorder are generally treated using similar methods
    d. this axis relates to biologically influenced conditions

    ANS: A   DIF: 1   REF: p. 508   OBJ: 7 TYPE: FACT

83. The DSM-IV criteria for mental retardation are:
    a. IQ approximately 70 or below and onset prior to age 18
    b. IQ approximately 70 or below, deficits in adaptive functioning, and onset prior to age 18
    c. IQ approximately 60 or below, deficits in communication, and onset prior to age 18
    d. IQ approximately 65 or below and deficits in adaptive functioning

    ANS: B   DIF: 1   REF: p. 508   OBJ: 7 TYPE: FACT

84. Joe is 24-years old, lives in a rural area and works as a helper/stock boy in a small local store. Joe's IQ was tested when he was in elementary school and again in high school. His IQ score was about 65 and he did not finish high school. Joe lives in a guesthouse on his parents' farm and although he does spend lots of time with his family, he takes care of himself. Based on the information provided, Joe should receive a diagnosis of:
    a. mental retardation
    b. borderline mental retardation
    c. learning disorder
    d. no diagnosis

    ANS: D   DIF: 3   REF: p. 509   OBJ: 7 TYPE: APP

85. The diagnostic criteria for mental retardation include an assessment of adaptive functioning because an IQ score is:
    a. not a measure of intelligence
    b. an insufficient measure of impairment
    c. is not adjusted statistically for people of different ages
    d. score is always highly inaccurate

    ANS: B   DIF: 3   REF: p. 509   OBJ: 7 TYPE: CON

86. The DSM-IV criterion for mental retardation called "concurrent deficits or impairments in adaptive functioning" is defined as significant difficulty in at least _____ area(s) such as communication, self-care, home living, etc.
    a. one
    b. two
    c. three
    d. four

    ANS: B   DIF: 1   REF: p. 509   OBJ: 7 TYPE: FACT

87. The reason that "onset prior to age 18" is part of the DSM-IV diagnostic criteria for mental retardation is that:
    a. the diagnosis indicates that the individual was affected during the developmental period
    b. the diagnosis is not intended to include individuals who have suffered any form of brain damage
    c. the diagnosis has legal implications for children
    d. this diagnosis is reserved for children; other diagnostic terms are applied once the mentally retarded individual reaches the age of 18

    ANS: A   DIF: 3   REF: p. 509   OBJ: 7 TYPE: CON

88. Fran is a 25-year-old woman who has been having a great deal of difficulty taking care of herself. Her IQ score is 68, though this surprises her parents because they recall that her IQ was tested several times when she was in school and it was always in the 80s. The diagnosis of mental retardation for Fran is:
    a. appropriate because she meets the criteria for IQ and has difficulty with self care
    b. inappropriate because she does not meet the IQ criterion
    c. inappropriate because we do not have sufficient evidence of impairment
    d. inappropriate because she did not appear to meet criteria before age 18

    ANS: D   DIF: 1   REF: p. 509   OBJ: 7 TYPE: APP/WWW

89. The IQ score designated as the cutoff for the diagnosis of mental retardation is:
   a. fairly arbitrary
   b. based on medical considerations
   c. based on the significant differences found in individuals who are either just above or just below the designated IQ level
   d. based on studies showing that the designated level separates most individuals with brain deficits from those who are simply of below average intelligence

   ANS: A   DIF: 3   REF: p. 509   OBJ: 7 TYPE: FACT

90. An individual with an IQ score of 60 would be classified with:
   a. mild retardation
   b. moderate retardation
   c. severe retardation
   d. profound retardation

   ANS: A   DIF: 1   REF: p. 509   OBJ: 8 TYPE: FACT

91. An individual with an IQ score of 35 would be classified with:
   a. mild retardation
   b. moderate retardation
   c. severe retardation
   d. profound retardation

   ANS: C   DIF: 3   REF: p. 509   OBJ: 8 TYPE: FACT

92. The following statement is true regarding an individual who is classified as mildly retarded:
   a. she can definitely live independently
   b. she is very unlikely to be able to live independently
   c. she is very likely to be able to live independently
   d. she will never live completely independently

   ANS: C   DIF: 5   REF: p. 509   OBJ: 8 TYPE: APP

93. The major difference between the DSM-IV system of classification of levels of mental retardation and the American Association on Mental Retardation (AAMR) system is that the AAMR system is based on:
   a. abilities
   b. disabilities
   c. IQ
   d. support required

   ANS: D   DIF: 3   REF: p. 509   OBJ: 9 TYPE: FACT

94. The educational system classification of mental retardation that uses terms such as educable, trainable and severe is not generally used because it:
   a. is not empirically based
   b. creates negative expectations
   c. has not been subjected to research
   d. is too complex

   ANS: B   DIF: 3   REF: p. 509   OBJ: 9 TYPE: CON

95. The percentage of persons with mental retardation who are classified as mildly mentally retarded is approximately:
    a. 90%
    b. 70%
    c. 50%
    d. 25%

    ANS: A   DIF: 1   REF: p. 510   OBJ: 10 TYPE: FACT

96. Which is the most accurate statement regarding the causes of mental retardation?
    a. It is caused by genetics.
    b. It has four known causes.
    c. It is caused by either substances or trauma.
    d. It has hundreds of known causes.

    ANS: D   DIF: 1   REF: p. 510   OBJ: 10 TYPE:
    FACT/WWW

97. The vast majority of cases of mental retardation are due to:
    a. prenatal influences
    b. postnatal influences
    c. unknown causes
    d. head trauma

    ANS: C   DIF: 3   REF: p. 511   OBJ: 10 TYPE: FACT

98. Lesch-Nyhan syndrome is an example of a:
    a. genetic disorder that causes mental retardation
    b. cluster of symptoms displayed by some mentally retarded individuals
    c. form of cerebral palsy
    d. viral infection that causes mental retardation

    ANS: A   DIF: 5   REF: p. 511   OBJ: 10 TYPE: FACT

99. Down syndrome is caused by:
    a. an extra 21st chromosome
    b. a missing 21st chromosome
    c. lack of oxygen at birth
    d. unknown influences

    ANS: A   DIF: 3   REF: p. 511   OBJ: 11 TYPE: FACT

100. The incidence of a child being born with Down syndrome to a mother at age 35 is 1 in 500 births. The risk at maternal age 45 is 1 in ___ births.
    a. 1,000
    b. 500
    c. 100
    d. 18

    ANS: D   DIF: 5   REF: p. 511   OBJ: 11 TYPE: FACT

101. When there are no known genetic or organic influences, the causes of mild mental retardation are generally considered to be:
a. substances
b. cultural-familial
c. prenatal
d. completely unknown

ANS: B   DIF: 3   REF: p. 512   OBJ: 10 TYPE: CON

102. An appropriate treatment goal for an individual with mild or moderate mental retardation is:
a. resolution of symptoms by age 18
b. increase intellectual functioning by 15%
c. improve abilities to care for self
d. select an institution for long term care

ANS: C   DIF: 1   REF: p. 514   OBJ: 12 TYPE: FACT

103. The form of treatment that has been found to be most successful for individuals with mental retardation is:
a. interpersonal therapy
b. the behavioral approach to skills training
c. medication
d. the cognitive approach to self-care activities

ANS: B   DIF: 1   REF: p. 514   OBJ: 12 TYPE: FACT/WWW

104. Research regarding early intervention programs such as Head Start indicate that such programs:
a. are ineffective
b. may help improve the functioning of mentally retarded children
c. may help prevent "at risk" children from developing mental retardation
d. help parents manage the behavior of their mentally retarded children

ANS: C   DIF: 3   REF: p. 515   OBJ: 12 TYPE: FACT

105. Currently, the technology of gene therapy for mental retardation is:
a. a viable treatment for only a small number of cases
b. a potentially effective treatment, but the risks must be evaluated carefully
c. considered unethical
d. in the research stage only

ANS: D   DIF: 3   REF: p. 515   OBJ: 12 TYPE: FACT

106. In the video of Sean performing on stage with other children ("Abnormal Psychology Live" CD), his ADHD is apparent by his:
a. forgetting his lines
c. running back and forth across the stage during the presentation
b. failure to follow the apparently simple directions to hold hands
d. yelling and shouting during the play

ANS: B   DIF: 1   REF: CD

107. One thing that the Life Skills Training and Bullying programs have in common ("Abnormal Psychology Live" CD) is that they both focus on:
    a. home and school behaviors   c. helping victims
    b. prevention   d. criminal activity

    ANS: B   DIF: 1   REF: CD

108. During the interview in the segment on bullying of the "Abnormal Psychology Live" CD, it is mentioned that bullies often:
    a. out-grow their inappropriate behavior   c. become drug users
    b. have low self-esteem   d. become criminals in later life

    ANS: D   DIF: 3   REF: CD

109. Christina, the child with autism on the "Abnormal Psychology Live" CD is described as communicating with her teachers by:
    a. pictures   c. tantrums
    b. gestures   d. simple words

    ANS: A   DIF: 3   REF: CD

110. When asked to find the "8", the little girl with autism on the "Abnormal Psychology Live" CD:
    a. looked the other way   c. started laughing
    b. did not seem to understand the instruction   d. cried

    ANS: D   DIF: 3   REF: CD

ESSAY

1. Most models of developmental psychology suggest that normal childhood development progresses as a series of steps, with each new achievement building on prior development. Given this model, select any childhood developmental disorder and describe how it can influence current and future deficits for the individual.

2. Explain the statement "we are not sure whether academic difficulties of children with attention deficit/hyperactivity disorder are a result of the disorder or a result of the symptoms of the disorder."

3. Describe the typical social difficulties that a child with attention deficit/hyperactivity disorder might experience. Provide an explanation for a child with patterns of inattention and a separate explanation for a child with hyperactivity/impulsivity.

4. Describe the benefits and disadvantages of medication treatment versus non-medication treatments for attention deficit/hyperactivity disorder. Make sure to include discussion of the medications and therapy procedures used in the treatment of this disorder.

5. Explain why it is completely incorrect to state that learning disorder is just another way of saying "not bright". Make sure that your explanation includes the procedures to diagnose a learning disorder and a description of the categories of learning disorders.

6. Describe three pervasive developmental disorders. What do each of these disorders have in common? Why is the term "pervasive" used?

7. Describe a typical treatment plan for a newly diagnosed 4-year-old autistic boy. What are realistic short-term and long-term treatment goals? Assuming that this boy makes some progress in initial therapy, what would you suggest for his school education? Explain the rationale for your recommendations.   **WWW**

8. Describe the similarities and differences between Asperger's disorder and autism.

9. Explain why mental retardation (especially many cases of mild retardation) is often considered more of an arbitrary, culturally defined diagnosis than typical Axis I diagnoses such as schizophrenia or bipolar disorder. Make sure that your explanation includes discussion of the DSM-IV criteria for mental retardation.

10. Describe a typical treatment plan for a 10-year-old, mildly retarded girl. What are appropriate treatment goals? What treatment methods have been found to be successful to meet these goals?

MULTIPLE CHOICE

1. Asperger's disorder shares characteristics similar to autistic disorder except for
   a. the language delay present in autistic disorder.
   b. the language delay present in Asperger's disorder.
   c. impairments in social relationships seen in autistic disorder.
   d. impairments in social relationships seen in Asperger's disorder.

   ANS: A

2. _____ is found almost exclusively in females and is characterized by constant hand wringing, mental retardation, and impaired motor skills.
   a. Asperger's disorder
   b. Rett's disorder
   c. Childhood disintegrative disorder
   d. Autistic disorder

   ANS: B

3. Tics are involuntary movements that often occur in rapid succession, come about suddenly, and happen in very idiosyncratic or stereotyped ways. _____ is a disorder with these characteristics.
   a. Autistic disorder
   b. Selective mutism
   c. Tourette's disorder
   d. Coprolalia

   ANS: C

4. Which of the following is not a communication disorder?
   a. expressive language disorder
   b. selective mutism
   c. Asperger's disorder
   d. stuttering

   ANS: C

5. The four levels of mental retardation identified in DSM-IV are
   a. mild, moderate, severe, profound
   b. educable, trainable, severe, profound
   c. slight, moderate, profound, intensive
   d. borderline, custodial care, intermittent care, pervasive care

   ANS: A

6. The educational system has developed an additional method of classification for mental retardation which
   a. is used to identify the ability of students.
   b. is split into three categories: trainable, educable, and severe mental retardation.
   c. assumes that certain individuals will not benefit from academic or vocational training.
   d. all of the above

   ANS: D

7. Mary was 18 years old when she was involved in a serious car accident. Before the car accident her IQ was 95 and she was living independently. Now, her IQ is 50 and she has impairment in many of her adaptive functions. Under DSM-IV, what would Mary's diagnosis be?
   a. Mild Mental Retardation
   b. Moderate Mental Retardation
   c. Mental Retardation, Severity Unspecified
   d. none of the above

   ANS: D

8. All of the following are types of learning disorders in DSM-IV except
   a. reading disorder.
   b. mathematics disorder.
   c. school performance disorder.
   d. disorder of written expression.

   ANS: C

9. Learning disabilities are characterized by performance that is substantially
   a. above what would be expected given the person's age, IQ, and education.
   b. below what would be expected given the person's age, IQ, and education.
   c. diminished from one year to the next.
   d. lower than 50% of the person's peer group.

   ANS: B

10. Which of the following statements is true about ADHD?
    a. Children in the United States are more likely to receive a diagnosis of ADHD than are children in other places.
    b. Research consistently finds that maternal smoking increases the likelihood of having a child with ADHD.
    c. It is clear that a combination of behavioral and medical treatments is superior to medication alone.
    d. a and b only
    e. all of the above

    ANS: D

MULTIPLE CHOICE

1. Delirium, dementia and amnestic disorders typically develop:
    a. from complications of birth
    b. as part of the normal aging process
    c. in late adulthood
    d. as temporary conditions

    ANS: C   DIF: 1   REF: p. 521   OBJ: 1 TYPE: FACT

2. The three categories of cognitive disorders are:
    a. delirium, dementia and amnestic disorders
    b. delirium, dementia and Alzheimer's
    c. Alzheimer's, delirium and amnestic disorders
    d. Alzheimer's, organic and amnestic disorders

    ANS: A   DIF: 1   REF: p. 521   OBJ: 2 TYPE: FACT

3. The term "organic mental disorders" is no longer used to describe cognitive disorders because:
    a. there is nothing "organic" about these disorders
    b. cognitive disorders are actually thought disorders
    c. the term implies that there is no effective treatment
    d. we have found that most psychological disorders have an "organic" component

    ANS: D   DIF: 3   REF: p. 521   OBJ: 1 TYPE: CON/WWW

4. The cause of most cognitive disorders is:
    a. the normal process of aging
    b. brain dysfunction
    c. alcohol/substances
    d. medication side effects

    ANS: B   DIF: 1   REF: p. 521   OBJ: 1 TYPE: FACT

5. Cognitive disorders typically cause impairment in all of the following primary abilities EXCEPT:
    a. memory
    b. perception
    c. dreaming
    d. attention

    ANS: C   DIF: 1   REF: p. 521   OBJ: 1 TYPE: FACT

6. From the following choices, choose the the age group most likely to use prescription medications:
    a. infants and young children
    b. children and adolescents
    c. middle-aged adults
    d. older adults

    ANS: D   DIF: 3   REF: p. 522   OBJ: 1 TYPE: FACT

7. Impaired consciousness and cognition during the course of several hours or days defines:
   a. delirium
   b. dementia
   c. Alzheimer's
   d. Amnestic disorder

   ANS: A   DIF: 1   REF: p. 521   OBJ: 3 TYPE: FACT

8. Mr. Smith (age 72) is brought to the hospital emergency room. Mr. Smith's son explains that his father woke up this morning and was "not himself." Mr. Smith appears confused, agitated and a bit frightened. He does not know his own name and cannot recognize his son. Mr. Smith's son reports that his father had been completely fine with no symptoms prior to that morning. Mr. Smith appears to be suffering from:
   a. dementia
   b. Alzheimer's
   c. delirium
   d. amnestic disorder

   ANS: C   DIF: 1   REF: p. 521-522   OBJ: 3 TYPE: APP

9. The symptoms of delirium tend to develop:
   a. very slowly, over the course of several years
   b. very quickly, over the course of a few hours to a few days
   c. moderately slowly, over the course of several months
   d. either very quickly or very slowly, depending on the cause

   ANS: B   DIF: 3   REF: p. 522   OBJ: 3 TYPE: FACT

10. The symptoms of delirium tend to subside:
    a. very slowly, over the course of several years
    b. relatively quickly, over the course of a few days or weeks
    c. moderately slowly, over the course of several months
    d. very slowly, if they ever subside at all

    ANS: B   DIF: 3   REF: p. 522   OBJ: 3 TYPE: FACT

11. All of the following are common causes of delirium EXCEPT:
    a. medical conditions
    b. medication side effects
    c. head trauma
    d. dietary factors

    ANS: D   DIF: 3   REF: p. 522   OBJ: 3 TYPE: FACT

12. Substance related delirium is a major problem for the elderly because:
    a. they are more likely to take many medications
    b. their bodies are less able to process and eliminate drugs
    c. improper use of medication is likely to have serious side effects
    d. of all the reasons listed in a, b, and c

    ANS: D   DIF: 3   REF: p. 522-523   OBJ: 3 TYPE: CON

13. Which of the following individuals is most likely to develop delirium?
    a. Joe (age 76) takes multiple medications for various medical conditions. Two new medications have just been prescribed for him and he has already made a mistake taking the first dose.
    b. Jean (age 89) is in good physical and mental health. This morning she has a little bit of a head cold, but has not yet taken any medication for it.
    c. Mark (age 12) woke up with a low-grade fever from the viral infection that has been going around his class this past week.
    d. Sarah (age 40) was in a minor car accident but claims to feel fine.

    ANS: A   DIF: 5   REF: p. 522   OBJ: 3 TYPE: APP

14. Delirium is generally treated with:
    a. antibiotic medication
    b. benzodiazepine medication
    c. antidepressant medication
    d. a treatment based on the specific cause of the delirium

    ANS: D   DIF: 3   REF: p. 523   OBJ: 3 TYPE: FACT/WWW

15. Delirium brought on by withdrawal from alcohol or other drugs is generally treated with:
    a. rest and reassurance
    b. antipsychotic medication
    c. antidepressant medication
    d. restraining the patient until the withdrawal symptoms are over

    ANS: B   DIF: 5   REF: p. 523   OBJ: 3 TYPE: FACT

16. Typical psychosocial intervention for a patient with delirium includes:
    a. restraining the patient to prevent self harm
    b. placing the person in a new environment
    c. reassurance and surrounding with familiar belongings
    d. excluding the patient from any medical decision to avoid increased anxiety

    ANS: C   DIF: 3   REF: p. 523   OBJ: 3 TYPE: FACT

17. The gradual deterioration of brain functioning that affects judgement, memory, language and other cognitive processes is called:
    a. dementia
    b. delirium
    c. amnestic disorder
    d. mental retardation

    ANS: A   DIF: 1   REF: p. 523   OBJ: 4 TYPE: FACT

18. One of the major differences between dementia caused by Alzheimer's disease and dementia caused by depression is that Alzheimer's type dementia:
    a. is generally reversible
    b. is not reversible
    c. involves a slow increase in symptoms
    d. leads to a rapid decline in abilities

    ANS: B   DIF: 3   REF: p. 523   OBJ: 5 TYPE: FACT

19. All of the following are possible causes of dementia EXCEPT:
    a. Alzheimer's disease
    b. chemical substances (including medications)
    c. depression
    d. food additives and preservatives

    ANS: D   DIF: 1   REF: p. 523   OBJ: 4 TYPE: FACT

20. The most common cause of dementia is:
    a. a history of substance abuse
    b. Alzheimer's disease
    c. improper use of prescription drugs
    d. syphilis

    ANS: B   DIF: 3   REF: p. 523   OBJ: 5 TYPE: FACT

21. One major difference that is useful in the diagnosis of dementia or delirium is that:
    a. dementia symptoms develop slowly over time and delirium symptoms develop quickly
    b. dementia symptoms are usually associated with underlying medical conditions and delirium is usually the result of other factors
    c. the initial symptoms of dementia are generally more severe than the symptoms of delirium
    d. the symptoms of dementia involve memory but the symptoms of delirium are more likely to involve expressive language

    ANS: A   DIF: 3   REF: p. 523   OBJ: 4 TYPE: FACT

22. At the age of 50, Debra has begun to receive quite a bit of teasing from her family about being "absentminded." The truth is that Debra has been hiding the fact that each week she seems to remember less and less. For the last month she has been getting lost while driving home from work. Lately Debra has been relying on a hand- drawn map to get home. She has started having trouble recognizing the faces of people at work and frequently forgets why she started to do something. Debra appears to be developing:
    a. delirium
    b. amnestic disorder
    c. dementia
    d. medically induced dementia

    ANS: C   DIF: 1   REF: p. 523-524   OBJ: 4 TYPE: APP

23. One of the early signs of dementia is:
    a. loss of memory for recent events
    b. loss of memory for events from long ago
    c. inability to produce language
    d. inability to understand language

    ANS: A   DIF: 1   REF: p. 523   OBJ: 4 TYPE: FACT/WWW

24. People with dementia generally suffer from agnosia, which is defined as the inability to:
    a. use language
    b. understand language
    c. recognize and name objects
    d. remember events and places

    ANS: C   DIF: 3   REF: p. 524   OBJ: 4 TYPE: FACT

25. When a person has dementia, he or she may also experience delusions, depression, agitation, aggression and/or apathy, all of which are due to::
    a. progressive deterioration of brain functioning
    b. frustration experienced by these patients as they lose their cognitive abilities
    c. neither of the above
    d. both of the above

    ANS: D   DIF: 3   REF: p. 524-525   OBJ: 4 TYPE: CON

26. The outcome for patients with dementia due to Alzheimer's disease is usually:
    a. death
    b. slow recovery
    c. stabilization at some level of greatly reduced cognitive ability
    d. dependent on individual response to treatment

    ANS: A   DIF: 1   REF: p. 525   OBJ: 5 TYPE: FACT

27. The prevalence of dementia in adults between the ages of 64 and 74 is:
    a. .5%
    b. 1%
    c. 3%
    d. 5%

    ANS: B   DIF: 5   REF: p. 525   OBJ: 4 TYPE: FACT

28. The prevalence of dementia in adults over the age of 85 is:
    a. 1%
    b. 5%
    c. 7%
    d. more than 10%

    ANS: D   DIF: 5   REF: p. 525   OBJ: 4 TYPE: FACT

29. In the United States, the cost of caring for patients with Alzheimer's type dementia is estimated in _____ of dollars.
    a. thousands
    b. millions
    c. billions
    d. trillions

    ANS: C   DIF: 5   REF: p. 525   OBJ: 5 TYPE: FACT

30. How is Alzheimer's type dementia usually diagnosed?
    a. MRI findings
    b. ruling out alternative explanations
    c. functional brain scan
    d. psychological and neurological test results

    ANS: B   DIF: 3   REF: p. 525   OBJ: 5 TYPE: FACT/WWW

31. Alzheimer's type dementia is characterized by:
    a. multiple cognitive deficits that develop gradually and steadily
    b. a few severe cognitive deficits that develop gradually and steadily
    c. multiple cognitive deficits that develop quickly
    d. a few severe cognitive deficits that develop quickly

    ANS: A   DIF: 1   REF: p. 526   OBJ: 5 TYPE: FACT

32. Which of the following is used for a definitive diagnosis of Alzheimer's type dementia?
    a. psychological testing
    b. a mental status exam
    c. an autopsy
    d. reported observations of the patient by family members

    ANS: C   DIF: 3   REF: p. 526   OBJ: 5 TYPE: FACT

33. Research has indicated that clinicians are accurate in their diagnosis of Alzheimer's type dementia
    about _____ of the time on average.
    a. 100%
    b. 90%
    c. 80%
    d. 50%

    ANS: C   DIF: 3   REF: p. 526   OBJ: 5 TYPE: FACT

34. In the advanced stages of Alzheimer's disease a phenomenon called "sundowner syndrome"
    occurs in which cognitive disturbances tend to:
    a. improve as the day goes on
    b. become worse toward evening
    c. come and go during the course of the day
    d. peak around mid-day

    ANS: B   DIF: 3   REF: p. 526   OBJ: 5 TYPE: FACT

35. Although the sample size is small, the results of a study that looked at the writings of a group of
    Catholic nuns (Massie et al., 1996), suggest that the development of Alzheimer's type dementia
    might be predicted in early life by analyzing the _____ present in an individual's writing.
    a. errors
    b. word usage
    c. idea density
    d. emotional tone

    ANS: C   DIF: 3   REF: p. 526-537   OBJ: 5 TYPE: FACT

36. If the findings from the study regarding the writings of a group of Catholic nuns (Massie et al., 1996) are correct, which of the following individuals is most likely to eventually develop Alzheimer's type dementia?
    a. John, whose writing is very descriptive and a bit bizarre
    b. Mary, whose writing has many religious themes
    c. Maureen, whose writing is mostly about animals
    d. Lisa, whose writing describes events in very brief terms

    ANS: D   DIF: 5   REF: p. 527   OBJ: 5 TYPE: APP

37. The progression of Alzheimer's type dementia is:
    a. slow during early stages and late stages, and rapid during middle stages
    b. rapid during early and late stages, and slow during middle stages
    c. slow and progressive throughout the individual's life
    d. slow in the early stages and rapid during late stages

    ANS: A   DIF: 3   REF: p. 527   OBJ: 5 TYPE: FACT

38. What is the percentage of dementia cases that are ultimately found to be of the Alzheimer's type?
    a. 25%
    b. 35%
    c. 50%
    d. 75%

    ANS: C   DIF: 3   REF: p. 527   OBJ: 5 TYPE: FACT

39. What is the approximate average survival time of a patient diagnosed with Alzheimer's type dementia?
    a. 4 years
    b. 8 years
    c. 15 years
    d. 20 years

    ANS: B   DIF: 3   REF: p. 527   OBJ: 5 TYPE: FACT

40. Symptoms of Alzheimer's type dementia typically appear between the ages of:
    a. 40 and 50
    b. 50 and 60
    c. 60 and 70
    d. 70 and 80

    ANS: C   DIF: 3   REF: p. 527   OBJ: 5 TYPE: FACT

41. Which of the following individuals has the greatest risk of developing Alzheimer's type dementia?
    a. Paul, who is wealthy and well educated
    b. Rena, who completed college although she has an average IQ
    c. Jason, who is extremely bright but never finished college
    d. Carrie, who dropped out of school when she was very young

    ANS: D   DIF: 3   REF: p. 527   OBJ: 5 TYPE: APP/WWW

42. One hypothesis to explain the observed differences in the rate of Alzheimer's type dementia for individuals of varying educational level is that:
    a. the abilities acquired through formal education help compensate for some of the deficits of the disorder
    b. the type of mental activity associated with formal education places an additional burden on the brain that makes symptoms worse once a person has the disorder
    c. knowledge acquired through formal education helps one avoid exposure to environmental stimuli that might influence the disorder
    d. the type of work that most college graduates pursue is less likely to expose the individual to the stressors associated with the disorder

    ANS: A   DIF: 5   REF: p. 528   OBJ: 5 TYPE: CON

43. In regard to dementia, the cognitive reserve hypothesis suggests that:
    a. skills acquired through formal education help compensate for the early symptoms of dementia
    b. the more synapses one develops throughout life, the more neuronal death required before the person becomes impaired
    c. individuals with Alzheimer's type dementia never had reserve neurons
    d. Alzheimer's type dementia is caused by a lack of formal education

    ANS: B   DIF: 3   REF: p. 528   OBJ: 6 TYPE: FACT

44. What is the biological version of the theory that states that formal education helps insulate people from the effects of Alzheimer's type dementia?
    a. mind-body hypothesis
    b. neuronal network theory
    c. cognitive reserve hypothesis
    d. cortical activity theory

    ANS: C   DIF: 5   REF: p. 528   OBJ: 6 TYPE: CON

45. Which of the following statements is true with regard to the rate of Alzheimer's type dementia for different demographic groups?
    a. Males and certain racial groups appear to have lower rates of the disorder.
    b. No differences are found in the rate of Alzheimer's type dementia by gender, but some racial differences have been noted.
    c. No differences are found in the rate of Alzheimer's type dementia by race, but women appear to have a slightly higher rate of the disorder than men.
    d. No differences in the rate of the disorder by race or gender have been noted.

    ANS: A   DIF: 3   REF: p. 528   OBJ: 5 TYPE: FACT

46. _____ is the most frequent cause of dementia and _____ is the second most frequent cause.
    a. Vascular disease; head trauma
    b. Vascular disease; Alzheimer's disease
    c. Alzheimer's disease; vascular disease
    d. Alzheimer's disease; head trauma

    ANS: C   DIF: 3   REF: p. 528   OBJ: 7 TYPE: FACT

47. Why are the symptoms of vascular dementia so different in each patient?
    a. It is not known why patients with vascular dementia have different symptoms.
    b. The symptoms relate to the area of the brain damaged.
    c. The symptoms depend upon the person's other medical conditions.
    d. Patients tend to be elderly and easily confused.

    ANS: B   DIF: 3   REF: p. 528   OBJ: 7 TYPE: CON

48. Sixty-year-old Fred has the typical early symptoms of dementia. The fact that he has abnormalities in walking and weakness in his limbs suggests that his dementia is:
    a. the Alzheimer's type
    b. influenced by a medication
    c. due to multiple influences
    d. the vascular type

    ANS: D   DIF: 5   REF: p. 528   OBJ: 7 TYPE: APP

49. In contrast to patients with Alzheimer's type dementia, patients with vascular dementia are more likely to have symptoms such as:
    a. abnormalities in walking or muscle weakness during early stages
    b. abnormalities in walking or muscle weakness during late stages
    c. memory impairment during the early stages
    d. memory impairment during the late stages

    ANS: A   DIF: 3   REF: p. 528   OBJ: 7 TYPE: FACT

50. The risk of developing vascular dementia is:
    a. greater for women than men
    b. greater for men than women
    c. equal for men and women
    d. greater for men in Western cultures, but equal for men and women in other cultures

    ANS: B   DIF: 3   REF: p. 528   OBJ: 7 TYPE: FACT

51. Which of the following statements is true regarding the different types of dementia?
    a. All forms of dementia have the same onset, symptoms and course.
    b. Vascular dementia has a more rapid onset and patients suffer a much more rapid demise that with the other forms of dementia.
    c. Vascular dementia has a more rapid onset and results in fewer deficits than Alzheimer's type dementia.
    d. Vascular dementia has a more rapid onset than Alzheimer's type dementia, although the course and outcome are similar.

    ANS: D   DIF: 3   REF: p. 528   OBJ: 7 TYPE: CON

52. All of the following are causes of dementia EXCEPT:
    a. HIV
    b. vitamin B12 deficiency
    c. pneumonia
    d. head trauma

    ANS: C   DIF: 1   REF: p. 529   OBJ: 7 TYPE: FACT

53. Dementia caused by HIV appears to be due to:
   a. the HIV infection itself
   b. side effects of medications used to treat HIV
   c. opportunistic infections that occur in HIV patients
   d. chemical imbalances in the brain

   ANS: A   DIF: 5   REF: p. 529   OBJ: 7 TYPE: FACT/WWW

54. The dementia experienced by HIV patients primarily affects areas of the brain in the:
   a. cortex
   b. hindbrain
   c. subcortex
   d. brain stem

   ANS: C   DIF: 3   REF: p. 530   OBJ: 7 TYPE: FACT

55. Dementia due to HIV is more likely to cause _____ than Alzheimer's type dementia.
   a. death
   b. short term memory loss
   c. long term memory loss
   d. severe depression

   ANS: D   DIF: 3   REF: p. 530   OBJ: 7 TYPE: FACT

56. The differing patterns of impairment associated with Alzheimer's type dementia and HIV caused dementia are primarily attributable to:
   a. the different areas of the brain affected
   b. the immune response to the virus in HIV patients
   c. psychosocial differences in the lives of the typical patients with each disorder
   d. unexplained causes

   ANS: A   DIF: 3   REF: p. 530   OBJ: 7 TYPE: FACT

57. If Jane's dementia is caused by a process that has damaged her brain's dopamine pathways, it can be assumed that this condition is caused by:
   a. head trauma
   b. Parkinson's disease
   c. Huntington's disease
   d. Alzheimer's type dementia

   ANS: B   DIF: 5   REF: p. 530   OBJ: 7 TYPE: APP

58. Only some of the patients diagnosed with _____ and _____ go on to develop dementia.
   a. Alzheimer's; Huntington's disease
   b. Pick's disease; Huntington's disease
   c. Huntington's disease; Parkinson's disease
   d. Parkinson's disease; Pick's disease

   ANS: C   DIF: 3   REF: p. 530   OBJ: 7 TYPE: FACT

59. Compared to most disorders, Huntington's disease is very unusual because it is:
    a. the result of one gene
    b. influenced by many genes
    c. always a cause of dementia
    d. associated with subcortical impairment

    ANS: A   DIF: 5   REF: p. 531   OBJ: 7 TYPE: FACT

60. The disorder that causes a form of dementia called bovine spongiform encephalopathy (BSE) or "mad cow disease" is a variant of:
    a. Huntington's disease
    b. Pick's disease
    c. Alzheimer's type dementia
    d. Creutzfeldt-Jacob disease

    ANS: D   DIF: 3   REF: p. 531   OBJ: 7 TYPE: FACT

61. The symptoms of dementia associated with substance dependence are most similar to the symptoms observed in:
    a. vascular dementia
    b. Alzheimer's type dementia
    c. Huntington's disease
    d. HIV induced dementia

    ANS: B   DIF: 3   REF: p. 531   OBJ: 7 TYPE: FACT

62. When symptoms of dementia occur with substance dependence, they are generally associated with:
    a. toxic effects of the substances
    b. temporary impairment in brain functioning
    c. permanent brain damage
    d. poor diet and self-care behaviors

    ANS: C   DIF: 1   REF: p. 531   OBJ: 7 TYPE: FACT

63. Research regarding the relationship between aluminum and Alzheimer's disease has:
    a. not demonstrated a causal link
    b. demonstrated that excessive aluminum can cause Alzheimer's type dementia
    c. proven that high aluminum levels observed in Alzheimer's patients brain tissues are due to lab procedures
    d. demonstrated that the disease process of Alzheimer's results in elevated aluminum in patients' brain tissue

    ANS: A   DIF: 3   REF: p. 532   OBJ: 6 TYPE: FACT

64. The research finding of a negative correlation between smoking and the Alzheimer's type of dementia, i.e., smokers were less likely to develop Alzheimer's type dementia, is generally interpreted to mean that:
    a. research findings are sometimes in error
    b. nicotine protects against dementia for most people
    c. smoking may be helpful in protecting people at high risk for Alzheimer's
    d. smoking may shorten the lives of smokers so they do not live long enough to develop dementia

    ANS: D   DIF: 3   REF: p. 532-533   OBJ: 6 TYPE: CON

65. Which disorder is associated with the formation of neurofibrillary tangles and amyloid plaques in the brain?
    a. Huntington's disease
    b. Pick's disease
    c. Alzheimer's type dementia
    d. Creutzfeldt-Jacob disease

    ANS: C   DIF: 1   REF: p. 533   OBJ: 6 TYPE: FACT

66. The neurofibrillary tangles associated with Alzheimer's type dementia are best described as:
    a. tangled, strandlike filaments in the cortex
    b. tangled, strandlike filaments throughout the nervous system
    c. gummy protein deposits in the cortex
    d. gummy protein deposits throughout the nervous system

    ANS: A   DIF: 1   REF: p. 533   OBJ: 6 TYPE: FACT

67. The amyloid plaques that accumulate in the brain of Alzheimer's type dementia patients are best described as:
    a. tangled, strandlike filaments
    b. gummy protein deposits
    c. plaques of dead nerve cells
    d. mineral deposits

    ANS: B   DIF: 1   REF: p. 533   OBJ: 6 TYPE: FACT

68. The neurofibrillary tangles and amyloid plaques associated with Alzheimer's type dementia are observed only:
    a. on MRI or CT brain scans
    b. on functional brain scans (fMRI)
    c. during an autopsy
    d. during an EEG examination

    ANS: C   DIF: 1   REF: p. 533   OBJ: 6 TYPE: FACT

69. Research into the causes of Alzheimer's type dementia indicates the influence of:
    a. multiple genes
    b. a single gene
    c. environmental toxins
    d. high levels of aluminum

    ANS: A   DIF: 1   REF: p. 533   OBJ: 6 TYPE: FACT/WWW

70. Genetic research on the causes of Alzheimer's type dementia suggests that there are:
    a. too many complex interactions to ever understand the causes of Alzheimer's type dementia
    b. many forms of Alzheimer's type dementia and each type may have somewhat different features and different genetic influences
    c. one or two forms of Alzheimer's type dementia and each type may have a different genetic cause
    d. three identifiable forms of Alzheimer's type dementia, each with its own specific genetic influences

    ANS: B   DIF: 3   REF: p. 533   OBJ: 6 TYPE: FACT

71. One theory about the development of Alzheimer's type dementia suggests that the formation of solid waxy proteins in the brain causes the disorder in a process similar to:
    a. cholesterol build up in blood vessels causing cardiovascular disease
    b. vascular spasms causing migraines
    c. head trauma causing neuronal death
    d. formation of scar tissue following an injury

    ANS: A   DIF: 3   REF: p. 533   OBJ: 6 TYPE: CON

72. The gene responsible for producing amyloid precursor protein (APP) appears to explain the development of:
    a. Alzheimer's type dementia in general
    b. Alzheimer's type dementia that develops very late in life
    c. non-Alzheimer's type dementia that tends to affect unique populations, such as those with strong family history of the disorder
    d. early onset Alzheimer's type dementia and the higher frequency of the disorder in Down syndrome patients

    ANS: D   DIF: 5   REF: p. 533   OBJ: 6 TYPE: FACT

73. The greater the number of apolipoprotein (apoE) genes an individual possesses, the:
    a. more likely the individual is to develop vascular dementia
    b. less likely the individual is to develop vascular dementia
    c. more likely the individual is to develop Alzheimer's type dementia
    d. less likely the individual is to develop Alzheimer's type dementia

    ANS: C   DIF: 3   REF: p. 534   OBJ: 6 TYPE: FACT/WWW

74. Apolipoprotein (apoE) is associated with the development of dementia because apoE:
    a. helps insulate neurons from various toxins
    b. results in neurofibrillary tangles
    c. causes aluminum to concentrate in the brain
    d. helps transport amyloid protein through the bloodstream

    ANS: D   DIF: 5   REF: p. 534   OBJ: 6 TYPE: CON

75. In regard to dementia of the Alzheimer type, having two genes for apolipoprotein (apoE):
    a. increases the risk of developing Alzheimer's type dementia, but does not relate to the age of onset
    b. decreases the risk of developing Alzheimer's type dementia and raises the average age of onset
    c. decreases the risk of developing Alzheimer's type dementia but lowers the average age of onset
    d. increases the risk of developing Alzheimer's type dementia and decreases the average age of onset

    ANS: D   DIF: 5   REF: p. 534   OBJ: 6 TYPE: FACT

76. The condition called *dementia pugilistica* is diagnosed in _____.
    a. baseball players
    b. boxers
    c. bowlers
    d. basketball players

    ANS: B   DIF: 3   REF: p. 534   OBJ: 6 TYPE: FACT

77. Some types of Down Syndrome predisopose the individual to developing:
    a. dementia pugilistica
    b. Parkinson's Disease
    c. Alzheimer's Disease
    d. vascular dementia

    ANS: C   DIF: 2   REF: p. 533   OBJ: 6 TYPE: FACT

78. Individuals who have the APoE4 gene _____ of developing Alzheimer's disease.
    a. are at slightly increased risk
    b. have nearly a 100% chance
    c. are not at risk
    d. may or may not be at risk

    ANS: A   DIF: 2   REF: p. 533   OBJ: 6 TYPE: FACT

79. All of the following are considered deterministic genes EXCEPT:
    a. Presenilin-1
    b. Presenilin-2
    c. ApoE4
    d. ß-amyloid precursor

    ANS: C   DIF: 2   REF: p. 533   OBJ: 6 TYPE: FACT

80. Which of the following environmental stressors appears to be a significant factor in the later development of dementia (including the Alzheimer's type)?
    a. smoking
    b. low blood pressure
    c. repeated head trauma
    d. exposure to high levels of aluminum

    ANS: C   DIF: 1   REF: p. 534   OBJ: 4 TYPE: FACT

81. Recent research regarding the biological processes and genetic factors associated with Alzheimer's type dementia is best viewed as:
    a. absolute facts
    b. preliminary findings that need to be studied further
    c. hypotheses that have yet to be tested
    d. interesting theories regarding influences, though of little potential use for finding a way to predict and treat dementia

    ANS: B   DIF: 1   REF: p. 534   OBJ: 6 TYPE: CON

82. The best way to think about the psychological and social influences involved in dementia is that they:
    a. help determine the onset and course
    b. are direct causes
    c. have no influence
    d. have not been studied

    ANS: A   DIF: 1   REF: p. 534   OBJ: 4 TYPE: CON

83. The risk for developing dementia is influenced by all of the following psychological or social factors EXCEPT:
    a. food preferences
    b. participation in sports such as boxing
    c. personality traits such as extroversion
    d. level of formal education

    ANS: C   DIF: 3   REF: p. 534   OBJ: 4 TYPE: FACT

84. Treatment for Alzheimer's disease utilizes drugs that prevent the breakdown of acetylcholine including all of the following EXCEPT:
    a. paroxetine (Paxil)
    b. tacrine hydrochloride (Cognex)
    c. donepezil (Aricept)
    d. galantamine (Reminyl)

    ANS: A   DIF: 3   REF: p. 535   OBJ: 4 TYPE: APP

85. With the best treatment available today, dementia is generally:
    a. reversible
    b. controllable but not curable
    c. curable
    d. not very responsive to treatment

    ANS: D   DIF: 1   REF: p. 535   OBJ: 4 TYPE: FACT

86. What is the main reason that we do not have an effective treatment for dementia?
    a. The disorder affects the elderly who generally have many other health problems.
    b. We do not have a way to replace damaged neurons.
    c. The amount of treatment research is considerably less for dementia than for other disorders.
    d. The cause is genetic.

    ANS: B   DIF: 1   REF: p. 535   OBJ: 4 TYPE: CON

87. Appropriate treatment goals for a patient recently diagnosed with dementia include all of the following EXCEPT:
   a. reverse the neurological damage already done
   b. improve lifestyle to prevent further neurological damage
   c. reduce the current rate of decline
   d. learn strategies to compensate for existing limitations

   ANS: A   DIF: 1   REF: p. 536   OBJ: 4 TYPE: FACT

88. Of the following which is NOT one of the potential consequences associated with caregiving for patients with dementia?
   a. burnout
   b. depression
   c. contagion
   d. elder abuse

   ANS: C   DIF: 3   REF: p. 536   OBJ: 4 TYPE: CON

89. The primary treatment for Alzheimer's type dementia is:
   a. anti-depressant medication such as SSRIs
   b. diet and exercise
   c. vitamin B-12 supplements
   d. medications such as Cognex or Aricept

   ANS: D   DIF: 1   REF: p. 535   OBJ: 4 TYPE: FACT

90. Patients with Alzheimer's type dementia benefit from medications that work by:
   a. preventing the breakdown of acetylcholine
   b. enhancing the level of dopamine
   c. preventing the reuptake of serotonin
   d. unknown mechanisms

   ANS: A   DIF: 5   REF: p. 535   OBJ: 4 TYPE: FACT/WWW

91. What is the typical response to medication that can be expected for an Alzheimer's type dementia patient?
   a. about one year without symptoms
   b. doubling of life expectancy
   c. temporary improvement in abilities
   d. relief of physical but not cognitive symptoms

   ANS: C   DIF: 1   REF: p. 535   OBJ: 4 TYPE: FACT

92. John was recently diagnosed with Alzheimer's type dementia. After researching his treatment options, he decides to try medication and attempt to make the most of his remaining abilities. John plans to stay as physically and mentally active as possible for as long as he can, and to use compensation strategies if necessary. His decision:
    a. makes little sense as there are more aggressive biological treatments that are effective
    b. seems reasonable given the fact that there are no effective treatments available
    c. ignores the additional demands that his decision will ultimately place on his caregivers
    d. makes little sense since intensive psychosocial intervention has been shown to be effective

    ANS: B   DIF: 1   REF: p. 537   OBJ: 4 TYPE: APP

93. Which of the following are problems associated with the medications used to treat Alzheimer's type dementia?
    a. Abilities only improve to the same point where they were 6 months prior to treatment.
    b. Any gains in ability are temporary.
    c. Many patients discontinue medication because of severe side effects and expense.
    d. All of these are significant problems with the medications used to treat Alzheimer's type dementia.

    ANS: D   DIF: 1   REF: p. 535   OBJ: 4 TYPE: FACT

94. What is the primary goal of most psychosocial treatments for dementia?
    a. relieve depression
    b. help the patient compensate for lost abilities
    c. treat the anxiety associated with knowing that the disorder is progressive
    d. enhance family functioning

    ANS: B   DIF: 1   REF: p. 536   OBJ: 4 TYPE: FACT

95. During the late stages of dementia, the _____ probably experiences the greatest need for psychosocial treatment.
    a. caregiver
    b. patient
    c. family
    d. health care provider

    ANS: A   DIF: 1   REF: p. 537   OBJ: 8 TYPE: CON

96. The main deficit of amnestic disorder is an inability to:
    a. transfer information into long-term memory
    b. remember significant events from the distant past
    c. perform basic mathematical calculations
    d. remember one's own name

    ANS: A   DIF: 1   REF: p. 538   OBJ: 9 TYPE: FACT/WWW

97. The feature that separates amnestic disorder from dementia is that amnestic disorder:
    a. produces a wider array of cognitive deficits
    b. is caused by brain damage
    c. is the result of an accident
    d. affects memory but may leave other cognitive abilities intact

    ANS: D   DIF: 1   REF: p. 538   OBJ: 9 TYPE: FACT

98. Seventy-two-year-old Mrs. Kane recently hit her head during an auto accident. Ever since then, she has been unable to remember the most basic things. For example, when shown a pencil, a ruler and a phone, Mrs. Kane can name each object, but can not recall these objects five minutes later. In all other ways, she appears normal. Mrs. Kane's diagnosis would probably be:
   a. dementia
   b. delirium
   c. amnestic disorder
   d. organic brain damage

   ANS: C   DIF: 1   REF: p. 538-539   OBJ: 9 TYPE: APP

99. Wernicke-Korsakoff syndrome is a type of amnestic disorder commonly caused by:
   a. depression
   b. nicotine addiction
   c. genetics
   d. alcohol abuse

   ANS: D   DIF: 3   REF: p. 539   OBJ: 9 TYPE: FACT

100. Potential causes of amnestic disorder include all of the following EXCEPT:
   a. nicotine
   b. alcohol abuse
   c. head trauma
   d. a medical condition

   ANS: A   DIF: 1   REF: p. 539   OBJ: 9 TYPE: FACT

101. In the "Abnormal Psychology Live" CD for Chapter 15, the Alzheimer's patient named Tom was shown to be:
   a. delusional   c. memory impaired
   b. angry and aggressive   d. mute

   ANS: C   REF: CD

102. While watching the patient named Tom on the "Abnormal Psychology Live" CD for Chapter 15, it becomes apparent that his Alzheimer's symptoms are worsening because he:
   a. urinated on the floor   c. did not dress himself completely
   b. was unable to use a spoon or fork d. yelled at his grandchildren

   ANS: C   REF: CD

103. When Tom, the patient with Alzheimer's disease ("Abnormal Psychology Live" CD), is asked, "Who is in your family?" he says:
   a. "my grandchildren"   c. "the people who take care of me"
   b. "people I see on TV"   d. "I have no family"

   ANS: C   REF: CD

104. On the "Abnormal Psychology Live" CD, Mike, the patient with amnestic disorder, has difficulty with:
    a. old memories
    b. new learning
    c. word retrieval
    d. reading and writing

    ANS: B   REF: CD

ESSAY

1. Describe the symptoms of dementia, delirium and amnestic disorder, noting similarities and differences. What do the symptoms of each of these disorders have in common? What features are unique to each disorder?

2. Describe the typical causes of delirium and how it is treated.

3. Describe the typical causes of amnestic disorder.

4. Describe the differences and similarities of Alzheimer's type dementia and vascular dementia. Explain ways of determining if dementia is of the Alzheimer's type or of the vascular type. Why it is not always possible to determine the actual cause of dementia while the patient is alive?

5. Describe some research findings regarding the possible influences on the development of Alzheimer's type dementia. Make sure that your description covers genetic findings as well as information regarding the degenerative process that occurs in the brain.

6. Explain how Alzheimer's type dementia is usually treated. Include information about medication and psychosocial therapies. How would you characterize the success of the currently available treatment options for Alzheimer's type dementia?   **WWW**

7. What are some of the issues that caregivers must face when dealing with a patient with Alzheimer's disease? Describe some support services that may be useful for caregivers.

8. The increase in the rate of dementia in modern civilized society may be due the fact that people are living longer, social factors such as the role of the elderly in our culture, and/or the increased complexity of modern times. Using a cross-cultural example, explain how dementia is far less likely to be diagnosed in a society very different from that in the United States. What cultural features would make the diagnosis of dementia far less likely even though many of the people in the other society live to old age?

9. Explain the relationship that has been observed between formal education and the development of Alzheimer's type dementia. What theoretical and neurological explanations have been offered for this observation?

10. Assume that you had a relative who was beginning to develop significant deficits associated with early Alzheimer's type dementia. Describe several compensating strategies that you could help develop to aid the individual's functioning. What kinds of tools could the patient use to keep from getting lost, remember important information and stay safe? Be creative!

11. Describe the symptoms of Alzheimer's disease displayed by Tom on the "Abnormal Psychology Live" CD. Note the changes indicating that his condition is worsening. Discuss how this disease affects the family as well as the patient.

    REF: CD

MULTIPLE CHOICE

1. Which of the following is characteristic of delirium?
   a. Delirium is characterized by reduced clarity of consciousness and cognition.
   b. Delirium develops over a course of several hours or days.
   c. Delirium was one of the first disorders to be recounted in history.
   d. all of the above

   ANS: D

2. _____ is a gradual deterioration of brain functioning that affects judgment, memory, language, and other advanced cognitive processes.
   a. Delirium
   b. Dementia
   c. Amnestic disorder
   d. none of the above

   ANS: B

3. Alzheimer's disease progresses _____ and eventually accounts for approximately _____ percent of all cases of dementia.
   a. rapidly; 40
   b. gradually; 50
   c. rapidly; 60
   d. gradually; 70

   ANS: B

4. The average survival time for someone with Alzheimer's disease is estimated to be approximately
   a. 8 years.
   b. 10 years.
   c. 12 years.
   d. 20 years.

   ANS: A

5. Biological treatments for dementia are usually ineffective because
   a. there is no effective treatment for the primary disorder.
   b. no medications exist that provide even temporary symptom relief.
   c. vitamin E treatments have proven ineffective.
   d. persons with dementia rarely participate in treatment.

   ANS: A

6. Which of the following chromosomes has *not* been linked to the onset of Alzheimer's disease?
   a. 21
   b. 19
   c. 2
   d. 14

   ANS: C

7. A type of amnestic disorder that results from prolonged and excessive alcohol use is
   a. Broca-Mandling syndrome.
   b. Wernicke-Korsakoff syndrome.
   c. McGowin-Swenson syndrome.
   d. Monger-Rolland syndrome.

   ANS: B

8. The disorders grouped under the category of cognitive disorders share the common impairment of
   a. memory.
   b. thinking.
   c. perception.
   d. all of the above

   ANS: D

9. After Mr. Khalil's 85th birthday he began to experience difficulties that appeared to be characteristic of delirium. His psychologist is careful about making a diagnosis, as she realizes that a diagnosis of delirium in the elderly is difficult
   a. since the majority of assessment techniques that are used to make such a diagnosis were designed primarily for use with children.
   b. since the DSM-IV criteria are so rigid that many people with the disorder do not get properly diagnosed.
   c. due to the combination of medical illnesses and medications used to treat illnesses within the elderly population.
   d. all of the above

   ANS: C

10. The most plausible explanation for the negative correlation between cigarette smoking and Alzheimer's disease is that
    a. nonsmokers are likely to eat a healthier diet, and diet has been implicated in the development of Alzheimer's disease.
    b. smokers are likely to eat a healthier diet, and diet has been implicated in the development of Alzheimer's disease.
    c. nicotine combats the Alzheimer's disease process.
    d. nonsmokers live longer, and are thus more likely to develop Alzheimer's disease, which appears in later life.

    ANS: D

MULTIPLE CHOICE

1. In the textbook case of Arthur, who was diagnosed with brief psychotic disorder after talking about his secret plans both to save the world's starving children and to break into a foreign embassy, his parents were unable to have him admitted to a psychiatric hospital because Arthur was:
   a. diagnosed incorrectly
   b. not considered dangerous to himself or others
   c. no longer covered by their health insurance
   d. a minor child

   ANS: B   DIF: 3   REF: p. 545   OBJ: 1 TYPE: APP/WWW

2. Which of the following is (are) specified in civil commitment laws?
   a. when a person can be legally declared to have a mental illness
   b. when a person can be placed in a mental hospital for treatment
   c. both of these
   d. neither of these

   ANS: C   DIF: 1   REF: p. 545   OBJ: 2 TYPE: CON

3. Which of the following is (are) the primary issue(s) in mental health law today?
   a. the rights of mentally ill individuals
   b. the rights of society to be protected
   c. both of these
   d. neither of these

   ANS: C   DIF: 3   REF: p. 546   OBJ: 2 TYPE: CON

4. Each of the following statements correctly describes the circumstances of mentally ill persons prior to the late 19th century EXCEPT:
   a. The community often took on the care of mentally ill persons.
   b. Family members often cared for a mentally ill person at home.
   c. Mentally ill persons received specialized care in psychiatric hospitals.
   d. Often mentally ill persons were left to care for themselves.

   ANS: C   DIF: 3   REF: p. 546   OBJ: 2 TYPE: CON

5. In the late 19th century the enactment of civil commitment laws resulted in:
   a. only a few cases of involuntary commitment to mental hospitals
   b. people being committed who were not mentally ill
   c. wives committing their husbands to mental hospitals
   d. a decrease in the number of large public mental hospitals

   ANS: B   DIF: 3   REF: p. 546   OBJ: 2 TYPE: CON/WWW

6. State laws permit involuntary commitment when all of the following conditions have been met EXCEPT:
   a. A person has a mental illness and is in need of treatment.
   b. A person is dangerous to herself/himself or others and is in need of treatment.
   c. A person is unable to care for himself/herself.
   d. A person asks to be admitted to a mental hospital.

   ANS: D   DIF: 3   REF: p. 546   OBJ: 2 TYPE: CON

7. Authorities can use police power to hold criminal offenders if they are a threat to society. However, if the power called *parens patriae* is used to take someone into custody, it means that:
   a. a person has already committed a crime
   b. a person is not acting in his or her own best interest
   c. the safety of the community is in jeopardy
   d. individual rights are more important than societal rights

   ANS: B   DIF: 5   REF: p. 546   OBJ: 2 TYPE: CON/WWW

8. When *parens patriae* is used to take a mentally ill individual into custody, it means that the state is acting as a:
   a. mental health counselor
   b. surrogate parent
   c. legal advisor
   d. social worker

   ANS: B   DIF: 1   REF: p. 546   OBJ: 2 TYPE: CON

9. The formal process of civil commitment begins with a petition directed to a(n):
   a. attorney
   b. psychiatrist
   c. judge
   d. prosecutor

   ANS: C   DIF: 3   REF: p. 547   OBJ: 2 TYPE: FACT

10. When a person is the subject of civil commitment proceedings, the rights and protections provided by law include all of the following EXCEPT:
    a. notification that civil commitment proceedings are taking place
    b. required presence during the proceedings
    c. representation by an attorney
    d. selection of a judge who will determine the outcome of the case

    ANS: D   DIF: 5   REF: p. 547   OBJ: 2 TYPE: FACT

11. According to mental health law, what happens if a family member or a police officer certifies that a mentally disturbed person "presents a clear and immediate danger?"
    a. a long-term commitment can be made
    b. a short-term commitment can be made
    c. the person can be given psychotropic medication immediately
    d. the person can be put in jail

    ANS: B   DIF: 3   REF: p. 547   OBJ: 2 TYPE: FACT

12. The term "mental illness" is considered a legal concept and is defined:
    a. differently from state to state
    b. exactly the same in every state
    c. by the United States government
    d. by the hospital where the patient is being committed

    ANS: A   DIF: 3   REF: p. 547   OBJ: 1 TYPE: FACT

13. In some states the legal definition of mental illness excludes:
    a. mental retardation and substance-related disorders
    b. anxiety disorders and alcoholism
    c. personality disorders and gender dysphoria
    d. post-traumatic stress disorder

    ANS: A   DIF: 3   REF: p. 547   OBJ: 1 TYPE: CON

14. Receiving a DSM-IV-TR diagnosis means that the person:
    a. is considered dangerous
    b. fits the legal definition of mental illness
    c. does not necessarily fit the legal definition of mental illness
    d. must be either civilly or criminally committed

    ANS: C   DIF: 1   REF: p. 547   OBJ: 1 TYPE: FACT

15. In regard to the mentally ill, popular opinion holds that:
    a. the mentally ill are more dangerous than those who are not mentally ill
    b. the mentally ill are less dangerous than those who are not mentally ill
    c. normal people and mentally ill people are equally dangerous
    d. normal people are more dangerous than the mentally ill

    ANS: A   DIF: 3   REF: p. 547   OBJ: 4 TYPE: CON

16. The popular opinion that the mentally ill are more dangerous than those who are not mentally ill
    is probably the result of:
    a. data from medical records
    b. public knowledge of DSM-IV-TR diagnostic criteria
    c. media reports
    d. statistics on homicide and other violent crimes

    ANS: C   DIF: 1   REF: p. 547   OBJ: 4 TYPE: APP

17. The risk of violence among mentally ill patients increases if specific symptoms such as
    _____ are present.
    a. hallucinations
    b. delusions
    c. both of these
    d. neither of these

    ANS: C   DIF: 3   REF: p. 547   OBJ: 4 TYPE: FACT

18. Which of the following is a FALSE statement in regard to prediction of dangerousness?
    a. Mental health professionals can predict with certainty if a particular person will become violent.
    b. Generally speaking, persons with a previous history of violence are more likely to be dangerous than individuals without a past history of violence.
    c. Generally speaking, substance abusers are more likely to be violent than those individuals without a history of drug or alcohol dependence.
    d. Research suggests that mental health professionals are better at determining relative risk than determining dangerousness on a case-by-case basis.

    ANS: A   DIF: 5   REF: p. 548   OBJ: 4 TYPE: CON

19. In 1976, Kenneth Donaldson, who was not considered dangerous, successfully sued the director of the hospital in which he had been confined for fifteen years and where he had received:
    a. SSRI medication
    b. ECT
    c. no treatment
    d. abusive treatment

    ANS: C   DIF: 3   REF: p. 548   OBJ: 4 TYPE: FACT

20. According to the 1975 case of O'Connor v. Donaldson, a non-dangerous mentally ill individual:
    a. must be given medication to control the possibility of dangerous tendencies developing
    b. cannot be confined in an institution if capable of functioning safely on the outside
    c. must be confined in an institution in case a violent episode occurs
    d. can be released from an institution only if relatives agree to provide care

    ANS: B   DIF: 3   REF: p. 548   OBJ: 4 TYPE: APP

21. Provisions of the Supreme Court decision known as Addington v. Texas (1979) included all of the following EXCEPT:
    a. more than just the promise of improving one's quality of life is required for involuntary commitment
    b. if non-dangerous persons can survive in the community with the help of others, they should not be detained against their will
    c. needing treatment or having a grave disability is sufficient to commit someone with a mental illness
    d. the government has limited ability to commit individuals unless they are dangerous

    ANS: C   DIF: 5   REF: p. 548   OBJ: 4 TYPE: APP

22. In the 1970s and 1980s, tightened restrictions on involuntary commitment resulted in:
    a. the criminal justice system becoming responsible for mentally ill people
    b. fewer mentally ill patients living in the community
    c. family members having increased access to treatment services for their loved ones
    d. mentally ill patients receiving needed mental health services

    ANS: A   DIF: 5   REF: p. 548   OBJ: 4 TYPE: APP/WWW

23. According to the U.S. Department of Health and Human Services (2003), the number of homeless people on any given night in the United States is:
    a. 125,00
    b. 300,000
    c. 600,000
    d. 1 million

    ANS: C   DIF: 1   REF: p. 548   OBJ: 4 TYPE: FACT

24. What percentage of homeless people has a previous history of hospitalization for mental problems?
    a. 5%
    b. 15%
    c. 25%
    d. 50%

    ANS: C   DIF: 1   REF: p. 548   OBJ: 4 TYPE: FACT

25. During the 1970s and 1980s, the trend toward deinstitutionalization resulted in:
    a. an increased number of patients in psychiatric institutions
    b. a decreased number of patients in psychiatric institutions
    c. better treatment of institutionalized mentally ill patients
    d. decreased numbers of homeless mentally ill people

    ANS: B   DIF: 3   REF: p. 548   OBJ: 4 TYPE: CON

26. During the 1980s, homelessness was blamed on strict civil commitment criteria and deinstitutionalization, two policies that included all of the following EXCEPT:
    a. limits on conditions for involuntary commitment
    b. limits placed on how long a mentally ill patient could stay in a hospital
    c. closing of large psychiatric hospitals
    d. increased numbers of mental health professionals working in psychiatric hospitals

    ANS: D   DIF: 3   REF: p. 548   OBJ: 4 TYPE: CON

27. Which of the goals of deinstitutionalization have been accomplished?
    a. the closing of large psychiatric hospitals
    b. the creation of a network of community mental health centers
    c. both of these
    d. neither of these

    ANS: A   DIF: 3   REF: p. 549   OBJ: 4 TYPE: CON

28. The term transinstitutionalization refers to the movement of people with severe mental illness out of psychiatric hospitals and into any or all of the following EXCEPT:
    a. jails and prisons
    b. nursing homes
    c. group residences
    d. community health centers

    ANS: D   DIF: 3   REF: p. 549   OBJ: 4 TYPE: CON

29. Which of the following statements accurately describes the outcome of the policy known as deinstitutionalization?
   a. Previously hospitalized patients received adequate care in most communities.
   b. Funding for community mental health centers was sufficient to provide care for previously hospitalized patients.
   c. Deinstitutionalization is considered a success because patient care improved.
   d. Deinstitutionalization is considered a failure because patient care deteriorated.

   ANS: D   DIF: 3   REF: p. 549   OBJ: 4 TYPE: CON/WWW

30. Beginning in the mid-1970s, authorities were unable to confine non-dangerous mentally ill patients, a policy that emphasized:
   a. individual freedom
   b. society's rights
   c. both of these
   d. neither of these

   ANS: A   DIF: 3   REF: p. 549   OBJ: 4 TYPE: APP

31. The conflicting interests over civil commitment were illustrated by the 1988 case of Joyce Brown, a homeless woman diagnosed with paranoid schizophrenia, who was:
   a. medicated against her will
   b. hospitalized involuntarily
   c. dangerous
   d. suicidal

   ANS: B   DIF: 3   REF: p. 549   OBJ: 4 TYPE: APP

32. In Supreme Court rulings such as O'Connor v. Donaldson and Addington v. Texas, it was argued that the criteria for involuntary commitment should include:
   a. dangerousness
   b. mental illness
   c. both of these
   d. neither of these

   ANS: C   DIF: 3   REF: p. 550   OBJ: 4 TYPE: APP

33. In the late 1970s and early 1980s, legal reforms enacted by some states to make civil commitment easier resulted in:
   a. a decrease in the number of hospitalized mental patients
   b. more voluntary than involuntary admissions
   c. more patients admitted under *parens patriae* powers
   d. shorter hospital stays for mentally ill patients

   ANS: C   DIF: 5   REF: p. 550   OBJ: 4 TYPE: APP

34. In response to the strict civil commitment laws of the 1970s and 1980s, some states enacted legal reforms that:
    a. shortened hospital stays
    b. reduced the number of admissions
    c. changed the status under which patients were committed
    d. eliminated the doctrine of *parens patriae*

    ANS: C   DIF: 5   REF: p. 550   OBJ: 4 TYPE: APP

35. According to the authors of your textbook, the periodic changes in the laws regarding civil commitment are a sign of a:
    a. society that has no idea of what to do with this issue
    b. hospital system that is ineffective in treating uncooperative patients
    c. healthy system responding to the limits of previous decisions
    d. prior mistake that has now been successfully corrected

    ANS: C   DIF: 3   REF: p. 550   OBJ: 4 TYPE: CON

36. The "sexual psychopath laws" that were passed in the mid-1900s provided for:
    a. an indefinite period of hospitalization for sex offenders
    b. an indefinite prison term for sex offenders
    c. both of these
    d. neither of these

    ANS: A   DIF: 3   REF: p. 550   OBJ: 4 TYPE: FACT

37. The "sexual psychopath laws" enacted in the mid-1900s were based on the assumption that:
    a. criminal commitment proceedings should be invoked for sexual offenders
    b. sexual offenders could be successfully treated
    c. rapists and pedophiles deserved to be punished
    d. sexual psychopaths could be rehabilitated in a prison setting

    ANS: B   DIF: 3   REF: p. 550   OBJ: 4 TYPE: CON

38. You have read an article in the newspaper about a rapist who was convicted under a "sexual predator law." You know that this person will be:
    a. hospitalized immediately in a psychiatric institution that has a sexual offenders unit
    b. sentenced to an indefinite term in a prison that has a separate section for rapists
    c. hospitalized for treatment and then imprisoned if the treatment is not effective
    d. incarcerated for a specific term and then civilly committed if judged still dangerous

    ANS: D   DIF: 5   REF: p. 550   OBJ: 4 TYPE: APP

39. Which of the following is NOT a question that addresses the issues of civil (involuntary) commitment?
    a. Should a mentally ill person be involuntarily committed if he or she is not dangerous but in need of treatment?
    b. Should a mentally ill person be civilly committed if he or she has been convicted of a crime?
    c. Should a mentally ill person be involuntarily committed at the request of family or relatives who believe it is in the person's best interest?
    d. If a person is mentally ill, unable to care for oneself and in need of help, should the law allow for involuntary commitment?

ANS: B   DIF: 5   REF: p. 550   OBJ: 3 TYPE: CON

40. Andrew has been accused of committing a crime and is currently in a mental health facility. He will stay there until it is determined that he is fit to participate in legal proceedings against him. The commitment process by which Andrew is being held is called:
    a. civil
    b. criminal
    c. *parens patriae*
    d. *mens rea*

ANS: B   DIF: 1   REF: p. 551   OBJ: 3 TYPE: APP/WWW

41. Andrea is being held in a psychiatric hospital after being found guilty of criminal behavior. She is in this facility instead of in jail because:
    a. She has been found not guilty by reason of insanity.
    b. She has been found unable to participate in legal proceedings against her.
    c. Either of these
    d. Neither of these

ANS: C   DIF: 3   REF: p. 551   OBJ: 3 TYPE: APP

42. The outcome of Miguel's trial resulted in a finding of "not guilty by reason of insanity." According to criminal law, Miguel now will be sent to:
    a. prison
    b. a psychiatric hospital
    c. a community mental health center
    d. an insane asylum

ANS: B   DIF: 3   REF: p. 551   OBJ: 3 TYPE: APP/WWW

43. In the United States, persons convicted of criminal behavior:
    a. always receive a prison sentence
    b. always are considered responsible for their behavior
    c. sometimes are not considered responsible for their behavior
    d. sometimes have been found incompetent to stand trial

ANS: C   DIF: 3   REF: p. 551   OBJ: 3 TYPE: CON

44. The insanity defense is based on a historical case in England involving a man named:
    a. Durham
    b. Addington
    c. M'Naghten
    d. Tory

    ANS: C   DIF: F   REF: p. 551   OBJ: 3 TYPE: APP/FACT

45. Since the 19th century, the method of determining responsibility when a person's mental state is in question has been based on the _____ M'Naghten rule.
    a. American
    b. British
    c. Irish
    d. Scottish

    ANS: B   DIF: 1   REF: p. 551   OBJ: 3 TYPE: FACT

46. Which of the following is NOT related to the M'Naghten ruling decreed by an English court more than 150 years ago?
    a. It concerns a person's mental state at the time a crime is committed.
    b. It states that individuals are not responsible for criminal behavior if they do not know what they are doing.
    c. It states that individuals are not responsible for their behavior if they don't know that what they are doing is wrong.
    d. It is based on a case in which paranoid delusions influenced an individual to actually kill the British prime minister.

    ANS: D   DIF: 3   REF: p. 551   OBJ: 3 TYPE: APP

47. In the case of Durham v. United States (1954), the criteria for responsibility for determining criminal behavior were broadened to include:
    a. mental disease
    b. mental defect
    c. both of these
    d. neither of these

    ANS: C   DIF: 1   REF: p. 551   OBJ: 3 TYPE: FACT

48. Although the Durham ruling in 1954 allowed mental health professionals to present information about an accused person's mental state, it became apparent that:
    a. no mental health professional wanted to participate in court proceedings
    b. mental health professionals could not reliably assess whether mental illness caused criminal behavior
    c. judges were reluctant to include testimony from mental health professional in their decisions
    d. juries were reluctant to consider testimony from mental health professionals

    ANS: B   DIF: 5   REF: p. 551   OBJ: 3 TYPE: CON/WWW

49. The decision to include the presence of "a mental disease or defect" in determining an accused person's responsibility for a crime was part of a Supreme Court ruling known as:
    a. O'Connor v. Donaldson
    b. Addington v. Texas
    c. Durham v. United States
    d. M'Naghten v. Tory

    ANS: C   DIF: 3   REF: p. 551   OBJ: 3 TYPE: FACT

50. Criteria for the insanity defense were developed by a group from the American Law Institute that included all of the following EXCEPT:
    a. attorneys
    b. judges
    c. psychologists
    d. law scholars

    ANS: C   DIF: 1   REF: p. 551   OBJ: 3 TYPE: APP

51. Which of the following statements does NOT apply to the American Law Institute (ALI) study of the insanity defense?
    a. mentally ill persons must be distinguished from those without mental disorders
    b. the threat of punishment will usually deter a mentally ill person from committing a crime
    c. mentally ill persons who commit crimes should be treated for their illness until improved and then released from confinement
    d. mentally ill people who cannot control their behavior must be shielded from legal consequences

    ANS: B   DIF: 5   REF: p. 551   OBJ: 3 TYPE: APP

52. If an individual accidentally injures another person he or she cannot be convicted of a crime because there was no "criminal intent," a theoretical concept known legally as:
    a. *mens rea*
    b. *actus rea*
    c. sociopathic deviancy
    d. GBMI

    ANS: A   DIF: 3   REF: p. 552   OBJ: 3 TYPE: CON

53. Which of the following was NOT a provision of the American Law Institute recommendations regarding "diminished capacity?"
    a. a mentally ill criminal may actually not have criminal intent
    b. a mental illness could impair the ability to understand that one's behavior is criminal
    c. proof of either *mens rea* or *actus rea* is sufficient to convict someone of a crime
    d. mentally ill persons who commit crimes may not be responsible for their behavior

    ANS: C   DIF: 5   REF: p. 552   OBJ: 3 TYPE: APP

54. The legal concept of *mens rea* is generally used to mean:
   a. "guilty mind"
   b. criminal intent
   c. both of these
   d. neither of these

   ANS: A   DIF: 1   REF: p. 552   OBJ: 3 TYPE: CON

55. In the American legal system, the concept of diminished capacity is used to:
   a. keep mentally ill persons from being discharged from mental hospitals
   b. assess the responsibility of persons with mental illness
   c. evaluate the effects of medical treatments for schizophrenia
   d. determine the intelligence level of an individual accused of criminal behavior

   ANS: B   DIF: 5   REF: p. 552   OBJ: 3 TYPE: CON

56. In 1979, public opinion turned against the use of the insanity defense when it was used successfully to justify such behaviors as:
   a. child abuse
   b. stealing cars
   c. writing bad checks
   d. vandalism

   ANS: C   DIF: 1   REF: p. 552   OBJ: 3 TYPE: FACT

57. In the 1970s and 1980s, successful insanity defenses were based on all of the following EXCEPT:
   a. pathological gambling
   b. battered wife syndrome
   c. posttraumatic stress disorder
   d. borderline personality disorder

   ANS: D   DIF: 3   REF: p. 552   OBJ: 3 TYPE: FACT

58. What was the public reaction to the 1981 jury verdict that found John Hinckley, the attempted assassin of President Reagan, not guilty by reason of insanity?
   a. acceptance
   b. outrage
   c. disappointment
   d. disinterest

   ANS: B   DIF: 3   REF: p. 552   OBJ: 3 TYPE: FACT

59. What reason did John Hinckley give for his attempted assassination of President Reagan in 1981?
   a. he had an obsession about becoming President and thought he could be elected if President Reagan were dead
   b. he was obsessed with actress Jodie Foster and wanted to impress her
   c. he was anxious about homelessness and poverty in the world and thought Reagan wasn't doing enough to help poor people
   d. he thought that President Reagan was about to kill him so he acted in self-defense

   ANS: B   DIF: 3   REF: p. 552   OBJ: 3 TYPE: APP

60. What was one outcome of the attempted assassination of President Reagan in 1981?
    a. stricter gun control laws
    b. more secret service agents to protect the President of the United States
    c. improved screening procedures for the mentally ill
    d. greater public acceptance of the insanity defense

    ANS: A   DIF: 3   REF: p. 552   OBJ: 3 TYPE: APP

61. Following the NGRI verdict for John Hinckley in 1981, several states considered:
    a. abolishing the insanity defense
    b. using the insanity defense in every case
    c. using the insanity defense only for male criminals
    d. releasing all mentally ill patients who had successfully pleaded insanity

    ANS: A   DIF: 3   REF: p. 552   OBJ: 3 TYPE: APP

62. Cases in which the insanity defense has been used include those of all the following individuals EXCEPT:
    a. Charles Manson
    b. Jeffrey Dahmer
    c. Lee Harvey Oswald
    d. Ted Kaczynski

    ANS: C   DIF: 1   REF: p. 552   OBJ: 3 TYPE: FACT

63. A TV reporter is interviewing students about the insanity plea. If these students are similar to about 90% of the population, they will agree with the following statement:
    a. "The insanity defense is not used in enough cases. Too many mentally ill people are in jail instead of in hospitals."
    b. "Too many people escape responsibility for their crimes by pleading insanity."
    c. "If someone successfully pleads NGRI, he or she will spend more time in jail than in a mental hospital."
    d. "There are more mentally ill people in prisons than in mental hospitals."

    ANS: B   DIF: 5   REF: p. 553   OBJ: 3 TYPE: APP

64. As indicated by surveys of the general population, what percentage of people perceives that the insanity defense is used too often?
    a. 20%
    b. 45%
    c. 70%
    d. 90%

    ANS: D   DIF: 1   REF: p. 553   OBJ: 3 TYPE: FACT

65. Which of the following is an accurate statement in regard to public perception of the insanity defense?
    a. The public underestimates how often the insanity defense is used in criminal cases.
    b. The public overestimates how often the insanity defense is successfully used.
    c. The public overestimates the length of hospitalization of those who are found not guilty by reason of insanity (NGRI).
    d. The public underestimates how often people judged NGRI are set free.

    ANS: B   DIF: 5   REF: p. 553   OBJ: 3 TYPE: APP/WWW

66. Although surveys have shown that the public estimates that the insanity defense is used in 37% of felony cases, the actual figure is about:
    a. 1%
    b. 10%
    c. 57%
    d. 88%

    ANS: A   DIF: 1   REF: p. 553   OBJ: 3 TYPE: FACT

67. Pat has committed a non-violent crime and has been judged NGRI. According to statistical data, it is likely that Pat will be spending:
    a. a long time in prison
    b. a shorter time in a mental hospital than he/she would have spent in prison
    c. a short time in prison
    d. a longer time in a mental hospital than he/she would have spent in prison

    ANS: D   DIF: 5   REF: p. 553   OBJ: 3 TYPE: APP

68. The public perception that people with mental illness "beat the rap" as a result of being judged not guilty by reason of insanity (NGRI) is:
    a. incorrect
    b. correct
    c. true in murder cases only
    d. true for males who commit crimes but not for females who commit crimes

    ANS: A   DIF: 3   REF: p. 553   OBJ: 3 TYPE: CON

69. Major changes in the criteria for the insanity defense were made after:
    a. President Ronald Reagan sponsored legislative changes
    b. the Hinckley verdict in the early 1980s
    c. both of these
    d. neither of these

    ANS: B   DIF: 3   REF: p. 553   OBJ: 3 TYPE: FACT

70. When Congress passed the Insanity Defense Reform Act of 1984, it made successful use of the insanity defense:
    a. more difficult for all individuals
    b. easier for any individual
    c. more difficult for the mentally ill only
    d. easier for the non-mentally ill

    ANS: A   DIF: 3   REF: p. 553   OBJ: 3 TYPE: APP

71. In an attempt to replace the insanity plea, some states now use the "guilty but mentally ill" (GBMI) verdict, in which mentally ill criminals are usually:
    a. treated for their mental illnesses
    b. punished for committing crimes
    c. both of these
    d. neither of these

    ANS: C   DIF: 3   REF: p. 553   OBJ: 3 TYPE: CON

72. In contrast to the NGRI verdict, the GBMI verdict usually specifies all of the following EXCEPT:
    a. the accused is given a prison sentence just as if there were no mental illness present
    b. the accused may be either hospitalized or imprisoned, as determined by legal authorities
    c. the accused may be either hospitalized or imprisoned, as determined by medical authorities
    d. if the person recovers from the mental illness before the sentence has passed, he or she can be confined to prison for the maximum length of the term

    ANS: C   DIF: 5   REF: p. 553   OBJ: 3 TYPE: CON

73. Several years ago, Mary was arrested for participating in a crime. Since then she has been confined in a psychiatric hospital. Mary is periodically evaluated to see if she is still mentally ill. When it is determined that she is no longer mentally ill, Mary will be released. From your knowledge of mental health and the law, you would correctly state that the original verdict in Mary's case was:
    a. NGRI
    b. GBMI
    c. both of these
    d. neither of these

    ANS: A   DIF: 3   REF: p. 553   OBJ: 3 TYPE: APP

74. Several years ago, Mark was arrested for participating in a crime. Since then he has been confined to mental hospital, even though he was given a prison sentence. Mark is periodically evaluated to see if he is still mentally ill. If it is determined that he is no longer mentally ill, Mark will then be incarcerated to serve out his prison sentence. From your knowledge of mental health and the law, you would correctly state that Mark was originally found:
    a. innocent
    b. GBMI
    c. NGRI
    d. incompetent to stand trial

    ANS: B   DIF: 5   REF: p. 554   OBJ: 3 TYPE: APP

75. In 1994 the Supreme Court upheld Montana's abolition of the insanity defense. Since then, both Idaho and Utah as well as Montana have adopted a version of the GBMI verdict in which the accused:
    a. remains permanently in a psychiatric facility
    b. is imprisoned but is assured of receiving mental health services
    c. is imprisoned but is provided with mental health services only if they are available
    d. can choose either hospitalization or imprisonment

    ANS: C   DIF: 3   REF: p. 554   OBJ: 3 TYPE: APP

76. In comparison to persons judged NGRI, research studies have shown that those who are judged "guilty but mentally ill:"
    a. are more likely to be imprisoned
    b. receive shorter sentences
    c. get mental health services more frequently than other mentally ill prisoners
    d. spend more time in mental hospitals and less time in prisons

    ANS: A   DIF: 3   REF: p. 554   OBJ: 3 TYPE: CON

77. The term "therapeutic jurisprudence" refers to using what we know about behavior change to:
    a. punish those who break the law   c. protect society from dangerous individuals
    b. help people in trouble with the law   d. provide therapy to incarcerated individuals

    ANS: B   DIF: 1   REF: p. 554   OBJ: 3 TYPE: FACT

78. Problem-solving courts (Winick & Wexler, 2003) may be more helpful to both individuals with mental health problems who break the law and society because they:
    a. are not based on an adversarial system   c. provide for treatment and not punishment
    b. are based on an adversarial system   d. put the interests of the accused above the interests of society

    ANS: A   DIF: 3   REF: p. 554   OBJ: 3 TYPE: CON

79. According to the Supreme Court, persons are assessed as being competent to stand trial if they can:
    a. assist in their own defense
    b. understand the charges against them
    c. both of these
    d. neither of these

    ANS: C   DIF: 1   REF: p. 555   OBJ: 3 TYPE: CON

80. In regard to mental health and the law, which of the following is an accurate statement?
    a. a person can be found incompetent to stand trial and still be convicted of the crime
    b. a person can be found NGRI but competent to stand trial
    c. more individuals are found NGRI than are found incompetent to stand trial
    d. a person found incompetent to stand trial is placed in a mental hospital for an indefinite period of time

    ANS: B   DIF: 5   REF: p. 555   OBJ: 3 TYPE: CON

81. Before a person can be tried for a crime, a determination of competence must be made. For this reason, most individuals with obvious and severe impairments who commit crimes are:
    a. found NGRI
    b. found GBMI
    c. never tried
    d. medicated before trial

    ANS: C   DIF: 3   REF: p. 555   OBJ: 3 TYPE: CON

82. Margaret has been schizophrenic for many years and has been hospitalized several times. She has paranoid delusions and hallucinations. Her speech is rambling and incoherent. Most recently Margaret got hold of a gun and shot several people, believing that they were her enemies. Following her arrest, what is the most likely scenario for Margaret?
    a. if convicted, she will go to prison
    b. following a trial, she will be hospitalized again
    c. her case will never go to trial
    d. she will be found competent to stand trial

    ANS: C   DIF: 3   REF: p. 555   OBJ: 3 TYPE: APP/WWW

83. Since Roberto has been found incompetent to stand trial, he will be committed to a mental health facility. After a reasonable period of time, the law requires any one of the following outcomes EXCEPT:
    a. he must be found competent
    b. he must be set free
    c. he must be medicated
    d. he must be committed under civil law

    ANS: C   DIF: 3   REF: p. 555   OBJ: 3 TYPE: APP

84. Data indicate that the crimes committed by mentally ill persons are most likely to be:
    a. violent
    b. nonviolent
    c. rapes and murders
    d. assaults

    ANS: B   DIF: 1   REF: p. 555   OBJ: 4 TYPE: APP

85. The 1970s case, Tarasoff v. Regents of the University of California, in which a student killed his ex-girlfriend, involved the issue called:
    a. patients' rights
    b. duty to warn
    c. competency
    d. restrictive environment

    ANS: B   DIF: 1   REF: p. 555   OBJ: 4 TYPE: FACT

86. According to the ruling in the 1970s Tarasoff case, a therapist is required to:
    a. advise a patient of his or her rights
    b. have each patient sign a consent form
    c. warn a patient's potential victim(s)
    d. file a police report if threatened by a patient

    ANS: C   DIF: 3   REF: p. 555   OBJ: 4 TYPE: APP

87. During civil commitment proceedings, juries rely on mental health professionals as expert witnesses to assess a person's potential for future violence. Research suggests that mental health professionals can make reliable predictions about dangerousness over the:
    a. short term (2-20 days)
    b. long term (>20 days)
    c. both of these
    d. neither of these

    ANS: A   DIF: 3   REF: p. 555   OBJ: 4 TYPE: CON

88. According to the textbook, mental health professionals appear to have expertise in all of the following areas EXCEPT (Tardiff, 2003):
    a. identifying malingering
    b. assessing competence to stand trial
    c. predicting long term risk of violence
    d. making reliable diagnoses according to DSM-IV-TR criteria

    ANS: C   DIF: 3   REF: p. 555   OBJ: 4 TYPE: APP

89. Which of the following psychological tests has been used to accurately identify malingering in persons claiming to have posttraumatic stress disorder?
    a. Minnesota Multiphasic Personality Inventory (MMPI)
    b. Wechsler Adult Scale of Intelligence (WAIS)
    c. Rorschach Inkblot Test
    d. Thematic Apperception Test (TAT)

    ANS: A   DIF: 3   REF: p. 556   OBJ: 4 TYPE: FACT

90. Information about mental institutions indicates that up until the 1980s, patients had:
    a. civil rights
    b. personal rights
    c. legal rights
    d. virtually no rights

    ANS: D   DIF: 3   REF: p. 556   OBJ: 5 TYPE: FACT

91. Wyatt v. Stickney (1972), a class action lawsuit filed on behalf of mental patients addressed all of the following EXCEPT:
    a. adequate shower and toilet facilities
    b. treatment goals
    c. staff-patient ratios
    d. methods of administering medication

    ANS: D   DIF: 3   REF: p. 557   OBJ: 5 TYPE: APP

92. As specified by Wyatt v. Stickney (1972), among the least restrictive conditions for mentally retarded individuals were all of the following EXCEPT:
    a. more structured living
    b. smaller facilities
    c. integration into the community
    d. independent living

    ANS: A   DIF: 5   REF: p. 557   OBJ: 5 TYPE: APP

93. In 1986 Congress passed the Protection and Advocacy for Mentally Ill Individuals Act to provide agencies in each state that would:
    a. act as legal advocates for the mentally ill
    b. investigate allegations of abuse and neglect
    c. both of these
    d. neither of these

    ANS: C   DIF: 3   REF: p. 557   OBJ: 5 TYPE: FACT

94. The question of whether a person can be "forced" to become competent to stand trial involves the issue of:
    a. medication
    b. research participants' rights
    c. a patient's right to treatment
    d. legal representation

    ANS: A   DIF: 3   REF: p. 557   OBJ: 5 TYPE: CON

95. In Riggins v. Nevada (1992), the Supreme Court ruled that a person cannot be forced to take antipsychotic medication because:
    a. it would be unconstitutional
    b. it would not be in the patient's best interests
    c. there is a potential for negative side effects
    d. it would interfere with the patient's competency to stand trial

    ANS: C   DIF: 5   REF: p. 557   OBJ: 5 TYPE: APP

96. When conducting research on people with psychological disorders, the American Psychological Association has stipulated all of the following rights EXCEPT:
    a. the right to privacy
    b. the right to anonymity
    c. the right to be protected from harm
    d. the right to be informed about the outcome of the study

    ANS: D   DIF: 3   REF: p. 557   OBJ: 6 TYPE: APP

97. When a person formally agrees to be a research participant after being apprised of all aspects of the study, it is known as:
    a. limited liability
    b. informed consent
    c. applied understanding
    d. participant consensus

    ANS: B   DIF: 1   REF: p. 557   OBJ: 6 TYPE: CON

98. Research based evidence in the form of recommendations on how to treat a particular psychological disorder are called:
    a. treatment requirements   c. clinical practice guidelines
    b. clinical standard treatments   d. standard treatment guidelines

    ANS: C   DIF: 3   REF: p. 558   OBJ: 6 TYPE: FACT

99. The clinical efficacy axis of the clinical practice guidelines established by the American Psychological Association in 1995 was designed to answer the question:
    a. "What kind of research should be done to determine the type of clinician best suited for particular patients in terms of their diagnosis and chronicity?"
    b. "Is the treatment effective compared to an alternative treatment or to no treatment in a controlled clinical research setting?"
    c. "How long should a treatment be continued if there is no improvement in the patient's condition or if the patient has serious side effects?"
    d. "What is the most efficient way of admitting patients to clinics or hospitals?"

    ANS: B   DIF: 3   REF: p. 559   OBJ: 7 TYPE: APP

100. Although the clinical efficacy axis is concerned with research settings, the clinical utility axis is concerned with:
    a. effectiveness of the intervention in clinical practice
    b. feasibility and cost-effectiveness
    c. both of these
    d. neither of these

    ANS: C   DIF: 3   REF: p. 559   OBJ: 7 TYPE: CON

101. The first major consideration on the clinical utility axis is feasibility, which asks all of the following questions EXCEPT:
    a. Will patients accept the intervention?
    b. Will patients comply with the requirements?
    c. Has research shown the treatment to be effective?
    d. Is the treatment relatively easy to administer?

    ANS: C   DIF: 3   REF: p. 559   OBJ: 7 TYPE: CON

102. Whether a particular intervention is effective with different patients, in different settings, or with different therapists is referred to as:
    a. generalizability
    b. feasibility
    c. external reliability
    d. clinical replication

    ANS: A   DIF: 3   REF: p. 559   OBJ: 7 TYPE: CON

103. Deception of research participants is often required in psychological research studies like the one shown on the "Abnormal Psychology Live" CD segment for Chapter 16. When a research subject is deceived during an experiment, it is necessary to:
    a. provide compensation   c. explain the deception in a de-briefing session after the experiment
    b. pre-screen subjects to make sure they can d. utilize a "deception" version of informed handle the potential stress   consent prior to the experiment

    ANS: C   DIF: 3   REF: CD

104. In the "Abnormal Psychology Live" CD video for Chapter 16, Dr. Elizabeth Loftus describes an "implanted" (false) memory that the research subject later describes in great detail. This type of experiment leads to some controversy with regard to the treatment of research subjects because implanting a false memory requires the researcher to _____ the subject.
    a. deceive
    b. harm
    c. pay
    d. fail to obtain informed consent from

    ANS: A   DIF: 3   REF: CD

ESSAY

1. Trace the historical changes in civil commitment procedures, noting previous and current criteria.

2. Define the terms "grave disability" and *parens patriae,* giving examples of each.

3. Explain the following statement: "Mental illness is not synonymous with psychological disorder." What are the implications of mental illness as a legal concept?

4. Discuss research studies on the relationship between mental illness and dangerousness. Describe symptoms that correlate with an increased risk of violence among the mentally ill.

5. Discuss how the restrictions on involuntary commitment in the 1970s and 1980s led to the "criminalization" of mental illness.   **WWW**

6. Explore the consequences of the policy known as "deinstitutionalization" noting specifically the effect on homelessness. Compare the intended outcome of this policy with the actual outcome.

7. Compare the "sexual psychopath laws" of the mid-20th century with the "sexual predator laws" of the 1990s. Describe how the effectiveness of treatment procedures for sexual offenders related to these rulings.

8. Discuss the historical development of the insanity defense beginning with the 1843 M'Naghten Rule in England and noting the findings of the American Law Institute in the 1960s. In your discussion, define *mens rea* and the concept of "diminished capacity."

9. Discuss the standards set forth by Wyatt vs. Stickney (1972), the ruling that focused on the "right to treatment" for mental patients. Compare this ruling with Riggins v. Nevada (1992), which focused on the "right to refuse treatment."

10. Discuss the potential benefits regarding the application of therapeutic jurisprudence in "problem-solving courts". How does this system differ in philosophy and potential consequence (for individuals and society) from the traditional court system? Make sure to indicate the types of problems that problem-solving courts are most likely to handle.

MULTIPLE CHOICE

1. A person would not be held responsible for criminal behavior if s/he is not aware of what s/he is doing or that it is wrong under the
   a. M'Naghten rule.
   b. Durham rule.
   c. American Law Institute rule.
   d. diminished capacity rule.
   e. none of the above

   ANS: A

2. Because a mental disorder may lessen a person's ability to understand his/her behavior and criminal intent, it is difficult to prove
   a. actus rea.
   b. mens rea.
   c. diminished capacity.
   d. involvement in the crime.
   e. none of the above

   ANS: B

3. A person who is deemed severely mentally ill before trial for a crime probably
   a. cannot assist in his/her own defense.
   b. cannot be expected to understand the charges against him/her.
   c. is not competent to stand trial.
   d. will be hospitalized instead of tried.
   e. all of the above

   ANS: D

4. The right to treatment
   a. includes minimum staff-patient ratios.
   b. requires the least restrictive treatment option possible.
   c. promotes patient movement from smaller to larger living units.
   d. promotes patient movement from dependent to independent living units.
   e. all but c

   ANS: E

5. The issue of the right to refuse treatment
   a. is a controversial one.
   b. seems to contradict the belief that mentally ill people may not be capable of making decisions in their best interest.
   c. appears to be supported by Riggins v. Nevada.
   d. all of the above

   ANS: D

6. In Congress, the laws were changed so that individuals could be committed to mental hospitals more easily if they were in need of treatment. This led to
   a. an increase in the number of patients admitted to mental hospitals.
   b. more patients admitted voluntarily.
   c. more patients admitted involuntarily.
   d. a decrease in the number of patients admitted to mental hospitals.
   e. deinstitutionalization.

   ANS: C

7. The criteria developed by the American Law Institute suggested that individuals were not responsible for their criminal behavior if
   a. they suffered from a mental disorder.
   b. due to mental illness, they could not control or recognize the inappropriateness of criminal behavior.
   c. they did not recognize that their behavior was wrong and could not control it.
   d. they could not remember it.

   ANS: B

8. As an attorney, you are trying to decide whether your client is competent to stand trial. Which of these is NOT an issue for this decision?
   a. Can the client assist in preparing the defense?
   b. Does the client appreciate that the act was wrong?
   c. Does the client understand the charges?
   d. Does the client understand the possible trial outcomes?

   ANS: B

9. A court case has established that psychologically disordered individuals who are incompetent to stand trial
   a. have a right to treatment.
   b. cannot be responsible for the burden of proof.
   c. cannot be forced to take psychotropic medications to make them competent to stand trial.
   d. must do as much as possible that might make them competent to stand trial.
   e. do not have a guaranteed right to treatment to make them competent.

   ANS: C

10. One reason that the APA is developing guidelines for clinical intervention is to
    a. reduce the pay rate for therapists.
    b. increase the use of expensive treatment.
    c. ensure that individuals receive effective and personalized treatment.
    d. reduce the level of skill needed by therapists.

    ANS: C